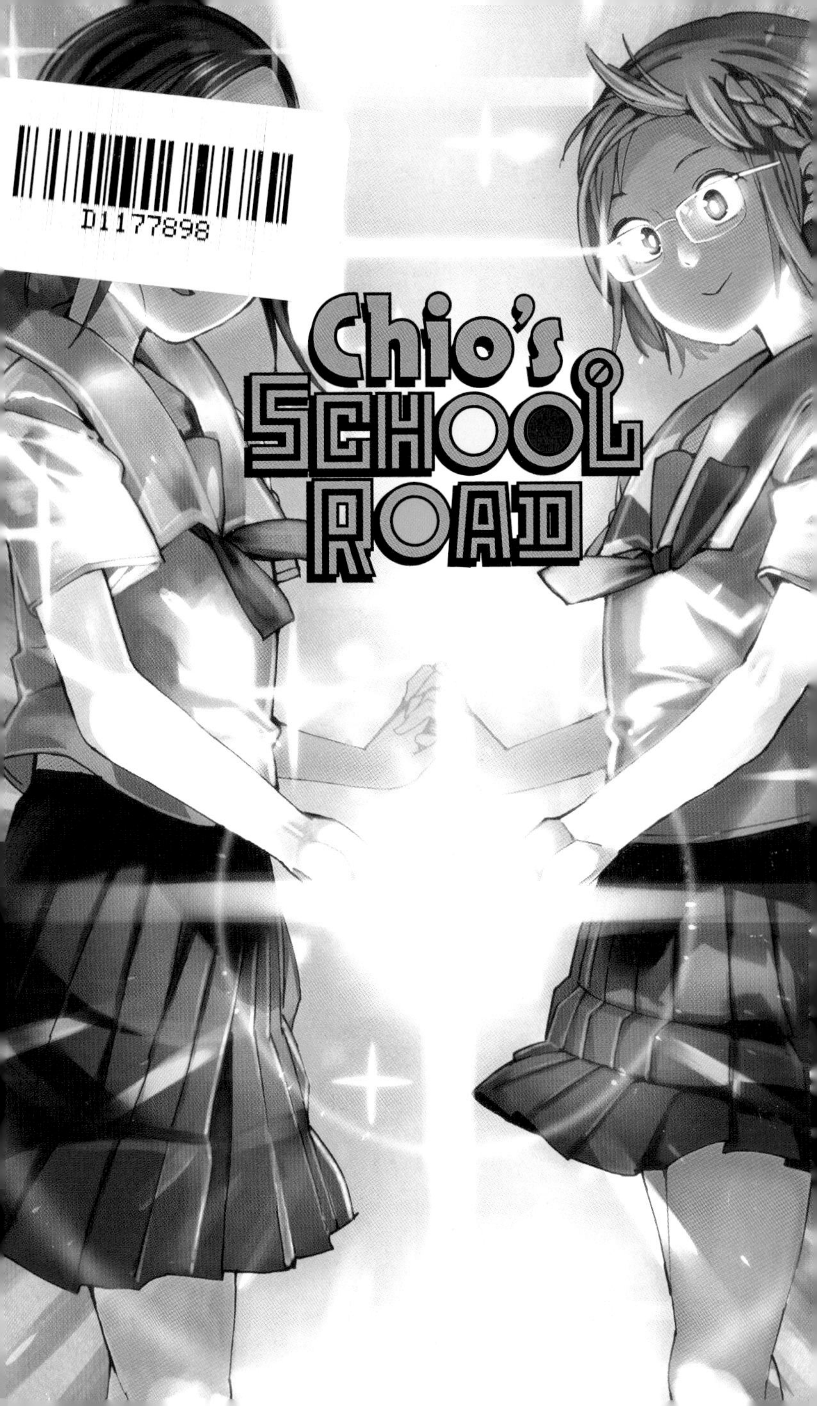
Chio's
SCHOOL
ROAD

CONTENTS

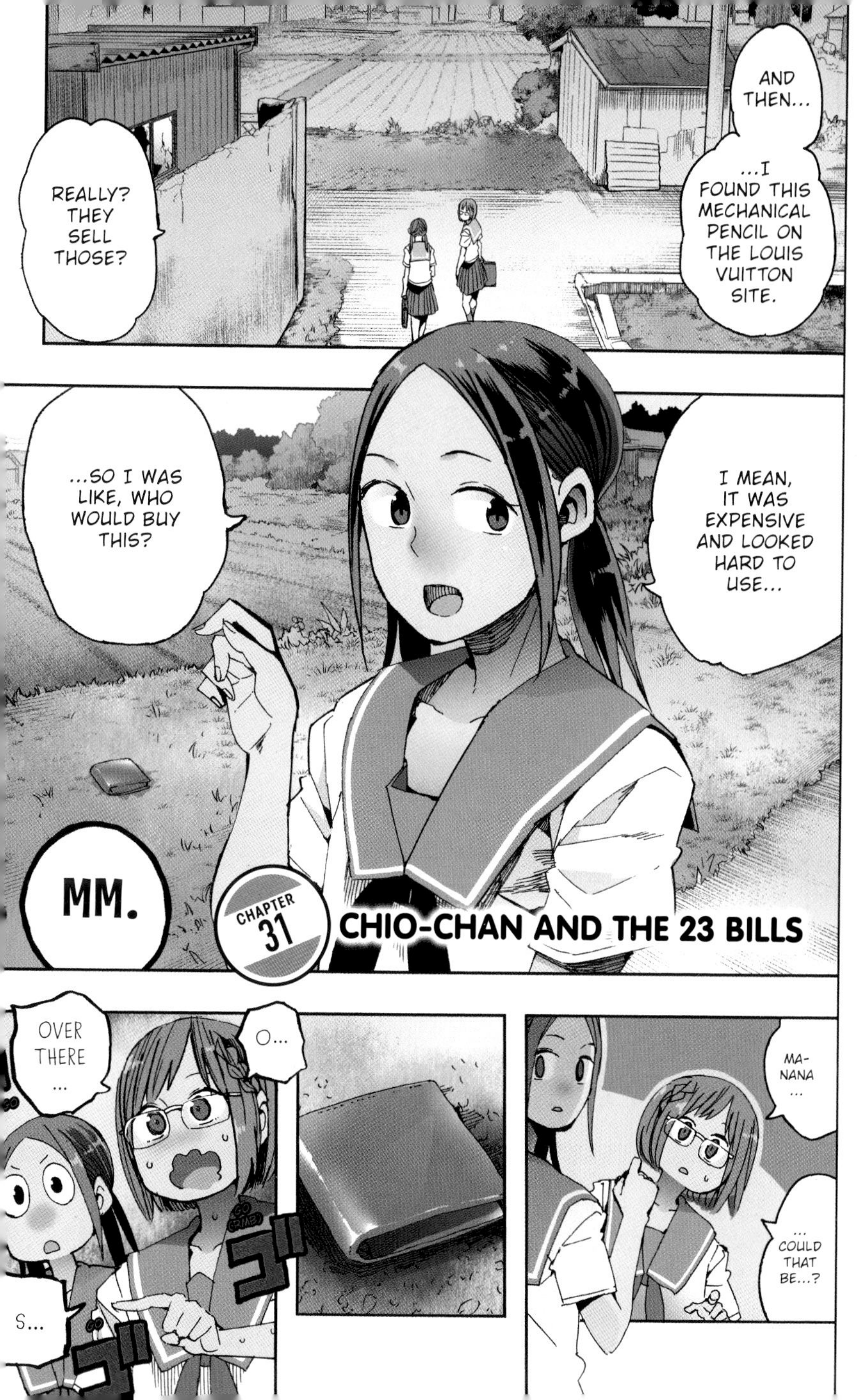
AND THEN...
...I FOUND THIS MECHANICAL PENCIL ON THE LOUIS VUITTON SITE.
REALLY? THEY SELL THOSE?
I MEAN, IT WAS EXPENSIVE AND LOOKED HARD TO USE...
...SO I WAS LIKE, WHO WOULD BUY THIS?
MM.
CHAPTER 31
CHIO-CHAN AND THE 23 BILLS
MA-NANA...
...COULD THAT BE...?
O...
OVER THERE...
S...

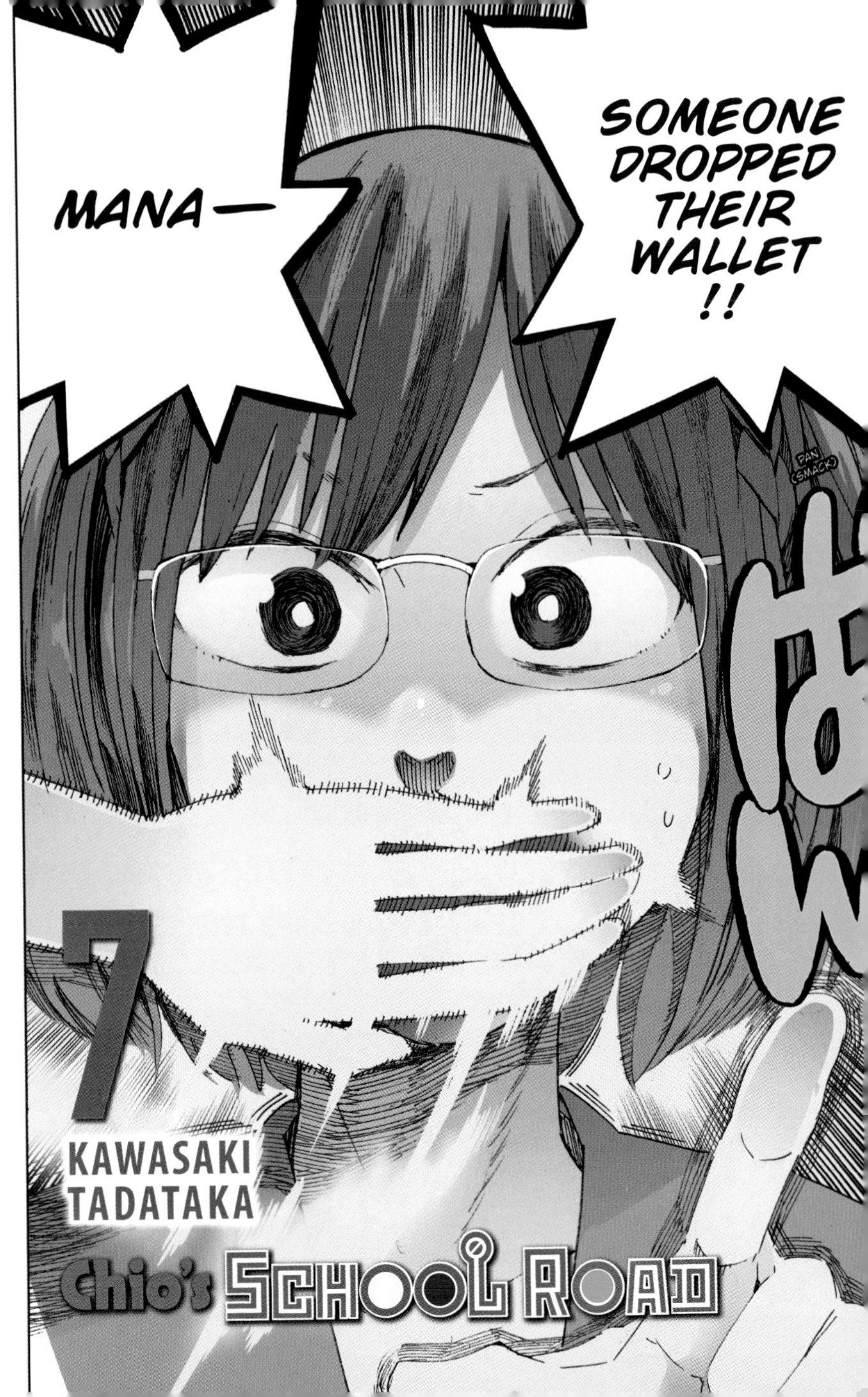
SOMEONE DROPPED THEIR WALLET !!
MANA—
PAN (SMACK)
7
KAWASAKI TADATAKA
Chio's SCHOOL ROAD

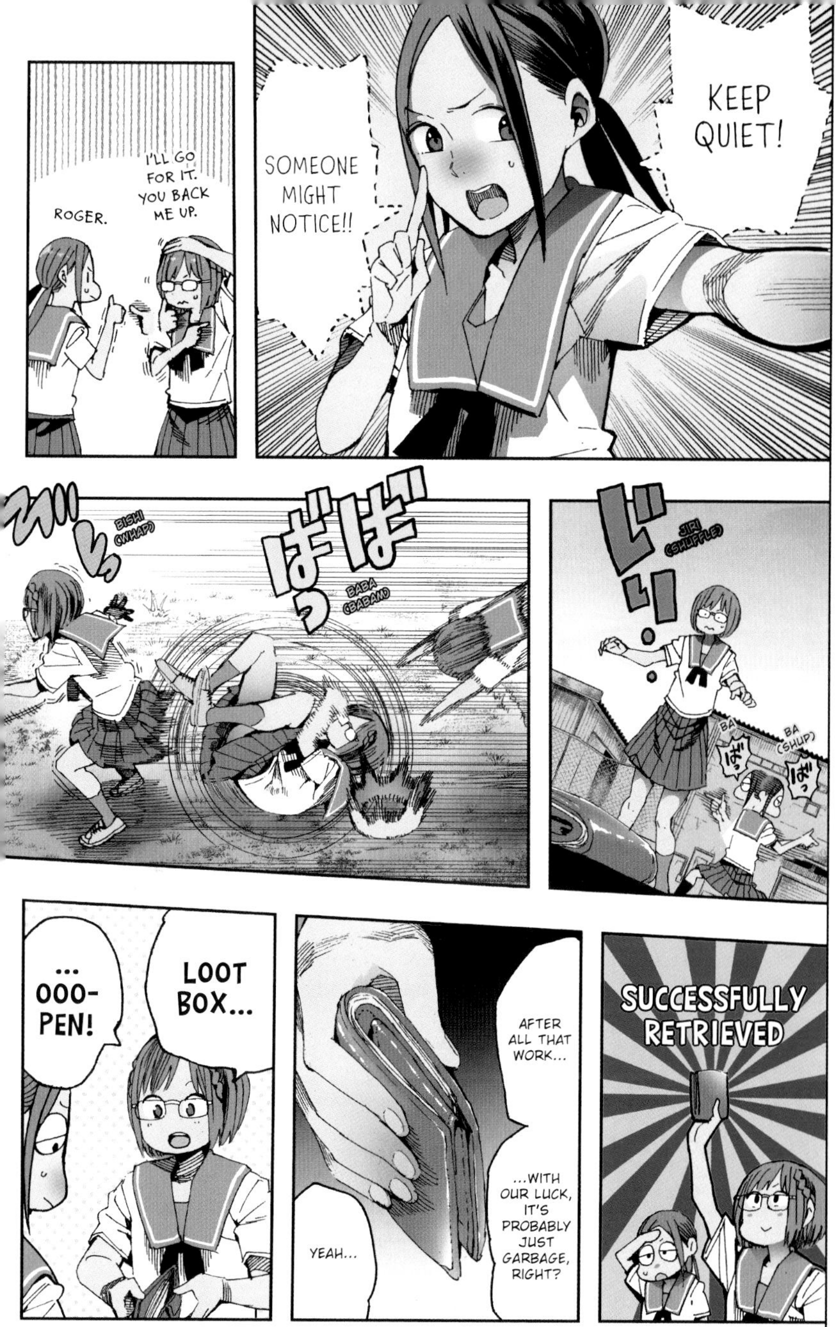
KEEP QUIET!
SOMEONE MIGHT NOTICE!!
I'LL GO FOR IT. YOU BACK ME UP.
ROGER.
JIRI (SHUFFLE)
BA
BA (SHUP)
BABA (BABAM)
BISHI (WHAP)
SUCCESSFULLY RETRIEVED
AFTER ALL THAT WORK...
...WITH OUR LUCK, IT'S PROBABLY JUST GARBAGE, RIGHT?
YEAH...
LOOT BOX...
...OOO-PEN!

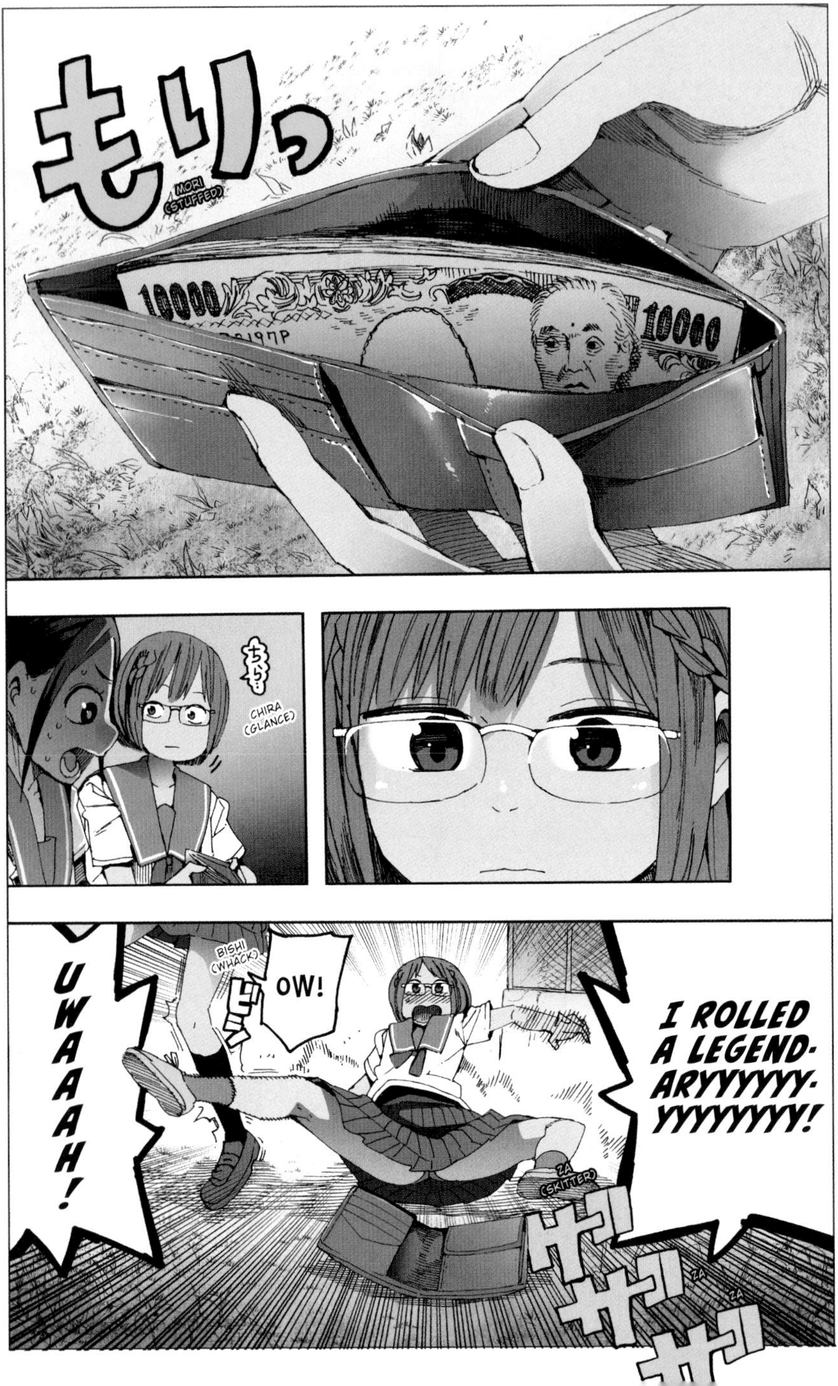
もりっ
MORI (STUFFED)
10000
10000
ちら…
CHIRA (GLANCE)
I ROLLED A LEGEND-ARYYYYYYY-YYYYYYYY!
OW!
BISHI (WHACK)
UWAAAAH!
ZA (SKITTER)
ZA
ZA

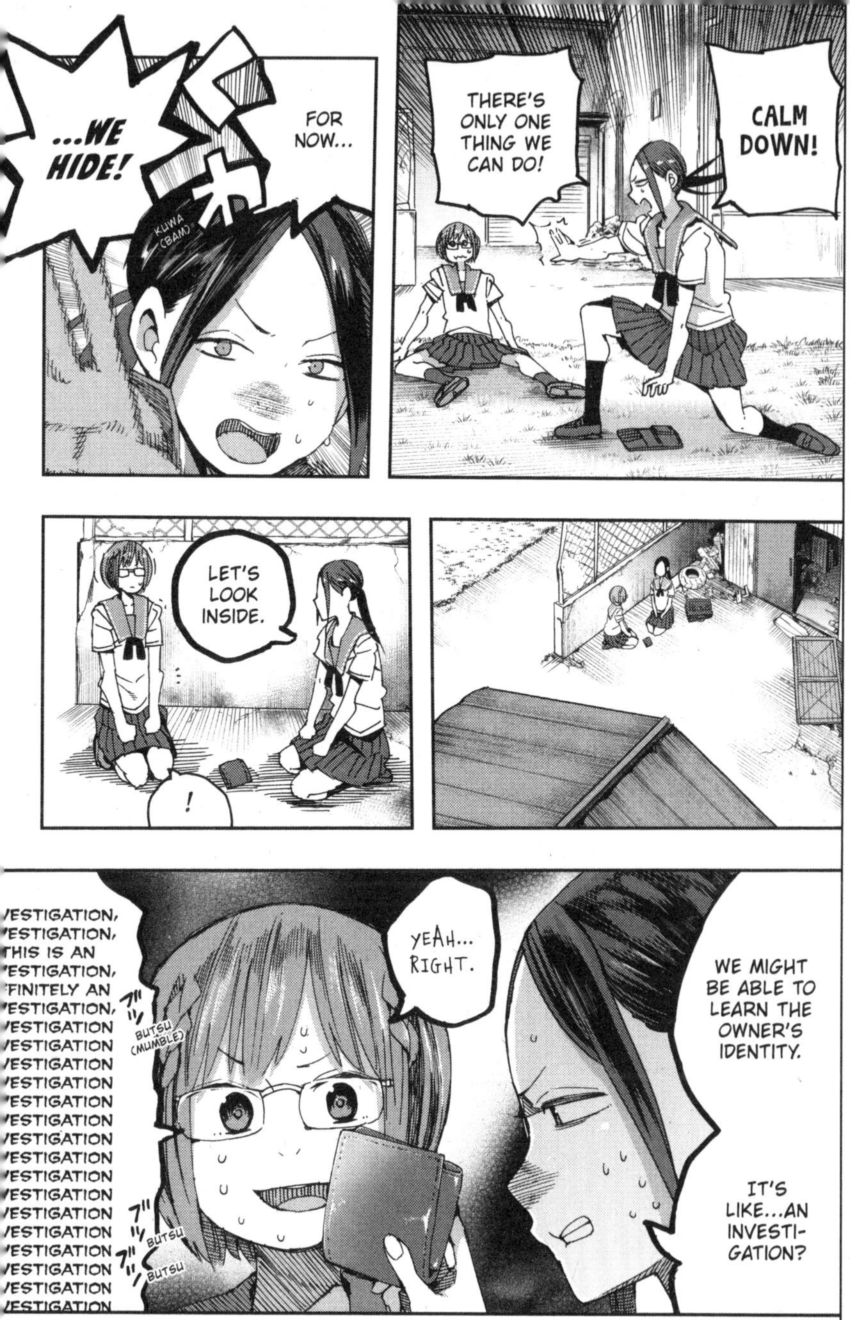
CALM DOWN!
THERE'S ONLY ONE THING WE CAN DO!
FOR NOW...
...WE HIDE!
KUWA (BAM)
LET'S LOOK INSIDE.
!
WE MIGHT BE ABLE TO LEARN THE OWNER'S IDENTITY.
IT'S LIKE...AN INVESTIGATION?
YEAH... RIGHT.
BUTSU (MUMBLE)
BUTSU
BUTSU
/ESTIGATION,
'ESTIGATION,
THIS IS AN
'ESTIGATION,
FINITELY AN
/ESTIGATION,
/ESTIGATION
/ESTIGATION
/ESTIGATION
/ESTIGATION
/ESTIGATION
/ESTIGATION
/ESTIGATION
/ESTIGATION
/ESTIGATION
/ESTIGATION
/ESTIGATION
/ESTIGATION
/ESTIGATION
/ESTIGATION
/ESTIGATION
/ESTIGATION

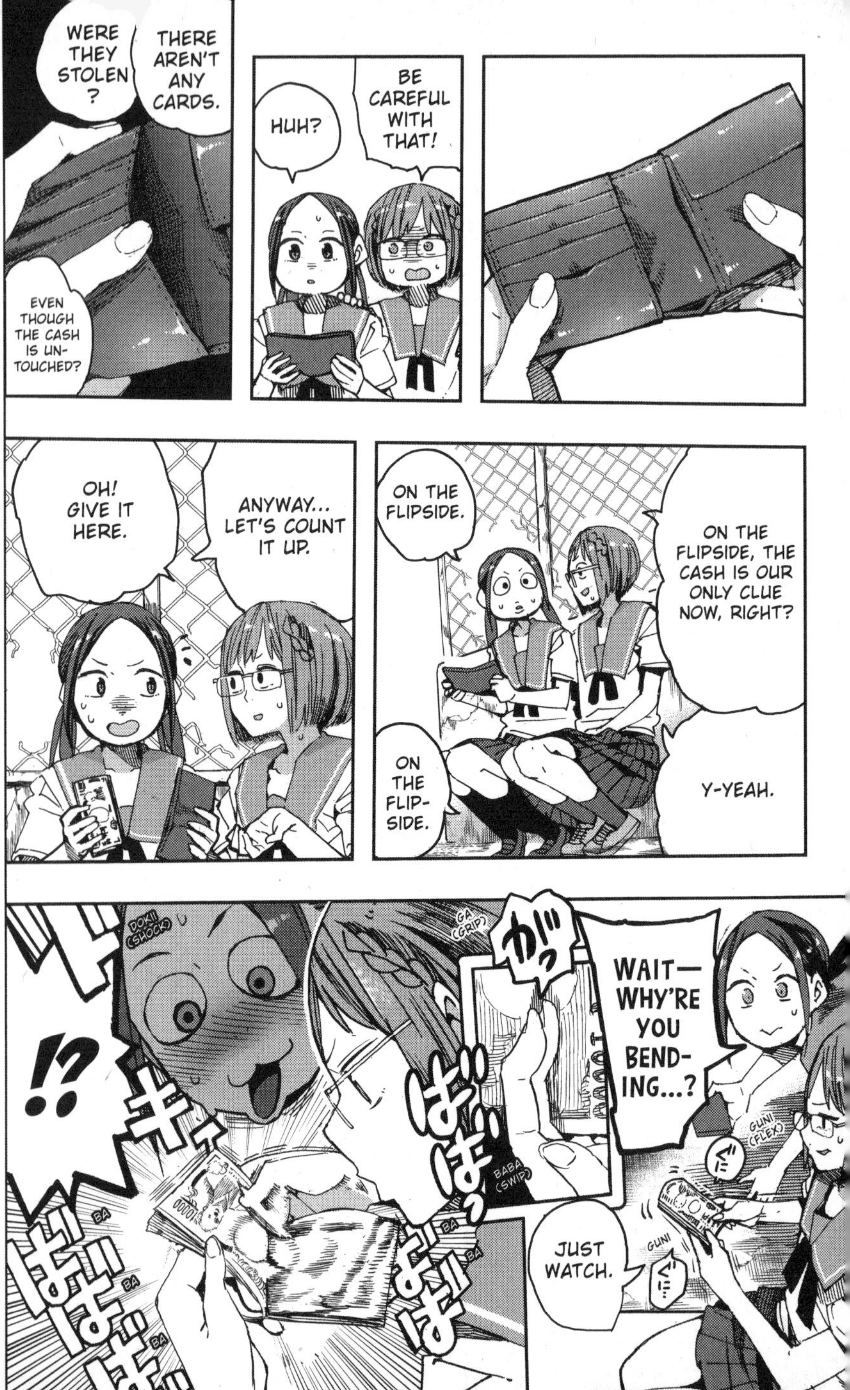

BE CAREFUL WITH THAT!
HUH?
THERE AREN'T ANY CARDS.
WERE THEY STOLEN?
EVEN THOUGH THE CASH IS UN-TOUCHED?
ON THE FLIPSIDE, THE CASH IS OUR ONLY CLUE NOW, RIGHT?
ON THE FLIPSIDE.
Y-YEAH.
ON THE FLIPSIDE.
ANYWAY... LET'S COUNT IT UP.
OH! GIVE IT HERE.
WAIT—WHY'RE YOU BENDING...?
GUNI (FLEX)
JUST WATCH.
GUNI
GA (GRIP)
BABA (SWIP)
DOKI! (SHOCK)
!?
BA
BA
BA
BA
BA

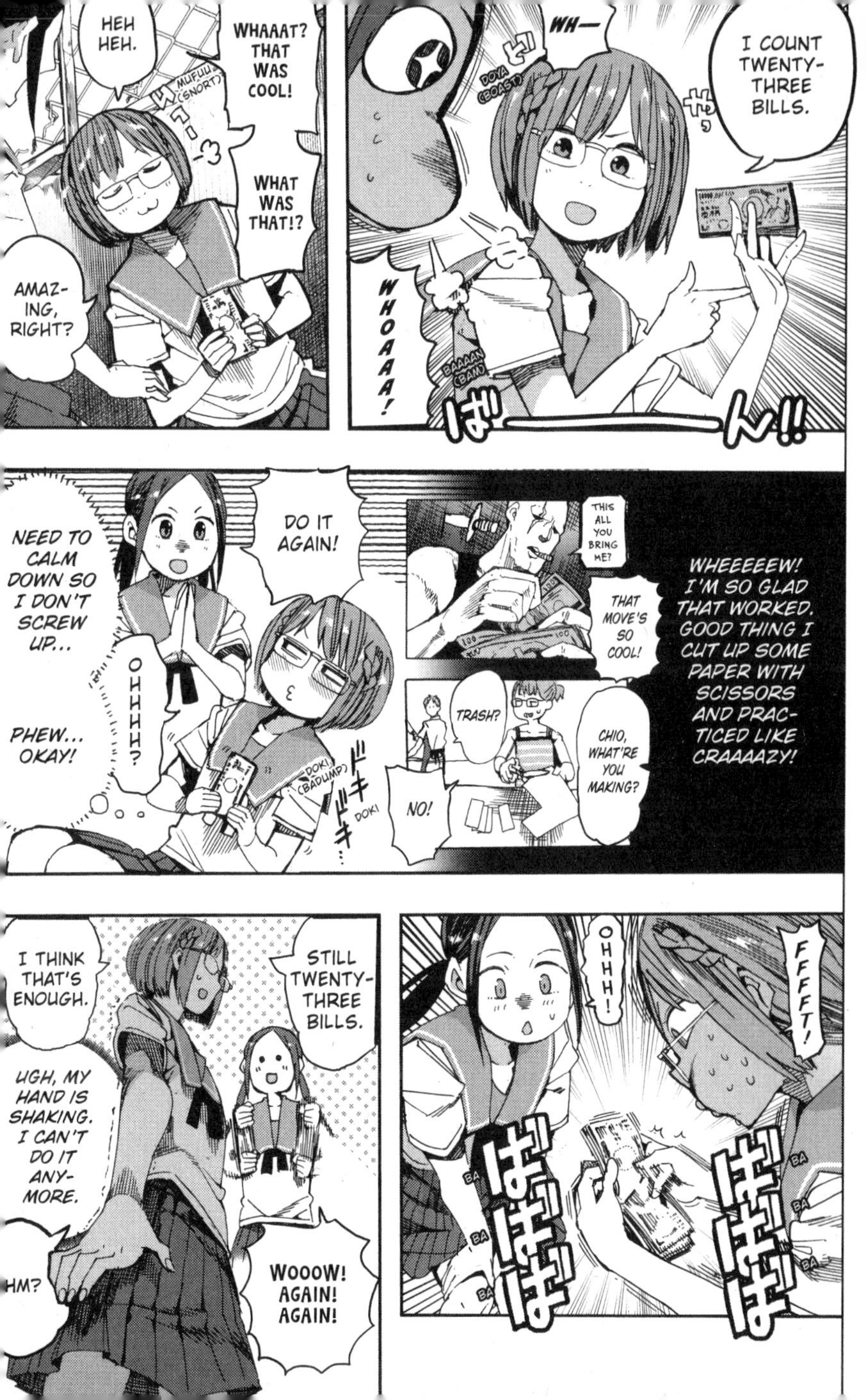
I COUNT TWENTY-THREE BILLS.
WH—
DOYA (BOAST)
BAAAAN (BAM)
WHOAAAA!
WHAAAT? THAT WAS COOL!
WHAT WAS THAT!?
HEH HEH.
MUFUU (SNORT)
AMAZ-ING, RIGHT?
WHEEEEEW! I'M SO GLAD THAT WORKED. GOOD THING I CUT UP SOME PAPER WITH SCISSORS AND PRAC-TICED LIKE CRAAAAZY!
THIS ALL YOU BRING ME?
THAT MOVE'S SO COOL!
CHIO, WHAT'RE YOU MAKING?
TRASH?
NO!
DO IT AGAIN!
OHHHH?
NEED TO CALM DOWN SO I DON'T SCREW UP...
PHEW... OKAY!
DOKI (BADUMP)
DOKI
FFFFT!
OHHH!
BA
BA
BA
BA
BA
BA
STILL TWENTY-THREE BILLS.
I THINK THAT'S ENOUGH.
WOOOW! AGAIN! AGAIN!
UGH, MY HAND IS SHAKING. I CAN'T DO IT ANY-MORE.
HM?

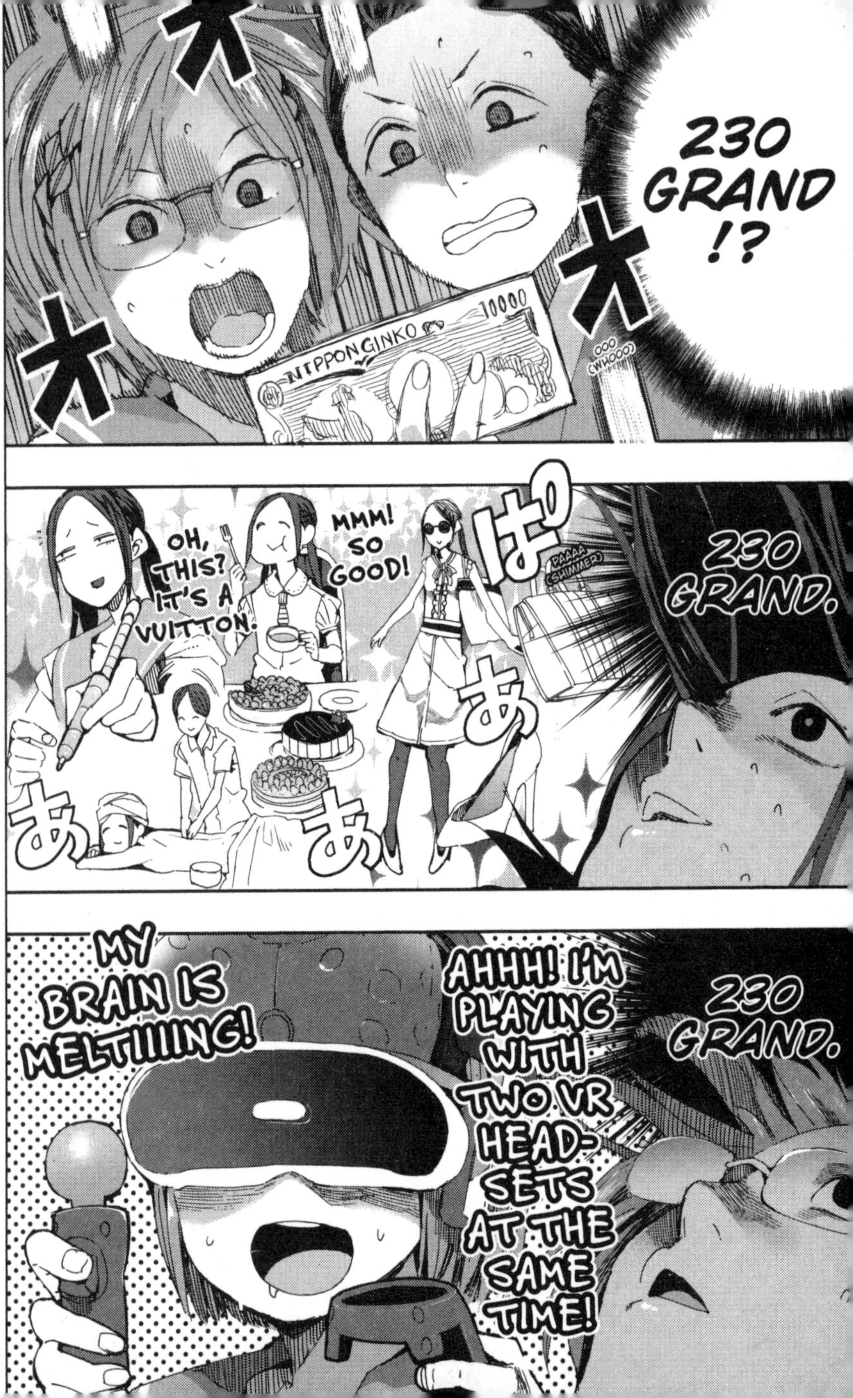
230 GRAND!?
オ
オ
OOO (WHOOO)
10000
NIPPON GINKO
オ
230 GRAND.
PAAAA (SHIMMER)
は
MMM! SO GOOD!
OH, THIS? IT'S A VUITTON.
あ
あ
あ
230 GRAND.
AHHHH! I'M PLAYING WITH TWO VR HEAD-SETS AT THE SAME TIME!
MY BRAIN IS MELTIIIIING!

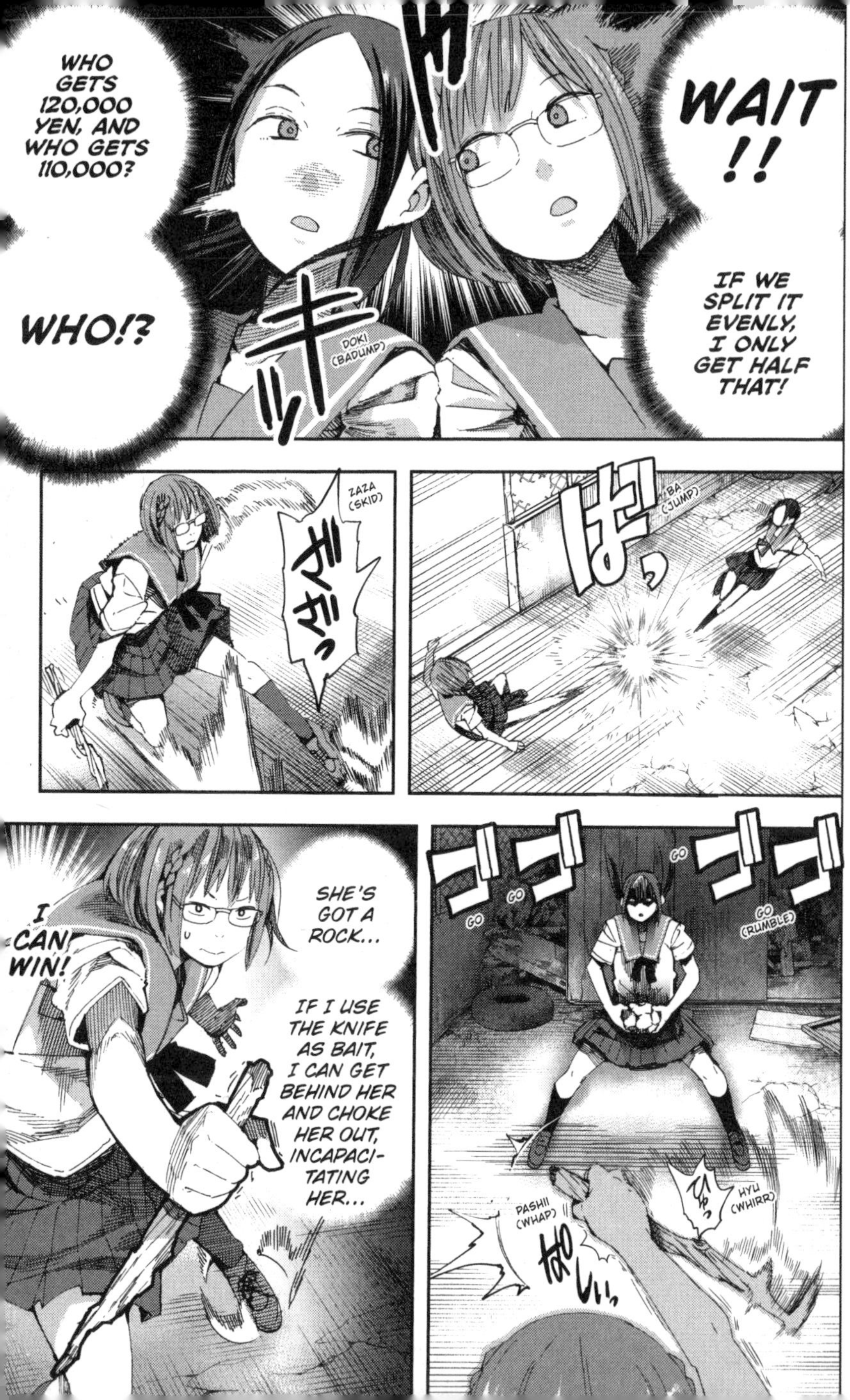
WAIT!!
WHO GETS 120,000 YEN, AND WHO GETS 110,000?
IF WE SPLIT IT EVENLY, I ONLY GET HALF THAT!
DOKI (BADUMP)
WHO!?
BA (JUMP)
ZAZA (SKID)
GO
GO
GO
GO (RUMBLE)
HYU (WHIRR)
PASHI (WHAP)
SHE'S GOT A ROCK...
IF I USE THE KNIFE AS BAIT, I CAN GET BEHIND HER AND CHOKE HER OUT, INCAPACITATING HER...
I CAN WIN!

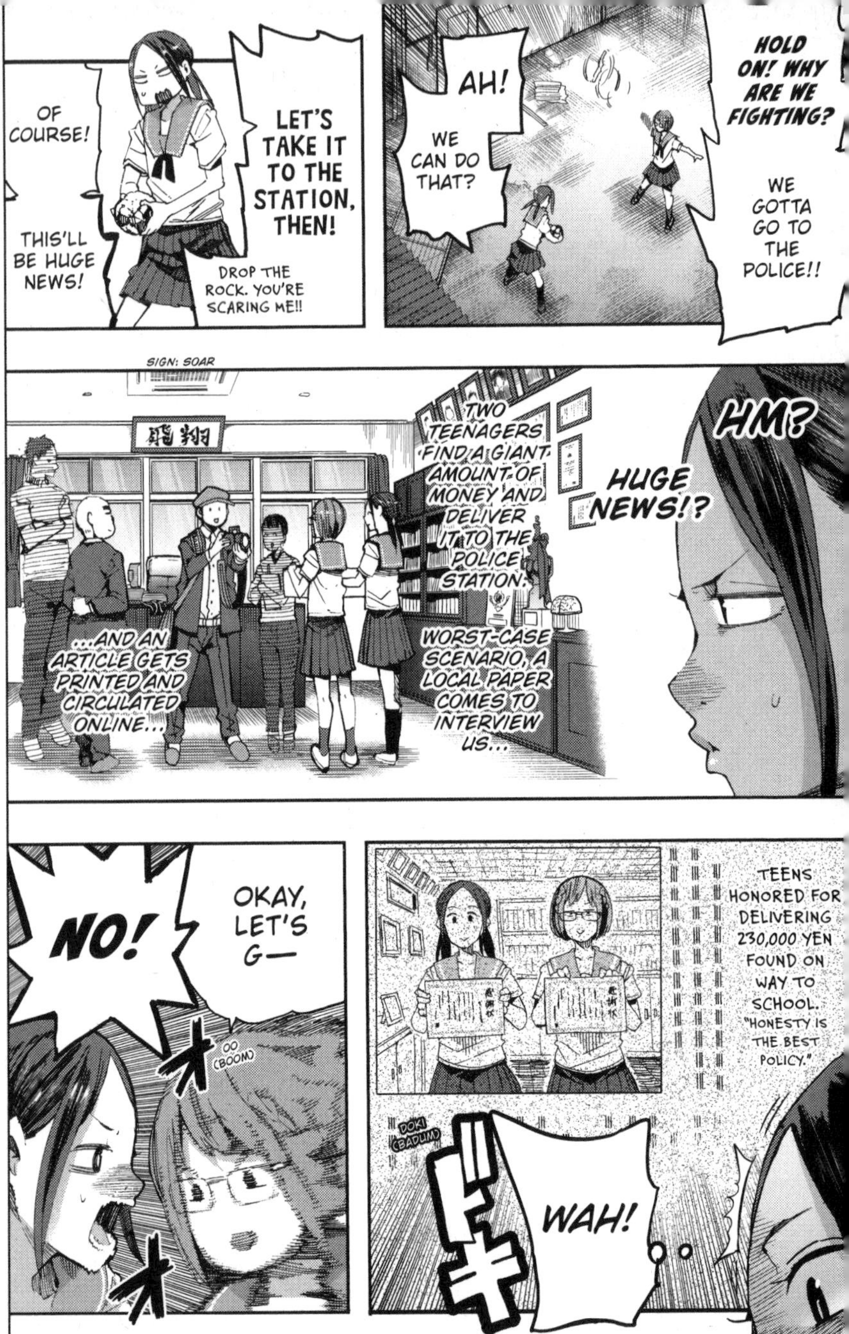

HOLD ON! WHY ARE WE FIGHTING?
WE GOTTA GO TO THE POLICE!!
AH!
WE CAN DO THAT?
LET'S TAKE IT TO THE STATION, THEN!
OF COURSE!
THIS'LL BE HUGE NEWS!
DROP THE ROCK. YOU'RE SCARING ME!!
HM?
HUGE NEWS!?
SIGN: SOAR
TWO TEENAGERS FIND A GIANT AMOUNT OF MONEY AND DELIVER IT TO THE POLICE STATION.
WORST-CASE SCENARIO, A LOCAL PAPER COMES TO INTERVIEW US...
...AND AN ARTICLE GETS PRINTED AND CIRCULATED ONLINE...
TEENS HONORED FOR DELIVERING 230,000 YEN FOUND ON WAY TO SCHOOL. "HONESTY IS THE BEST POLICY."
DOKI (BADUM)
WAH!
OKAY, LET'S G—
NO!
DO (BOOM)

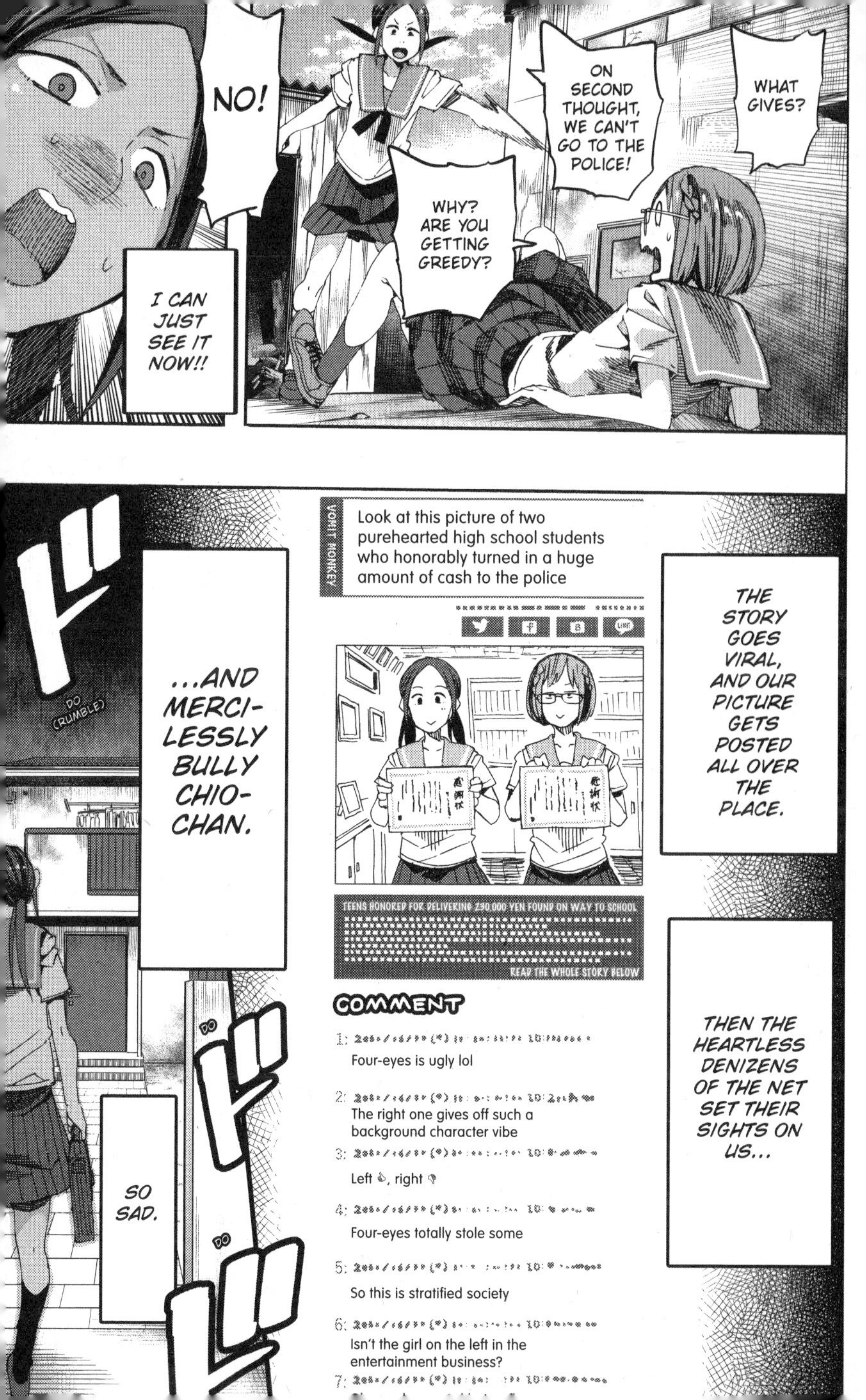

WHAT GIVES?
ON SECOND THOUGHT, WE CAN'T GO TO THE POLICE!
WHY? ARE YOU GETTING GREEDY?
NO!
I CAN JUST SEE IT NOW!!
THE STORY GOES VIRAL, AND OUR PICTURE GETS POSTED ALL OVER THE PLACE.
VOMIT MONKEY
Look at this picture of two purehearted high school students who honorably turned in a huge amount of cash to the police
TEENS HONORED FOR DELIVERING 230,000 YEN FOUND ON WAY TO SCHOOL
READ THE WHOLE STORY BELOW
COMMENT
1: Four-eyes is ugly lol
2: The right one gives off such a background character vibe
3: Left 👍, right 👎
4: Four-eyes totally stole some
5: So this is stratified society
6: Isn't the girl on the left in the entertainment business?
7:
THEN THE HEARTLESS DENIZENS OF THE NET SET THEIR SIGHTS ON US...
...AND MERCILESSLY BULLY CHIO-CHAN.
DO (CRUMBLE)
SO SAD.
DO
DO

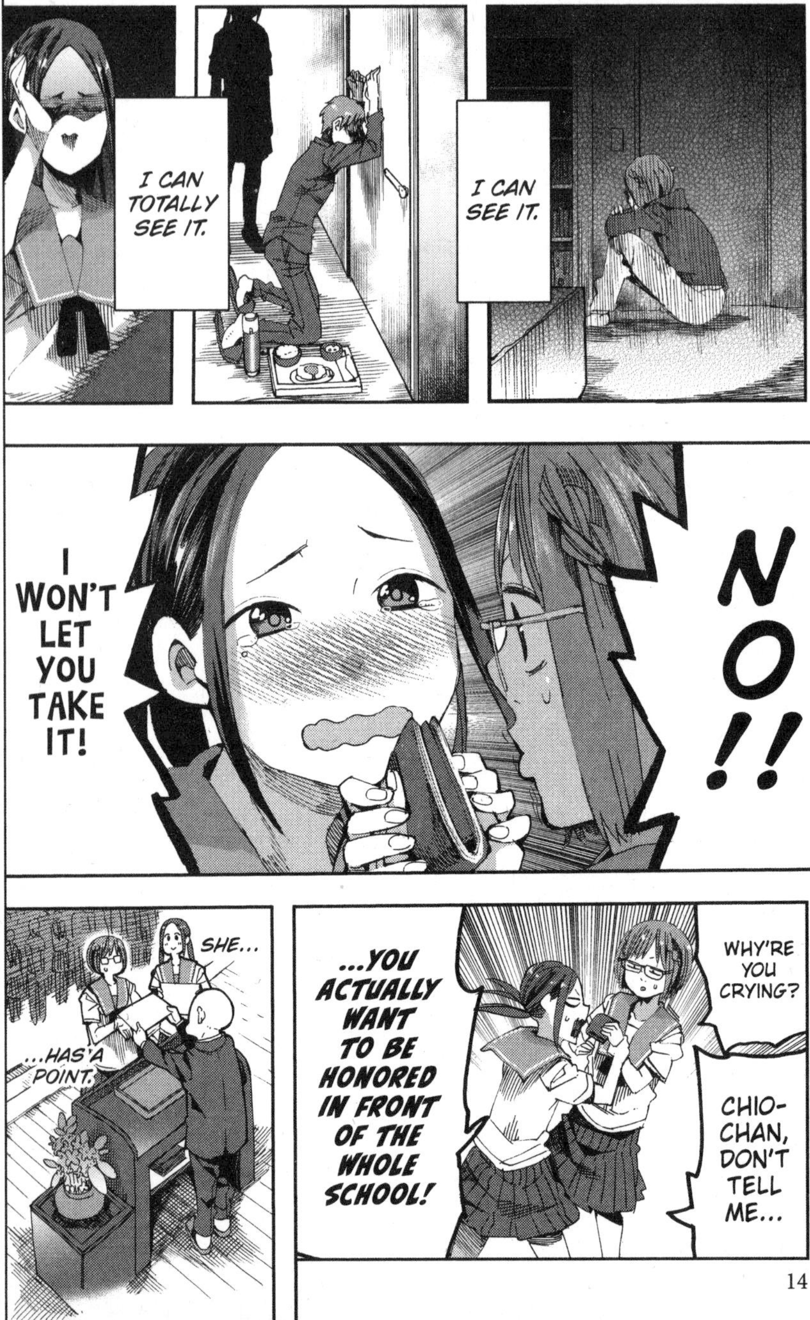
I CAN SEE IT.
I CAN TOTALLY SEE IT.
NO!!
I WON'T LET YOU TAKE IT!
WHY'RE YOU CRYING?
CHIO-CHAN, DON'T TELL ME...
...YOU ACTUALLY WANT TO BE HONORED IN FRONT OF THE WHOLE SCHOOL!
SHE...
...HAS A POINT.

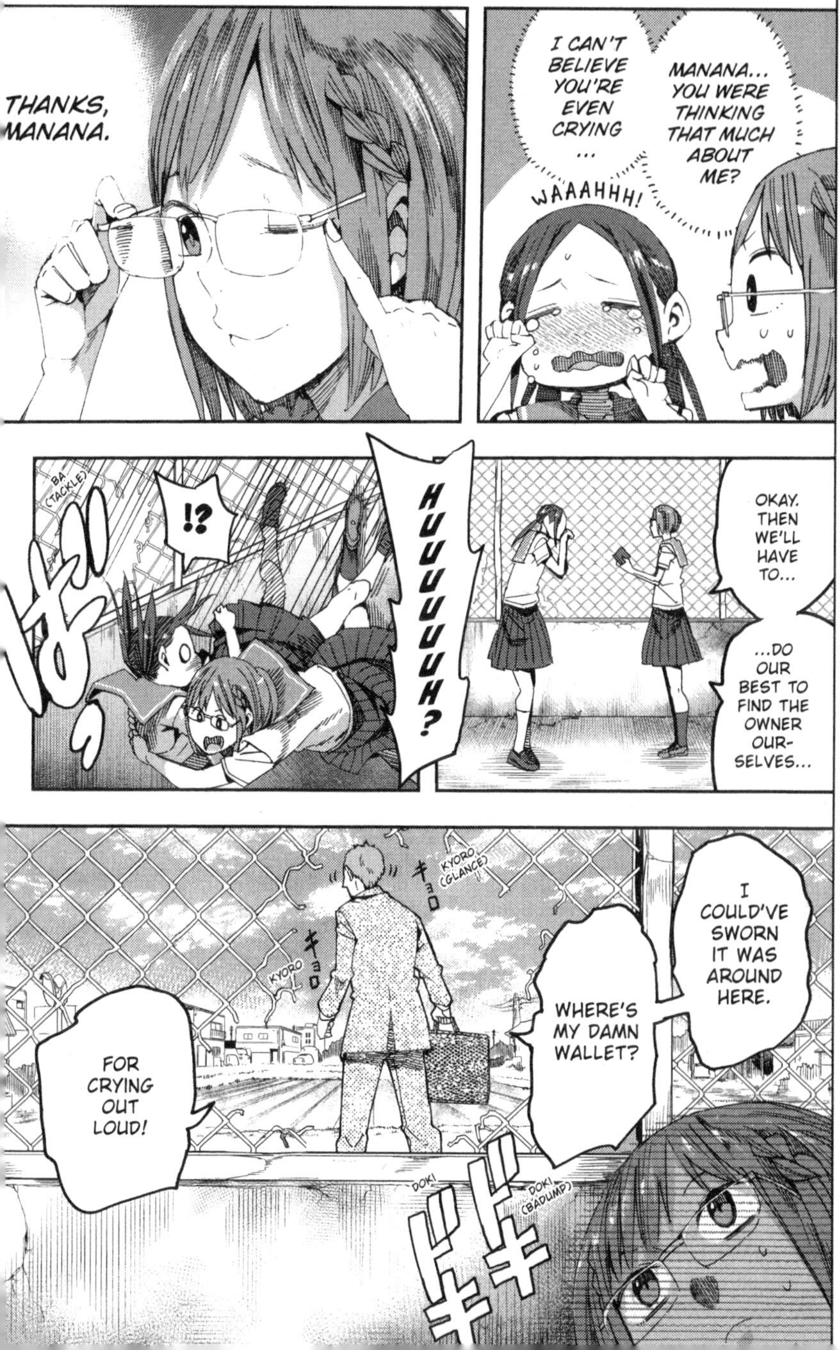
MANANA... YOU WERE THINKING THAT MUCH ABOUT ME?
I CAN'T BELIEVE YOU'RE EVEN CRYING...
WAAAHHH!
THANKS, MANANA.
OKAY. THEN WE'LL HAVE TO...
...DO OUR BEST TO FIND THE OWNER OURSELVES...
HUUUUUUUH?
!?
BA (TACKLE)
I COULD'VE SWORN IT WAS AROUND HERE.
KYORO (GLANCE)
WHERE'S MY DAMN WALLET?
KYORO
FOR CRYING OUT LOUD!
DOKI (BADUMP)
DOKI!

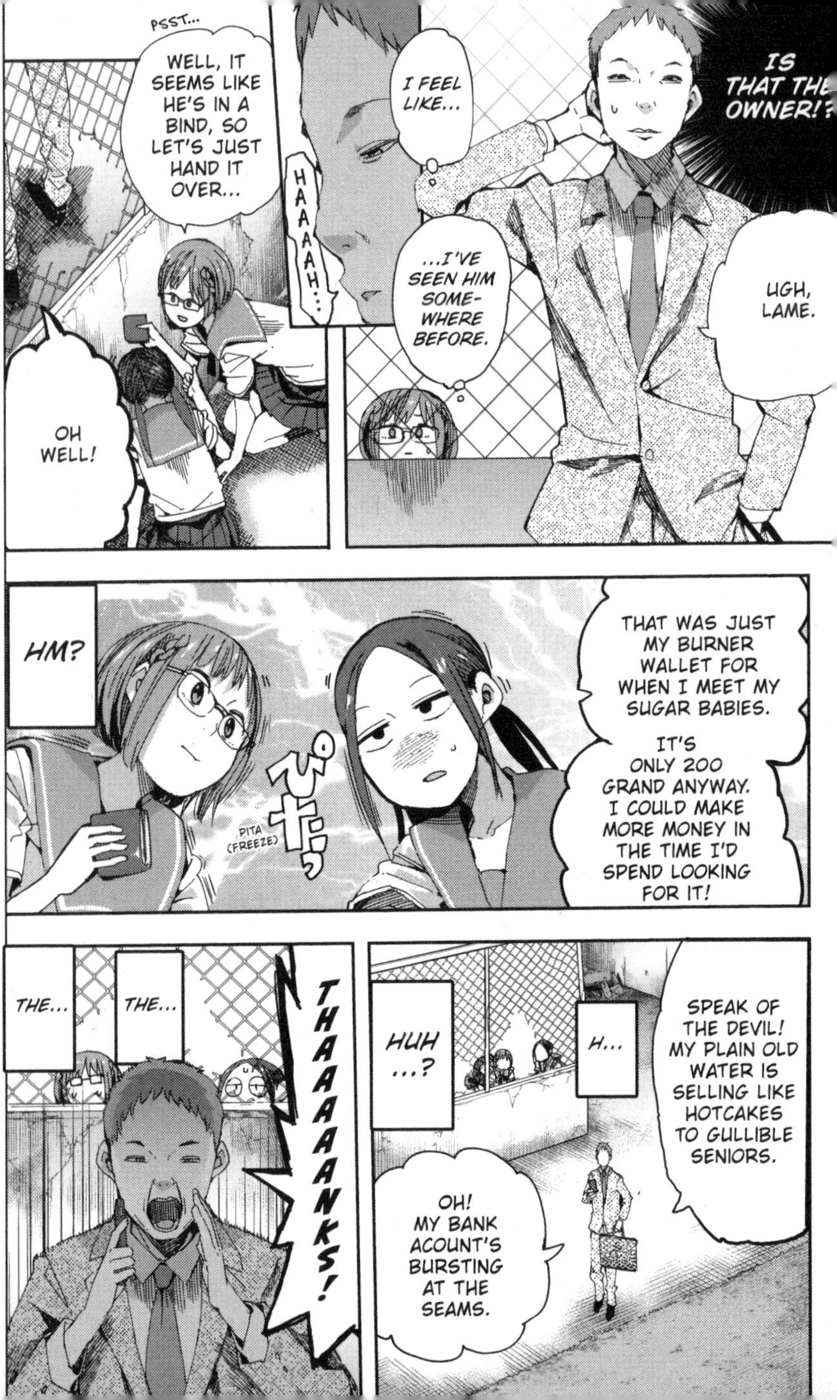
IS THAT THE OWNER!?
UGH, LAME.
HAAAAAH...
I FEEL LIKE...
...I'VE SEEN HIM SOMEWHERE BEFORE.
PSST...
WELL, IT SEEMS LIKE HE'S IN A BIND, SO LET'S JUST HAND IT OVER...
OH WELL!
THAT WAS JUST MY BURNER WALLET FOR WHEN I MEET MY SUGAR BABIES.
IT'S ONLY 200 GRAND ANYWAY. I COULD MAKE MORE MONEY IN THE TIME I'D SPEND LOOKING FOR IT!
PITA (FREEZE)
HM?
SPEAK OF THE DEVIL! MY PLAIN OLD WATER IS SELLING LIKE HOTCAKES TO GULLIBLE SENIORS.
H...
HUH ...?
OH! MY BANK ACOUNT'S BURSTING AT THE SEAMS.
THE...
THE...
THAAAAAAANKS!

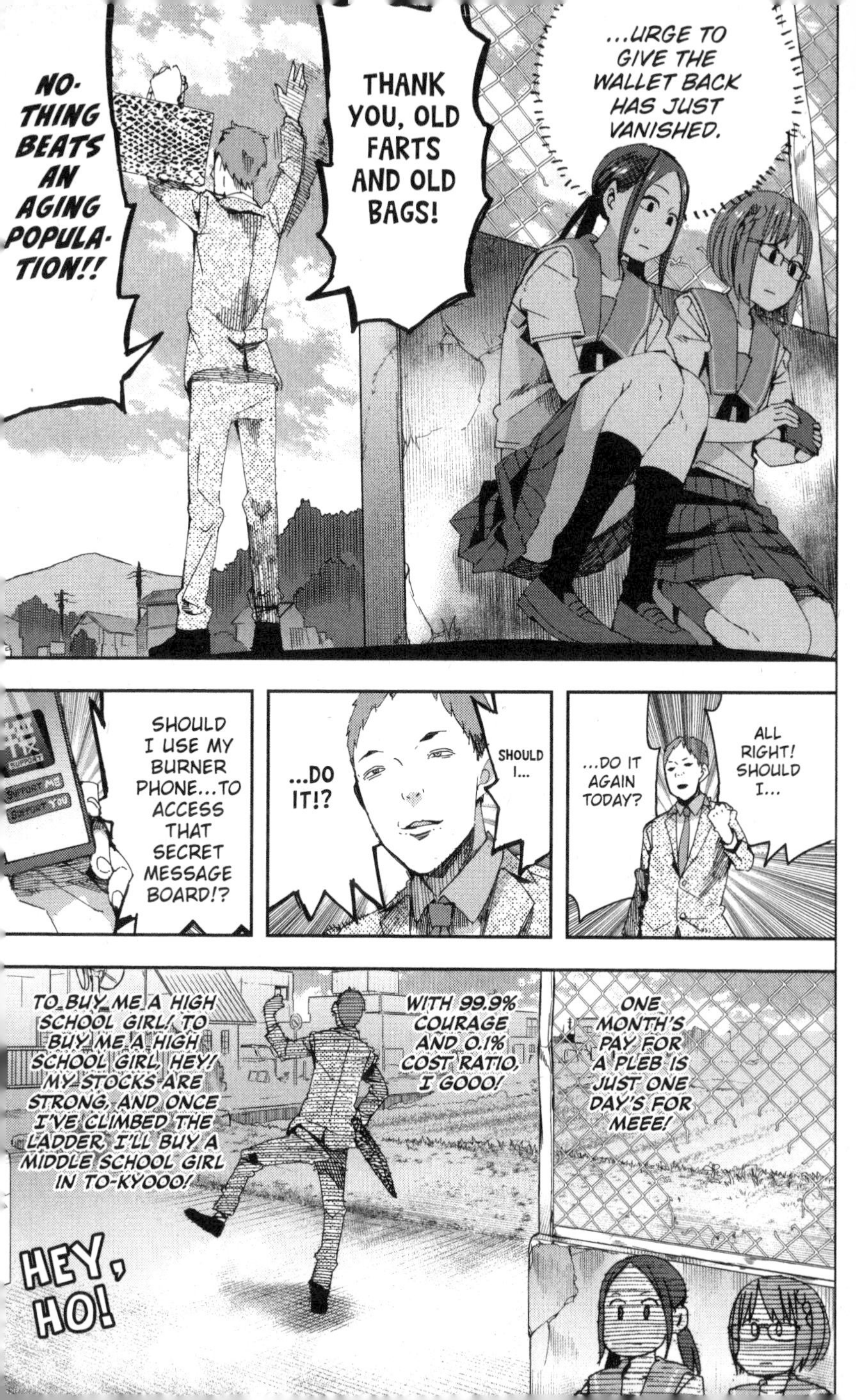
...URGE TO GIVE THE WALLET BACK HAS JUST VANISHED.
THANK YOU, OLD FARTS AND OLD BAGS!
NOTHING BEATS AN AGING POPULATION!!
ALL RIGHT! SHOULD I...
...DO IT AGAIN TODAY?
SHOULD I...
...DO IT!?
SHOULD I USE MY BURNER PHONE...TO ACCESS THAT SECRET MESSAGE BOARD!?
SUPPORT ME
SUPPORT YOU
ONE MONTH'S PAY FOR A PLEB IS JUST ONE DAY'S FOR MEEE!
WITH 99.9% COURAGE AND 0.1% COST RATIO, I GOOO!
TO BUY ME A HIGH SCHOOL GIRL! TO BUY ME A HIGH SCHOOL GIRL, HEY! MY STOCKS ARE STRONG, AND ONCE I'VE CLIMBED THE LADDER, I'LL BUY A MIDDLE SCHOOL GIRL IN TO-KYOOO!
HEY, HO!

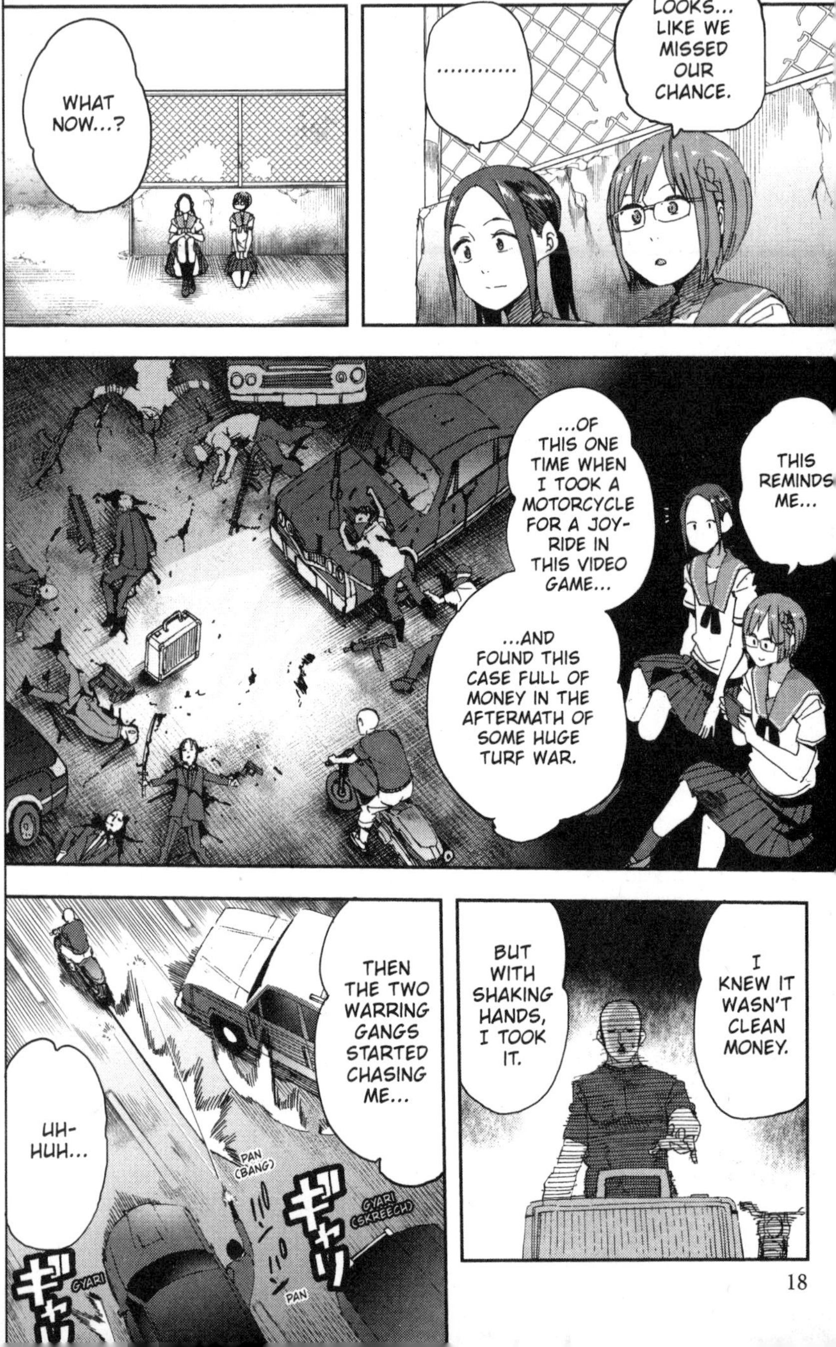
LOOKS... LIKE WE MISSED OUR CHANCE.
....
WHAT NOW...?
THIS REMINDS ME...
...OF THIS ONE TIME WHEN I TOOK A MOTORCYCLE FOR A JOY-RIDE IN THIS VIDEO GAME...
...AND FOUND THIS CASE FULL OF MONEY IN THE AFTERMATH OF SOME HUGE TURF WAR.
I KNEW IT WASN'T CLEAN MONEY.
BUT WITH SHAKING HANDS, I TOOK IT.
THEN THE TWO WARRING GANGS STARTED CHASING ME...
PAN (BANG)
GYARI (SKREECH)
UH-HUH...
GYARI
PAN

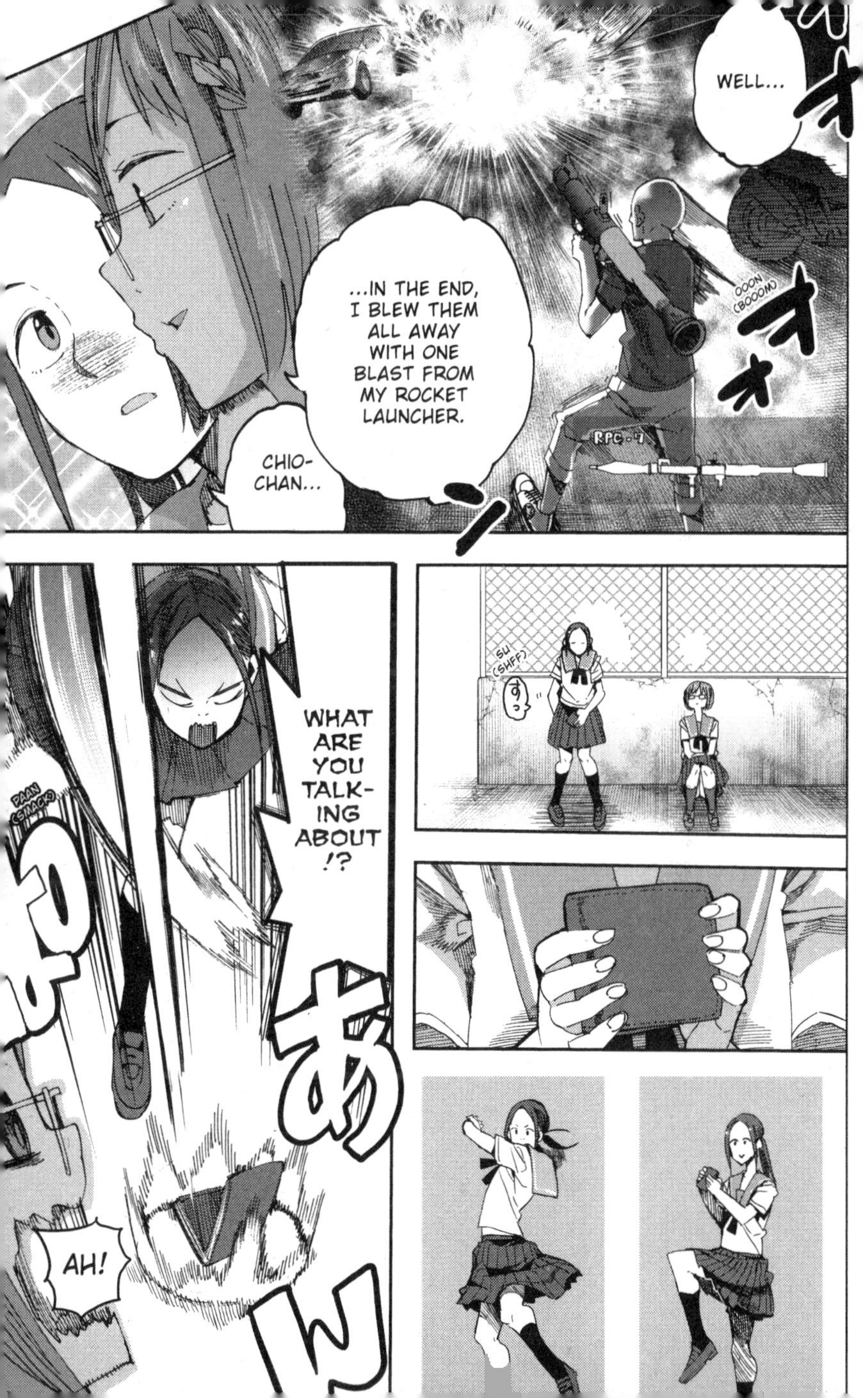
WELL...
...IN THE END, I BLEW THEM ALL AWAY WITH ONE BLAST FROM MY ROCKET LAUNCHER.
OOON (BOOOM)
RPG-7
CHIO-CHAN...
SU (SHFF)
WHAT ARE YOU TALKING ABOUT!?
PAAN (SMACK)
AH!

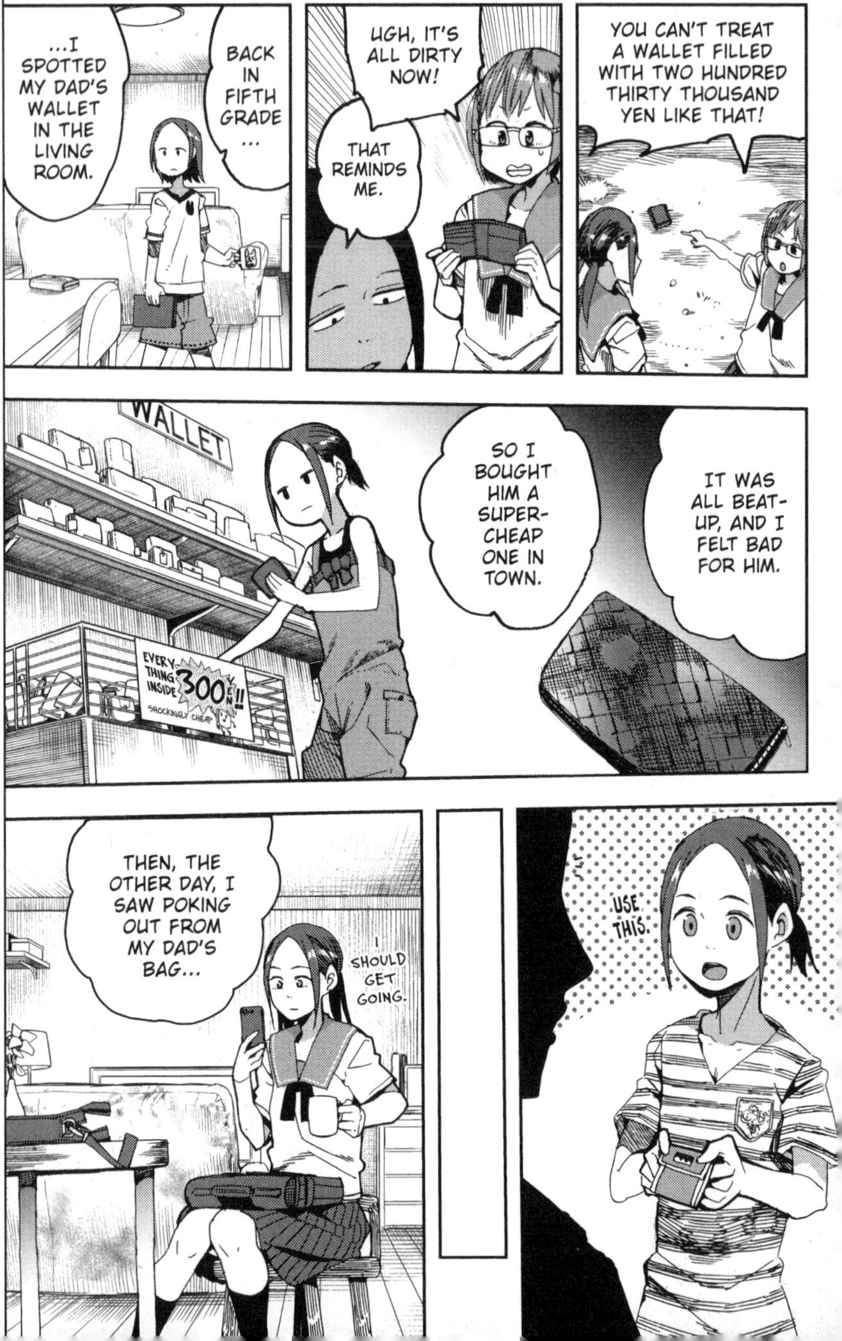
YOU CAN'T TREAT A WALLET FILLED WITH TWO HUNDRED THIRTY THOUSAND YEN LIKE THAT!
UGH, IT'S ALL DIRTY NOW!
THAT REMINDS ME.
BACK IN FIFTH GRADE...
...I SPOTTED MY DAD'S WALLET IN THE LIVING ROOM.
IT WAS ALL BEAT-UP, AND I FELT BAD FOR HIM.
SO I BOUGHT HIM A SUPER-CHEAP ONE IN TOWN.
WALLET
EVERYTHING INSIDE 300 YEN!!
SHOCKINGLY CHEAP
USE THIS.
THEN, THE OTHER DAY, I SAW POKING OUT FROM MY DAD'S BAG...
I SHOULD GET GOING.

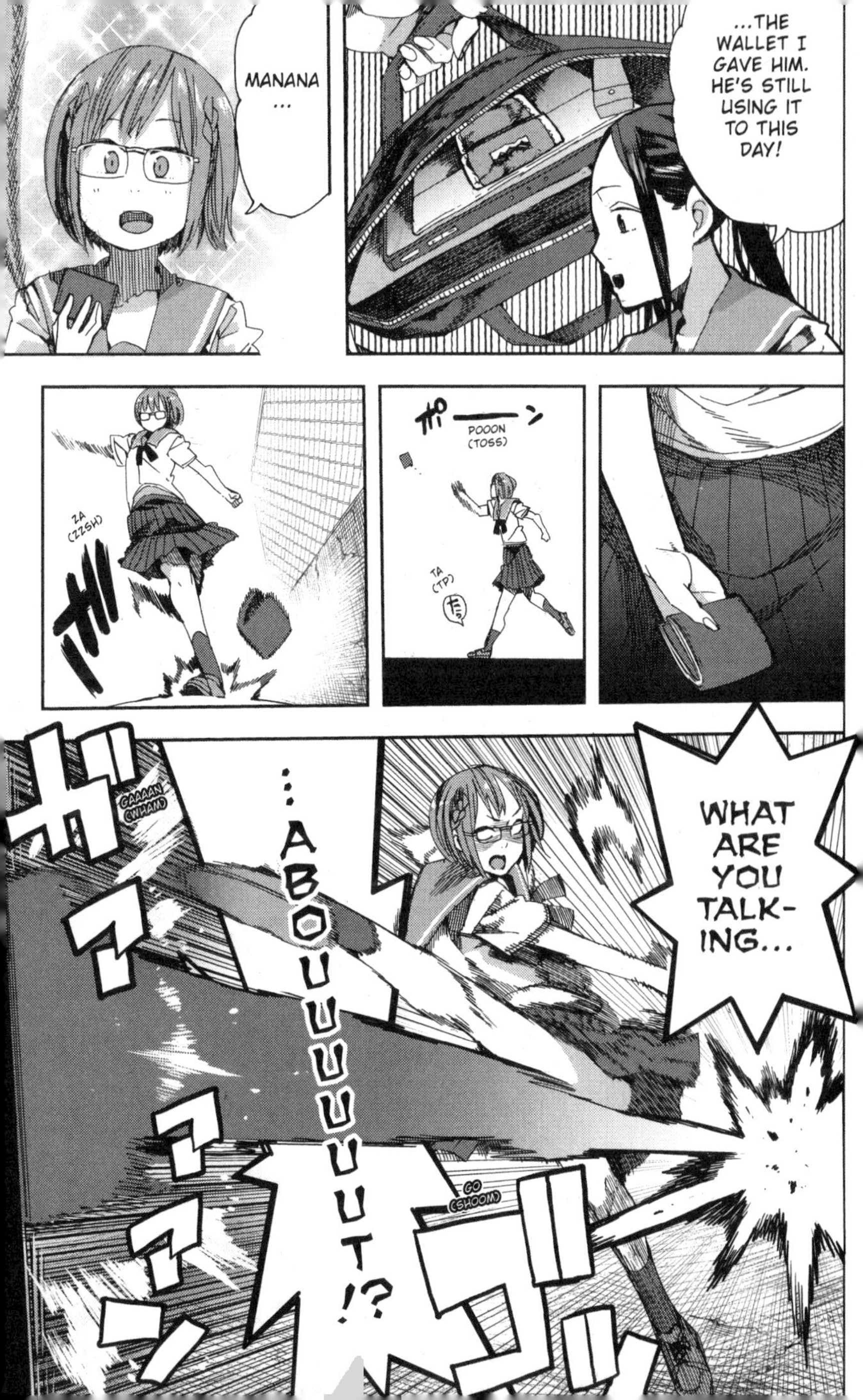
...THE WALLET I GAVE HIM. HE'S STILL USING IT TO THIS DAY!
MANANA ...
ポーン
POOON (TOSS)
TA (TP)
ZA (ZZZSH)
WHAT ARE YOU TALKING...
...ABOUUUUUT!?
GAAAAN (WHAM)
GO (SHOOM)

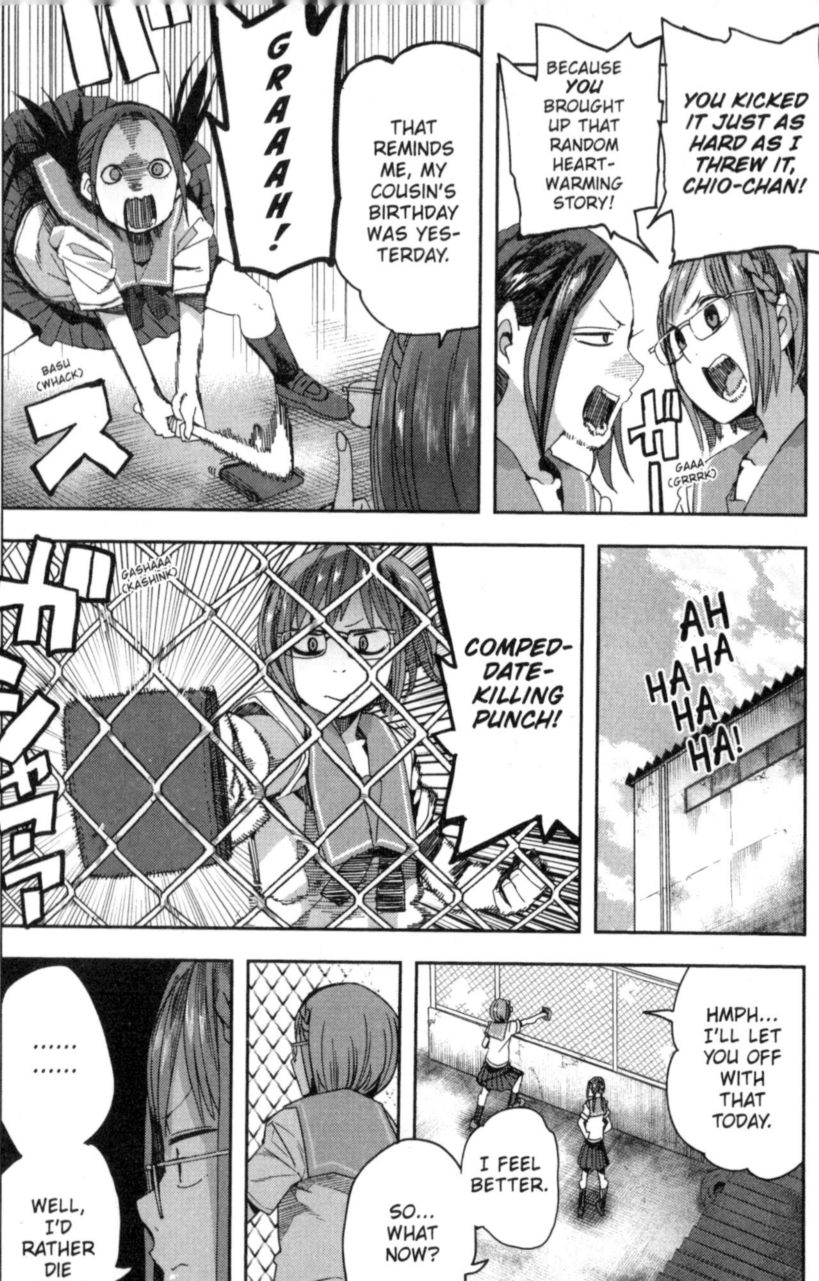
YOU KICKED IT JUST AS HARD AS I THREW IT, CHIO-CHAN!
BECAUSE YOU BROUGHT UP THAT RANDOM HEART-WARMING STORY!
GAAA (GRRRK)
THAT REMINDS ME, MY COUSIN'S BIRTHDAY WAS YES-TERDAY.
GRAAAAH!
BASU (WHACK)
AH HA HA HA HA HA!
COMPED-DATE-KILLING PUNCH!
GASHAAA (KASHINK)
HMPH... I'LL LET YOU OFF WITH THAT TODAY.
I FEEL BETTER.
SO... WHAT NOW?
......
......
WELL, I'D RATHER DIE THAN GIVE IT BACK.

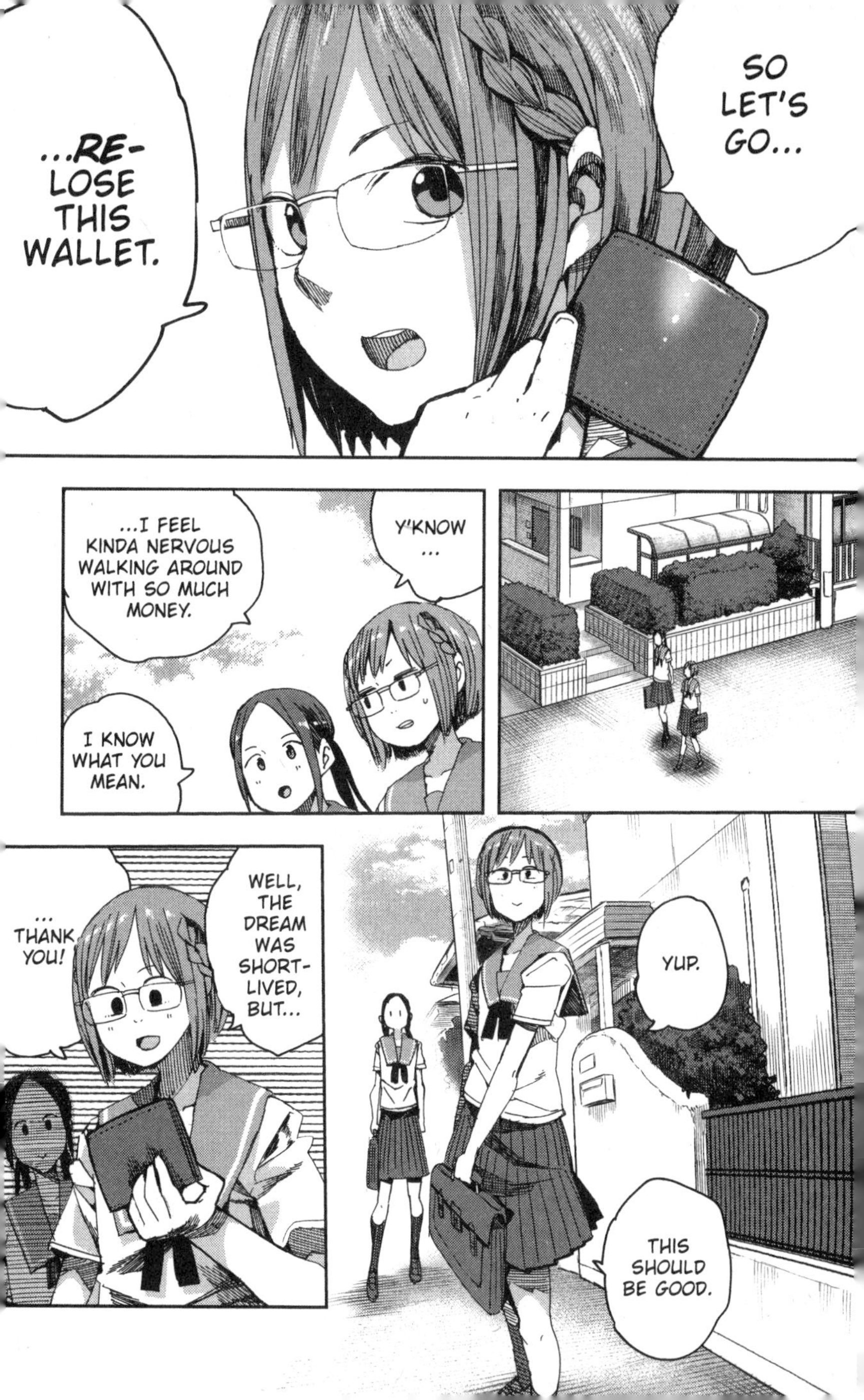
SO LET'S GO...
...RE-LOSE THIS WALLET.
Y'KNOW...
...I FEEL KINDA NERVOUS WALKING AROUND WITH SO MUCH MONEY.
I KNOW WHAT YOU MEAN.
YUP.
THIS SHOULD BE GOOD.
WELL, THE DREAM WAS SHORT-LIVED, BUT...
...THANK YOU!

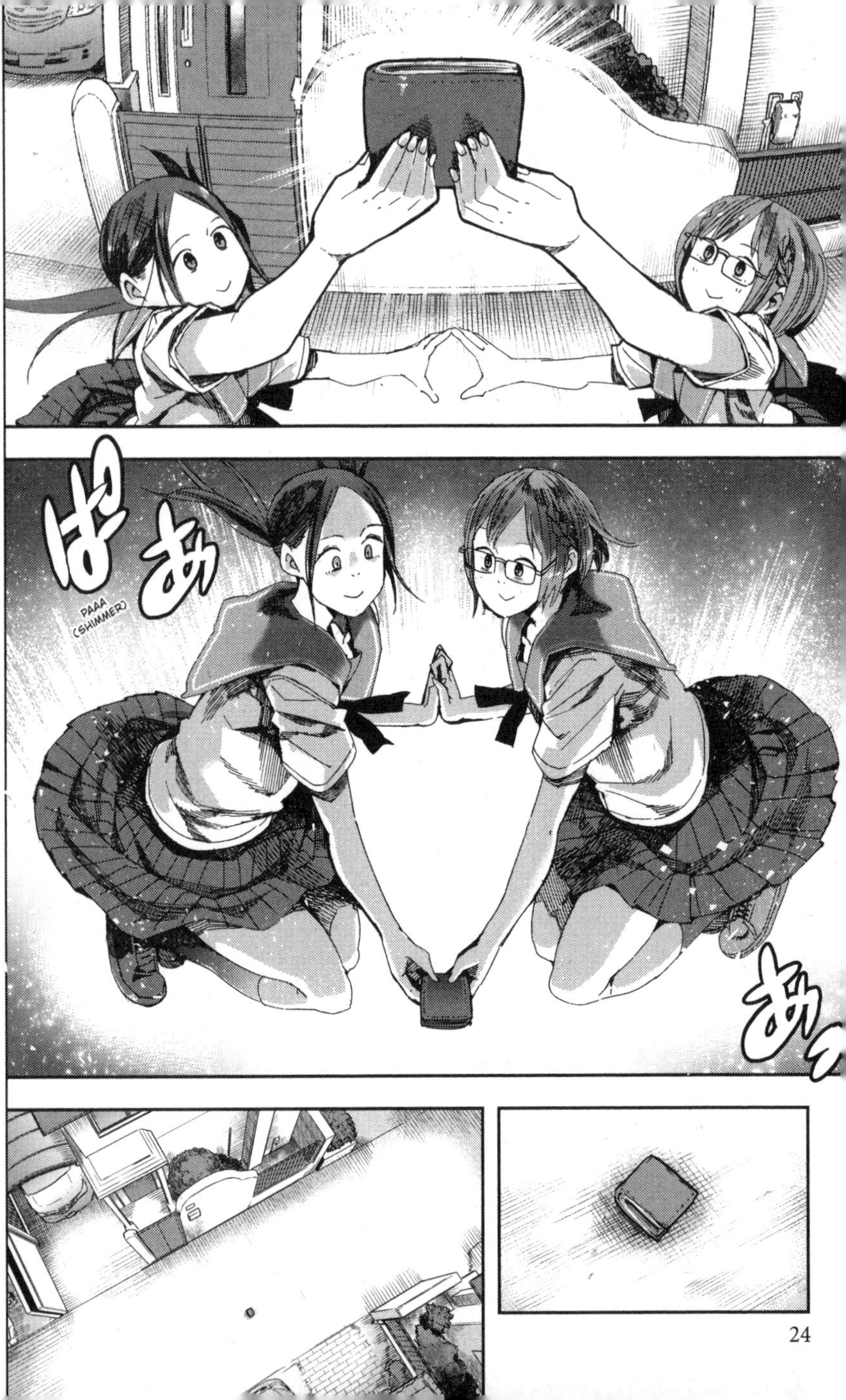
ぱあ
PAAA (SHIMMER)
あ

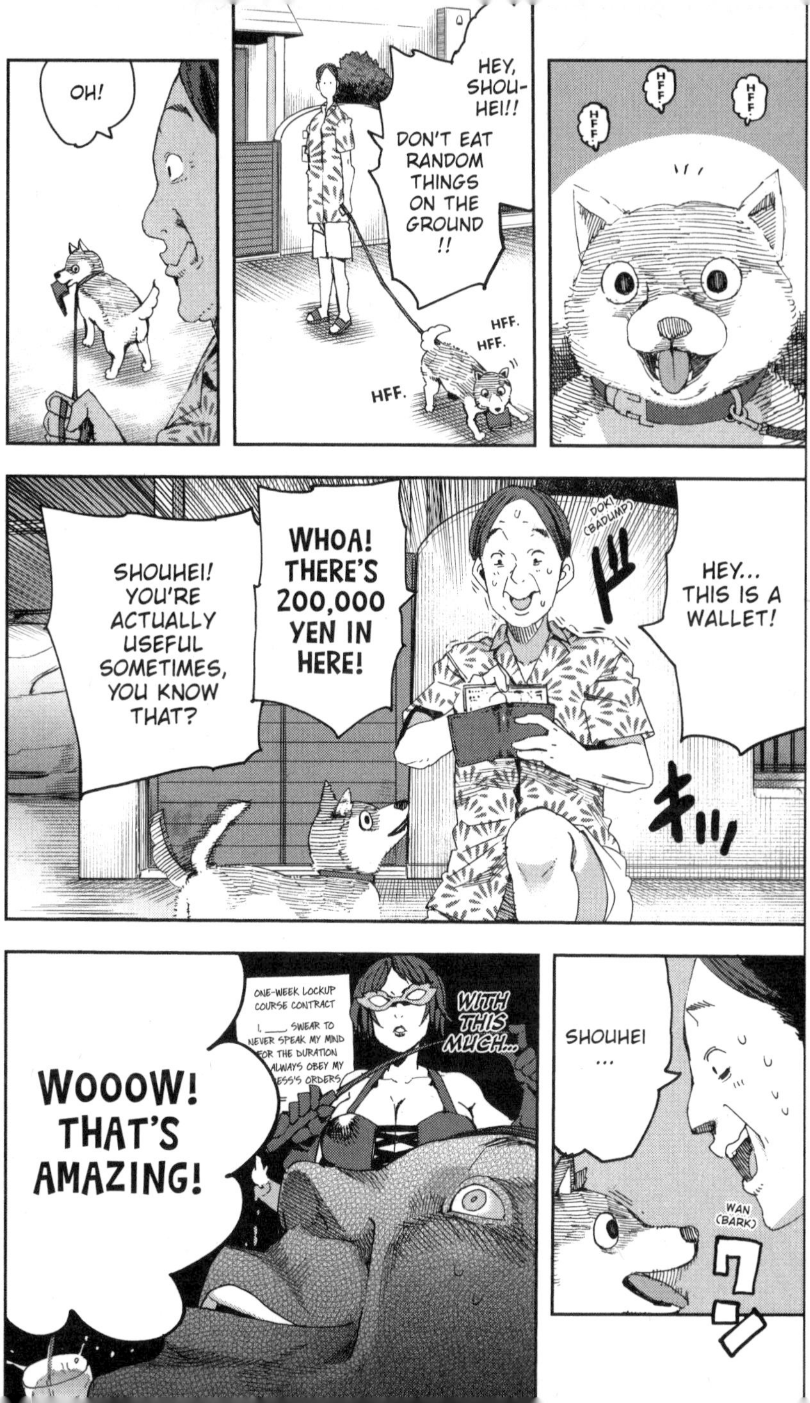
HFF.
HFF.
HFF.
HEY, SHOUHEI!!
DON'T EAT RANDOM THINGS ON THE GROUND!!
HFF.
HFF.
HFF.
OH!
HEY... THIS IS A WALLET!
DOKI (BADUMP)
WHOA! THERE'S 200,000 YEN IN HERE!
SHOUHEI! YOU'RE ACTUALLY USEFUL SOMETIMES, YOU KNOW THAT?
SHOUHEI...
WAN (BARK)
WITH THIS MUCH...
ONE-WEEK LOCKUP COURSE CONTRACT
SWEAR TO NEVER SPEAK MY MIND
WOOOW! THAT'S AMAZING!

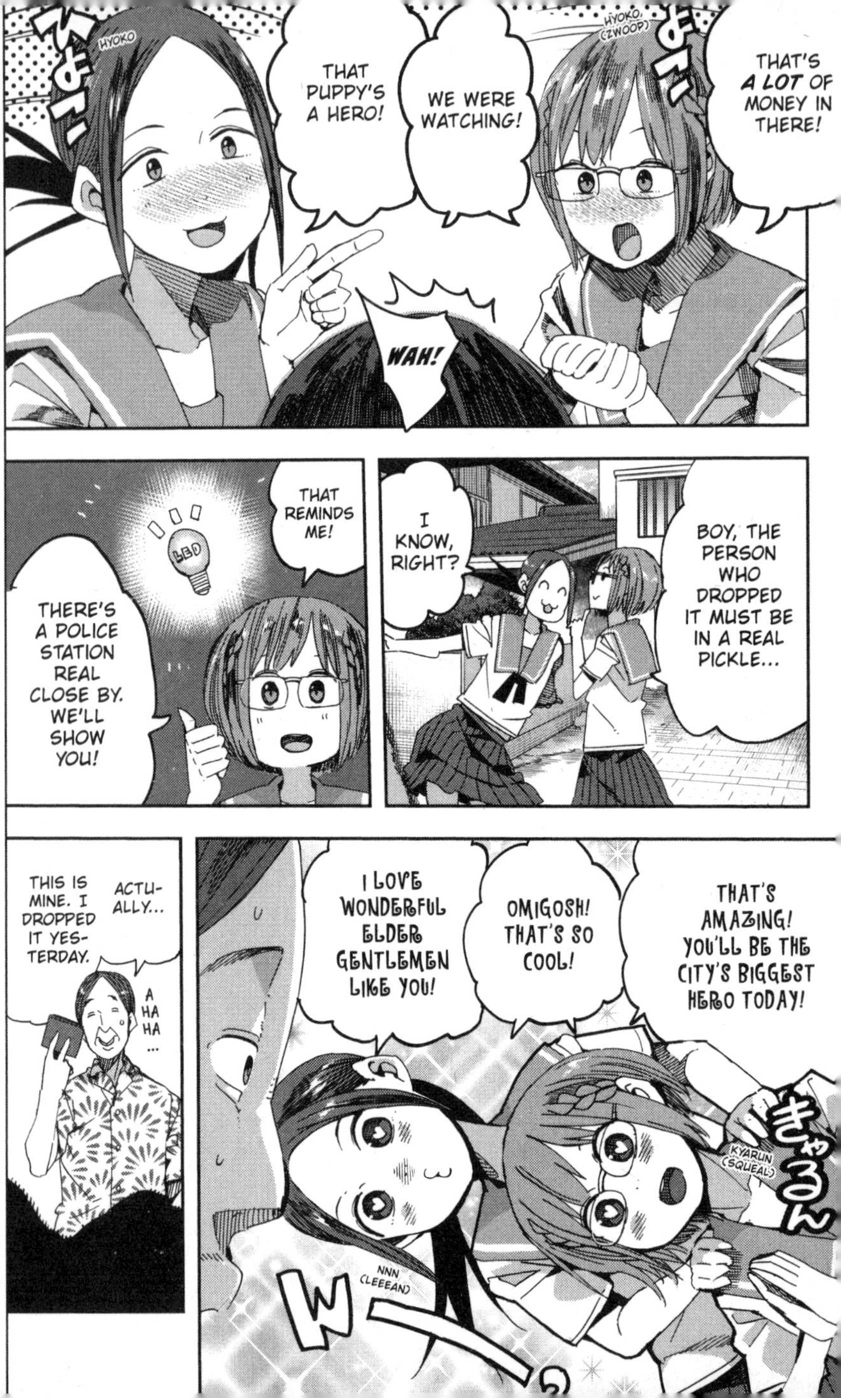
HYOKO (ZWOOP)
THAT'S **A LOT** OF MONEY IN THERE!
WE WERE WATCHING!
THAT PUPPY'S A HERO!
HYOKO
WAH!
BOY, THE PERSON WHO DROPPED IT MUST BE IN A REAL PICKLE...
I KNOW, RIGHT?
THAT REMINDS ME!
LED
THERE'S A POLICE STATION REAL CLOSE BY. WE'LL SHOW YOU!
THAT'S AMAZING! YOU'LL BE THE CITY'S BIGGEST HERO TODAY!
きゃるん
KYARUN (SQUEAL)
OMIGOSH! THAT'S SO COOL!
I LOVE WONDERFUL ELDER GENTLEMEN LIKE YOU!
NNN (LEEEAN)
ACTUALLY...
THIS IS MINE. I DROPPED IT YESTERDAY.
A HA HA...

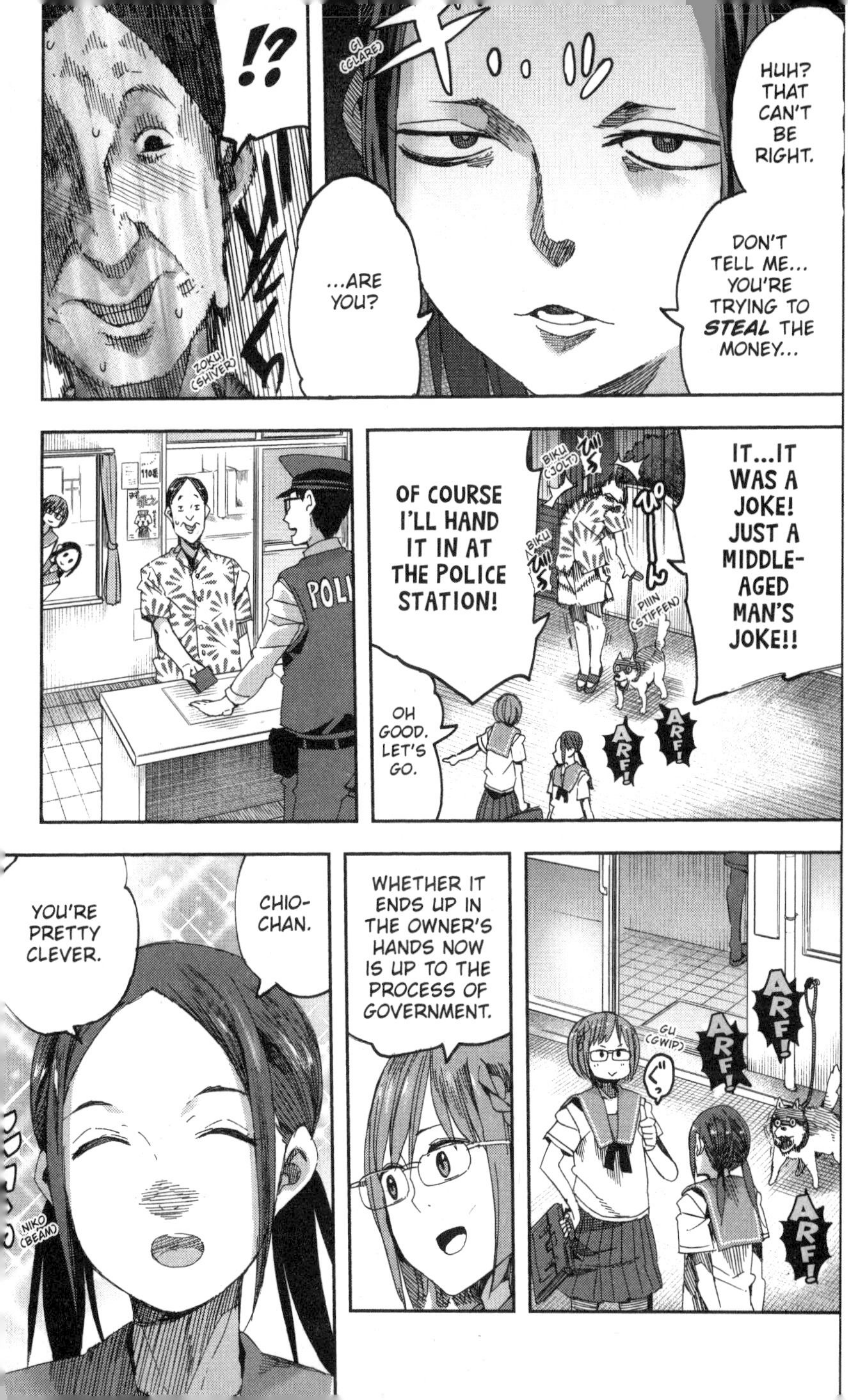

GI (GLARE)
HUH? THAT CAN'T BE RIGHT.
DON'T TELL ME... YOU'RE TRYING TO STEAL THE MONEY...
...ARE YOU?
!?
ZOKU (SHIVER)
IT...IT WAS A JOKE! JUST A MIDDLE-AGED MAN'S JOKE!!
BIKU (JOLT)
BIKU
OF COURSE I'LL HAND IT IN AT THE POLICE STATION!
PIIIN (STIFFEN)
ARF!
ARF!
OH GOOD. LET'S GO.
POLI
ARF!
ARF!
GU (GWIP)
ARF!
WHETHER IT ENDS UP IN THE OWNER'S HANDS NOW IS UP TO THE PROCESS OF GOVERNMENT.
CHIO-CHAN.
YOU'RE PRETTY CLEVER.
NIKO (BEAM)

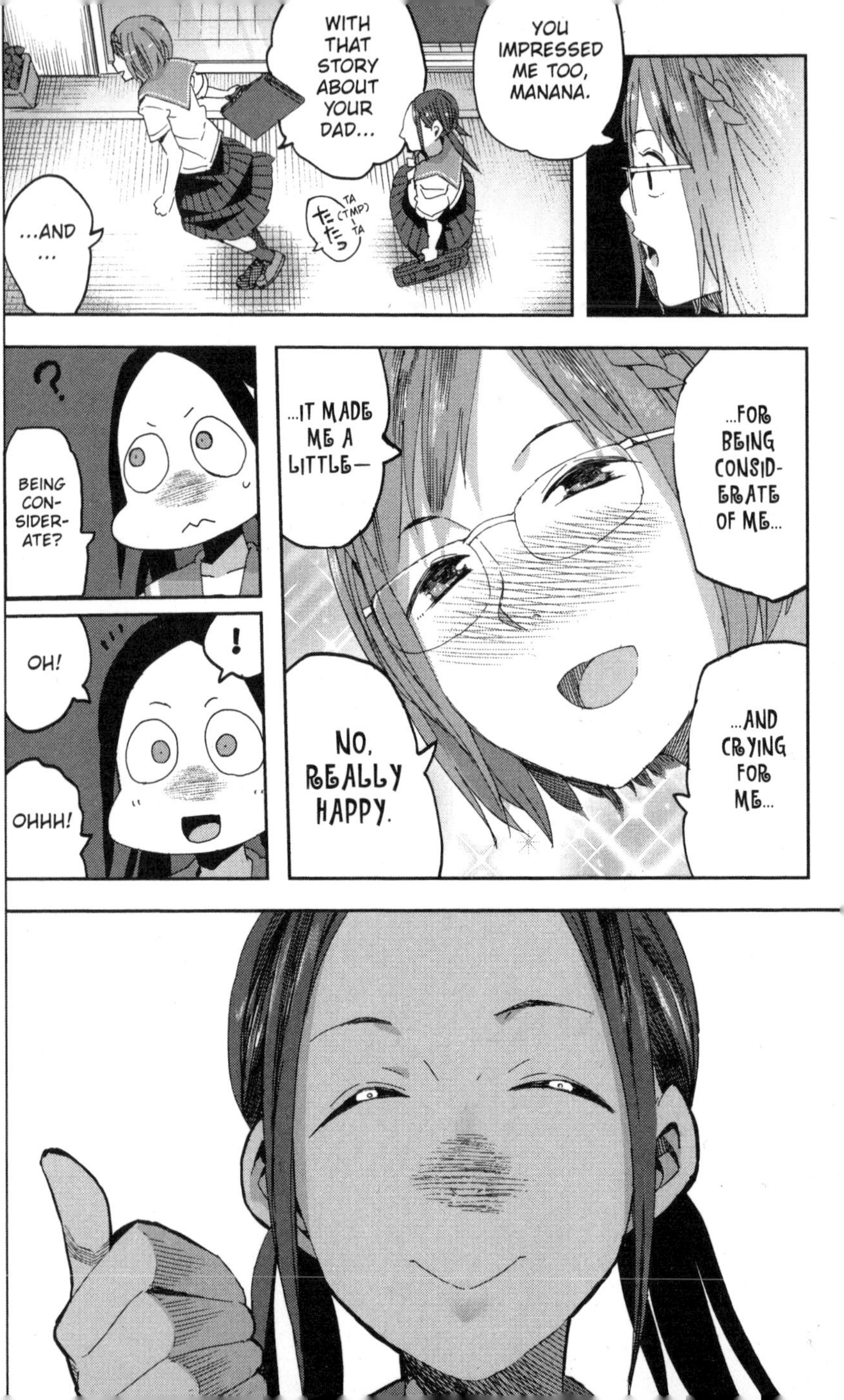
YOU IMPRESSED ME TOO, MANANA.
WITH THAT STORY ABOUT YOUR DAD...
たたっ TA (TMP) TA
...AND ...
...FOR BEING CONSID-ERATE OF ME...
...IT MADE ME A LITTLE—
...AND CRYING FOR ME...
NO, REALLY HAPPY.
?
BEING CON-SIDER-ATE?
!
OH!
OHHH!

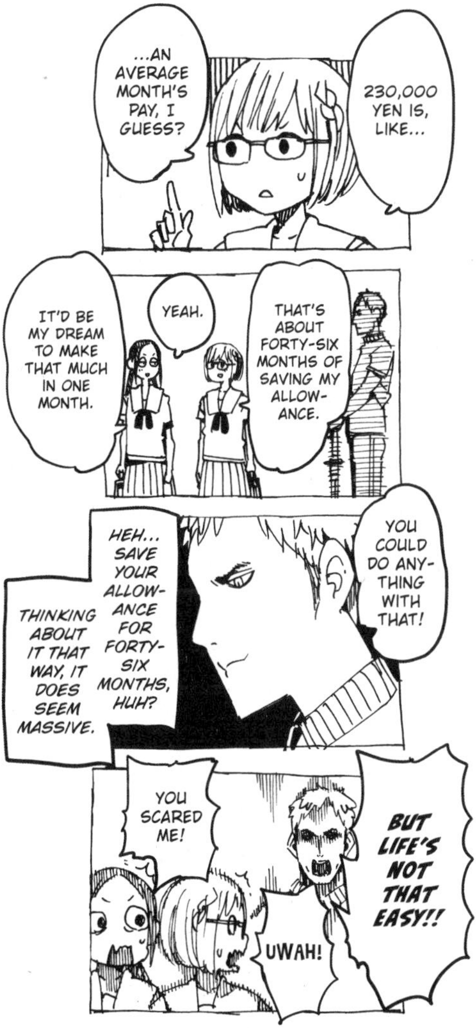
230,000 YEN IS, LIKE...
...AN AVERAGE MONTH'S PAY, I GUESS?
THAT'S ABOUT FORTY-SIX MONTHS OF SAVING MY ALLOWANCE.
YEAH.
IT'D BE MY DREAM TO MAKE THAT MUCH IN ONE MONTH.
YOU COULD DO ANYTHING WITH THAT!
HEH... SAVE YOUR ALLOWANCE FOR FORTY-SIX MONTHS, HUH?
THINKING ABOUT IT THAT WAY, IT DOES SEEM MASSIVE.
BUT LIFE'S NOT THAT EASY!!
YOU SCARED ME!
UWAH!

Chio's SCHOOL ROAD

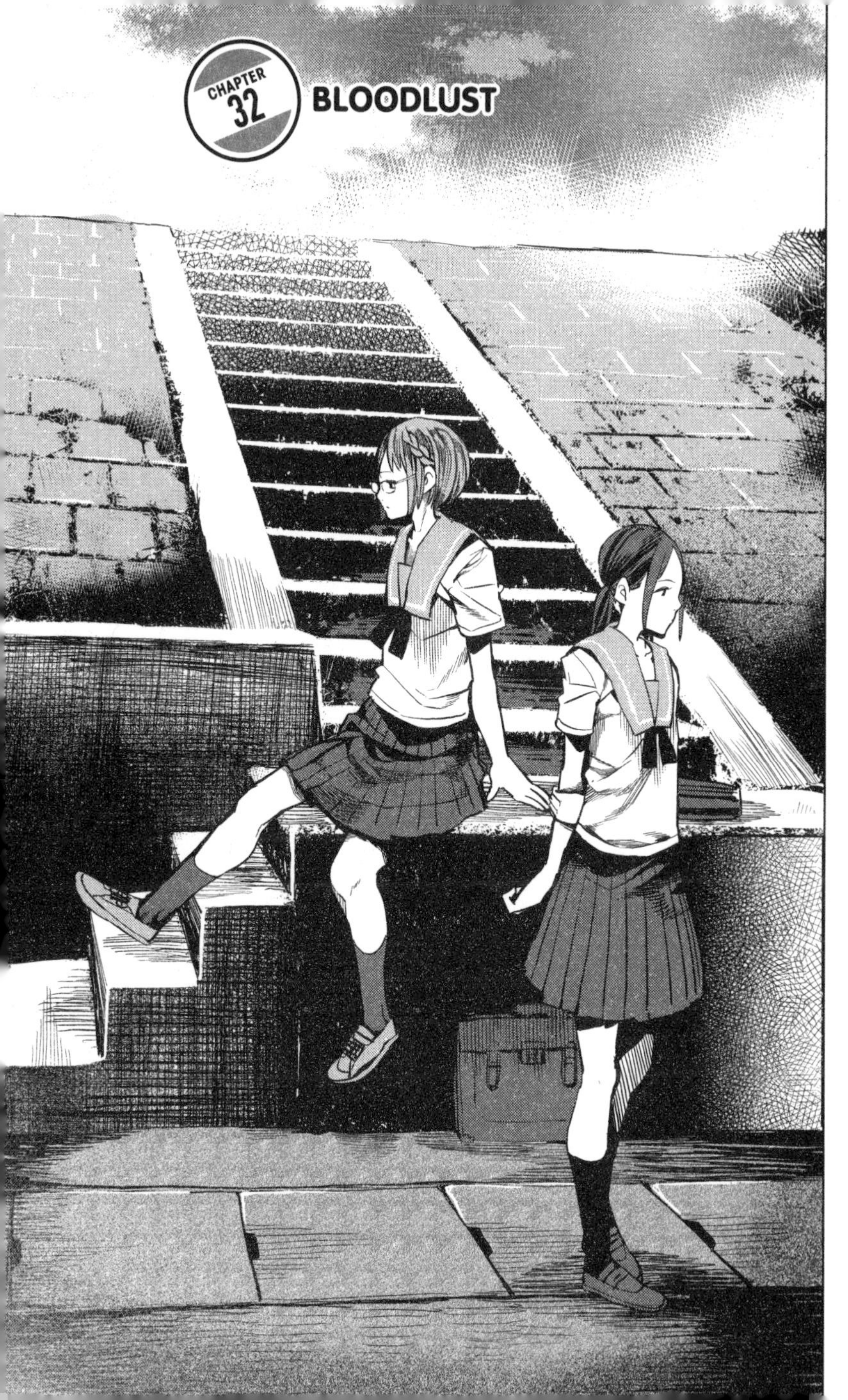
CHAPTER 32
BLOODLUST

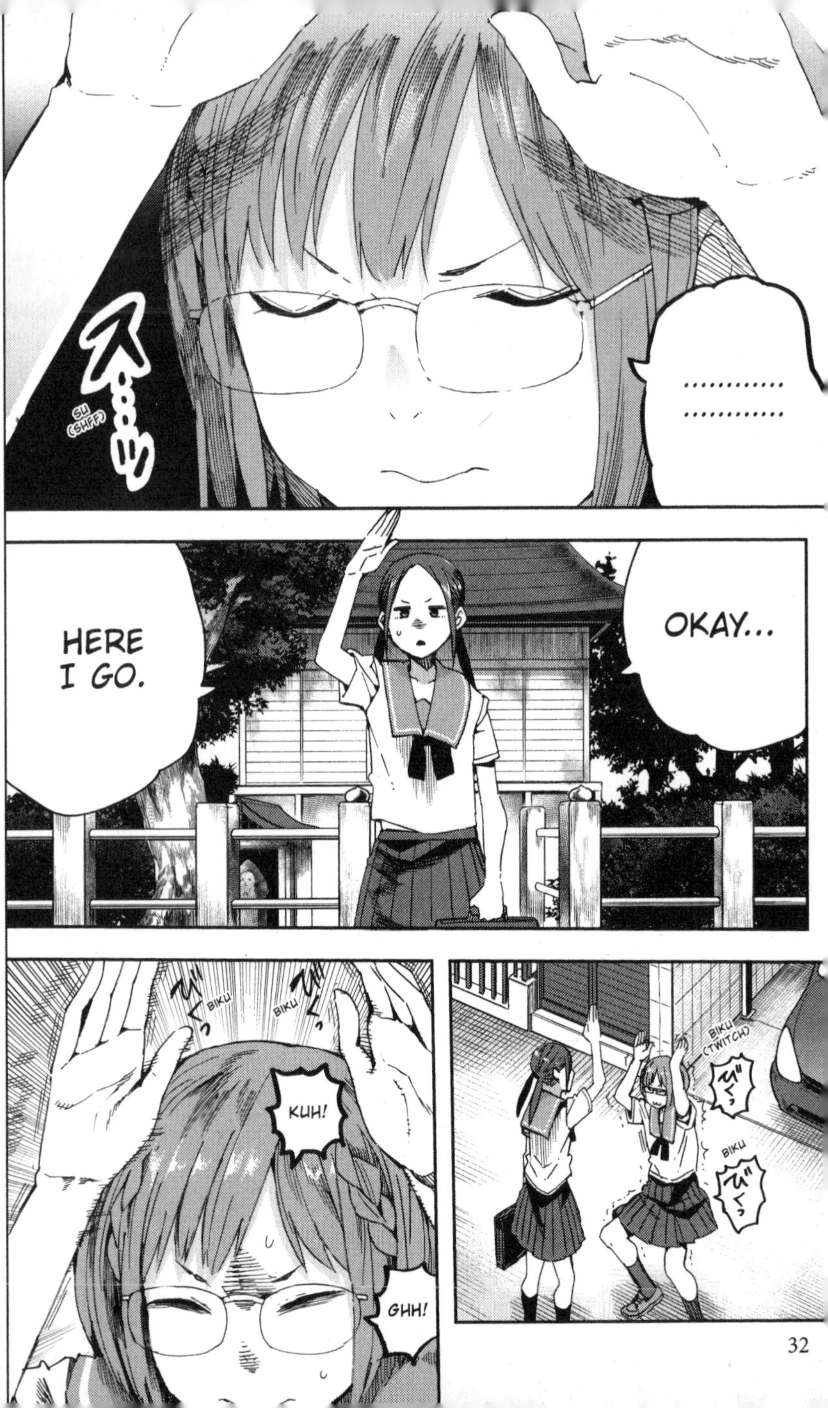
....
....
SU (SHFF)
OKAY...
HERE I GO.
BIKU (TWITCH)
びくっ
BIKU
びくっ
BIKU
BIKU
KUH!
GHH!

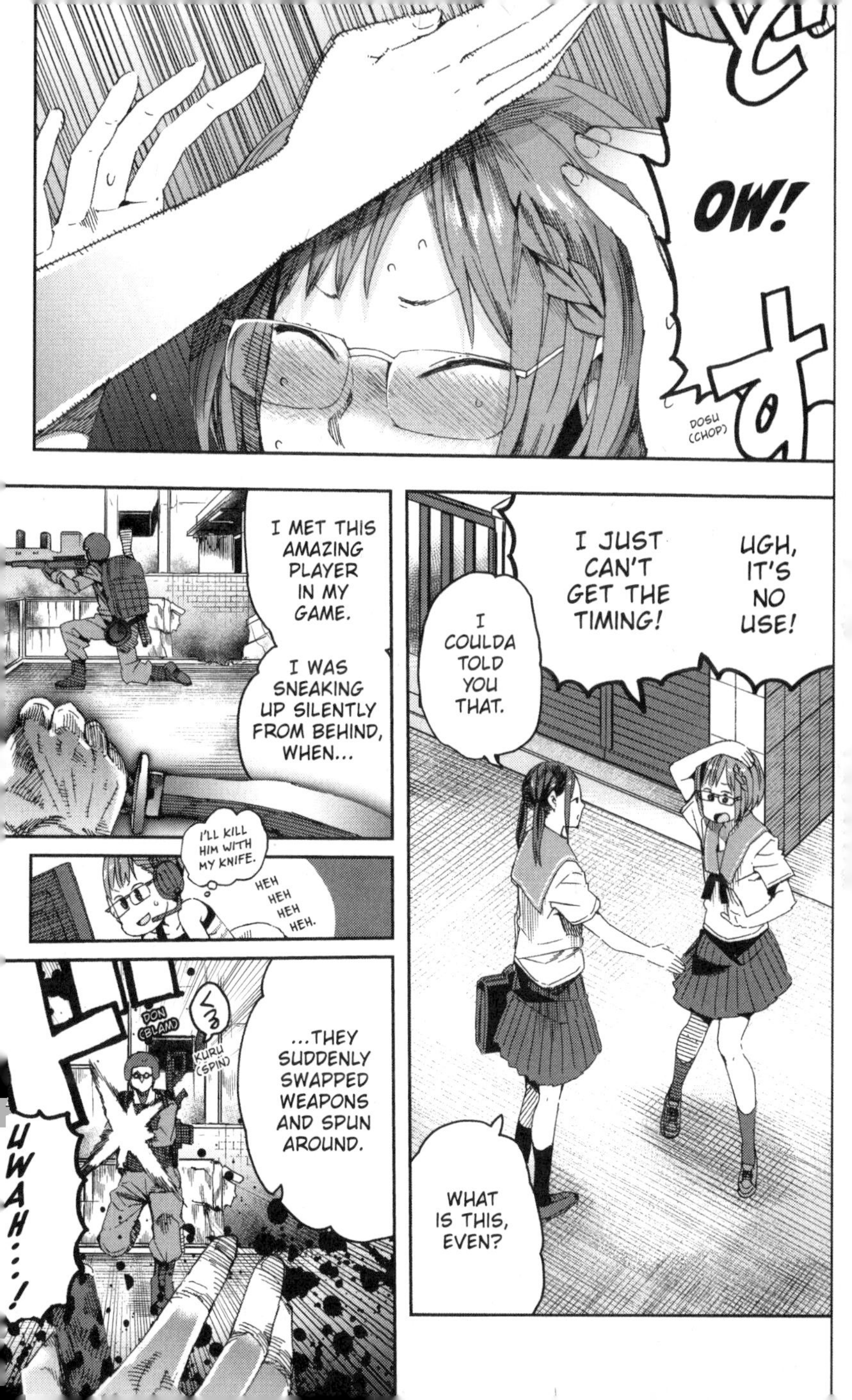

OW!
DOSU (CHOP)
UGH, IT'S NO USE!
I JUST CAN'T GET THE TIMING!
I COULDA TOLD YOU THAT.
WHAT IS THIS, EVEN?
I MET THIS AMAZING PLAYER IN MY GAME.
I WAS SNEAKING UP SILENTLY FROM BEHIND, WHEN...
I'LL KILL HIM WITH MY KNIFE.
HEH HEH HEH HEH.
KURU (SPIN)
DON (BLAM)
...THEY SUDDENLY SWAPPED WEAPONS AND SPUN AROUND.
UWAH...!

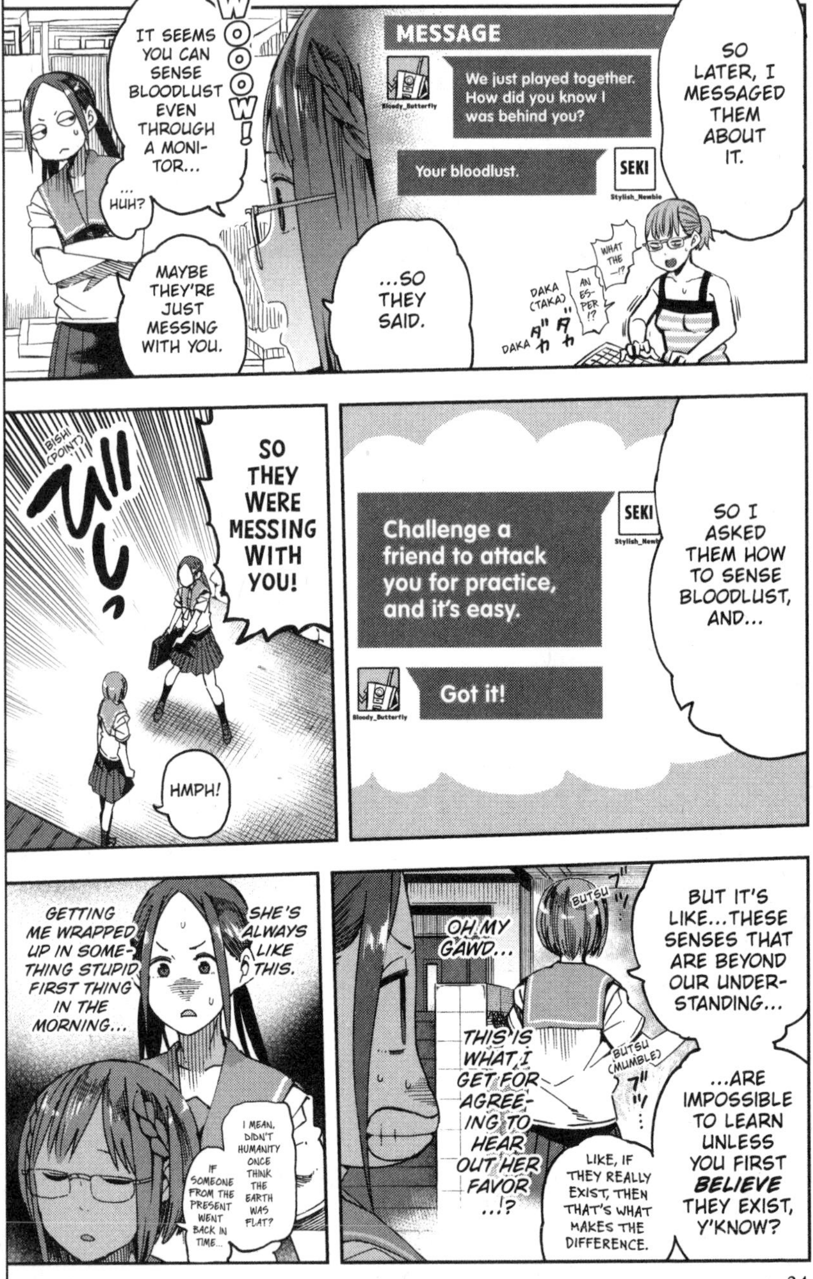
SO LATER, I MESSAGED THEM ABOUT IT.
MESSAGE
Bloody_Butterfly
We just played together. How did you know I was behind you?
SEKI
Stylish_Newbie
Your bloodlust.
WHAT THE—!?
AN ESPER!?
DAKA (TAKA)
DAKA
...SO THEY SAID.
IT SEEMS YOU CAN SENSE BLOODLUST EVEN THROUGH A MONITOR...
WOOOW!
...HUH?
MAYBE THEY'RE JUST MESSING WITH YOU.
SO I ASKED THEM HOW TO SENSE BLOODLUST, AND...
SEKI
Stylish_Newbie
Challenge a friend to attack you for practice, and it's easy.
Bloody_Butterfly
Got it!
SO THEY WERE MESSING WITH YOU!
BISHI (POINT)
HMPH!
BUT IT'S LIKE...THESE SENSES THAT ARE BEYOND OUR UNDERSTANDING...
...ARE IMPOSSIBLE TO LEARN UNLESS YOU FIRST *BELIEVE* THEY EXIST, Y'KNOW?
BUTSU
BUTSU (MUMBLE)
LIKE, IF THEY REALLY EXIST, THEN THAT'S WHAT MAKES THE DIFFERENCE.
OH MY GAWD...
THIS IS WHAT I GET FOR AGREEING TO HEAR OUT HER FAVOR...!?
SHE'S ALWAYS LIKE THIS.
GETTING ME WRAPPED UP IN SOMETHING STUPID FIRST THING IN THE MORNING...
I MEAN, DIDN'T HUMANITY ONCE THINK THE EARTH WAS FLAT?
IF SOMEONE FROM THE PRESENT WENT BACK IN TIME...

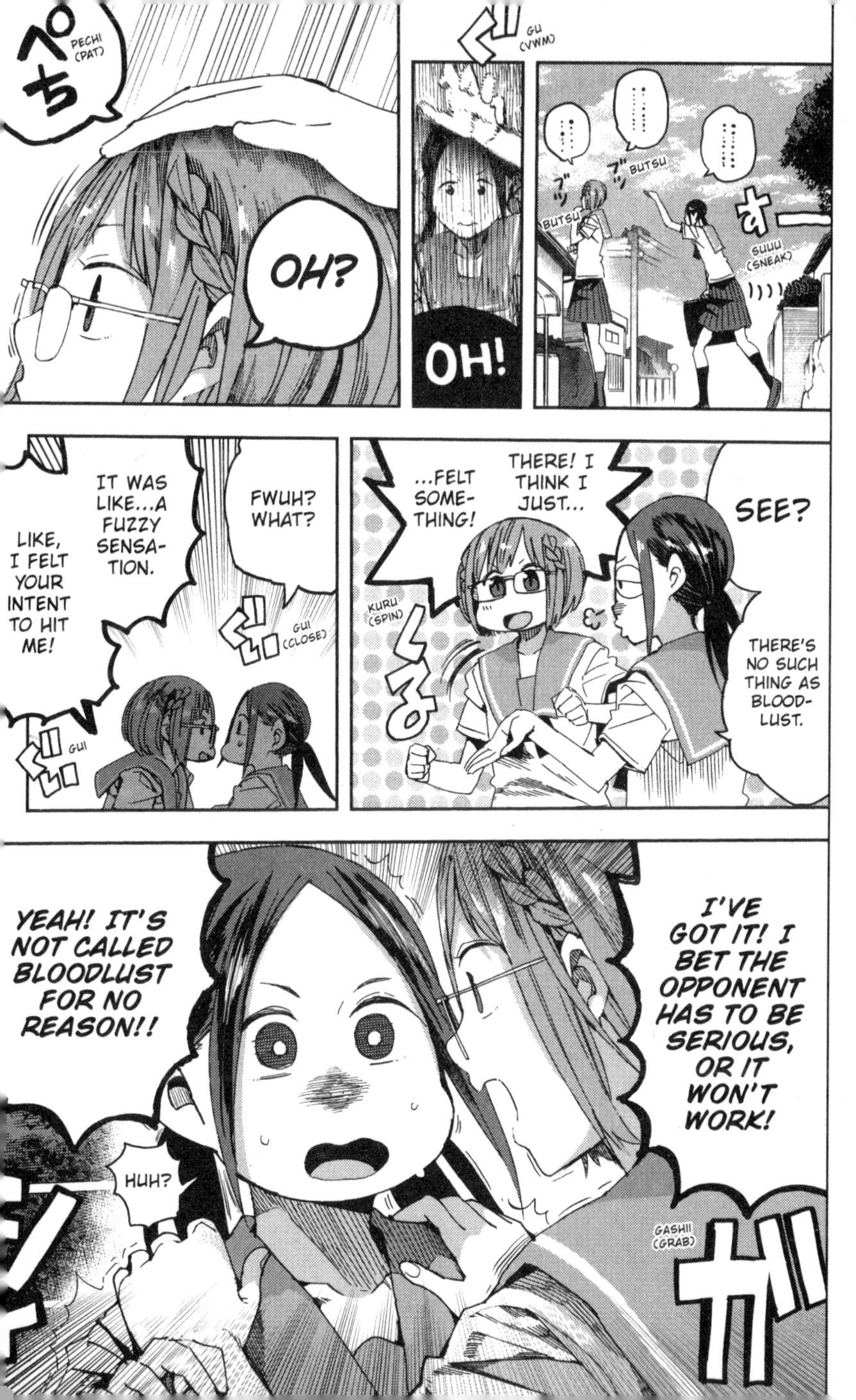

BUTSU
BUTSU
SUUU (SNEAK)
GU (VWM)
OH!
PECHI (PAT)
OH?
SEE?
THERE! I THINK I JUST...
...FELT SOMETHING!
KURU (SPIN)
THERE'S NO SUCH THING AS BLOODLUST.
FWUH? WHAT?
IT WAS LIKE...A FUZZY SENSATION.
LIKE, I FELT YOUR INTENT TO HIT ME!
GUI (CLOSE)
GUI
I'VE GOT IT! I BET THE OPPONENT HAS TO BE SERIOUS, OR IT WON'T WORK!
GASHII (GRAB)
YEAH! IT'S NOT CALLED BLOODLUST FOR NO REASON!!
HUH?

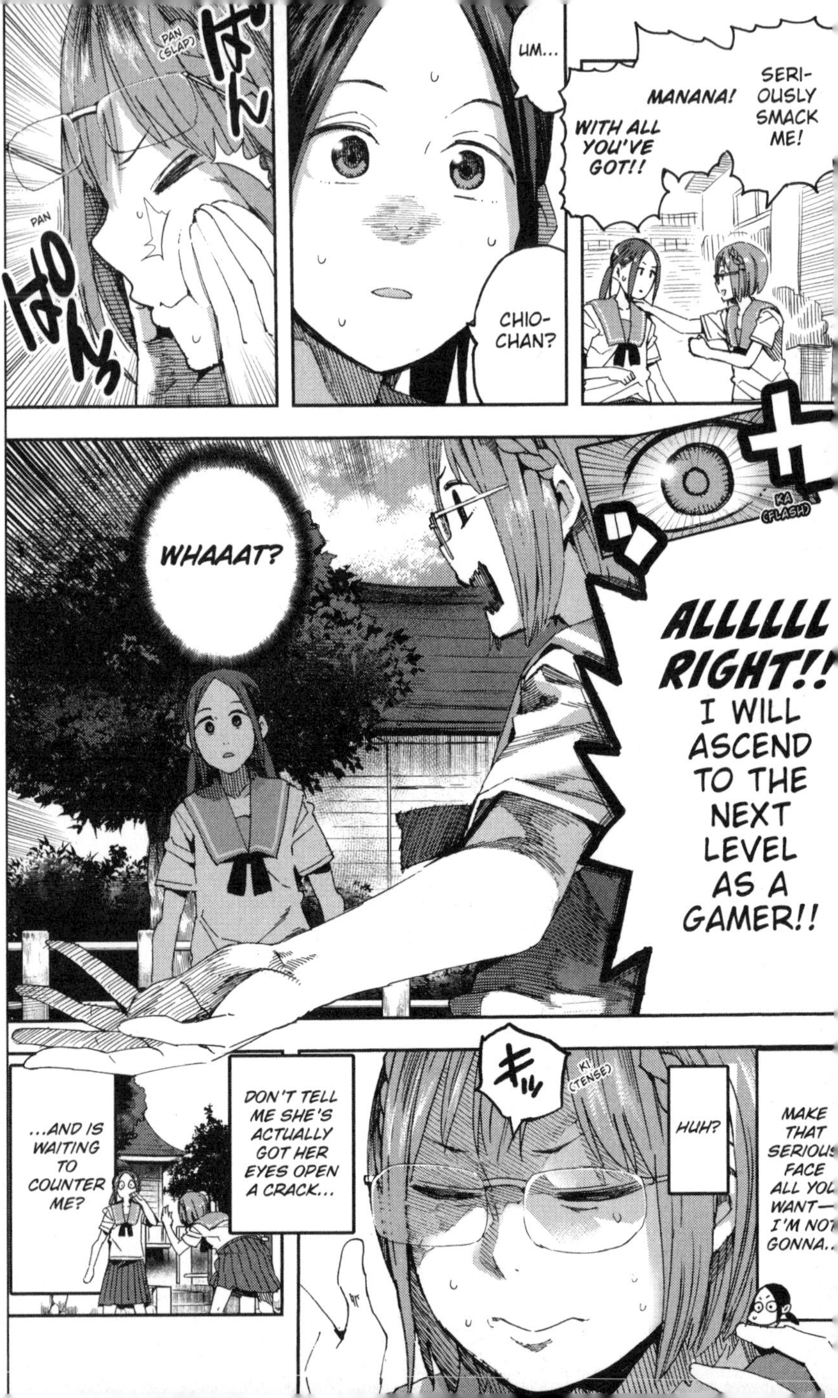
SERI-OUSLY SMACK ME!
MANANA!
WITH ALL YOU'VE GOT!!
UM...
CHIO-CHAN?
ぱん
PAN (SLAP)
ぱん
PAN
KA (FLASH)
ALLLLLL RIGHT!! I WILL ASCEND TO THE NEXT LEVEL AS A GAMER!!
WHAAAT?
MAKE THAT SERIOUS FACE ALL YOU WANT— I'M NOT GONNA...
HUH?
キッ
KI (TENSE)
DON'T TELL ME SHE'S ACTUALLY GOT HER EYES OPEN A CRACK...
...AND IS WAITING TO COUNTER ME?

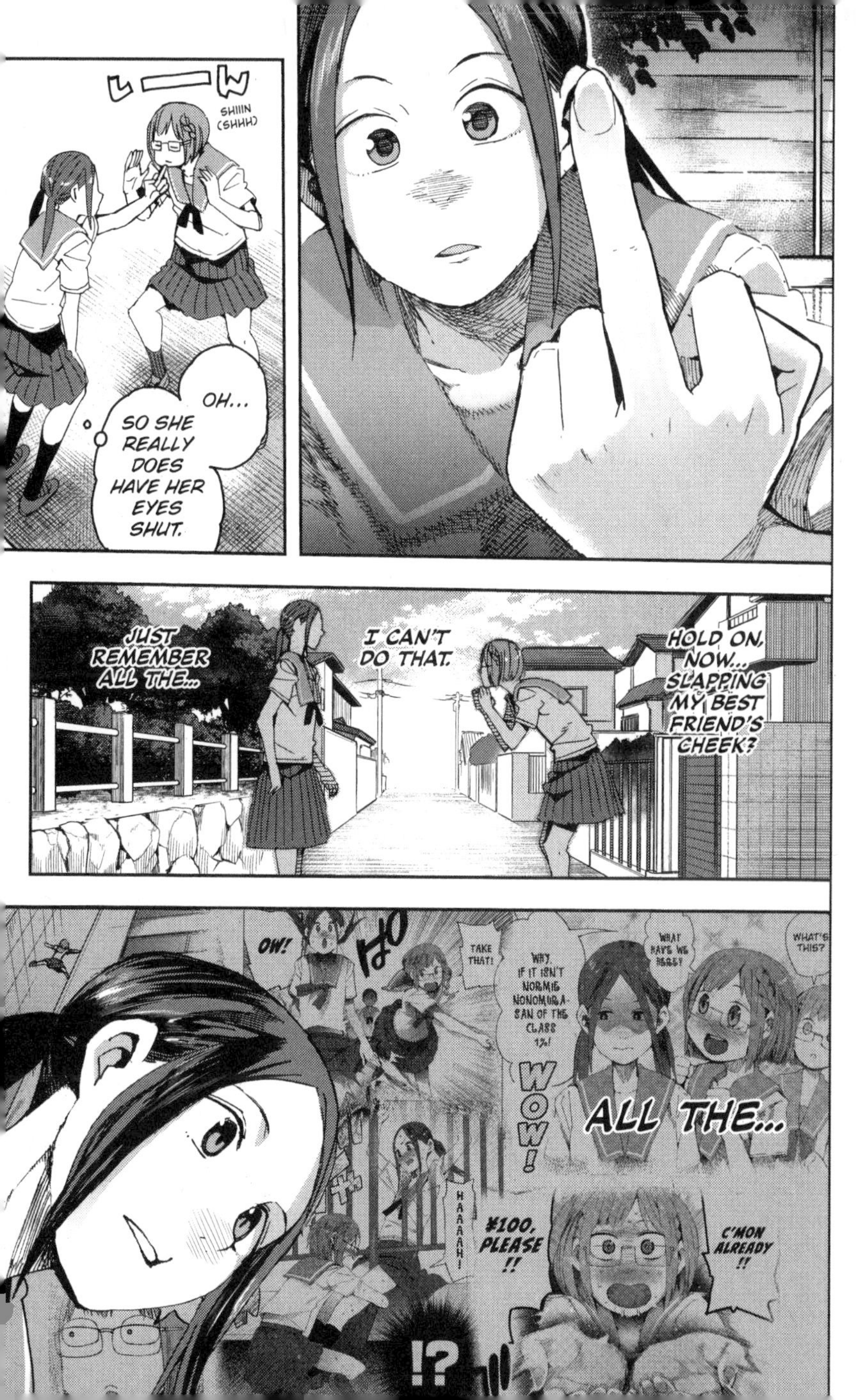
SHIIIN (SHHH)
OH... SO SHE REALLY DOES HAVE HER EYES SHUT.
HOLD ON, NOW... SLAPPING MY BEST FRIEND'S CHEEK?
I CAN'T DO THAT.
JUST REMEMBER ALL THE...
WHAT'S THIS?
WHAT HAVE WE HERE?
WHY, IF IT ISN'T NORMIE NONOMURA-SAN OF THE CLASS 1%!
WOW!
ALL THE...
TAKE THAT!
OW!
C'MON ALREADY!!
¥100, PLEASE!!
HAAAAH!
!?

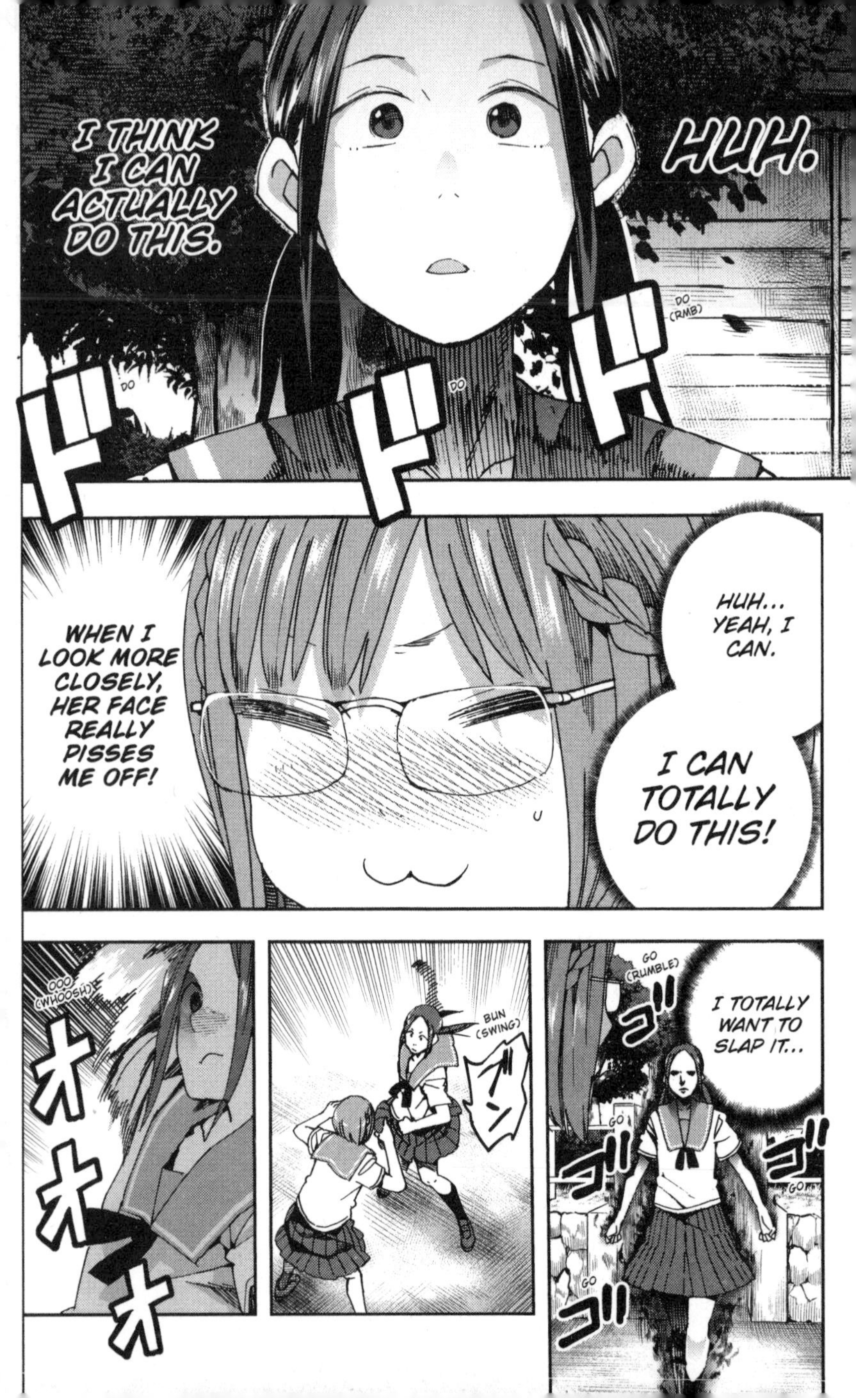
HUH.
I THINK I CAN ACTUALLY DO THIS.
DO (RMB)
DO
DO
HUH... YEAH, I CAN.
I CAN TOTALLY DO THIS!
WHEN I LOOK MORE CLOSELY, HER FACE REALLY PISSES ME OFF!
GO (RUMBLE)
I TOTALLY WANT TO SLAP IT...
GO
GO
GO
BUN (SWING)
OOO (WHOOSH)

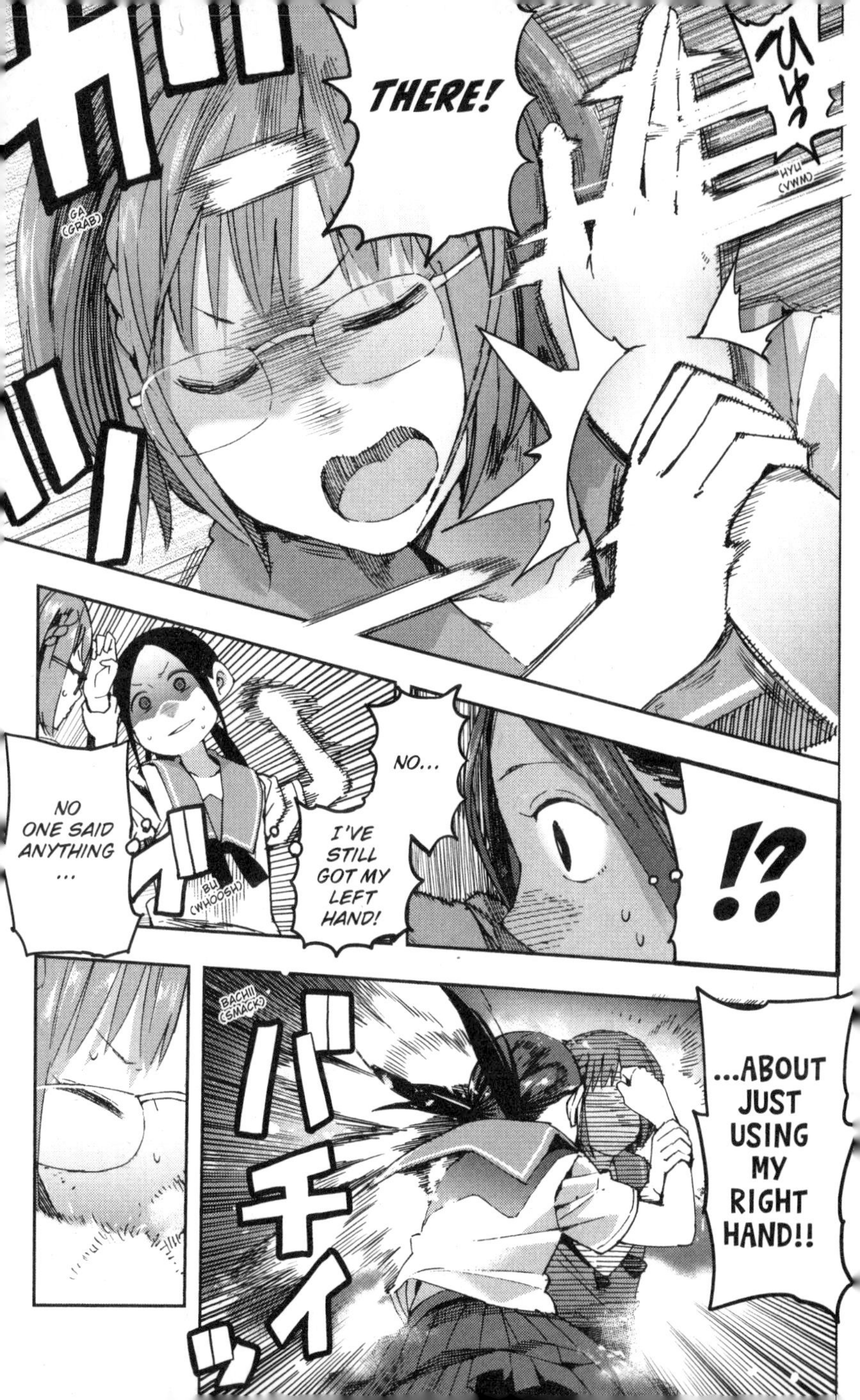
ひゅっ
HYU (VWM)
THERE!
GA (GRAB)
!?
NO...
I'VE STILL GOT MY LEFT HAND!
BU (WHOOSH)
NO ONE SAID ANYTHING ...
...ABOUT JUST USING MY RIGHT HAND!!
BACHII (SMACK)
バチィ

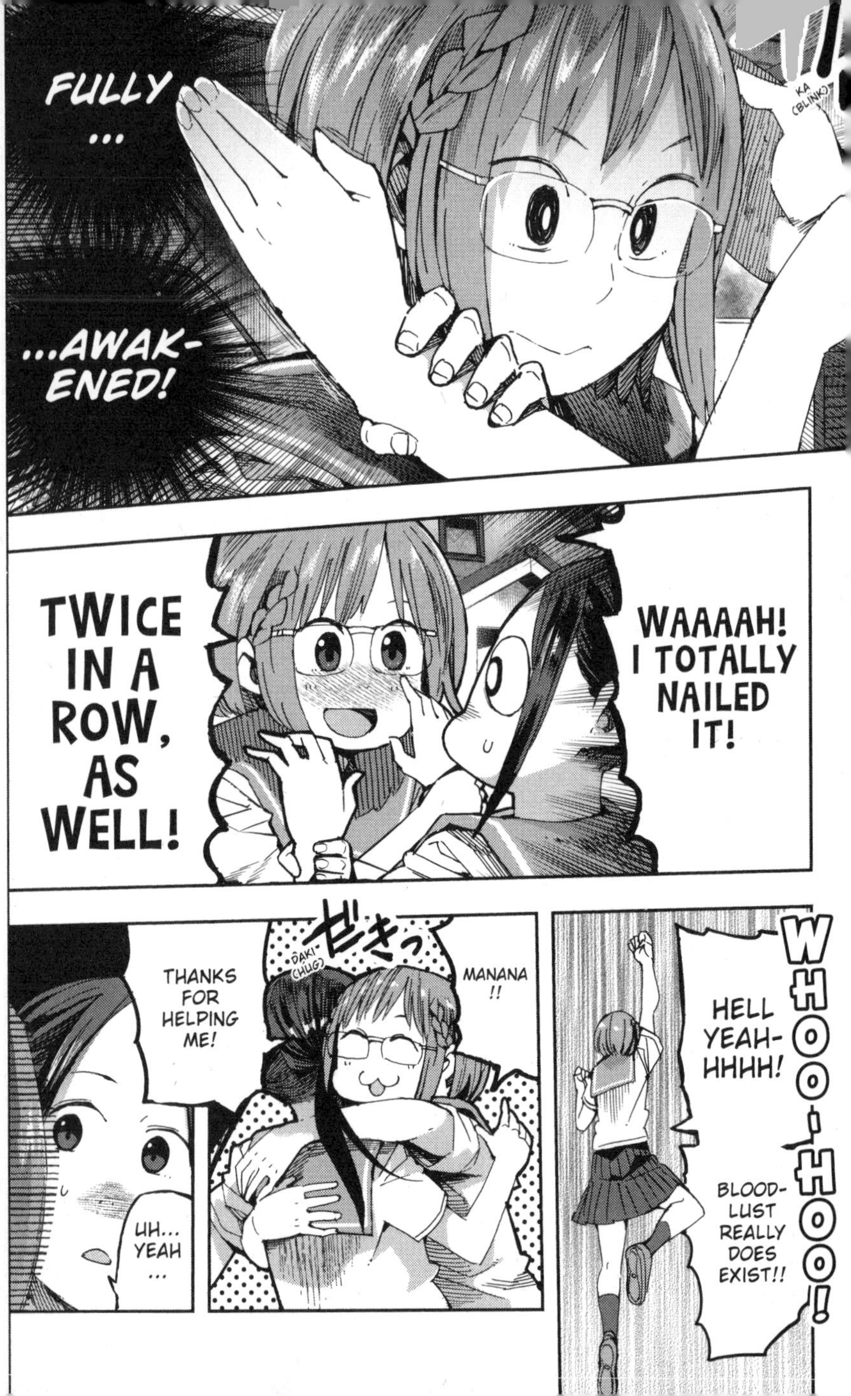
KA (BLINK)
FULLY ...
...AWAK-ENED!
WAAAAH! I TOTALLY NAILED IT!
TWICE IN A ROW, AS WELL!
WHOO-HOO!
HELL YEAH-HHHH!
BLOOD-LUST REALLY DOES EXIST!!
MANANA !!
だきっ
DAKI (HUG)
THANKS FOR HELPING ME!
UH... YEAH ...

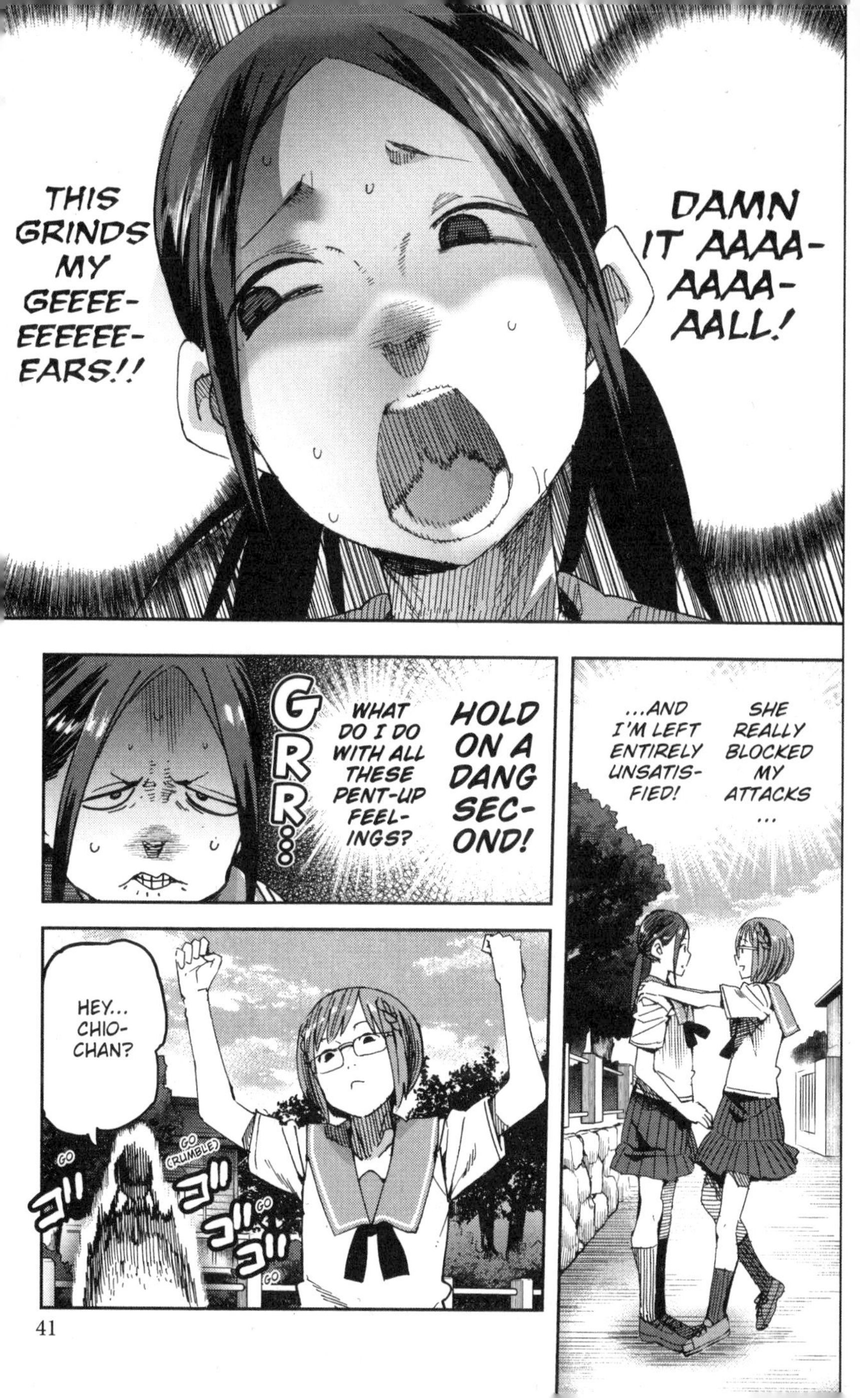
DAMN IT AAAA-AAAA-AALL!
THIS GRINDS MY GEEEE-EEEEEE-EARS!!
SHE REALLY BLOCKED MY ATTACKS...
...AND I'M LEFT ENTIRELY UNSATIS-FIED!
HOLD ON A DANG SEC-OND!
WHAT DO I DO WITH ALL THESE PENT-UP FEEL-INGS?
GRR...
HEY... CHIO-CHAN?
GO
GO (RUMBLE)
GO
GO

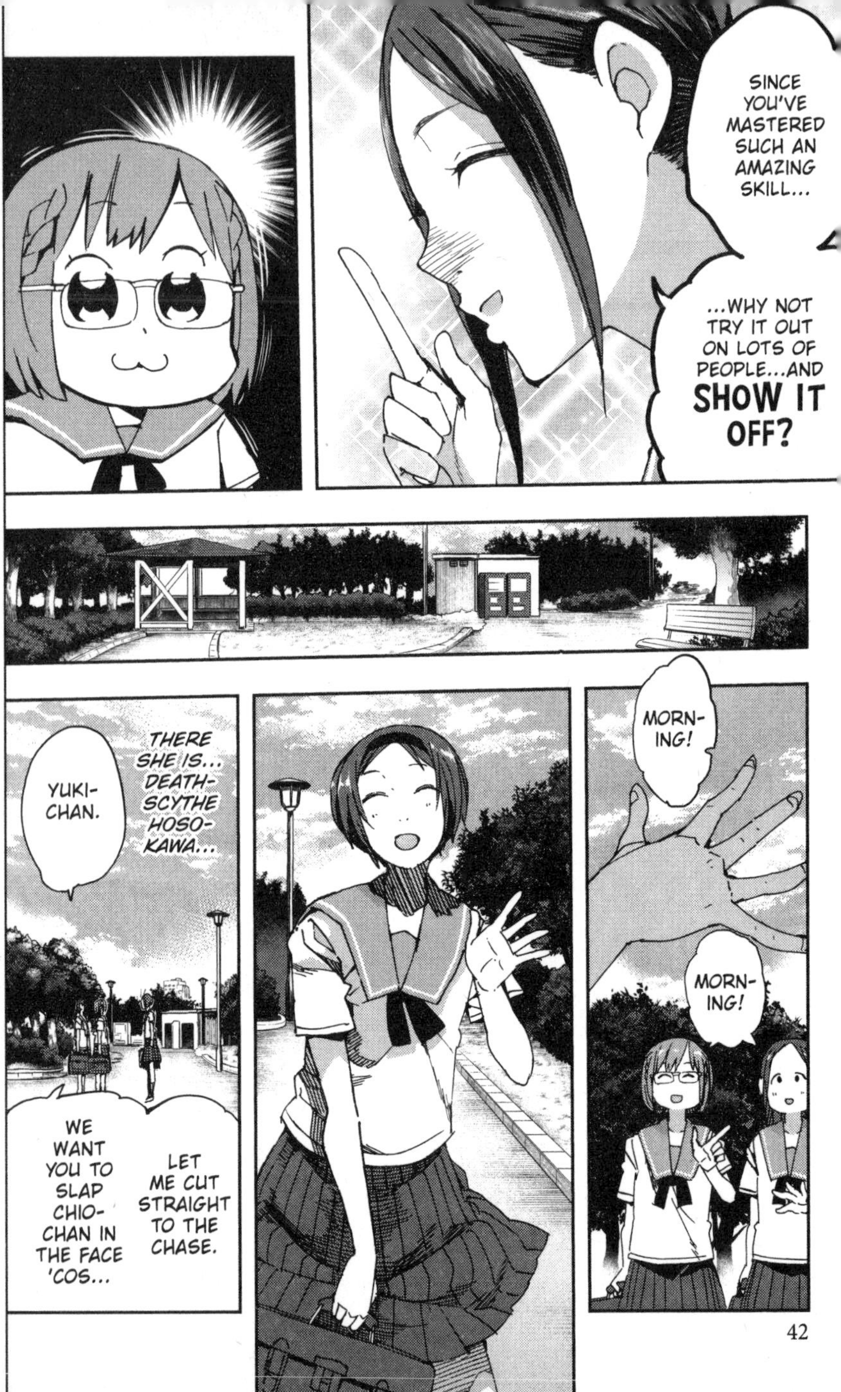

SINCE YOU'VE MASTERED SUCH AN AMAZING SKILL...
...WHY NOT TRY IT OUT ON LOTS OF PEOPLE...AND **SHOW IT OFF?**
MORN-ING!
MORN-ING!
THERE SHE IS... DEATH-SCYTHE HOSO-KAWA...
YUKI-CHAN.
LET ME CUT STRAIGHT TO THE CHASE.
WE WANT YOU TO SLAP CHIO-CHAN IN THE FACE 'COS...

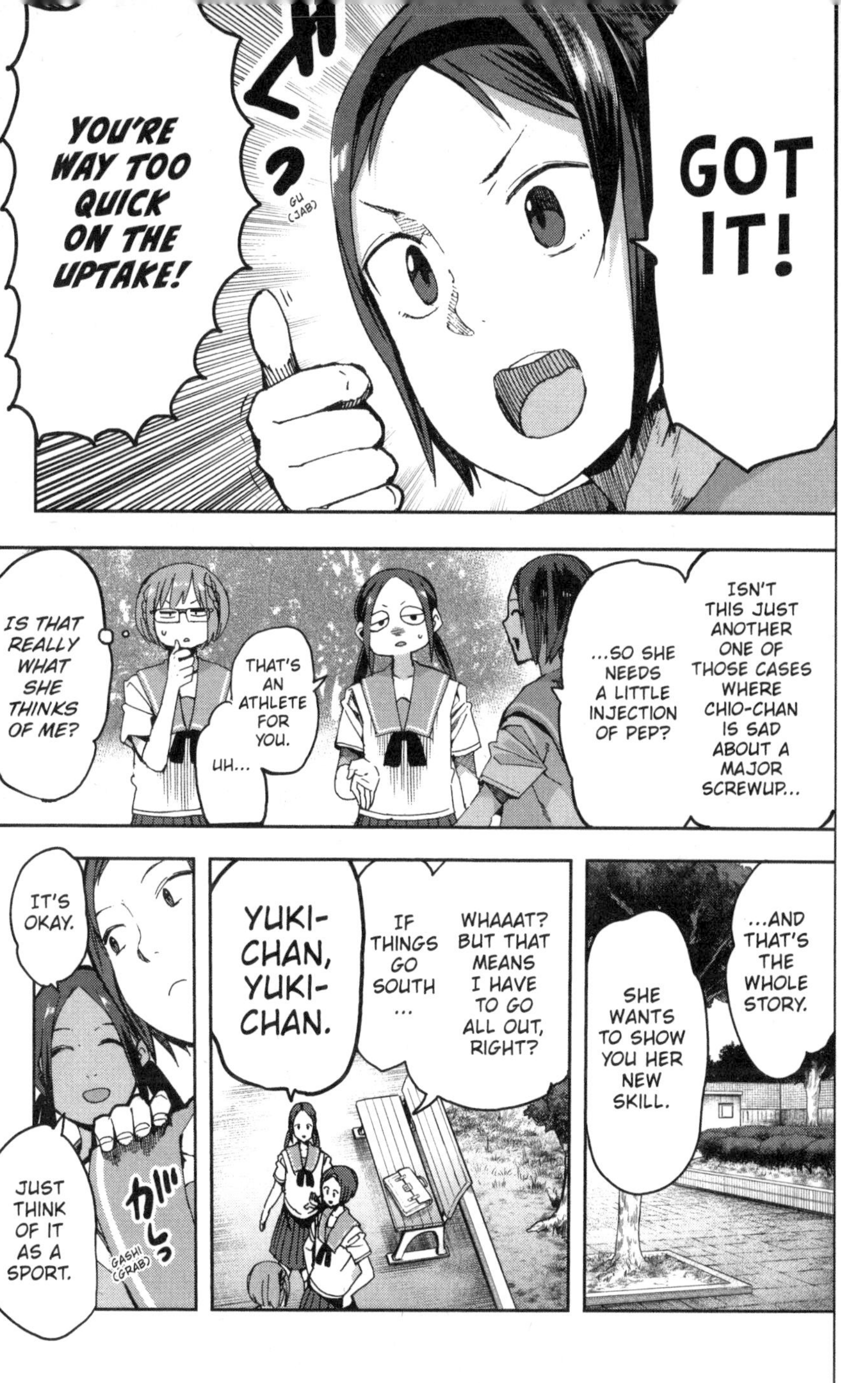
GOT IT!
GU (JAB)
YOU'RE WAY TOO QUICK ON THE UPTAKE!
ISN'T THIS JUST ANOTHER ONE OF THOSE CASES WHERE CHIO-CHAN IS SAD ABOUT A MAJOR SCREWUP...
...SO SHE NEEDS A LITTLE INJECTION OF PEP?
THAT'S AN ATHLETE FOR YOU.
UH...
IS THAT REALLY WHAT SHE THINKS OF ME?
...AND THAT'S THE WHOLE STORY.
SHE WANTS TO SHOW YOU HER NEW SKILL.
WHAAAT? BUT THAT MEANS I HAVE TO GO ALL OUT, RIGHT?
IF THINGS GO SOUTH ...
YUKI-CHAN, YUKI-CHAN.
IT'S OKAY.
GASHI (GRAB)
JUST THINK OF IT AS A SPORT.

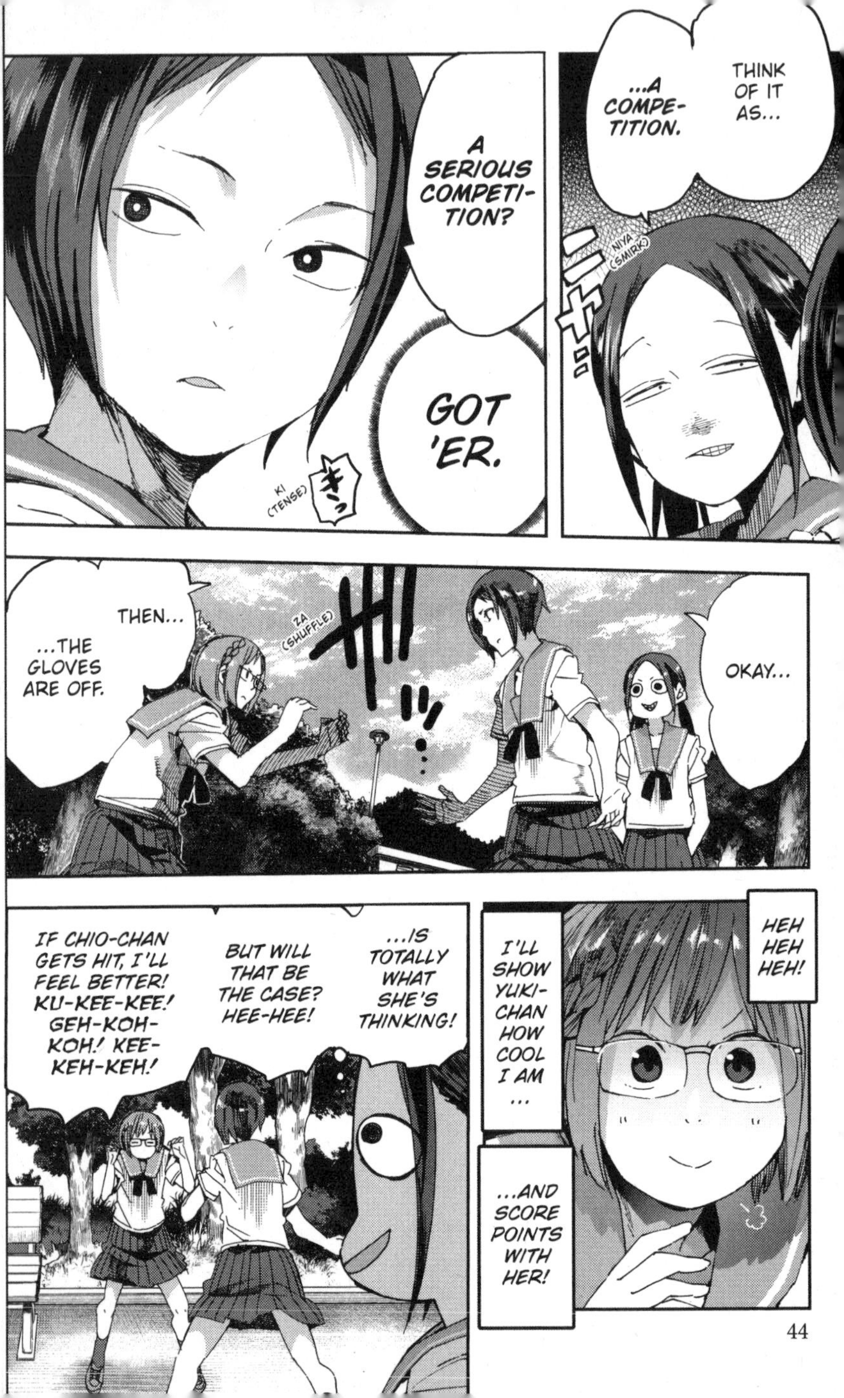
THINK OF IT AS...
...A COMPE-TITION.
NIYA (SMIRK)
A SERIOUS COMPETI-TION?
GOT 'ER.
KI (TENSE)
OKAY...
ZA (SHUFFLE)
THEN...
...THE GLOVES ARE OFF.
HEH HEH HEH!
I'LL SHOW YUKI-CHAN HOW COOL I AM ...
...AND SCORE POINTS WITH HER!
...IS TOTALLY WHAT SHE'S THINKING!
BUT WILL THAT BE THE CASE? HEE-HEE!
IF CHIO-CHAN GETS HIT, I'LL FEEL BETTER! KU-KEE-KEE! GEH-KOH-KOH! KEE-KEH-KEH!

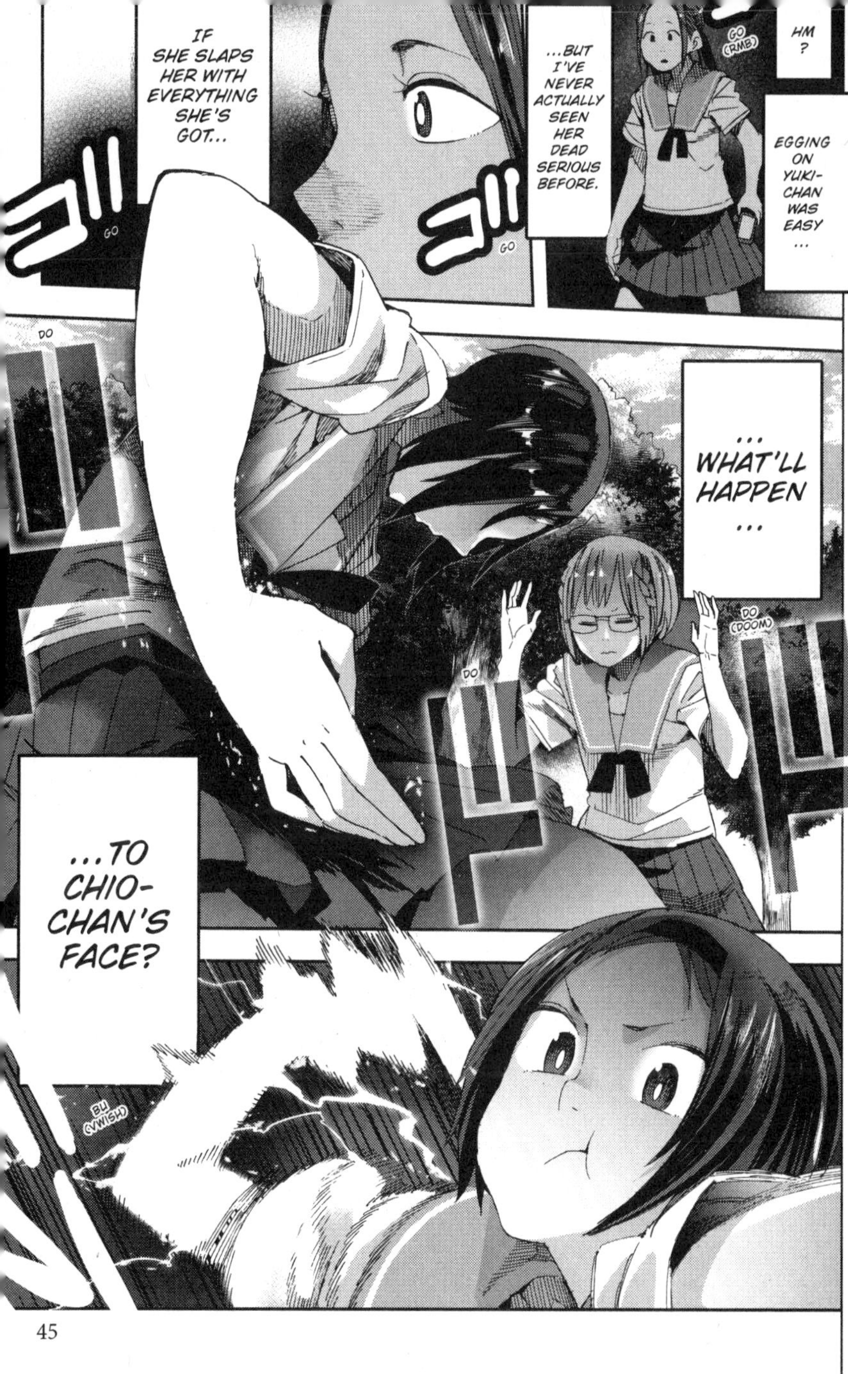

HM?
GO (RMB)
EGGING ON YUKI-CHAN WAS EASY...
...BUT I'VE NEVER ACTUALLY SEEN HER DEAD SERIOUS BEFORE.
IF SHE SLAPS HER WITH EVERYTHING SHE'S GOT...
GO
GO
...WHAT'LL HAPPEN...
DO (DOOM)
DO
DO
...TO CHIO-CHAN'S FACE?
BU (VWISH)

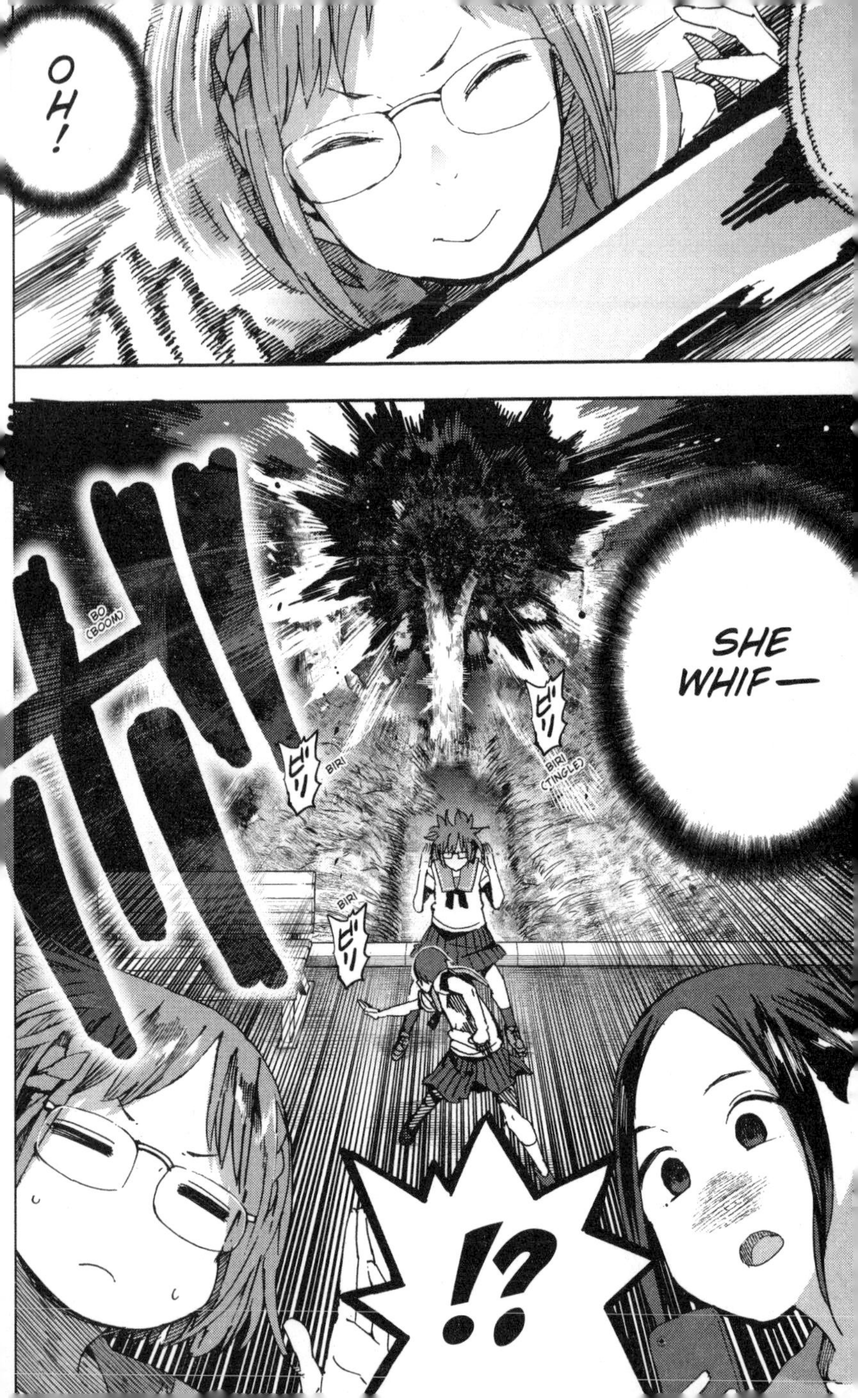
OH!
SHE WHIF—
BIRI (TINGLE)
BIRI
BIRI
BO (BOOM)
!?

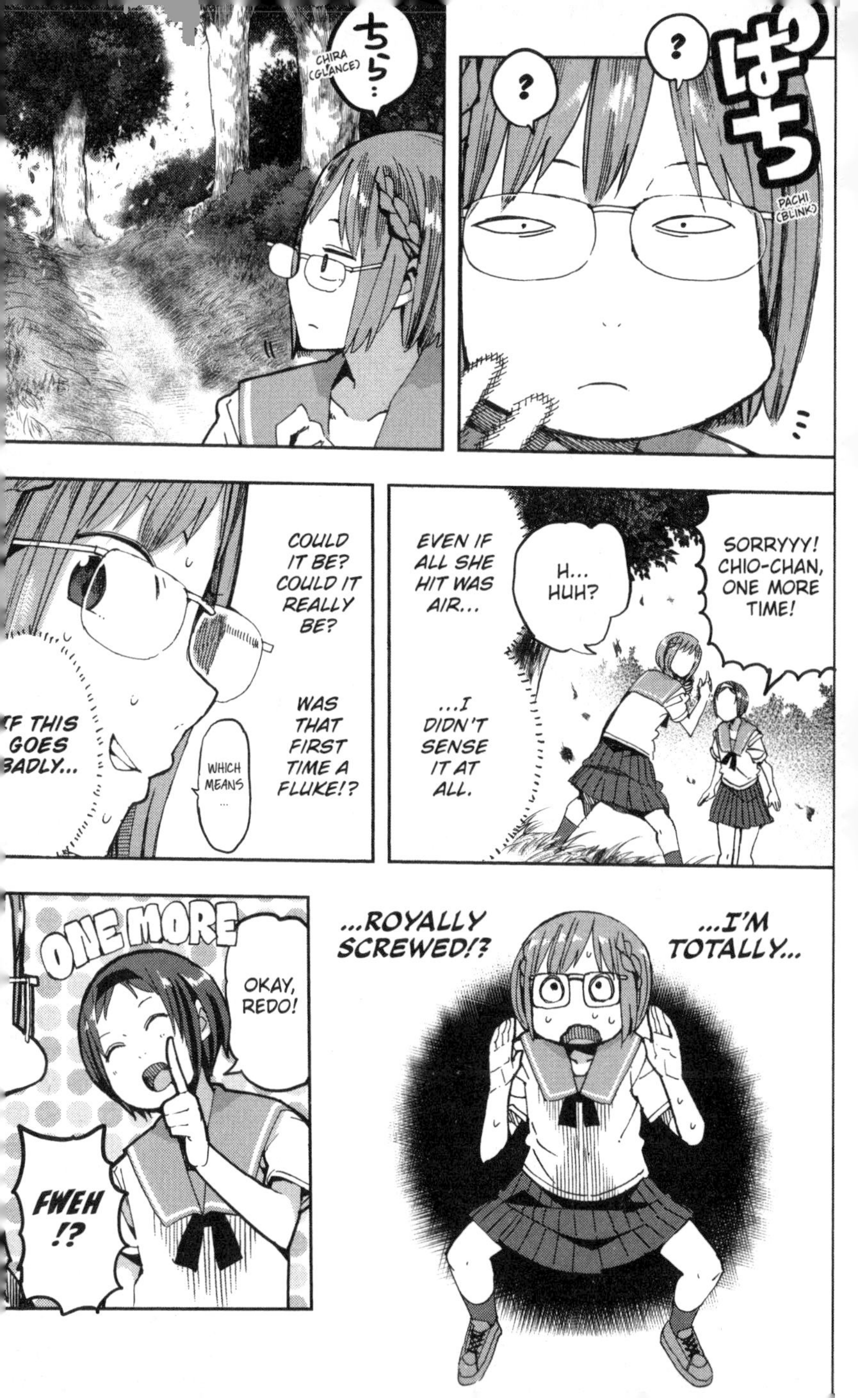
ぱち
PACHI (BLINK)
?
?
ちら..
CHIRA (GLANCE)
SORRYYY! CHIO-CHAN, ONE MORE TIME!
H... HUH?
EVEN IF ALL SHE HIT WAS AIR...
...I DIDN'T SENSE IT AT ALL.
COULD IT BE? COULD IT REALLY BE?
WAS THAT FIRST TIME A FLUKE!?
WHICH MEANS...
F THIS GOES BADLY...
...I'M TOTALLY...
...ROYALLY SCREWED!?
ONE MORE
OKAY, REDO!
FWEH!?

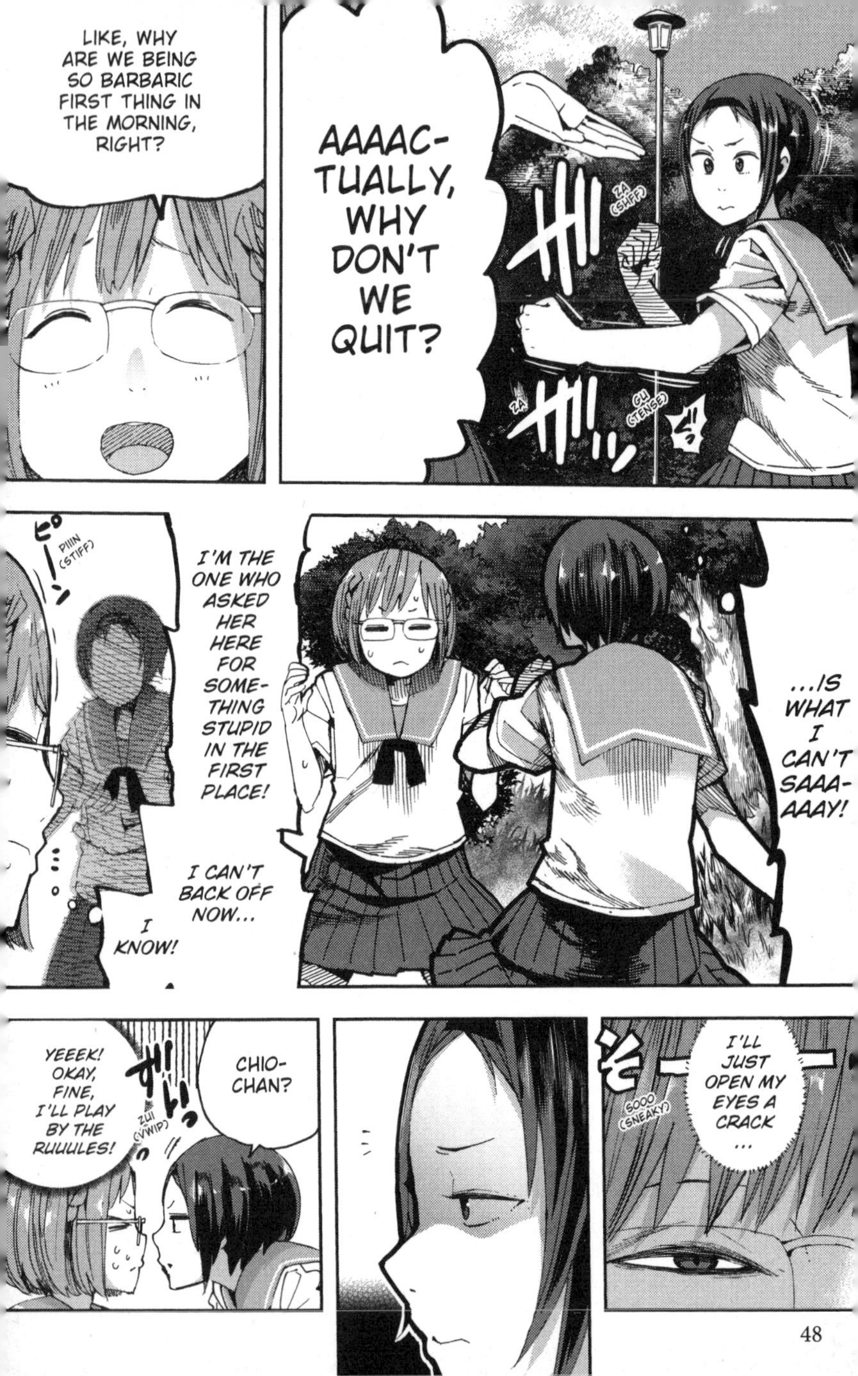
AAAAC-TUALLY, WHY DON'T WE QUIT?
ZA (SHFF)
ZA
GU (TENSE)
LIKE, WHY ARE WE BEING SO BARBARIC FIRST THING IN THE MORNING, RIGHT?
...IS WHAT I CAN'T SAAAAAAY!
I'M THE ONE WHO ASKED HER HERE FOR SOMETHING STUPID IN THE FIRST PLACE!
I CAN'T BACK OFF NOW...
I KNOW!
PIIIN (STIFF)
...
SOOO (SNEAKY)
I'LL JUST OPEN MY EYES A CRACK...
CHIO-CHAN?
ZUI (VWIP)
YEEEK! OKAY, FINE, I'LL PLAY BY THE RUUULES!

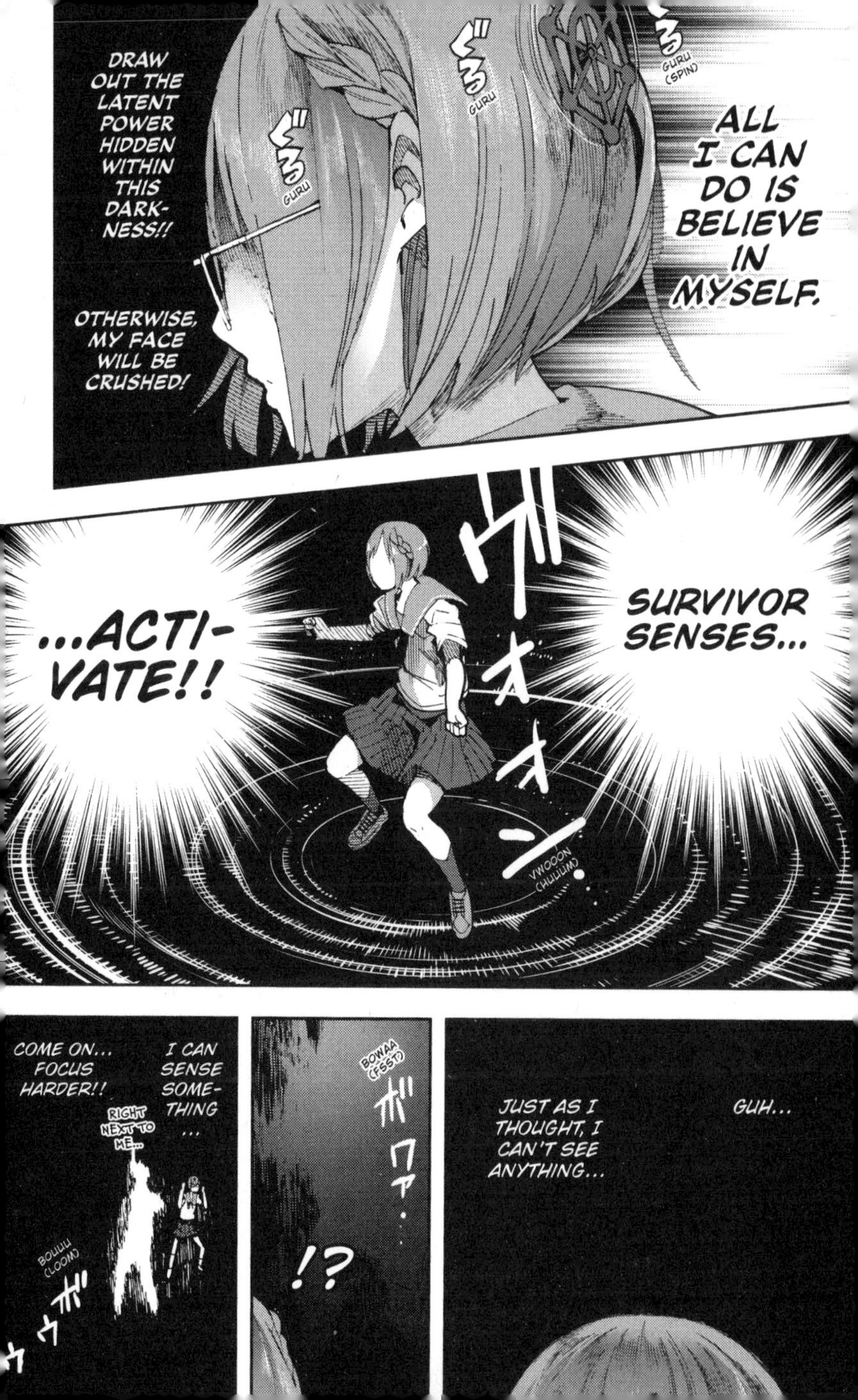
GURU (SPIN)
GURU
GURU
ALL I CAN DO IS BELIEVE IN MYSELF.
DRAW OUT THE LATENT POWER HIDDEN WITHIN THIS DARK-NESS!!
OTHERWISE, MY FACE WILL BE CRUSHED!
SURVIVOR SENSES...
VWOOON (WHUUUN)
...ACTI-VATE!!
GUH...
JUST AS I THOUGHT, I CAN'T SEE ANYTHING...
BOWAA (FSST)
!?
I CAN SENSE SOME-THING...
COME ON... FOCUS HARDER!!
RIGHT NEXT TO ME...
BOUUU (LOOM)

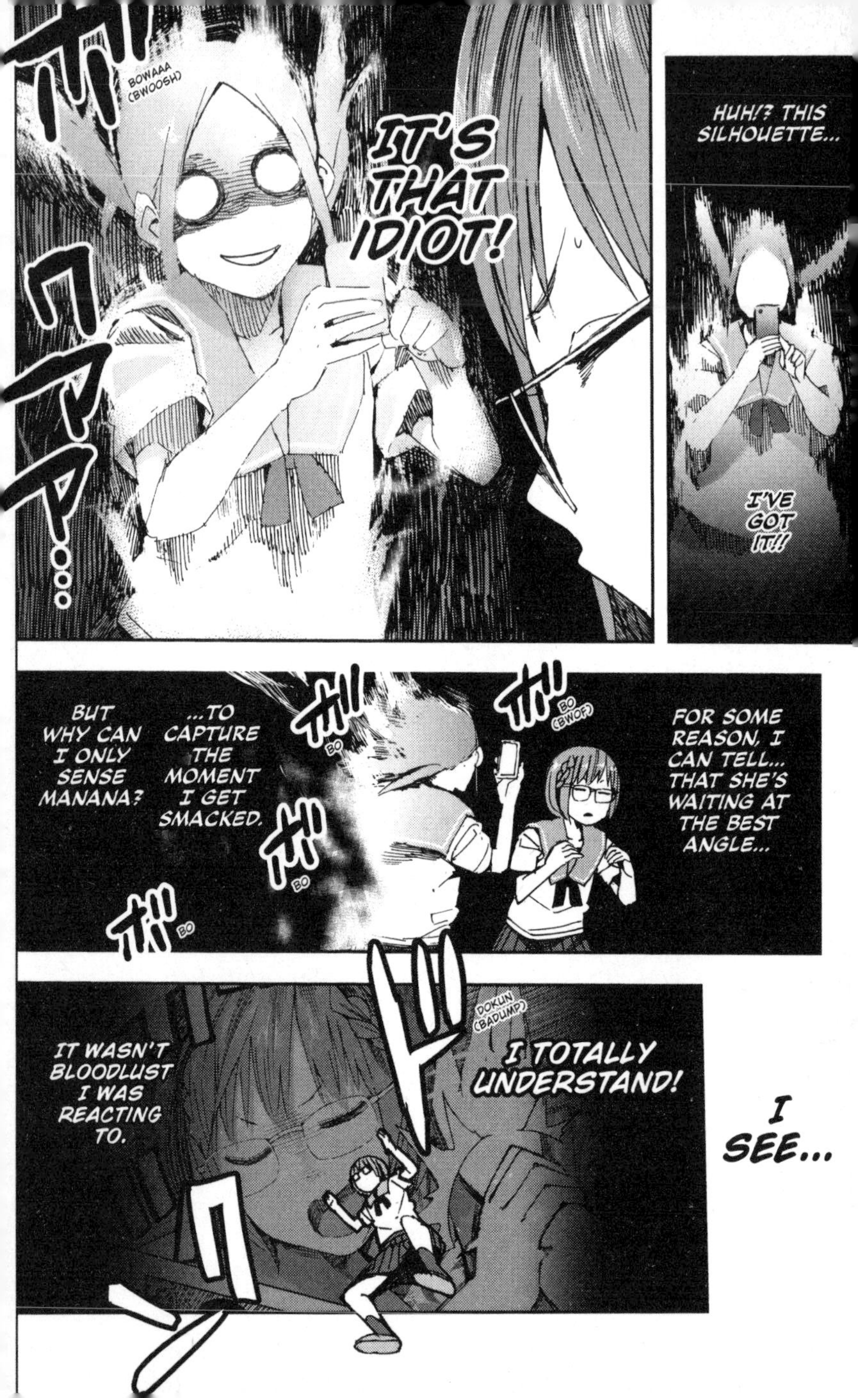
HUH!? THIS SILHOUETTE...
I'VE GOT IT!!
BOWAAA (BWOOSH)
IT'S THAT IDIOT!
FOR SOME REASON, I CAN TELL... THAT SHE'S WAITING AT THE BEST ANGLE...
BO (BWOF)
...TO CAPTURE THE MOMENT I GET SMACKED.
BUT WHY CAN I ONLY SENSE MANANA?
BO
BO
BO
I SEE...
DOKUN (BADUMP)
I TOTALLY UNDERSTAND!
IT WASN'T BLOODLUST I WAS REACTING TO.

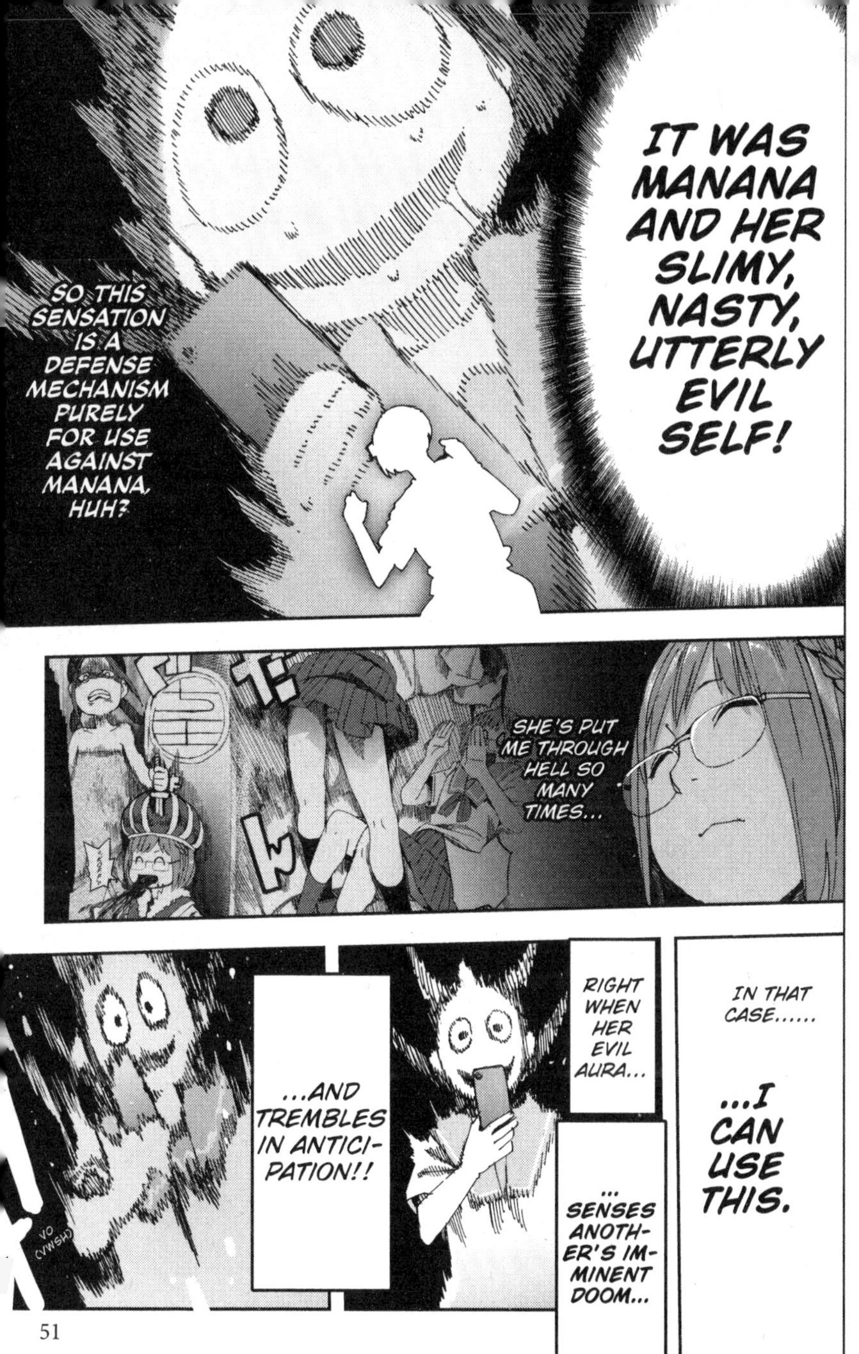
IT WAS MANANA AND HER SLIMY, NASTY, UTTERLY EVIL SELF!
SO THIS SENSATION IS A DEFENSE MECHANISM PURELY FOR USE AGAINST MANANA, HUH?
SHE'S PUT ME THROUGH HELL SO MANY TIMES...
IN THAT CASE......
...I CAN USE THIS.
RIGHT WHEN HER EVIL AURA...
...SENSES ANOTHER'S IMMINENT DOOM...
...AND TREMBLES IN ANTICIPATION!!
VO (VWSH)

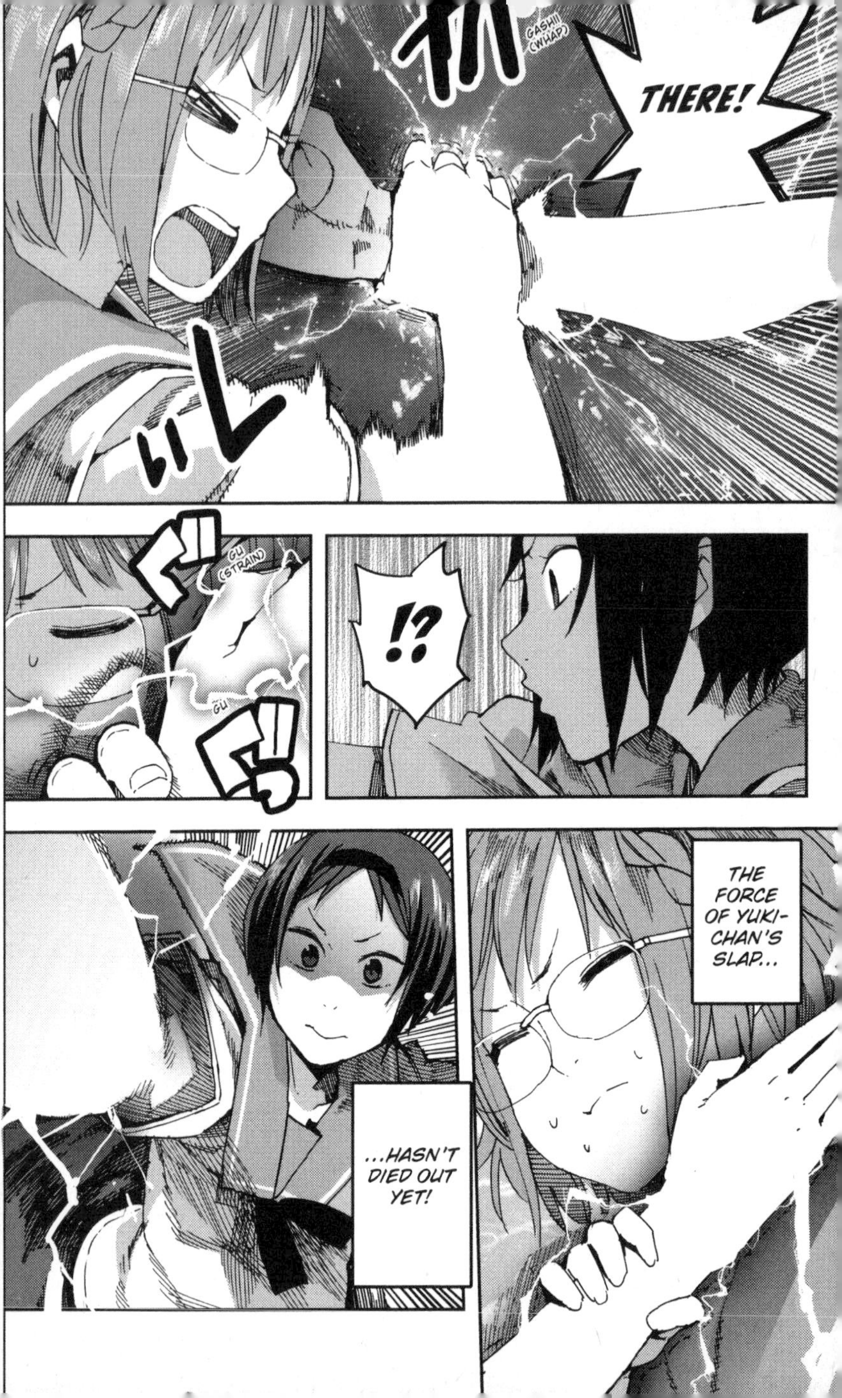
THERE!
GASHI! (WHAP)
!?
GU (STRAIN)
GU
THE FORCE OF YUKI-CHAN'S SLAP...
...HASN'T DIED OUT YET!

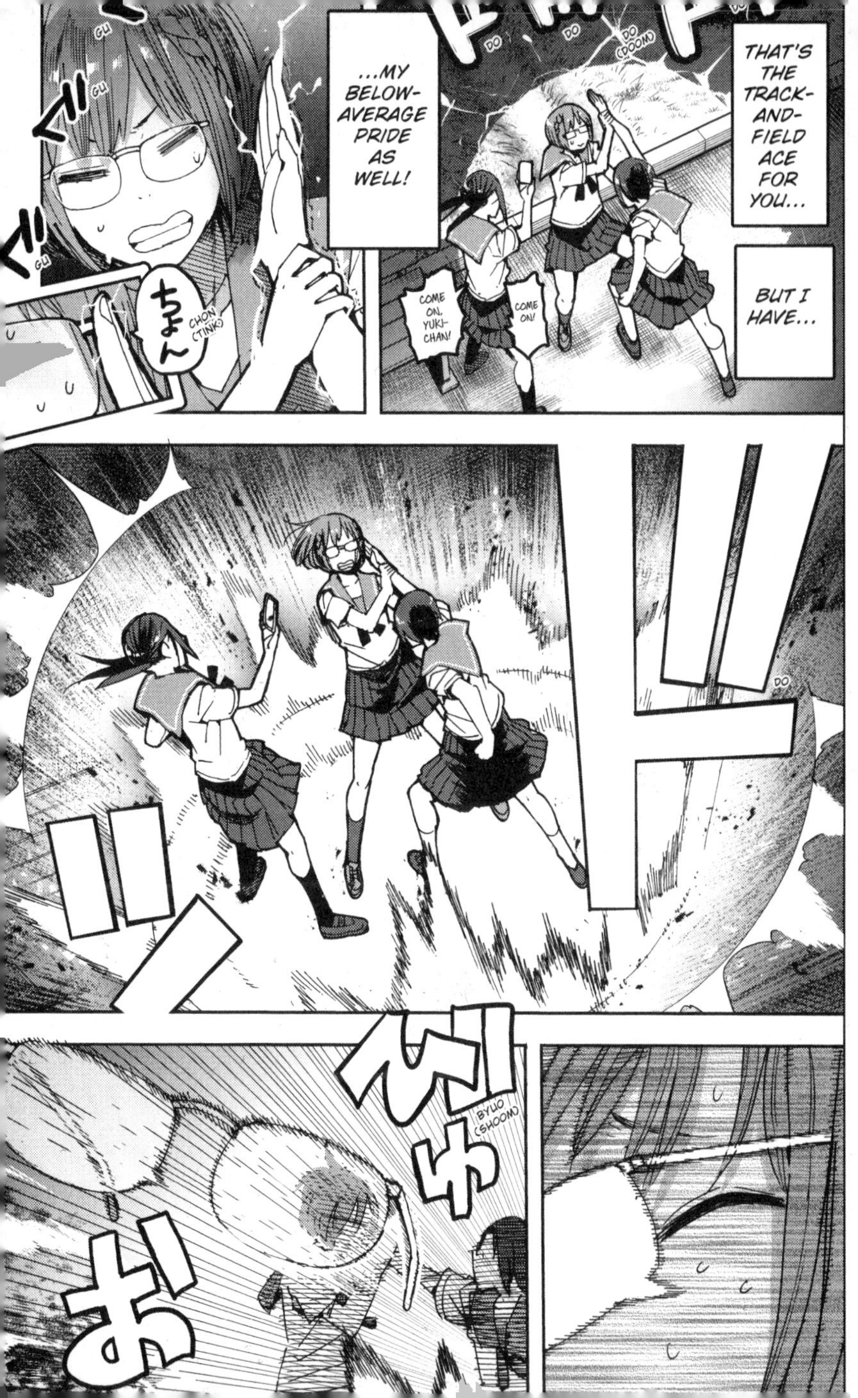
DO
DO
DO (DOOM)
THAT'S THE TRACK-AND-FIELD ACE FOR YOU...
BUT I HAVE...
COME ON!
COME ON, YUKI-CHAN!
...MY BELOW-AVERAGE PRIDE AS WELL!
GU
GU
GU
ちょん
CHON (TINK)
DO
BYUO (SHOOM)

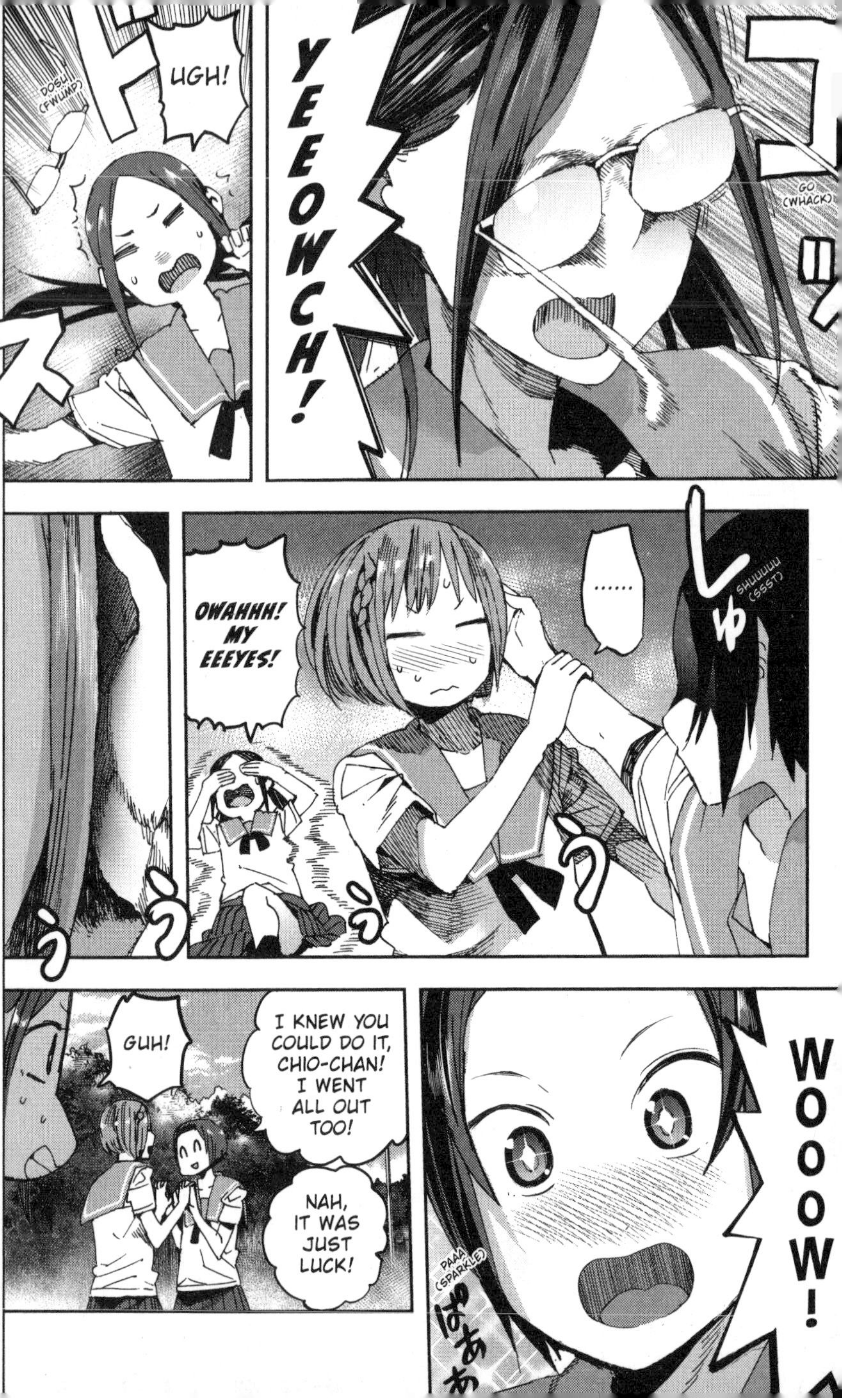
GO (WHACK)
YEEOWCH!
UGH!
DOSU (PWUMP)
......
SHUUUUU (SSST)
OWAHHH! MY EEEYES!
WOOOW!
PAAA (SPARKLE)
I KNEW YOU COULD DO IT, CHIO-CHAN! I WENT ALL OUT TOO!
GUH!
NAH, IT WAS JUST LUCK!

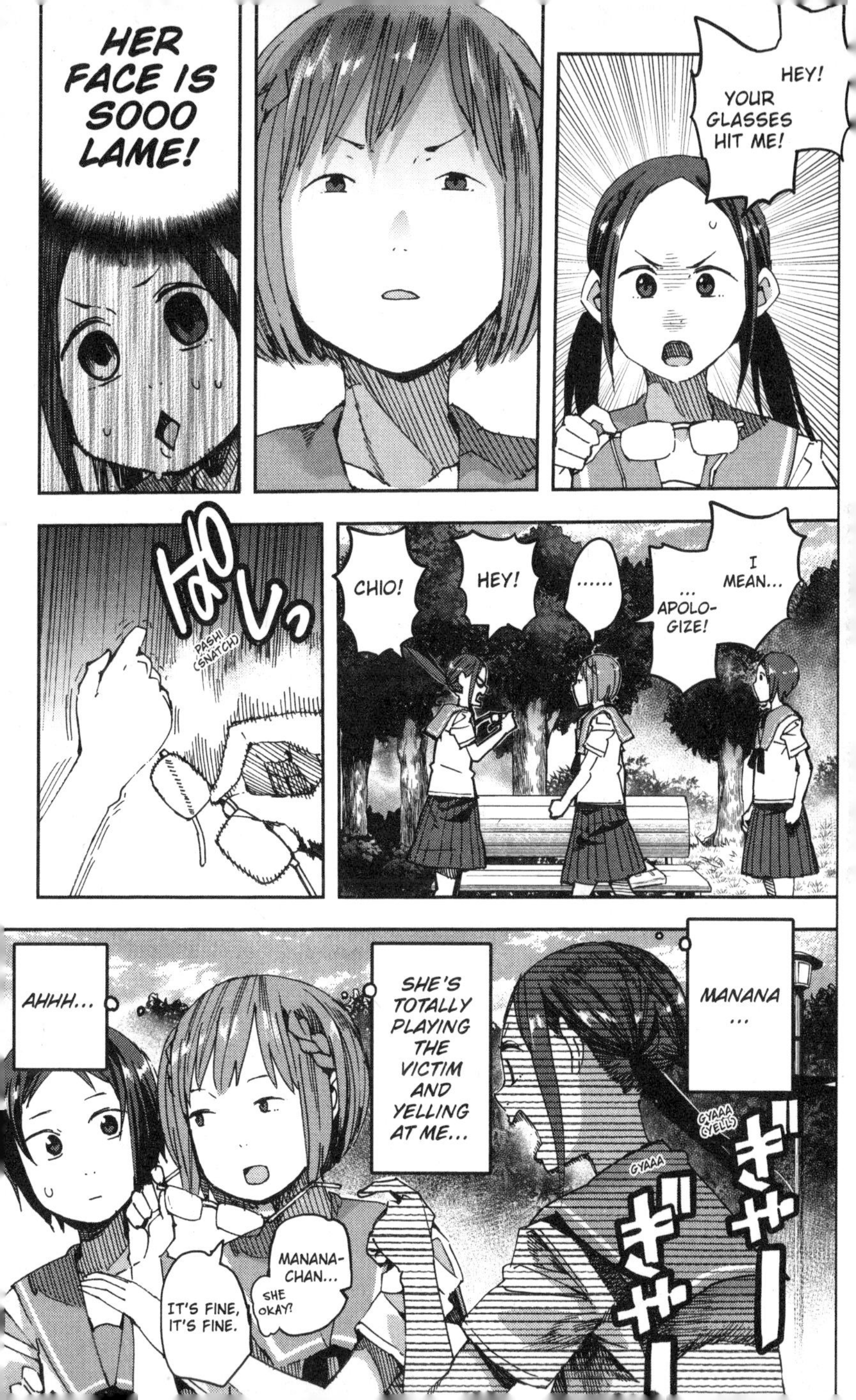

HEY! YOUR GLASSES HIT ME!
HER FACE IS SOOO LAME!
I MEAN... ...APOLOGIZE!
......
HEY!
CHIO!
ぱしっ
PASHI (SNATCH)
MANANA...
ぎゃーぎゃー
GYAAA (YELLS)
GYAAA
SHE'S TOTALLY PLAYING THE VICTIM AND YELLING AT ME...
MANANA-CHAN...
SHE OKAY?
IT'S FINE, IT'S FINE.
AHHH...

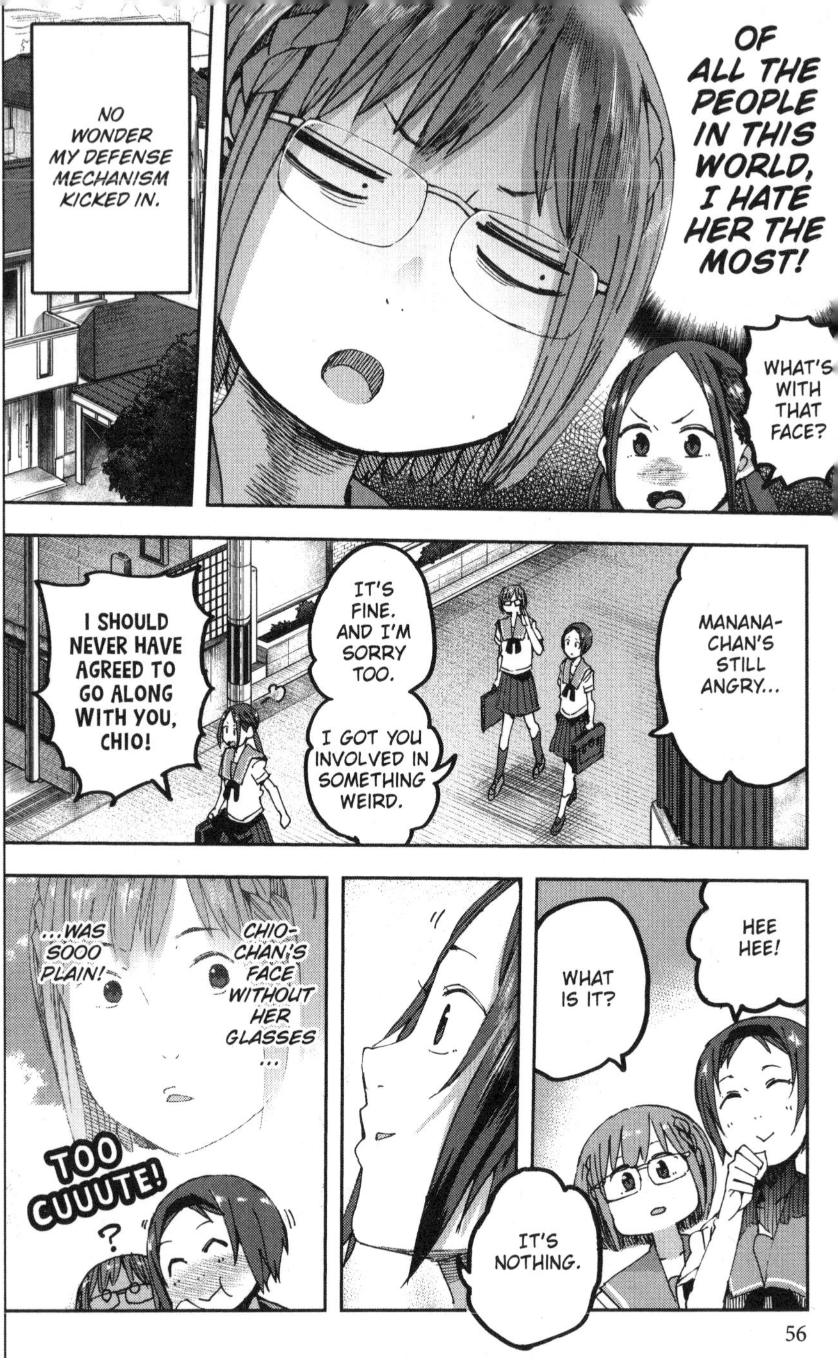
OF ALL THE PEOPLE IN THIS WORLD, I HATE HER THE MOST!
WHAT'S WITH THAT FACE?
NO WONDER MY DEFENSE MECHANISM KICKED IN.
MANANA-CHAN'S STILL ANGRY...
IT'S FINE. AND I'M SORRY TOO.
I GOT YOU INVOLVED IN SOMETHING WEIRD.
I SHOULD NEVER HAVE AGREED TO GO ALONG WITH YOU, CHIO!
HEE HEE!
WHAT IS IT?
IT'S NOTHING.
CHIO-CHAN'S FACE WITHOUT HER GLASSES...
...WAS SOOO PLAIN!
TOO CUUUTE!
?

HUH? WHERE DID MANANA GO?
THIS IS WHERE ...
...I GET MY REVENGE!
RAH!
BU (SWING)
SA (DODGE)
DAN-GER SENSE!
!?
WAIT!
GYURU
WAA-AAH!
ZASAA (SKIIID)
GYURU (SPIN)
I CAN'T STOP ...
NOT ONCE BUT TWICE?
IS THIS MY FAULT!?
GO
GO (RUMBLE)
GO

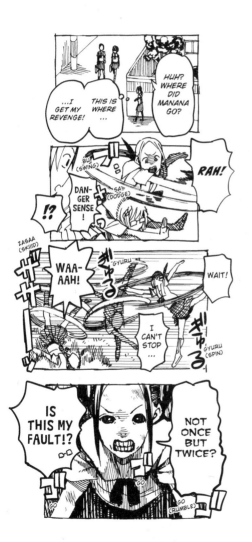

Chio's SCHOOL ROAD

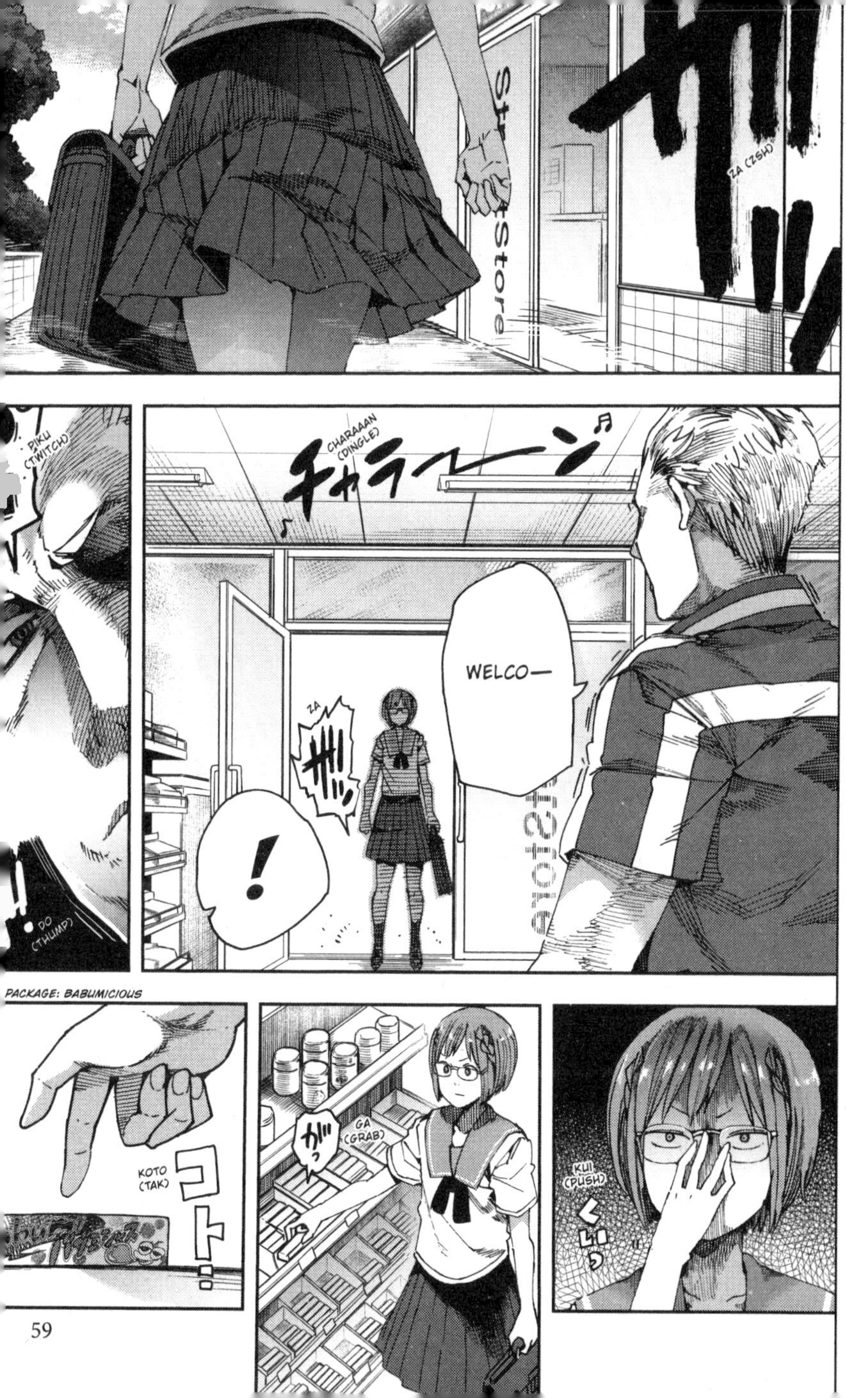
ZA (ZSH)
CHARAAAN (DINGLE)
WELCO—
ZA
!
PIKU (TWITCH)
DO (THUMP)
PACKAGE: BABUMICIOUS
KUI (PUSH)
GA (GRAB)
KOTO (TAK)

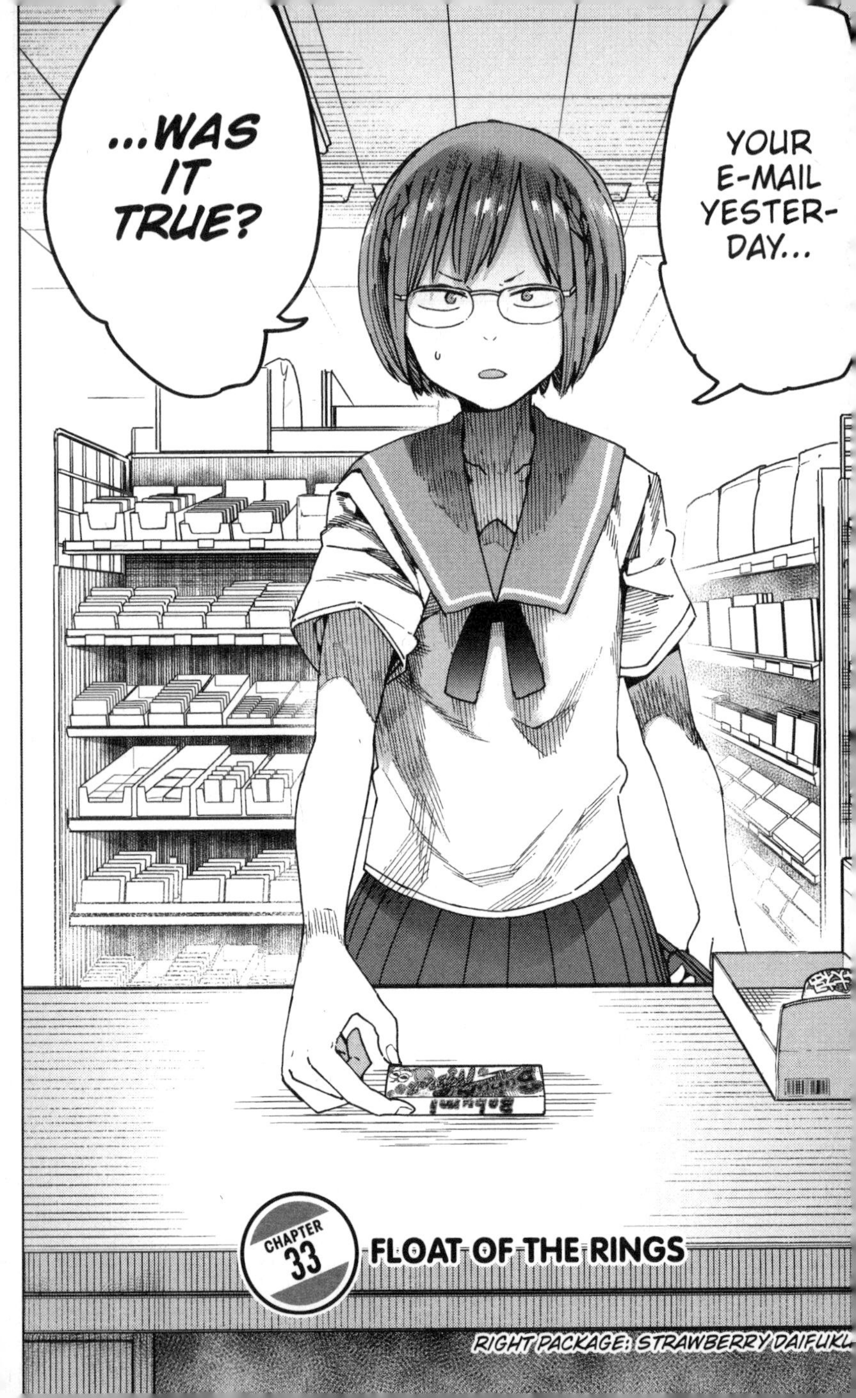
YOUR E-MAIL YESTER-DAY...
...WAS IT TRUE?
CHAPTER 33
FLOAT OF THE RINGS
RIGHT PACKAGE: STRAWBERRY DAIFUKU

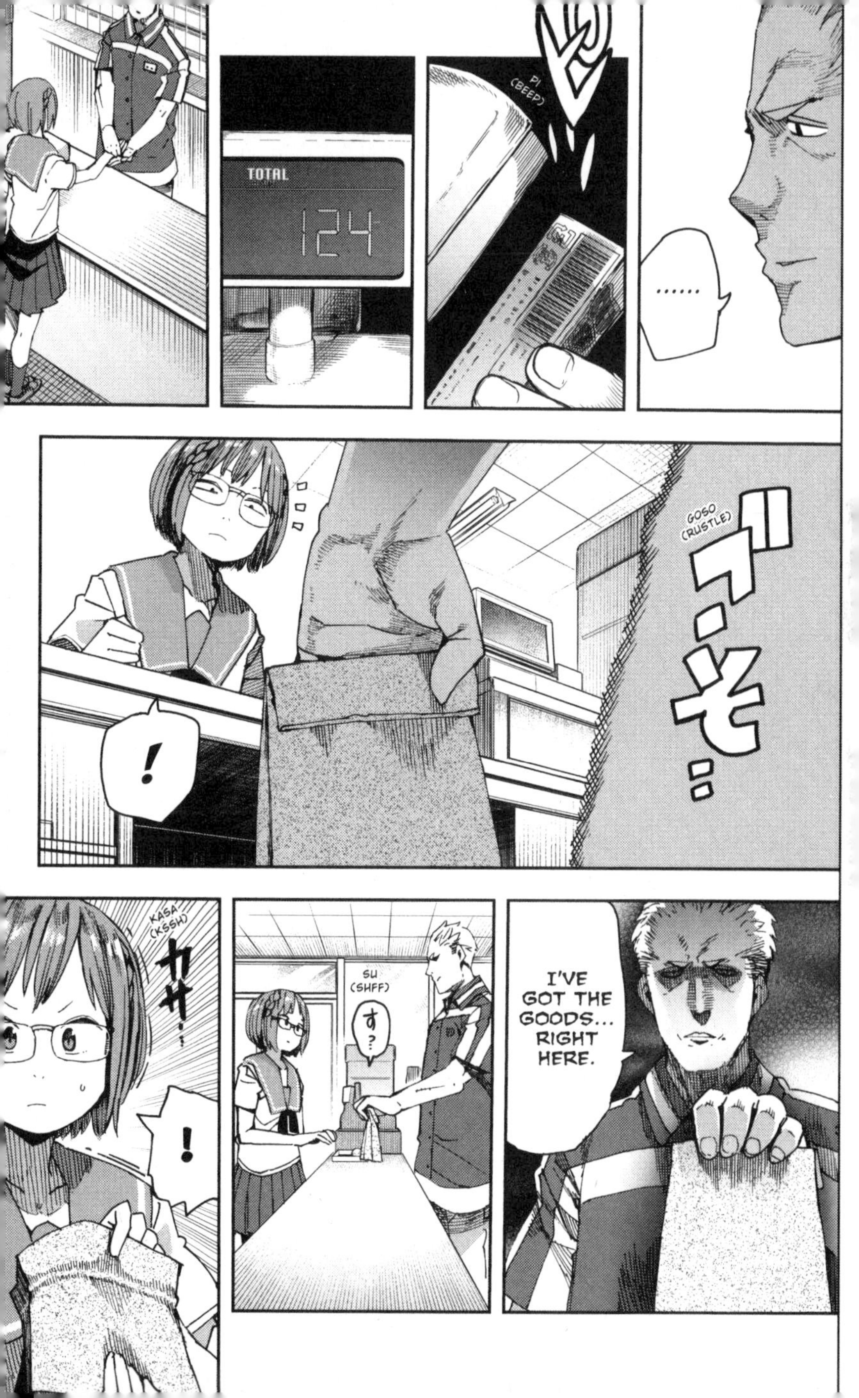
......
PI (BEEP)
TOTAL
124
GOSO (RUSTLE)
ゴソ…
!
I'VE GOT THE GOODS... RIGHT HERE.
SU (SHFF)
す？
KASA (KSSH)
カサ…
!

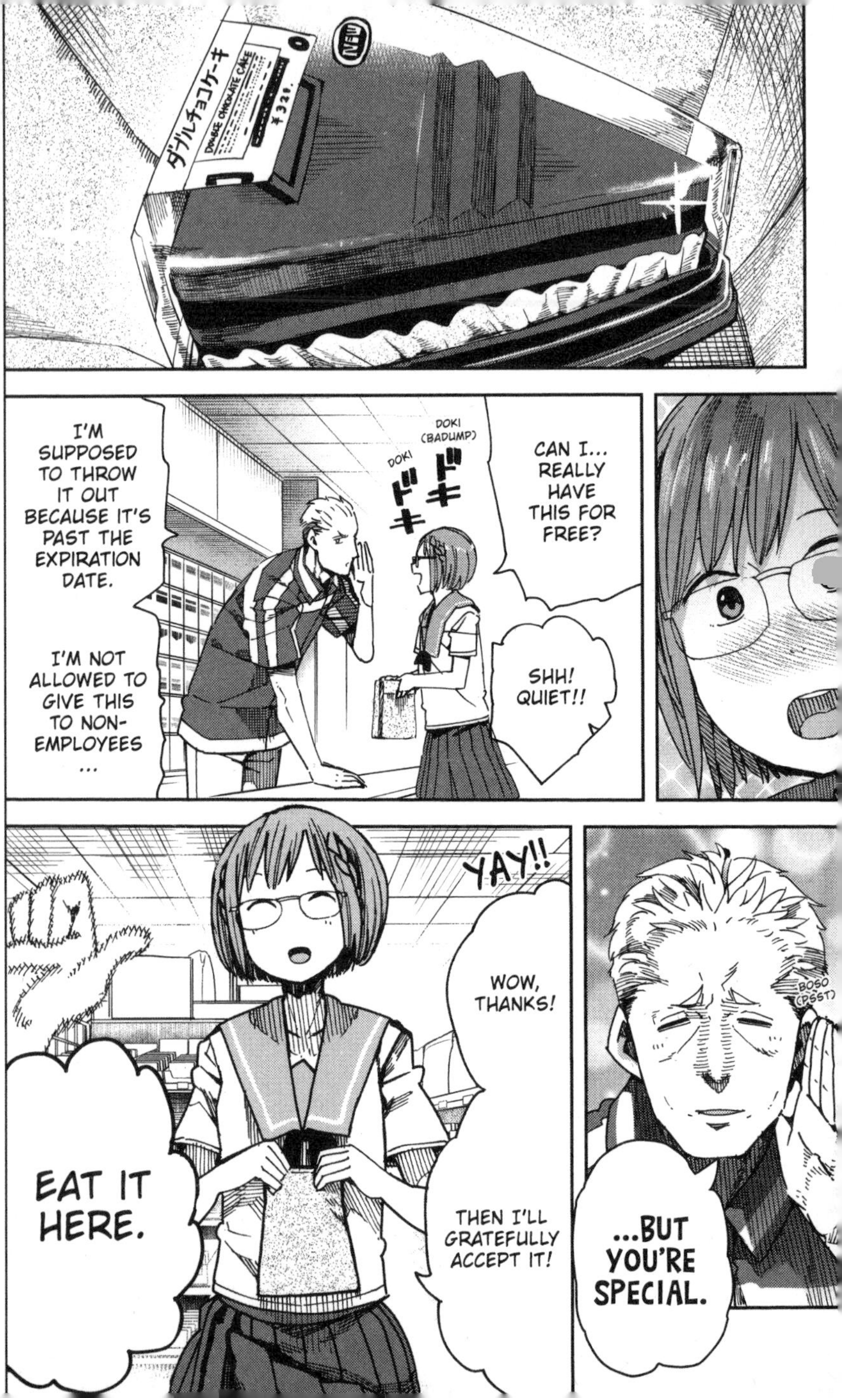
NEW
ダブルチョコケーキ
DOUBLE CHOCOLATE CAKE
¥321
CAN I... REALLY HAVE THIS FOR FREE?
DOKI (BADUMP) ドキ
DOKI ドキ
SHH! QUIET!!
I'M SUPPOSED TO THROW IT OUT BECAUSE IT'S PAST THE EXPIRATION DATE.
I'M NOT ALLOWED TO GIVE THIS TO NON-EMPLOYEES ...
BOSO (PSST)
...BUT YOU'RE SPECIAL.
YAY!!
WOW, THANKS!
THEN I'LL GRATEFULLY ACCEPT IT!
EAT IT HERE.

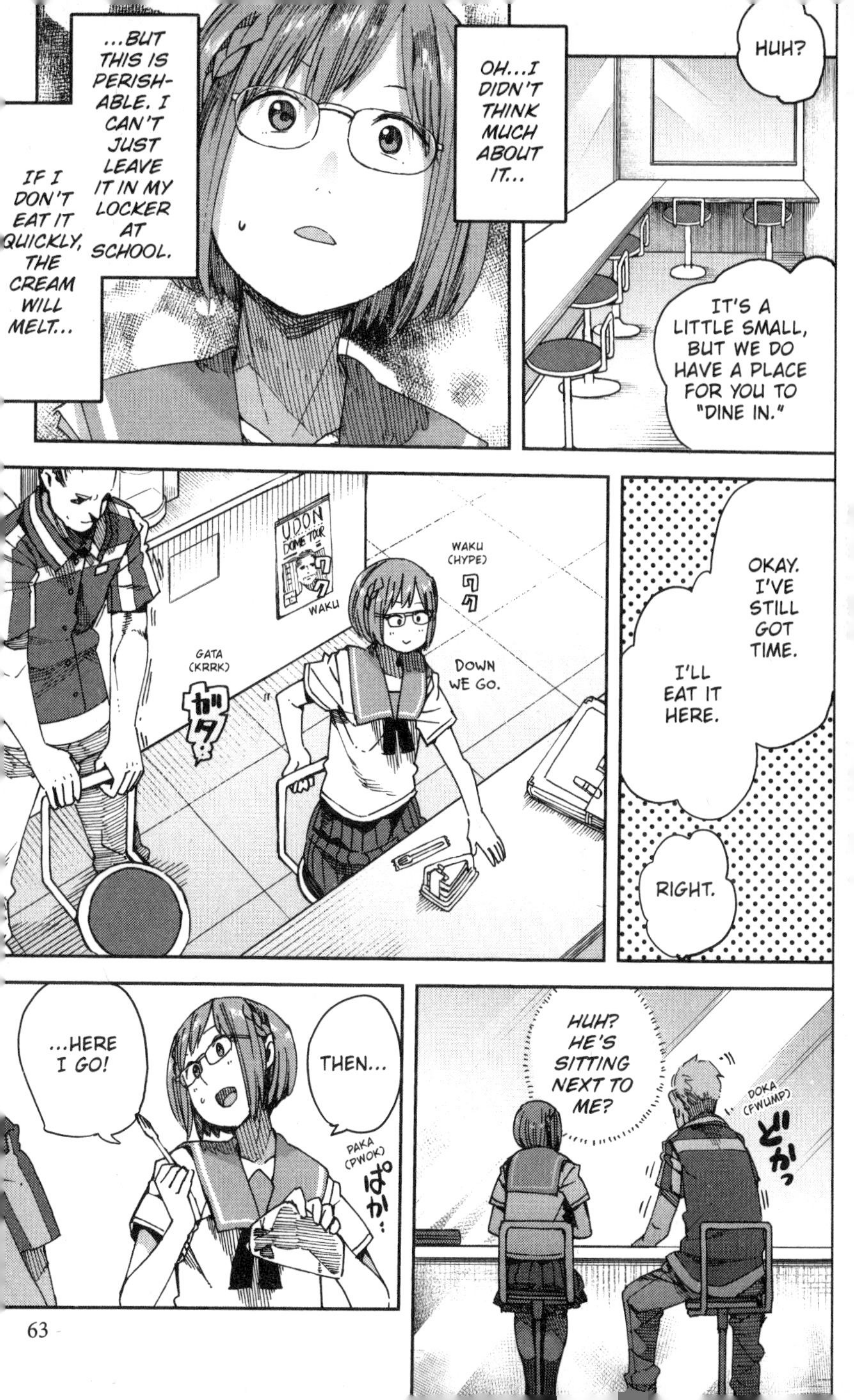
HUH?
IT'S A LITTLE SMALL, BUT WE DO HAVE A PLACE FOR YOU TO "DINE IN."
OH...I DIDN'T THINK MUCH ABOUT IT...
...BUT THIS IS PERISHABLE. I CAN'T JUST LEAVE IT IN MY LOCKER AT SCHOOL.
IF I DON'T EAT IT QUICKLY, THE CREAM WILL MELT...
OKAY. I'VE STILL GOT TIME.
I'LL EAT IT HERE.
RIGHT.
UDON DOME TOUR
WAKU (HYPE)
WAKU
DOWN WE GO.
GATA (KRRK)
HUH? HE'S SITTING NEXT TO ME?
DOKA (FWUMP)
THEN...
...HERE I GO!
PAKA (PWOK)

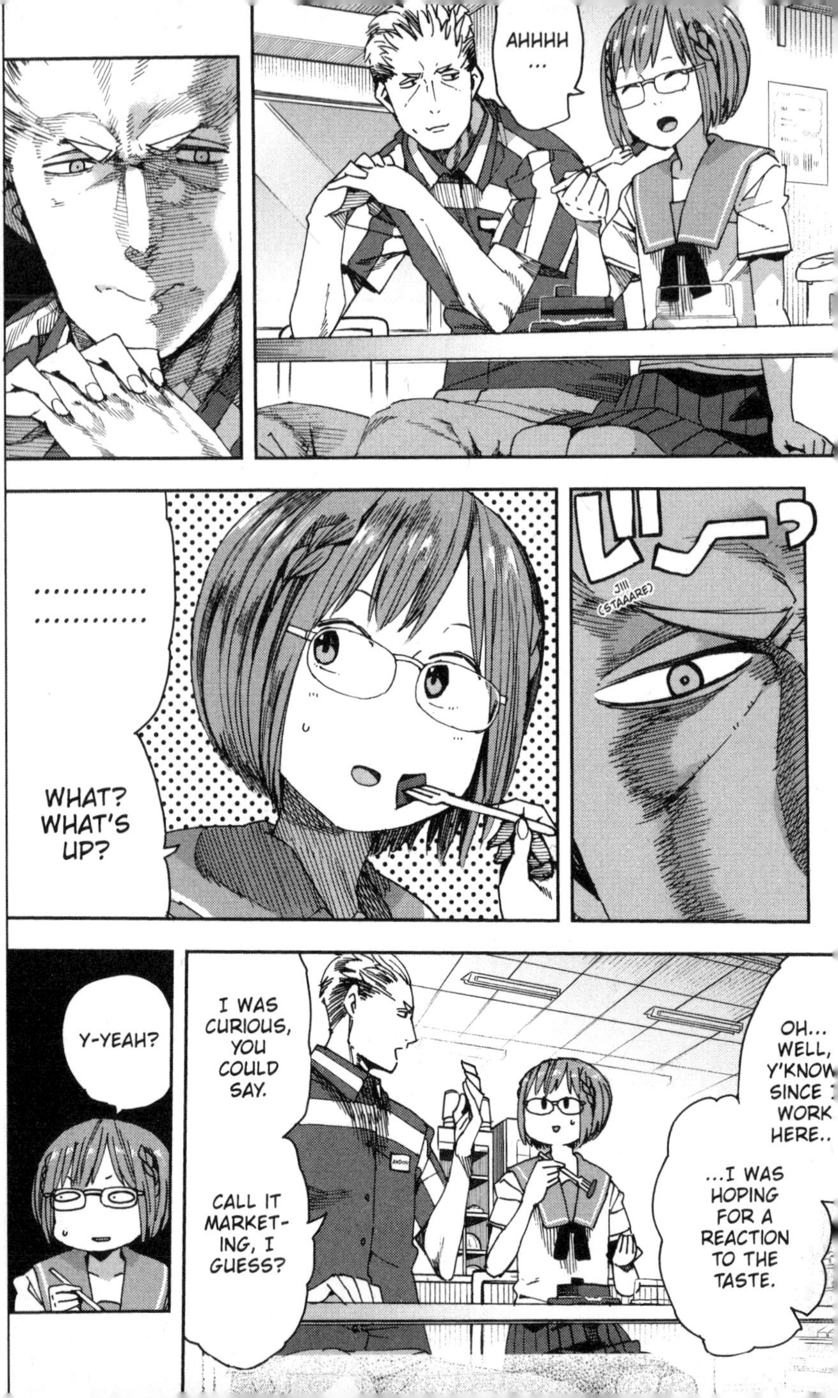
AHHHH ...
JIII (STAAARE)
....
....
WHAT? WHAT'S UP?
OH... WELL, Y'KNOW SINCE I WORK HERE..
...I WAS HOPING FOR A REACTION TO THE TASTE.
I WAS CURIOUS, YOU COULD SAY.
CALL IT MARKETING, I GUESS?
Y-YEAH?

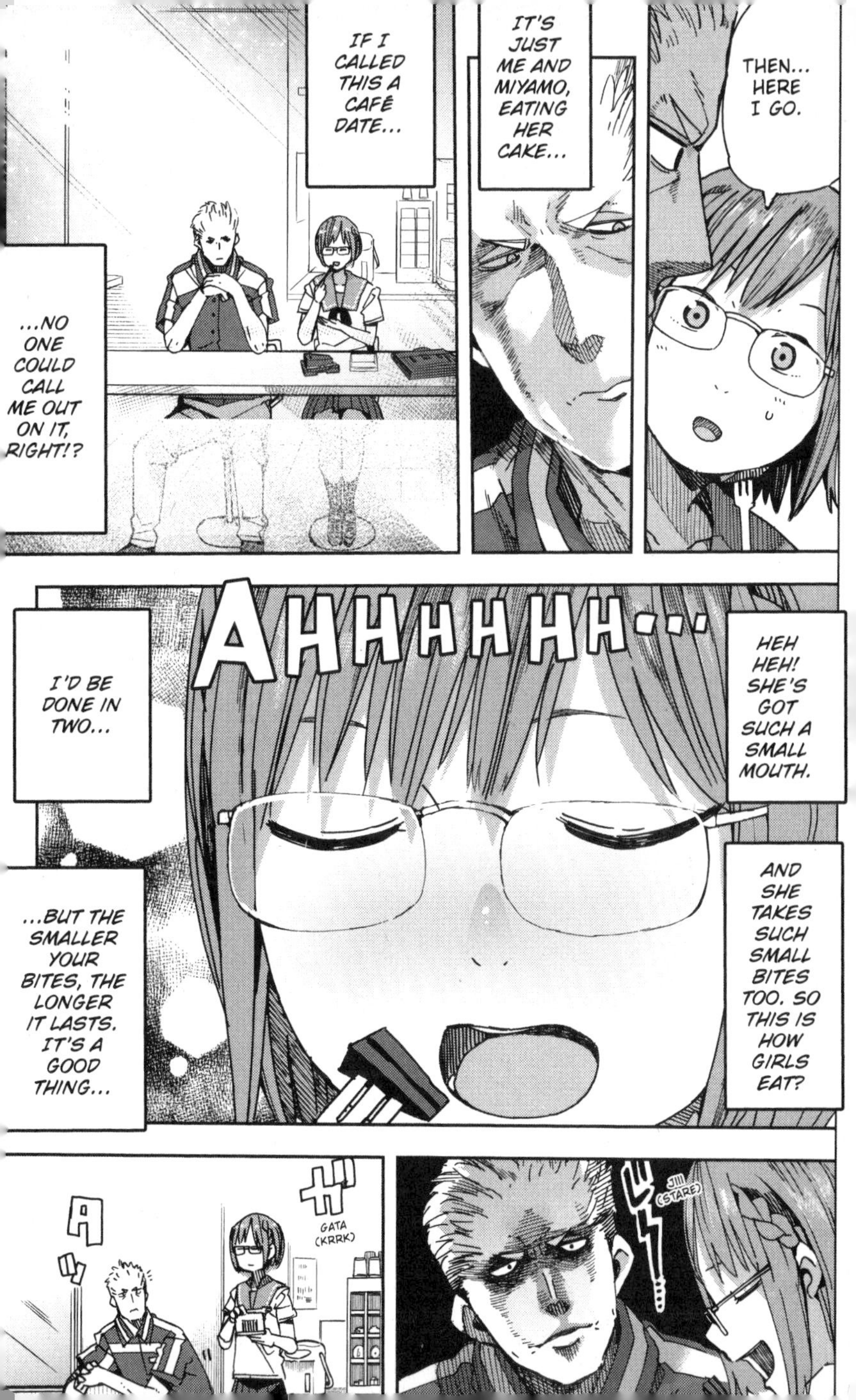
THEN... HERE I GO.
IT'S JUST ME AND MIYAMO, EATING HER CAKE...
IF I CALLED THIS A CAFÉ DATE...
...NO ONE COULD CALL ME OUT ON IT, RIGHT!?
AHHHHHH...
HEH HEH! SHE'S GOT SUCH A SMALL MOUTH.
I'D BE DONE IN TWO...
AND SHE TAKES SUCH SMALL BITES TOO. SO THIS IS HOW GIRLS EAT?
...BUT THE SMALLER YOUR BITES, THE LONGER IT LASTS. IT'S A GOOD THING...
JIII (STARE)
GATA (KRRK)

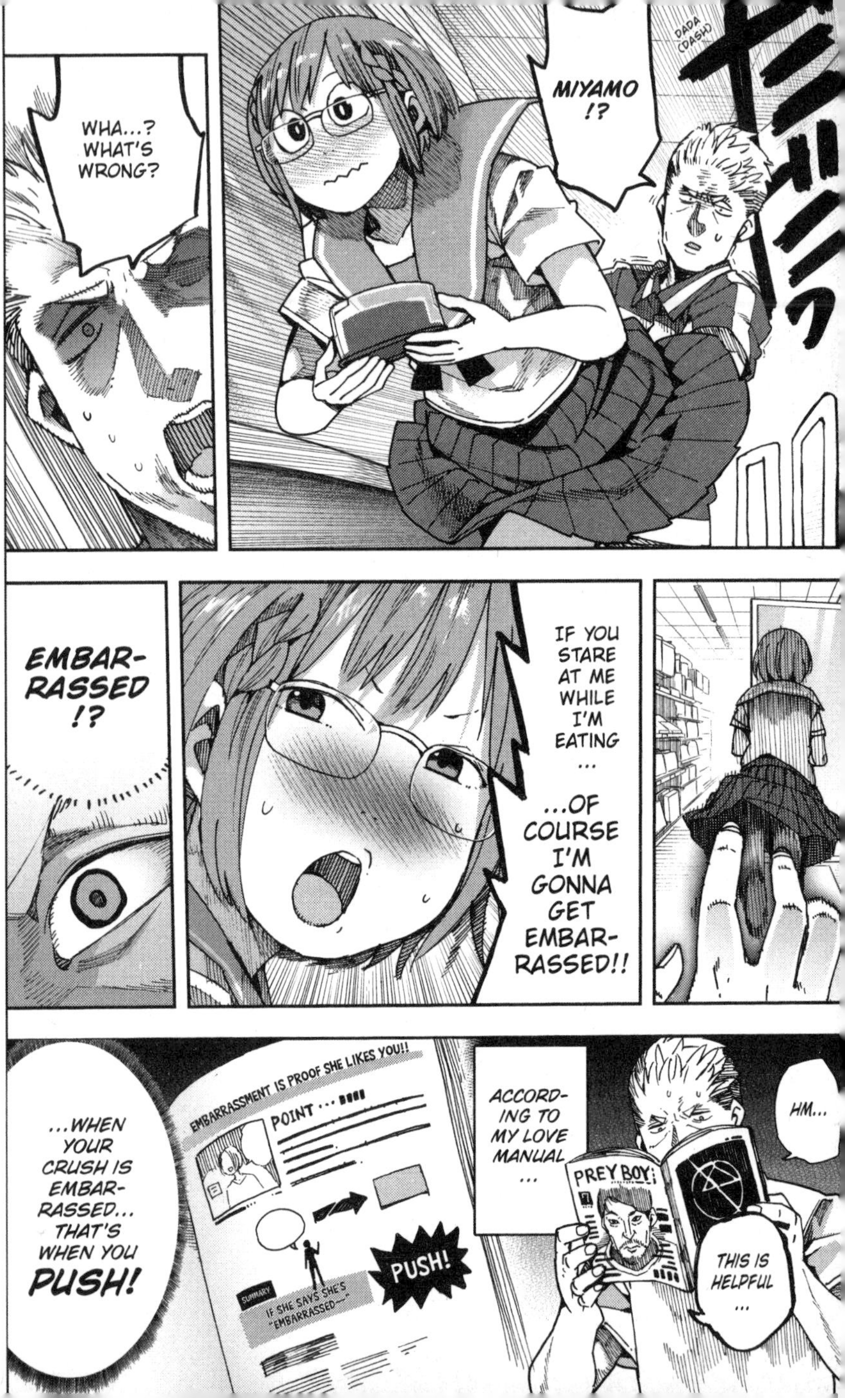
DADA (DASH)
MIYAMO !?
WHA...? WHAT'S WRONG?
IF YOU STARE AT ME WHILE I'M EATING ...
...OF COURSE I'M GONNA GET EMBAR-RASSED!!
EMBAR-RASSED !?
HM...
ACCORD-ING TO MY LOVE MANUAL ...
THIS IS HELPFUL ...
PREY BOY
EMBARRASSMENT IS PROOF SHE LIKES YOU!!
POINT ...
PUSH!
SUMMARY
IF SHE SAYS SHE'S "EMBARRASSED"—
...WHEN YOUR CRUSH IS EMBAR-RASSED... THAT'S WHEN YOU PUSH!

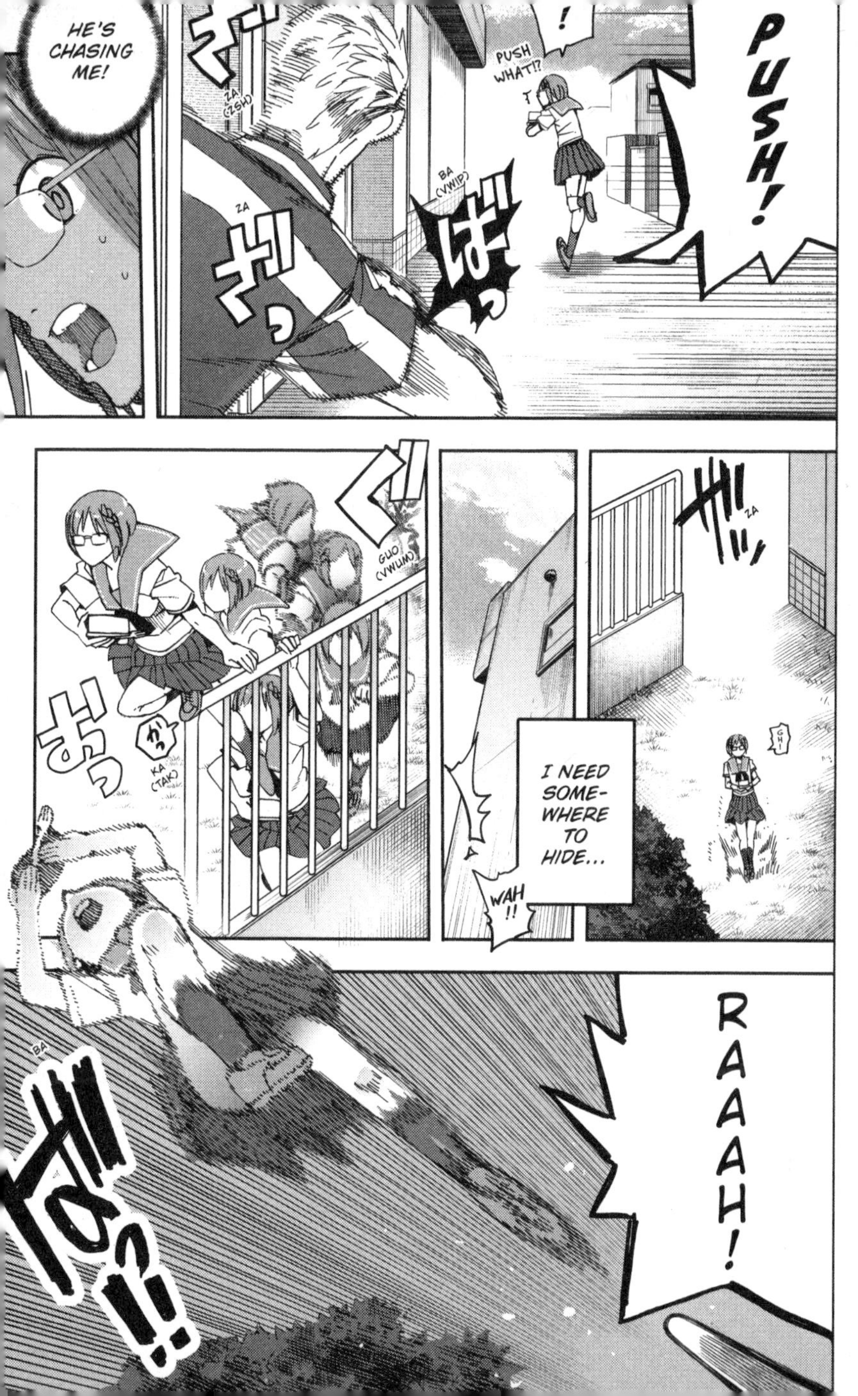
PUSH!
!
PUSH WHAT!?
BA (VWIP)
ZA
ZA (ZSH)
HE'S CHASING ME!
ZA
GHI
I NEED SOME-WHERE TO HIDE...
WAH !!
GUO (VWUM)
KA (TAK)
RAAAAH!
BA
?!!

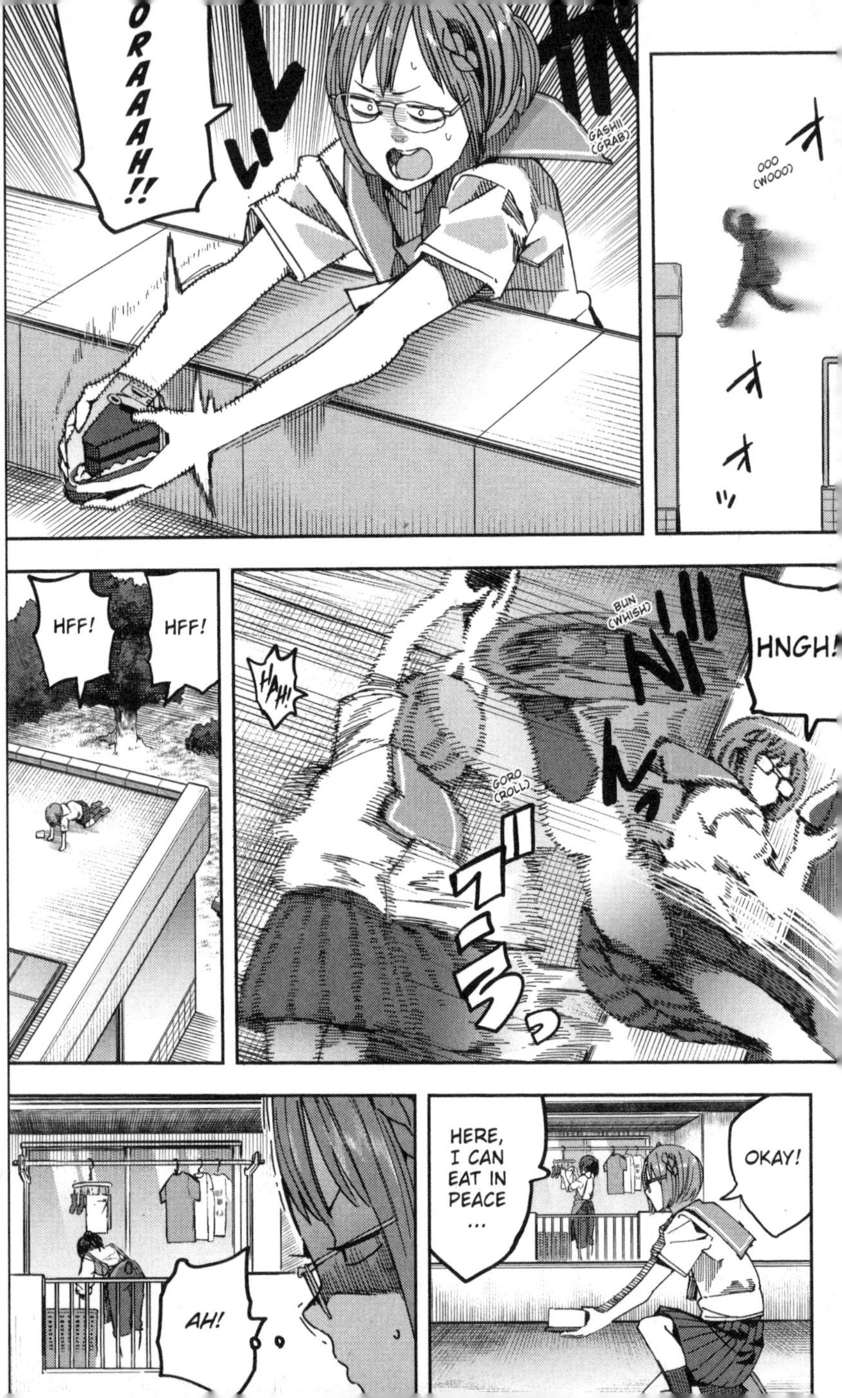
OOO (WOOO)
GASHII (GRAB)
ORAAAAH!!
HNGH!
BUN (WHISH)
HAH!
GORO (ROLL)
HFF!
HFF!
OKAY!
HERE, I CAN EAT IN PEACE ...
AH!

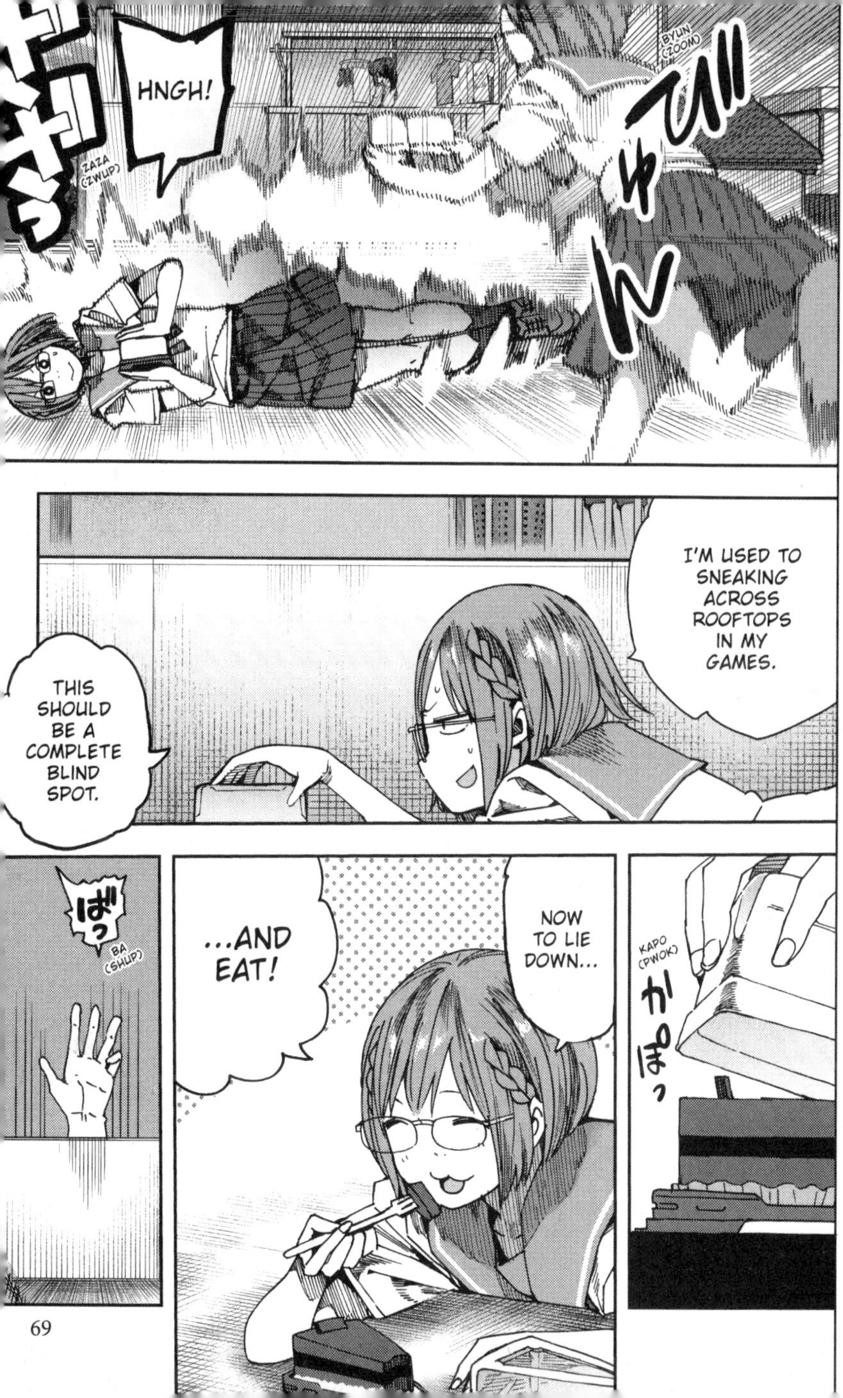
BYUN (ZOOM)
HNGH!
ZAZA (ZWUP)
I'M USED TO SNEAKING ACROSS ROOFTOPS IN MY GAMES.
THIS SHOULD BE A COMPLETE BLIND SPOT.
KAPO (PWOK)
かぽっ
NOW TO LIE DOWN...
...AND EAT!
ばっ
BA (SHUP)

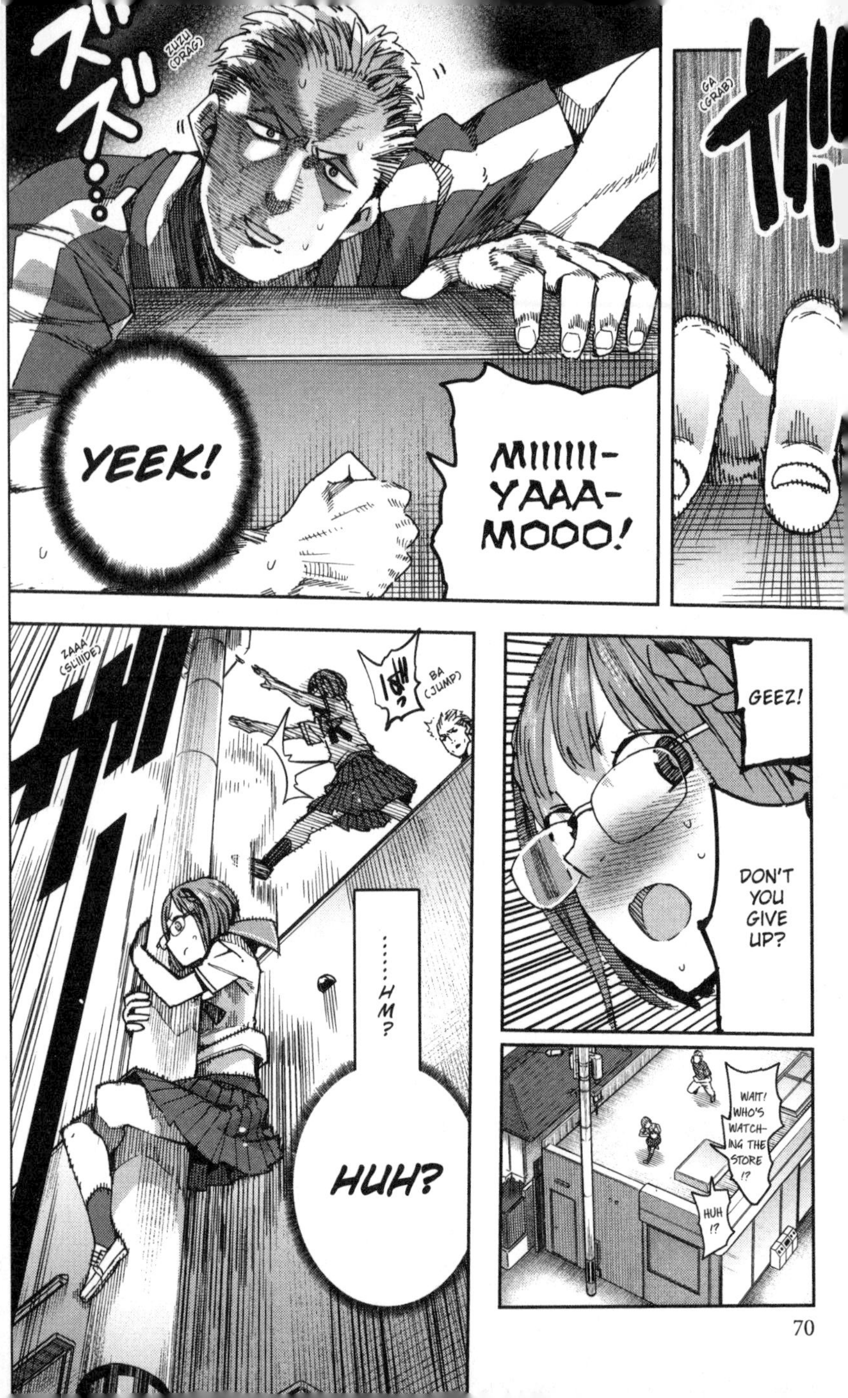
ガッ!!
GA (GRAB)
ズズズ…
ZUZU (DRAG)
YEEK!
MIIIIII-YAAA-MOOO!
GEEZ!
DON'T YOU GIVE UP?
WAIT! WHO'S WATCHING THE STORE!?
HUH!?
ZAAA (SLIIIDE)
はっ!?
BA (JUMP)
......HM?
HUH?

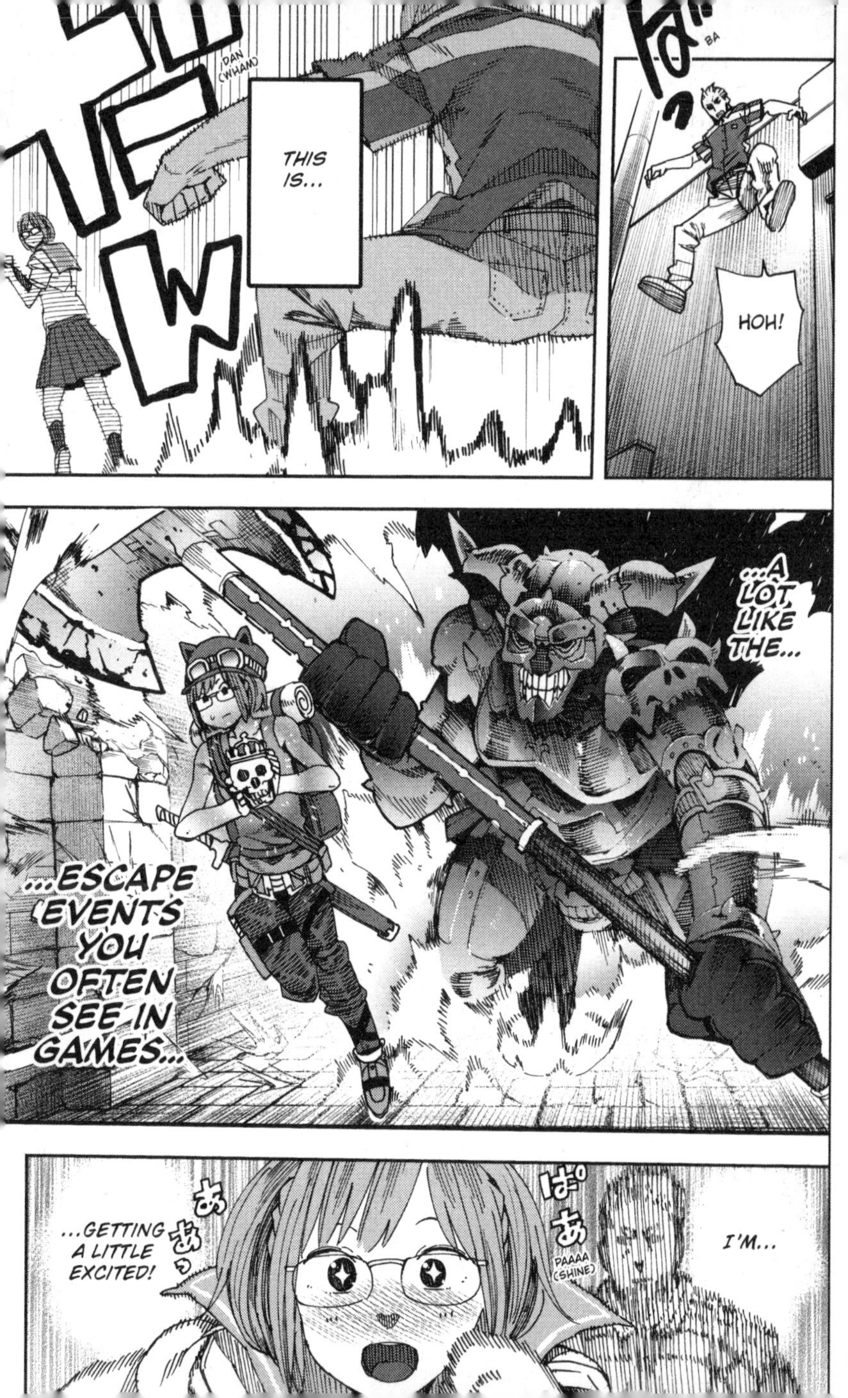

BA
HOH!
DAN (WHAM)
THIS IS...
...A LOT LIKE THE...
...ESCAPE EVENTS YOU OFTEN SEE IN GAMES...
I'M...
PAAAA (SHINE)
...GETTING A LITTLE EXCITED!

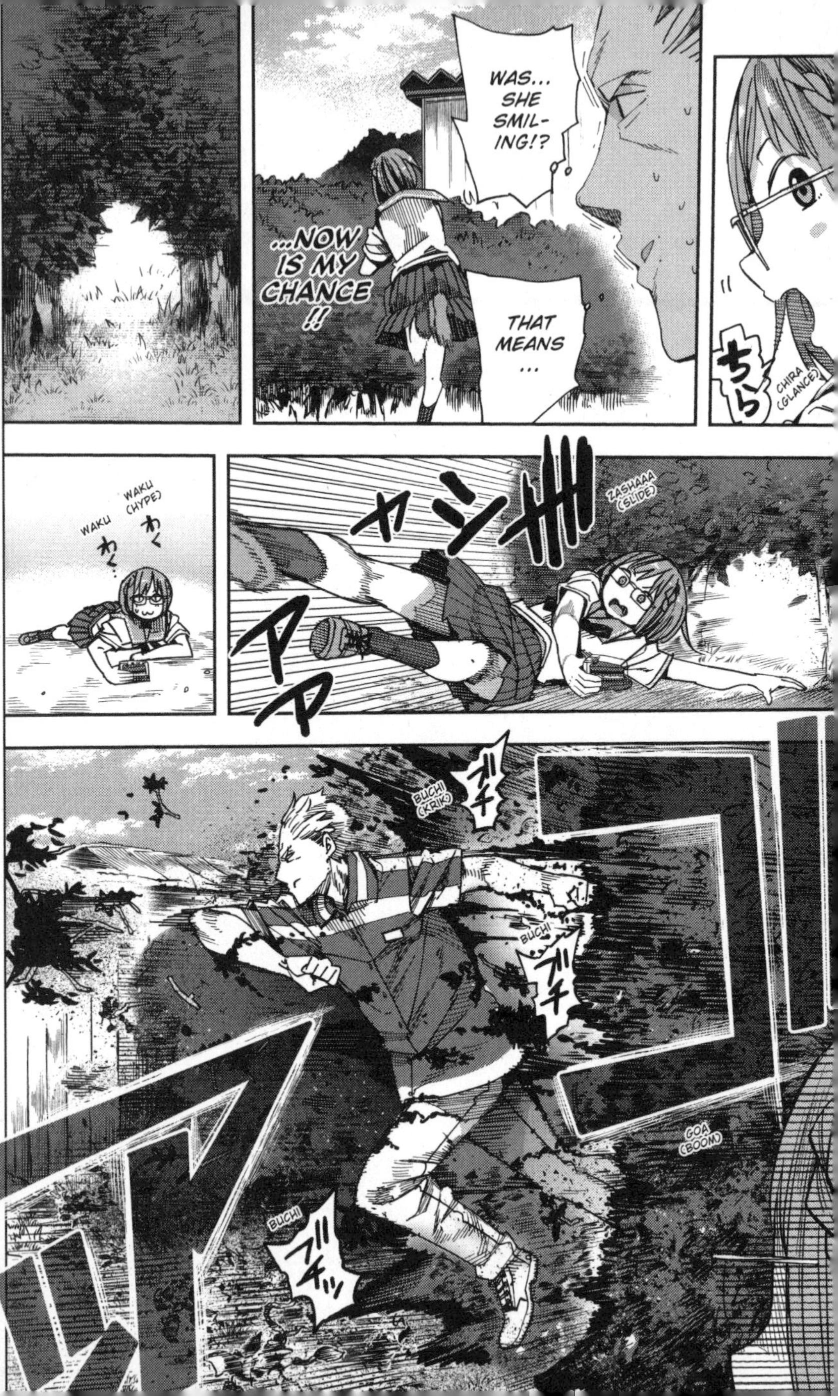
ちら
CHIRA (GLANCE)
WAS... SHE SMIL-ING!?
THAT MEANS...
...NOW IS MY CHANCE!!
ザシャアア
ZASHAAA (SLIDE)
わくわく
WAKU WAKU (HYPE)
ブチ
BUCHI (KRIK)
BUCHI
ブチ
BUCHI
ブチッ
GOA (BOOM)

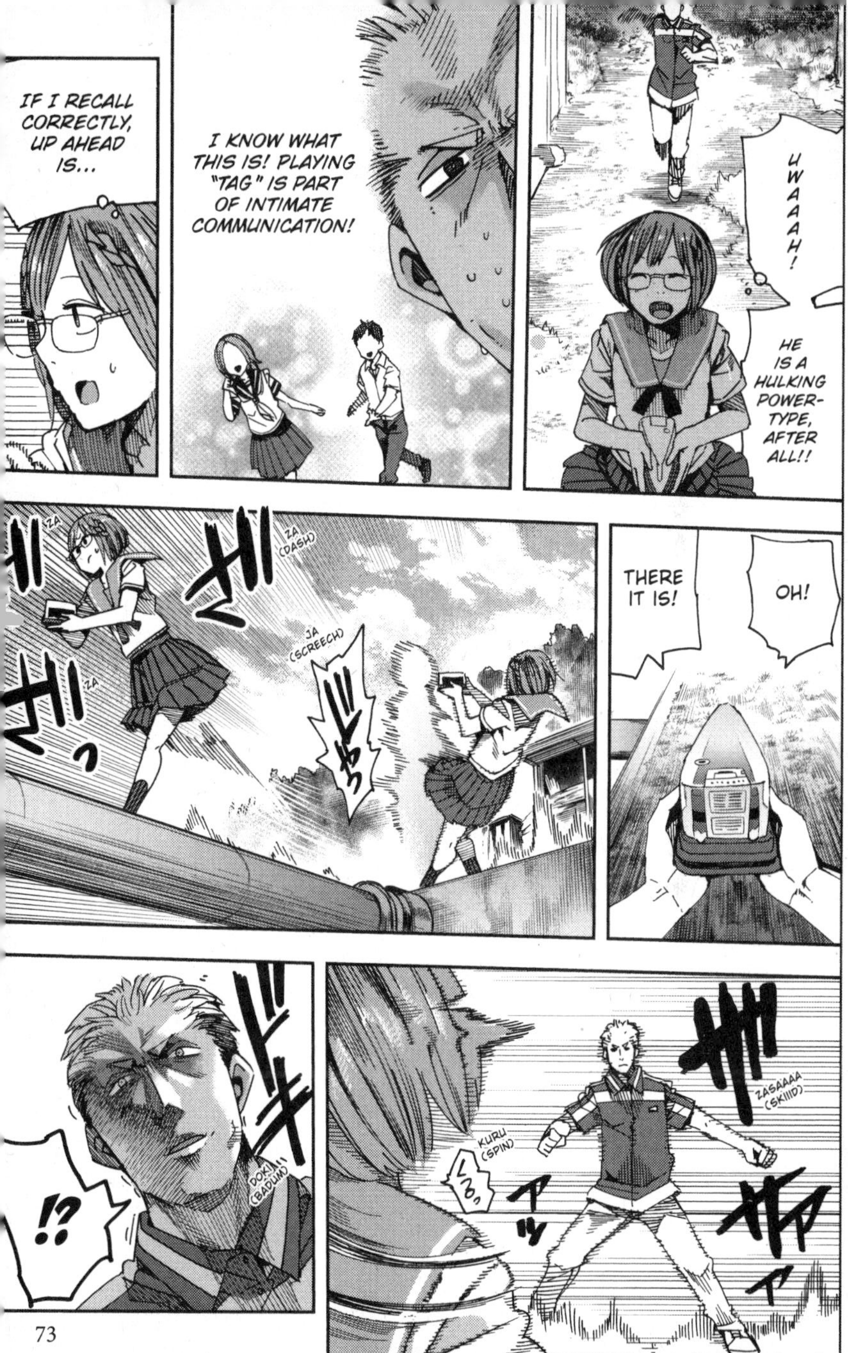
UWAAAAH!
HE IS A HULKING POWER-TYPE, AFTER ALL!!
I KNOW WHAT THIS IS! PLAYING "TAG" IS PART OF INTIMATE COMMUNICATION!
IF I RECALL CORRECTLY, UP AHEAD IS...
OH!
THERE IT IS!
ZA (DASH)
JA (SCREECH)
ZA
ZA
ZASAAAA (SKIIID)
KURU (SPIN)
DOKI (BADUMP)
!?

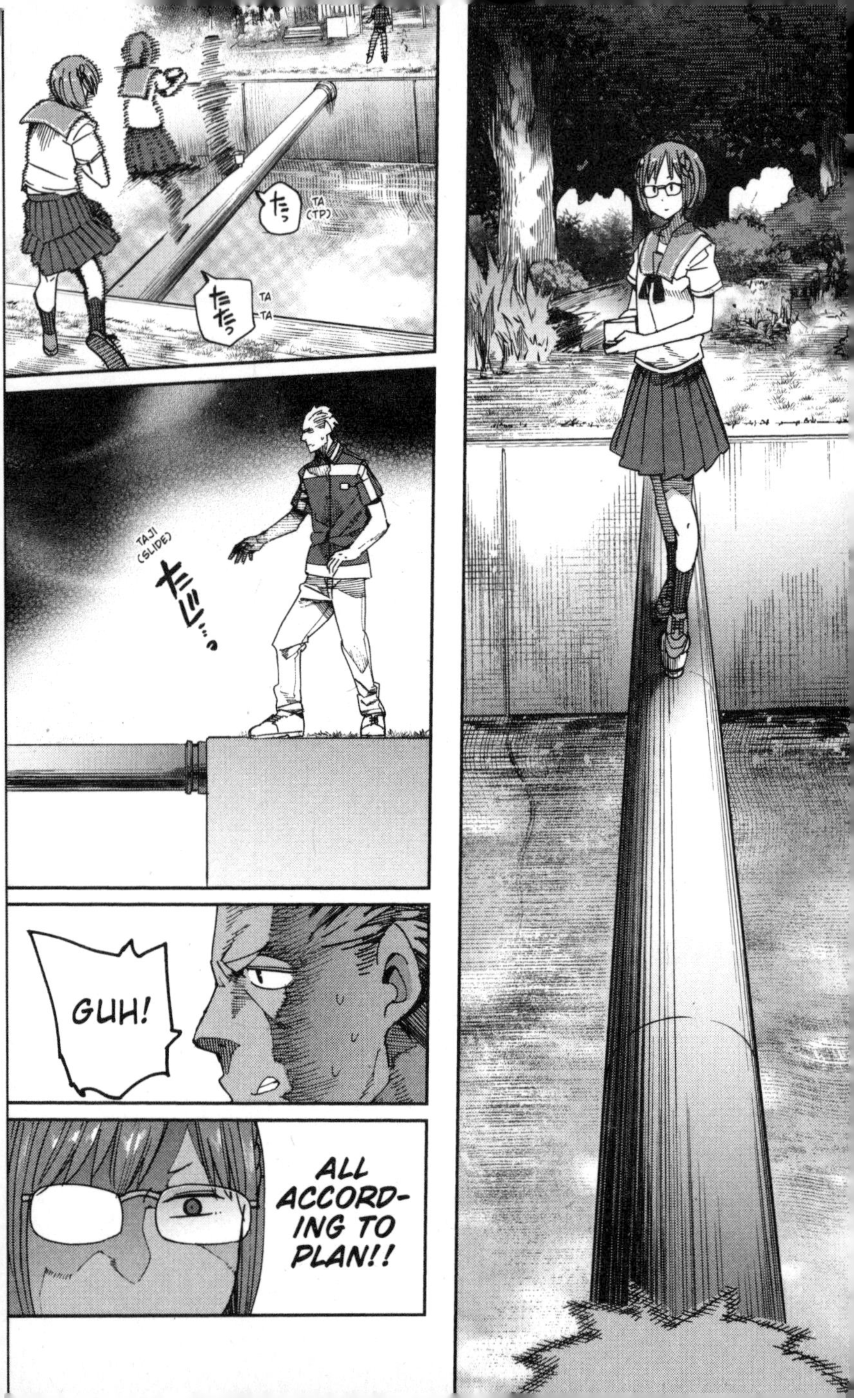
たっ
TA (TP)
たたっ
TA TA
TAJI (SLIDE)
たじ…
GUH!
ALL ACCORDING-ING TO PLAN!!

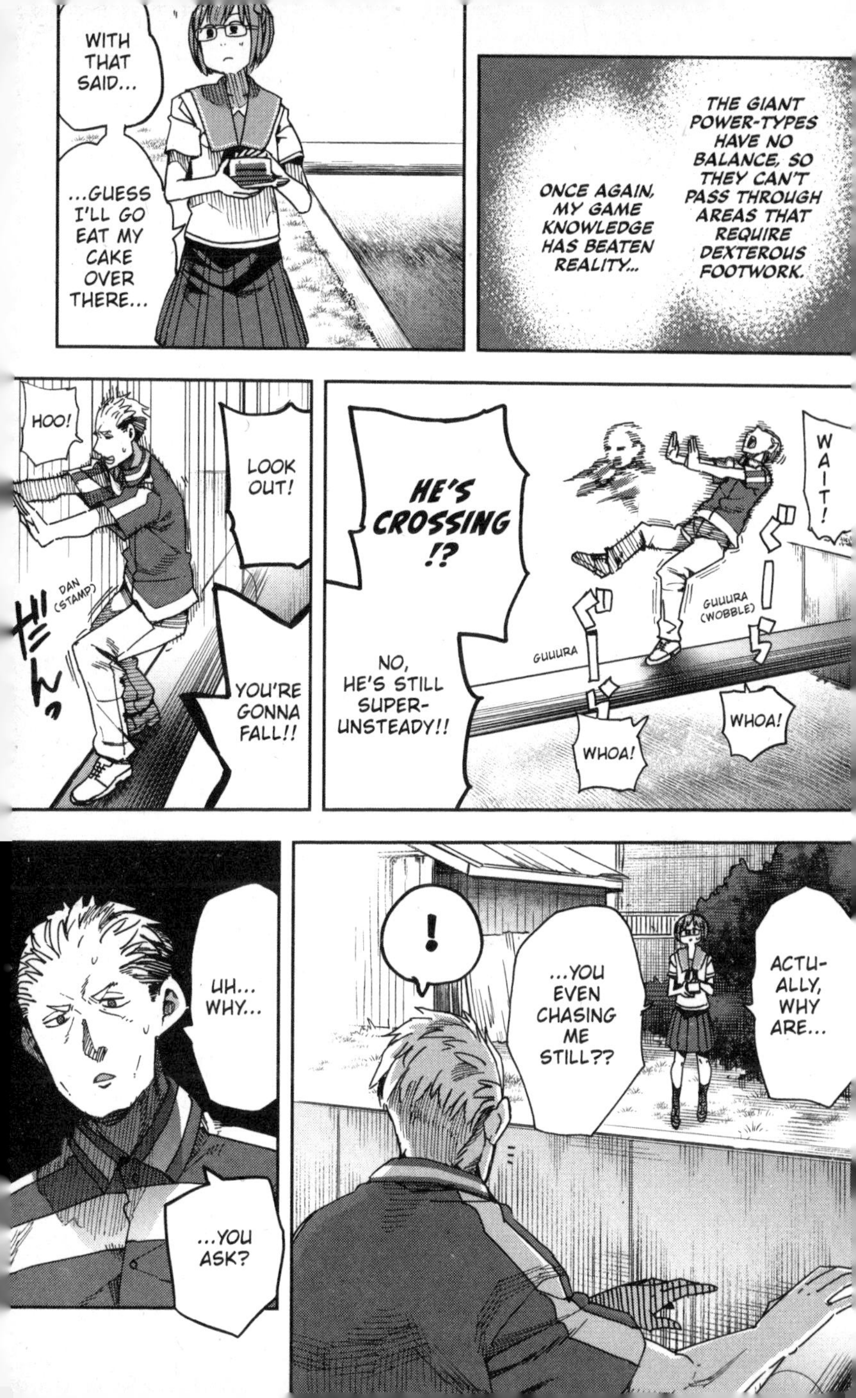
THE GIANT POWER-TYPES HAVE NO BALANCE, SO THEY CAN'T PASS THROUGH AREAS THAT REQUIRE DEXTEROUS FOOTWORK.
ONCE AGAIN, MY GAME KNOWLEDGE HAS BEATEN REALITY...
WITH THAT SAID...
...GUESS I'LL GO EAT MY CAKE OVER THERE...
WAIT!
HE'S CROSSING !?
GUUURA (WOBBLE)
WHOA!
GUUURA
WHOA!
NO, HE'S STILL SUPER-UNSTEADY!!
LOOK OUT!
HOO!
DAN (STAMP)
だんっ
YOU'RE GONNA FALL!!
ACTU-ALLY, WHY ARE...
...YOU EVEN CHASING ME STILL??
!
UH... WHY...
...YOU ASK?

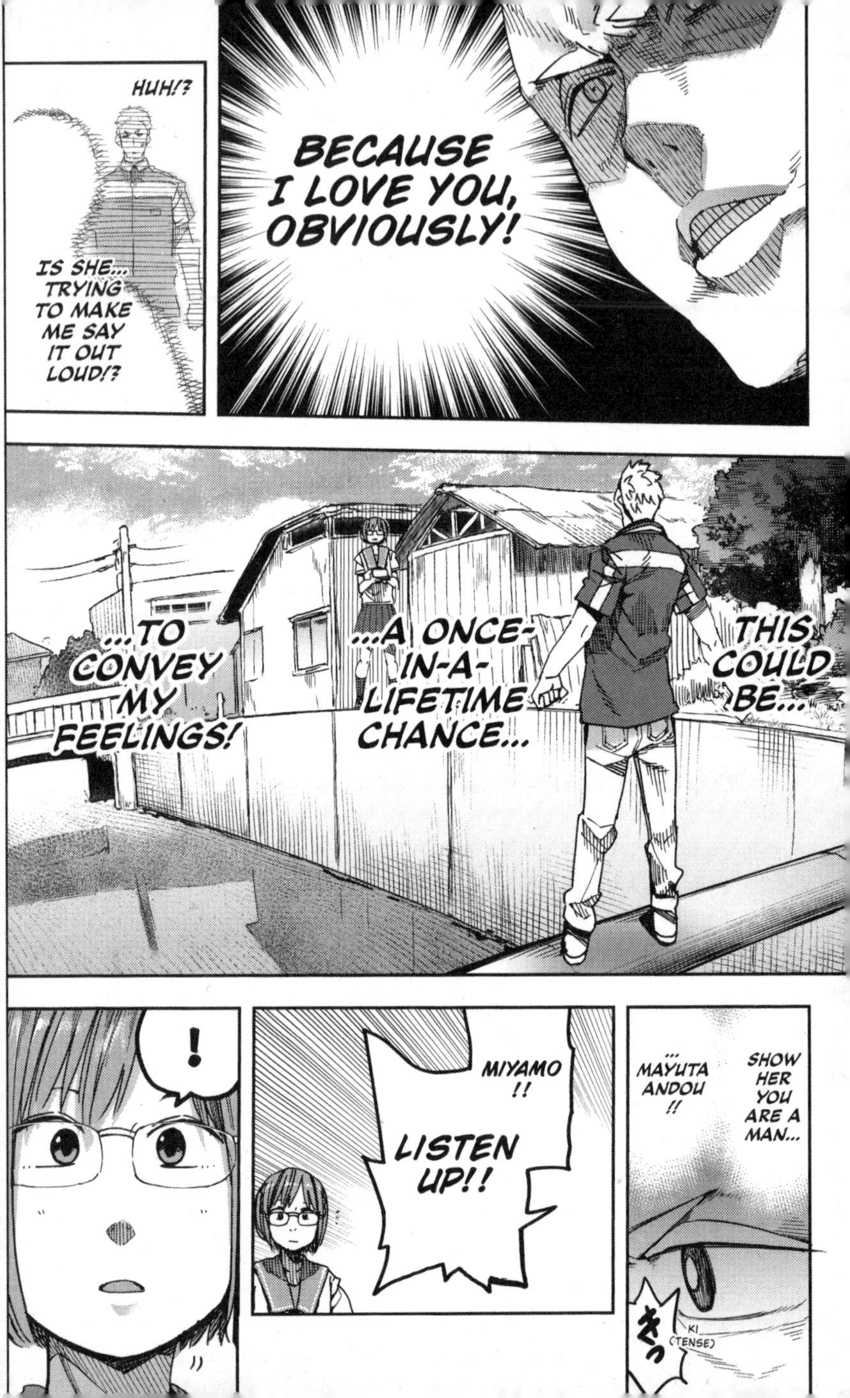
BECAUSE I LOVE YOU, OBVIOUSLY!
HUH!?
IS SHE... TRYING TO MAKE ME SAY IT OUT LOUD!?
THIS COULD BE...
...A ONCE-IN-A-LIFETIME CHANCE...
...TO CONVEY MY FEELINGS!
SHOW HER YOU ARE A MAN...
...MAYUTA ANDOU!!
KI (TENSE)
MIYAMO!!
LISTEN UP!!
!

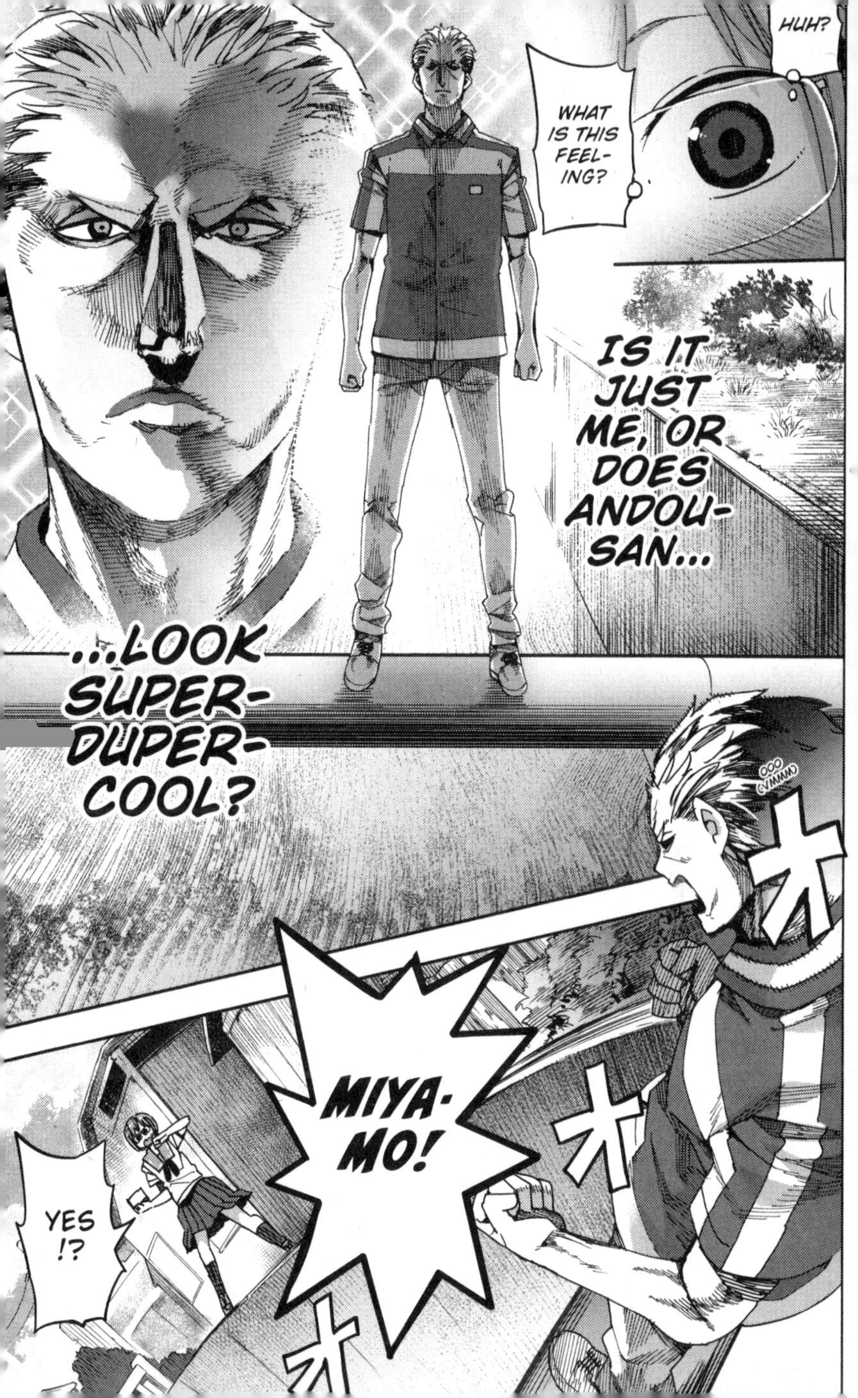
HUH?
WHAT IS THIS FEEL-ING?
IS IT JUST ME, OR DOES ANDOU-SAN...
...LOOK SUPER-DUPER-COOL?
MIYA-MO!
YES!?

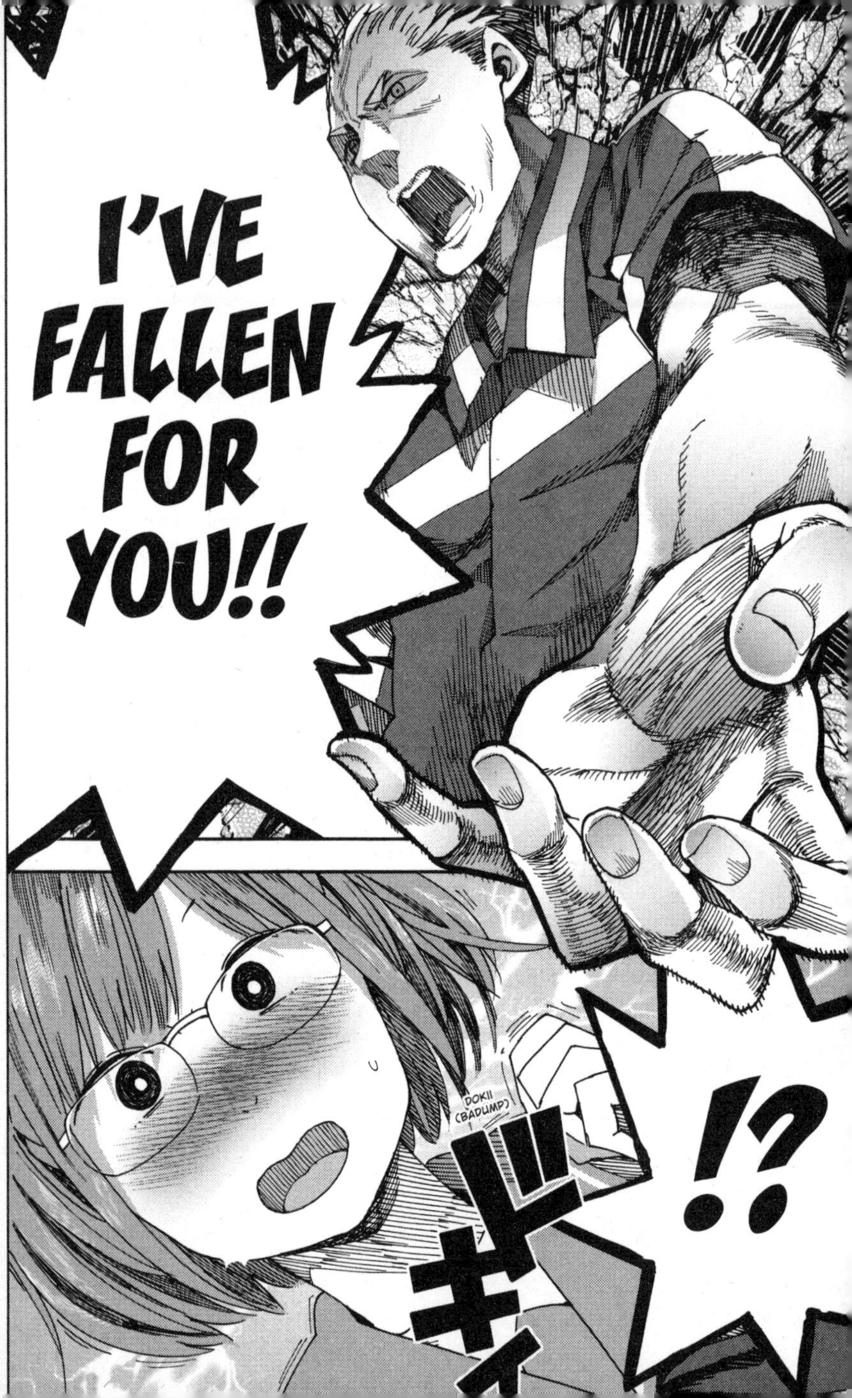
I'VE FALLEN FOR YOU!!
DOKI (BADUMP)
ドキ
!?

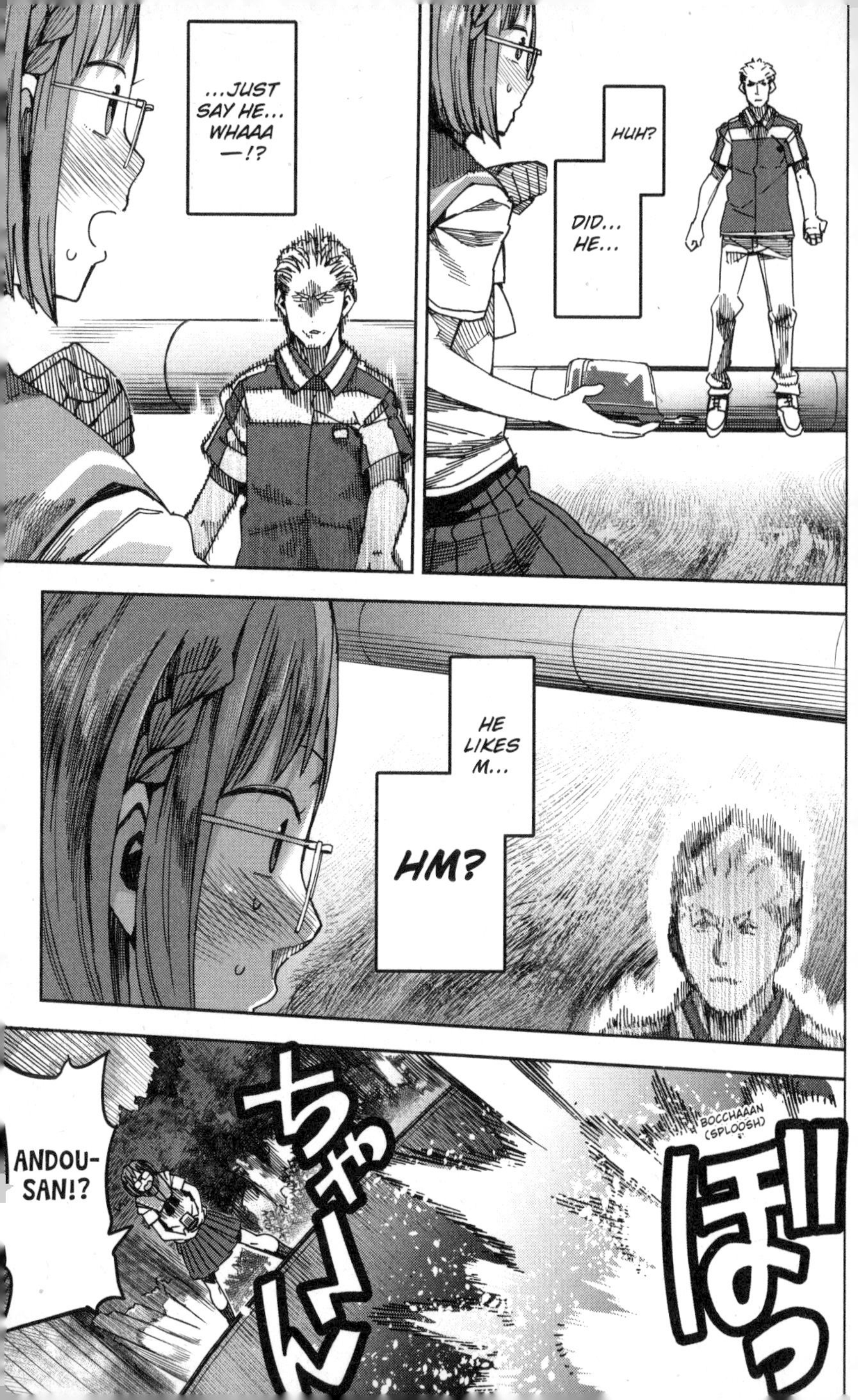
HUH?
DID... HE...
...JUST SAY HE... WHAAA—!?
HE LIKES M...
HM?
BOCCHAAAN (SPLOOSH)
ぼっ
ちゃ～ん
ANDOU-SAN!?

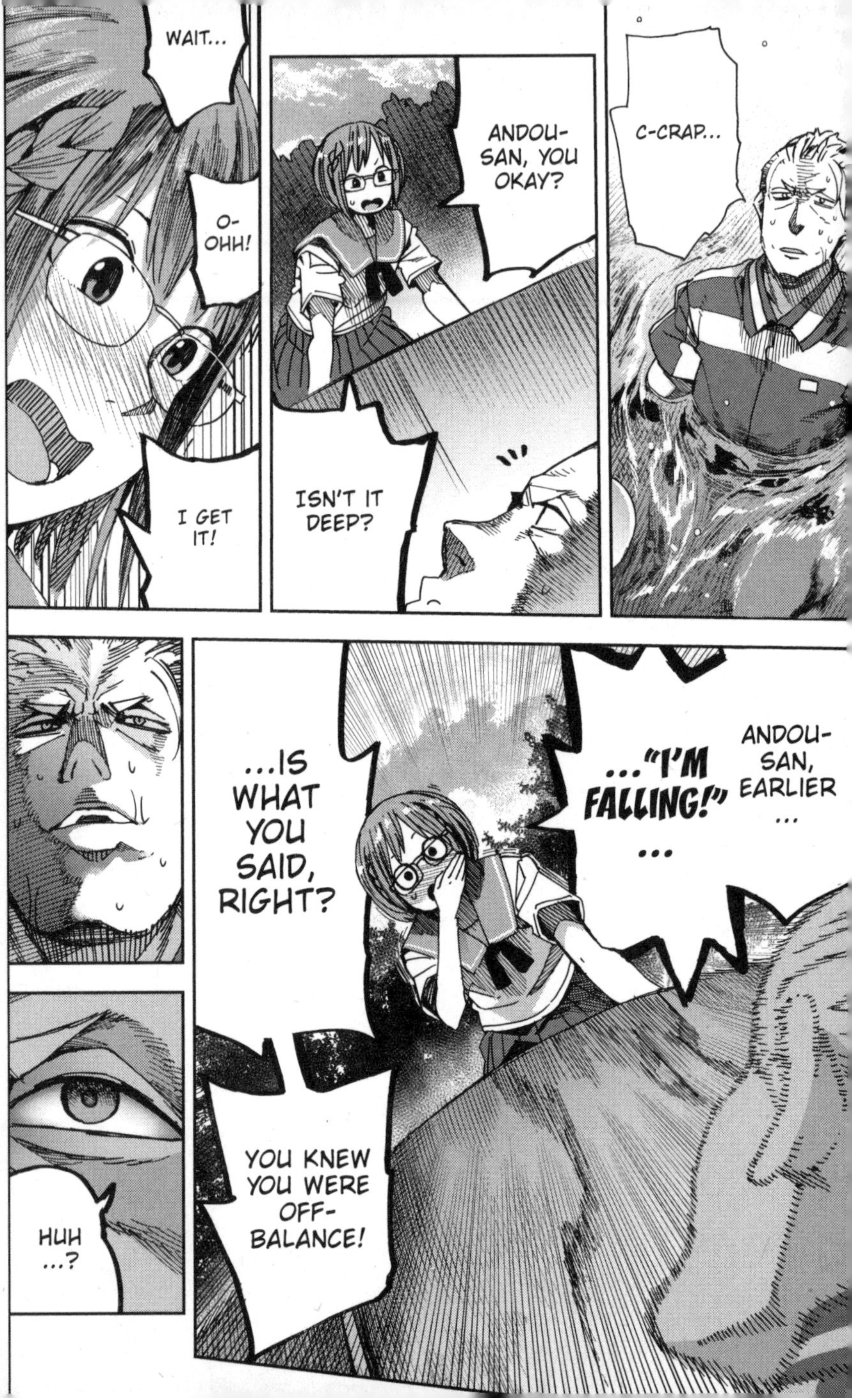
C-CRAP...
ANDOU-SAN, YOU OKAY?
ISN'T IT DEEP?
WAIT...
O-OHH!
I GET IT!
ANDOU-SAN, EARLIER...
..."I'M FALLING!"...
...IS WHAT YOU SAID, RIGHT?
YOU KNEW YOU WERE OFF-BALANCE!
HUH...?

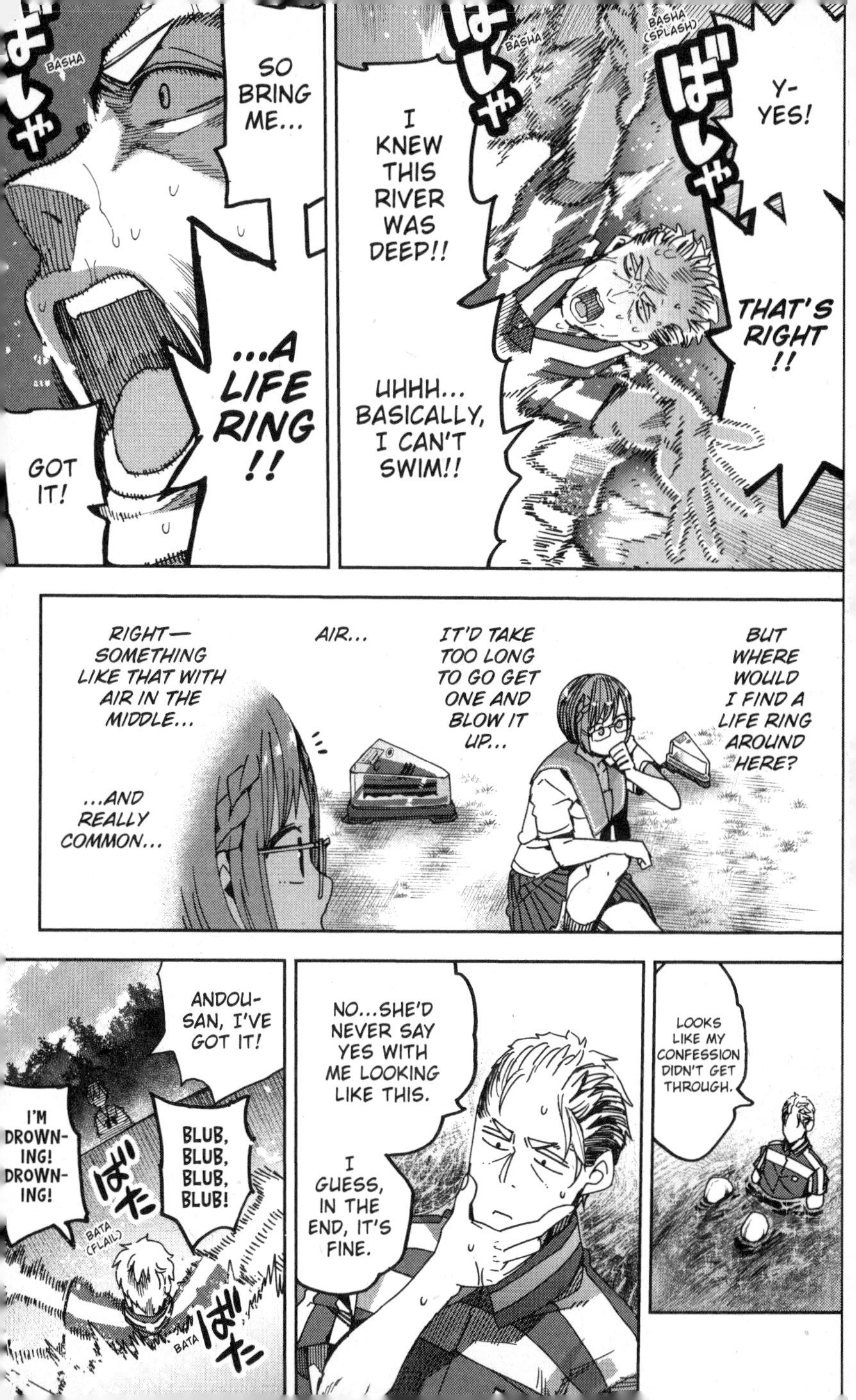
Y-YES!
ばしゃ
BASHA (SPLASH)
ばしゃ
BASHA
I KNEW THIS RIVER WAS DEEP!!
THAT'S RIGHT!!
UHHH... BASICALLY, I CAN'T SWIM!!
SO BRING ME...
ばしゃ
BASHA
...A LIFE RING!!
GOT IT!
BUT WHERE WOULD I FIND A LIFE RING AROUND HERE?
IT'D TAKE TOO LONG TO GO GET ONE AND BLOW IT UP...
AIR...
RIGHT—SOMETHING LIKE THAT WITH AIR IN THE MIDDLE...
...AND REALLY COMMON...
LOOKS LIKE MY CONFESSION DIDN'T GET THROUGH.
NO...SHE'D NEVER SAY YES WITH ME LOOKING LIKE THIS.
I GUESS, IN THE END, IT'S FINE.
ANDOU-SAN, I'VE GOT IT!
BLUB, BLUB, BLUB, BLUB!
I'M DROWNING! DROWNING!
ばた
BATA (FLAIL)
ばた
BATA

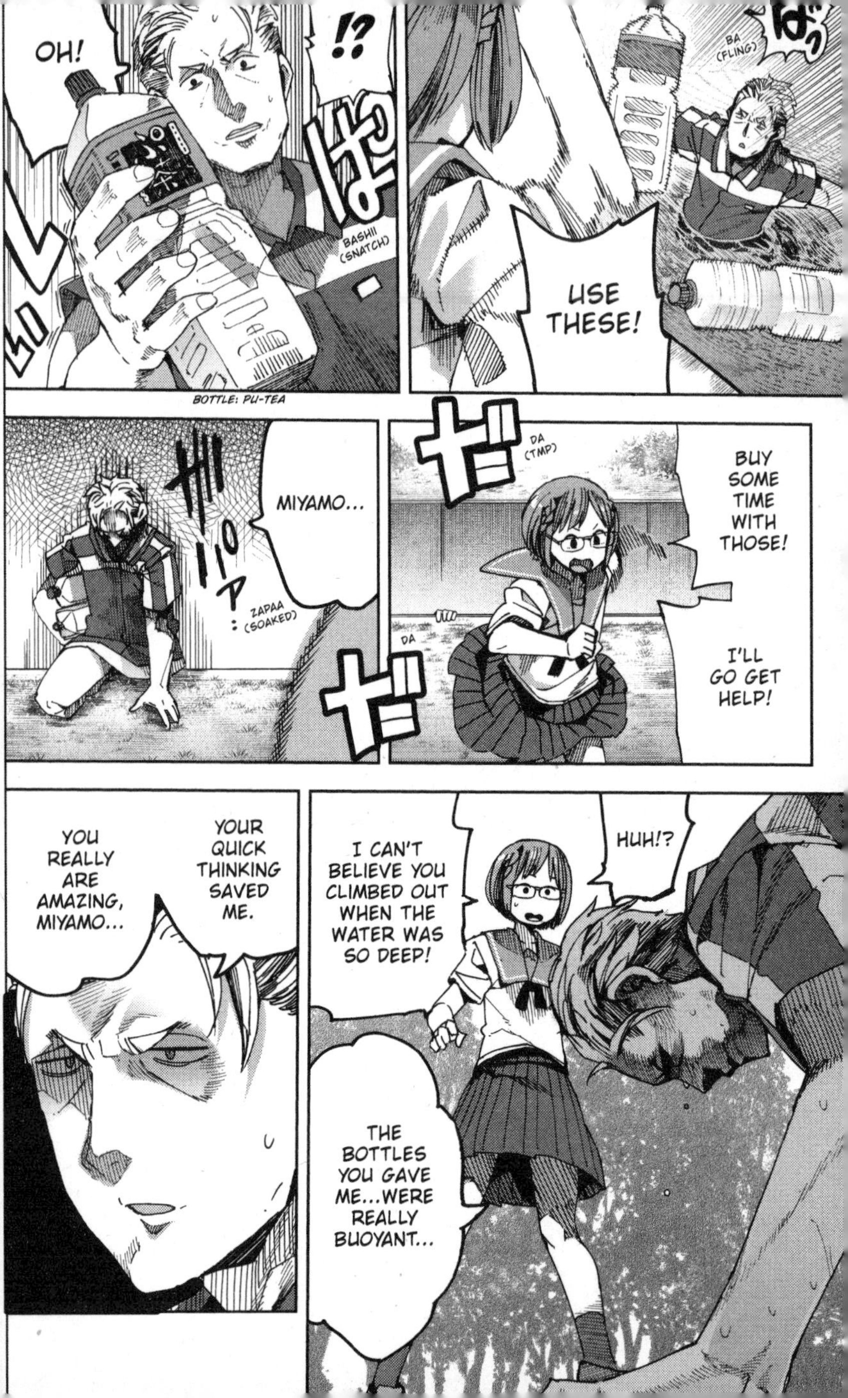
BA (FLING)
USE THESE!
OH!
!?
BASHII (SNATCH)
BOTTLE: PU-TEA
DA (TMP)
BUY SOME TIME WITH THOSE!
I'LL GO GET HELP!
DA
MIYAMO...
ZAPAA (SOAKED)
HUH!?
I CAN'T BELIEVE YOU CLIMBED OUT WHEN THE WATER WAS SO DEEP!
THE BOTTLES YOU GAVE ME...WERE REALLY BUOYANT...
YOUR QUICK THINKING SAVED ME.
YOU REALLY ARE AMAZING, MIYAMO...

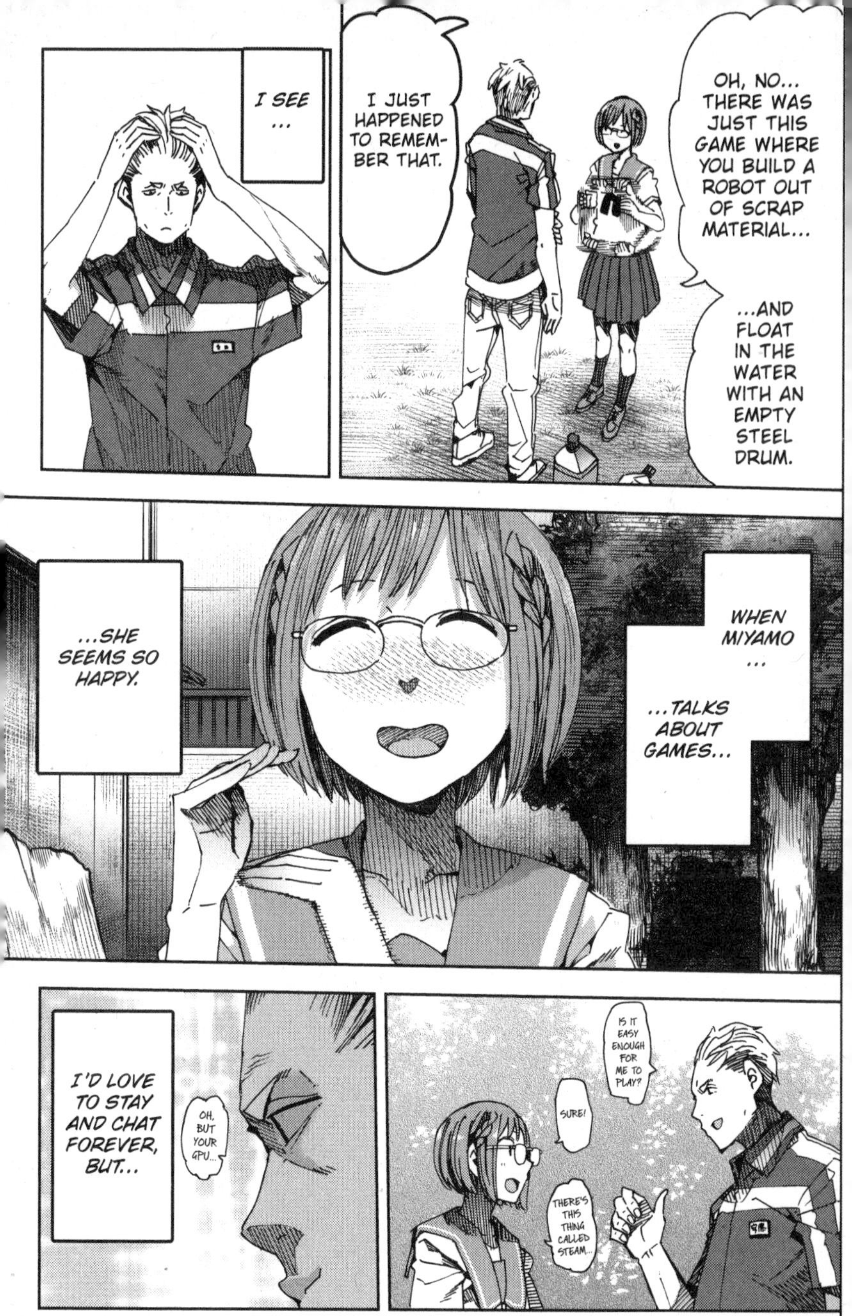
OH, NO... THERE WAS JUST THIS GAME WHERE YOU BUILD A ROBOT OUT OF SCRAP MATERIAL...
...AND FLOAT IN THE WATER WITH AN EMPTY STEEL DRUM.
I JUST HAPPENED TO REMEMBER THAT.
I SEE...
WHEN MIYAMO...
...TALKS ABOUT GAMES...
...SHE SEEMS SO HAPPY.
IS IT EASY ENOUGH FOR ME TO PLAY?
SURE!
THERE'S THIS THING CALLED STEAM...
I'D LOVE TO STAY AND CHAT FOREVER, BUT...
OH, BUT YOUR GPU...

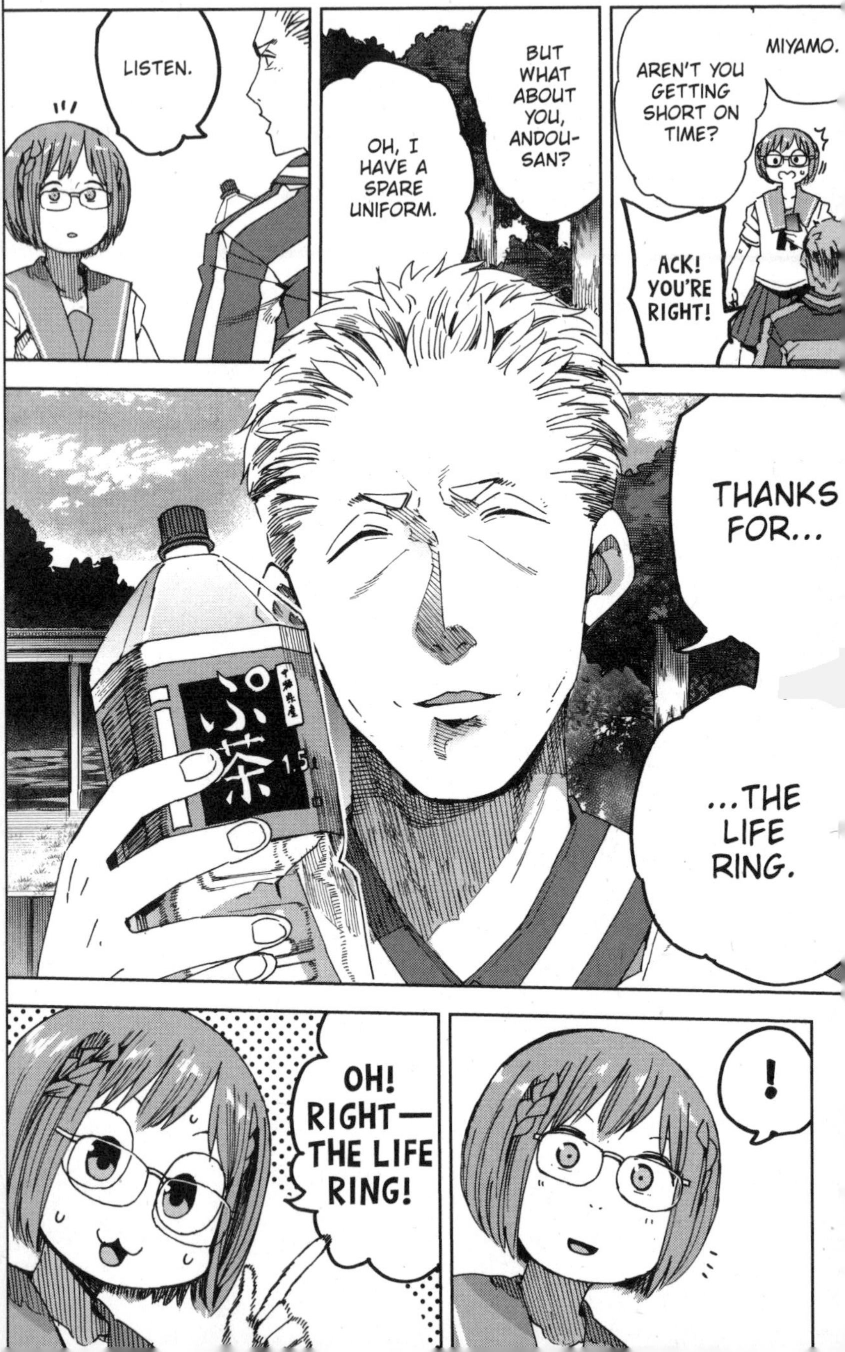
MIYAMO.
AREN'T YOU GETTING SHORT ON TIME?
ACK! YOU'RE RIGHT!
BUT WHAT ABOUT YOU, ANDOU-SAN?
OH, I HAVE A SPARE UNIFORM.
LISTEN.
THANKS FOR...
...THE LIFE RING.
ぷ茶
!
OH! RIGHT—THE LIFE RING!

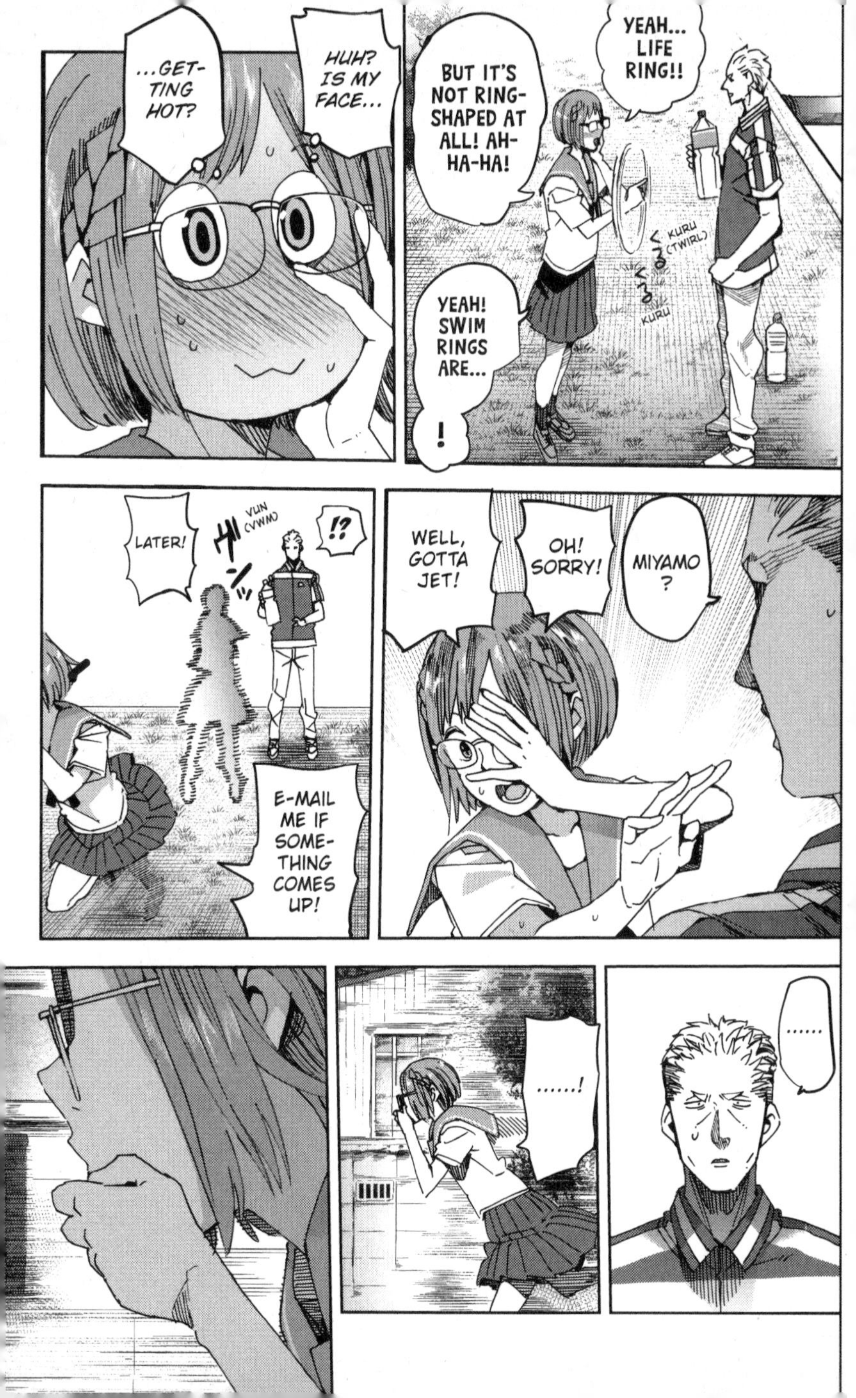
YEAH... LIFE RING!!
BUT IT'S NOT RING-SHAPED AT ALL! AH-HA-HA!
KURU (TWIRL)
KURU
YEAH! SWIM RINGS ARE...
!
HUH? IS MY FACE...
...GET-TING HOT?
MIYAMO?
OH! SORRY!
WELL, GOTTA JET!
!?
VUN (VWM)
LATER!
E-MAIL ME IF SOME-THING COMES UP!
......
......!

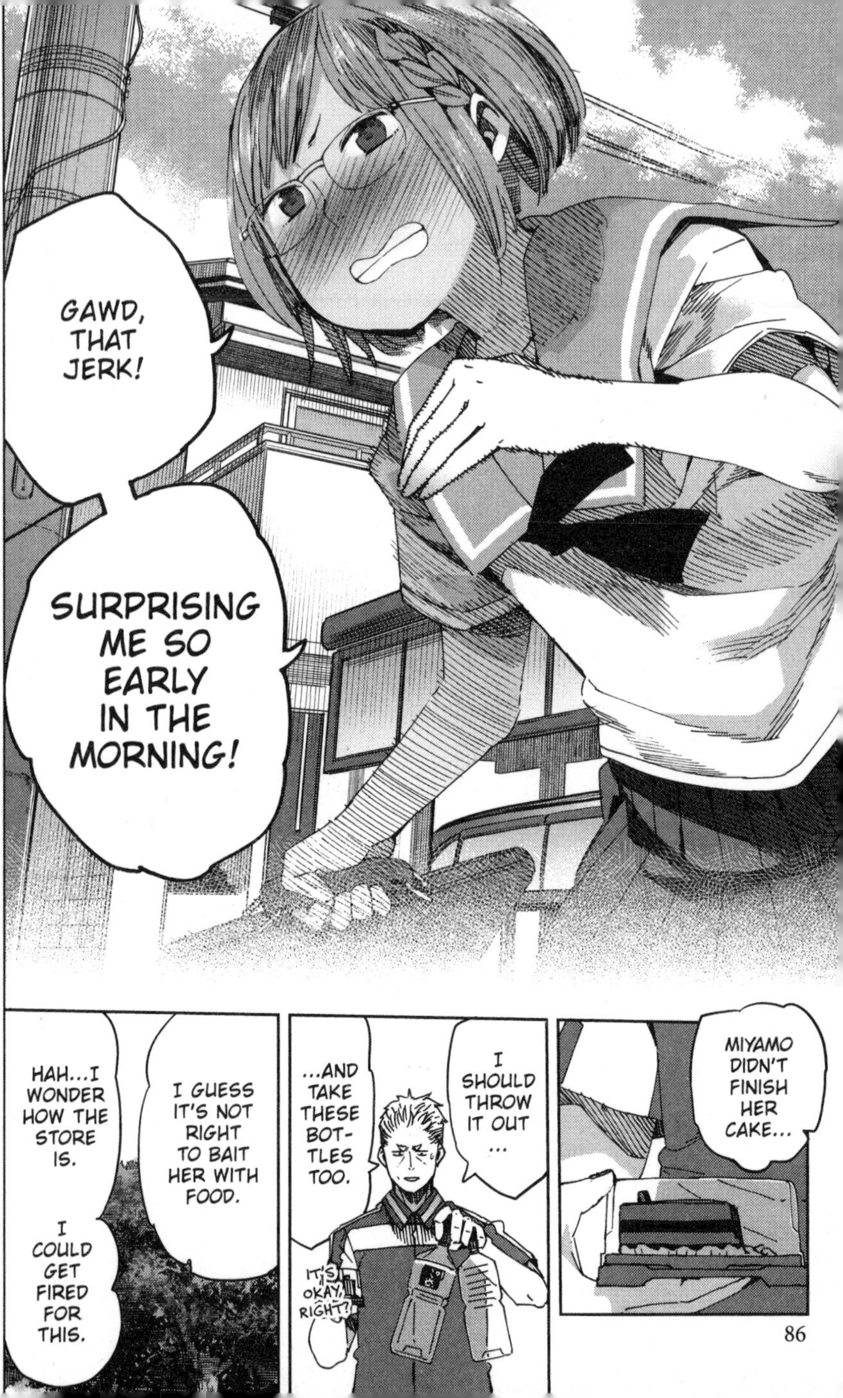
GAWD, THAT JERK!
SURPRISING ME SO EARLY IN THE MORNING!
MIYAMO DIDN'T FINISH HER CAKE...
I SHOULD THROW IT OUT ...
...AND TAKE THESE BOT-TLES TOO.
IT'S OKAY, RIGHT?
I GUESS IT'S NOT RIGHT TO BAIT HER WITH FOOD.
HAH...I WONDER HOW THE STORE IS.
I COULD GET FIRED FOR THIS.

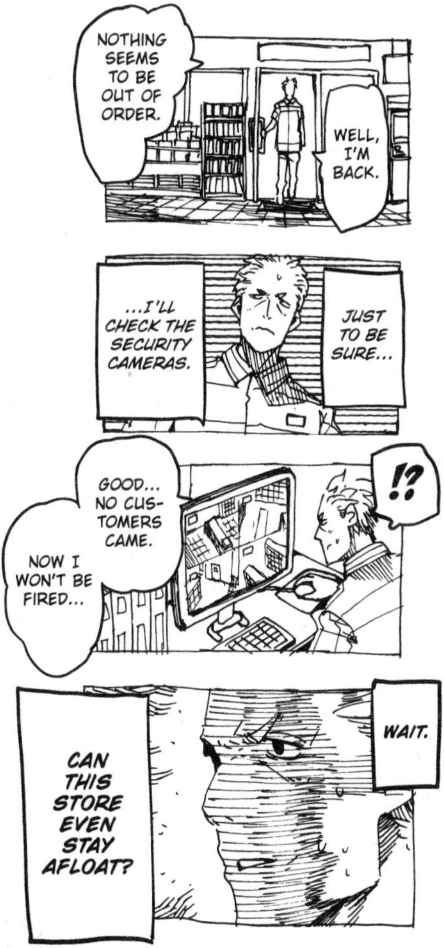
WELL, I'M BACK.
NOTHING SEEMS TO BE OUT OF ORDER.
JUST TO BE SURE...
...I'LL CHECK THE SECURITY CAMERAS.
!?
GOOD... NO CUS-TOMERS CAME.
NOW I WON'T BE FIRED...
WAIT.
CAN THIS STORE EVEN STAY AFLOAT?

Chio's SCHOOL ROAD

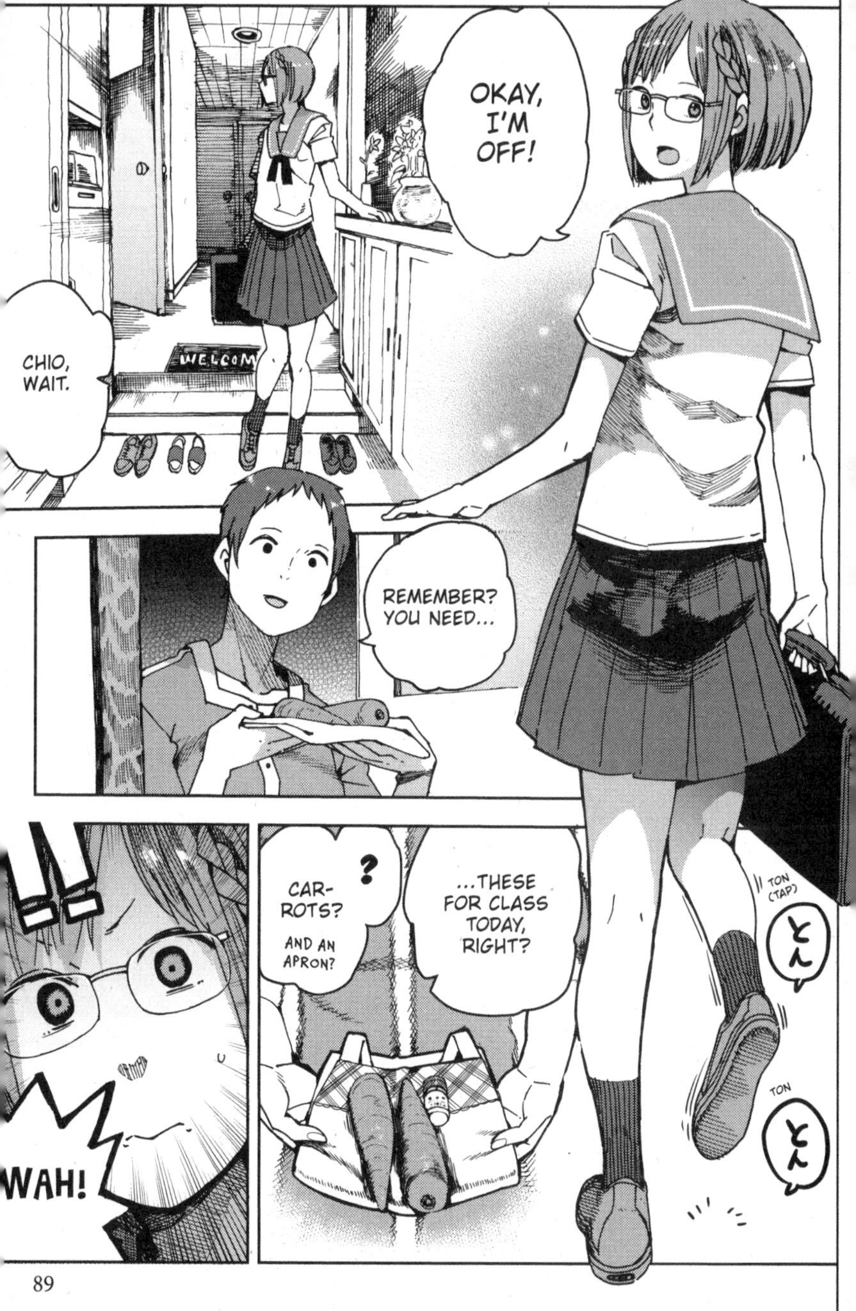
OKAY, I'M OFF!
TON (TAP)
とん
TON
とん
CHIO, WAIT.
REMEMBER? YOU NEED...
...THESE FOR CLASS TODAY, RIGHT?
?
CAR-ROTS?
AND AN APRON?
WAH!

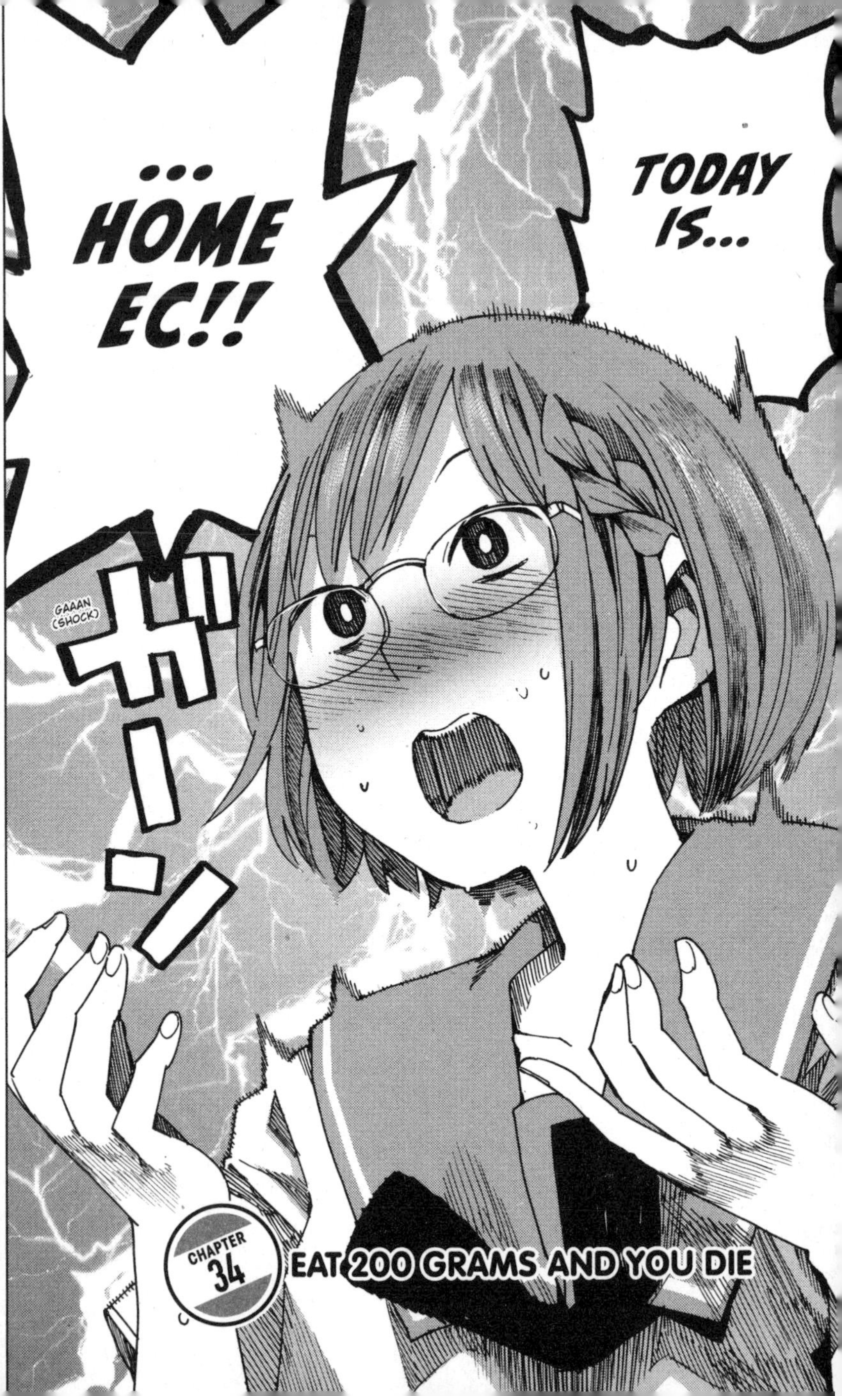
TODAY IS...
...HÖME EC!!
GAAAN (SHOCK)
CHAPTER 34
EAT 200 GRAMS AND YOU DIE

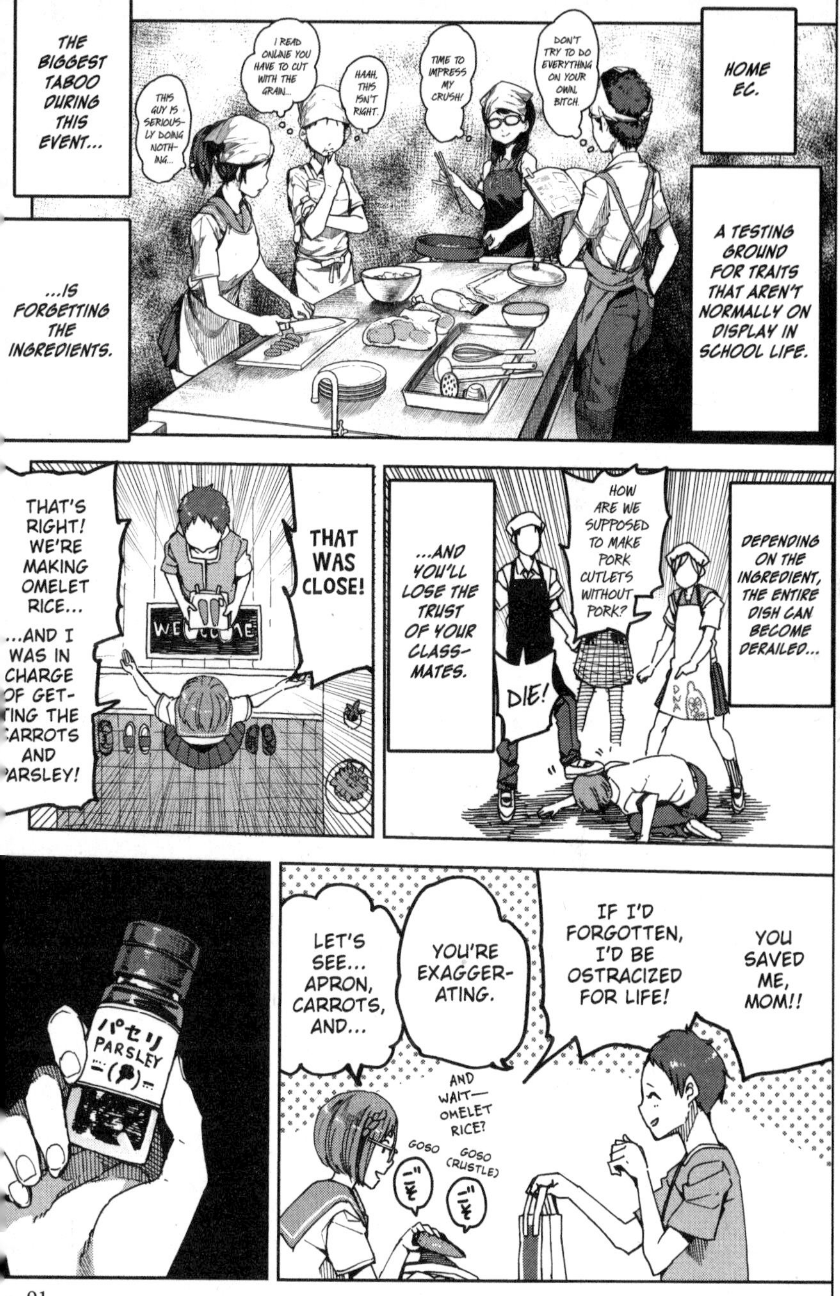
HOME EC.
A TESTING GROUND FOR TRAITS THAT AREN'T NORMALLY ON DISPLAY IN SCHOOL LIFE.
DON'T TRY TO DO EVERYTHING ON YOUR OWN, BITCH.
TIME TO IMPRESS MY CRUSH!
HAAH, THIS ISN'T RIGHT.
I READ ONLINE YOU HAVE TO CUT WITH THE GRAIN...
THIS GUY IS SERIOUS-LY DOING NOTH-ING...
THE BIGGEST TABOO DURING THIS EVENT...
...IS FORGETTING THE INGREDIENTS.
DEPENDING ON THE INGREDIENT, THE ENTIRE DISH CAN BECOME DERAILED...
HOW ARE WE SUPPOSED TO MAKE PORK CUTLETS WITHOUT PORK?
DIE!
...AND YOU'LL LOSE THE TRUST OF YOUR CLASS-MATES.
THAT WAS CLOSE!
THAT'S RIGHT! WE'RE MAKING OMELET RICE...
...AND I WAS IN CHARGE OF GET-TING THE CARROTS AND PARSLEY!
YOU SAVED ME, MOM!!
IF I'D FORGOTTEN, I'D BE OSTRACIZED FOR LIFE!
YOU'RE EXAGGER-ATING.
LET'S SEE... APRON, CARROTS, AND...
AND WAIT— OMELET RICE?
GOSO GOSO (RUSTLE)
パセリ PARSLEY

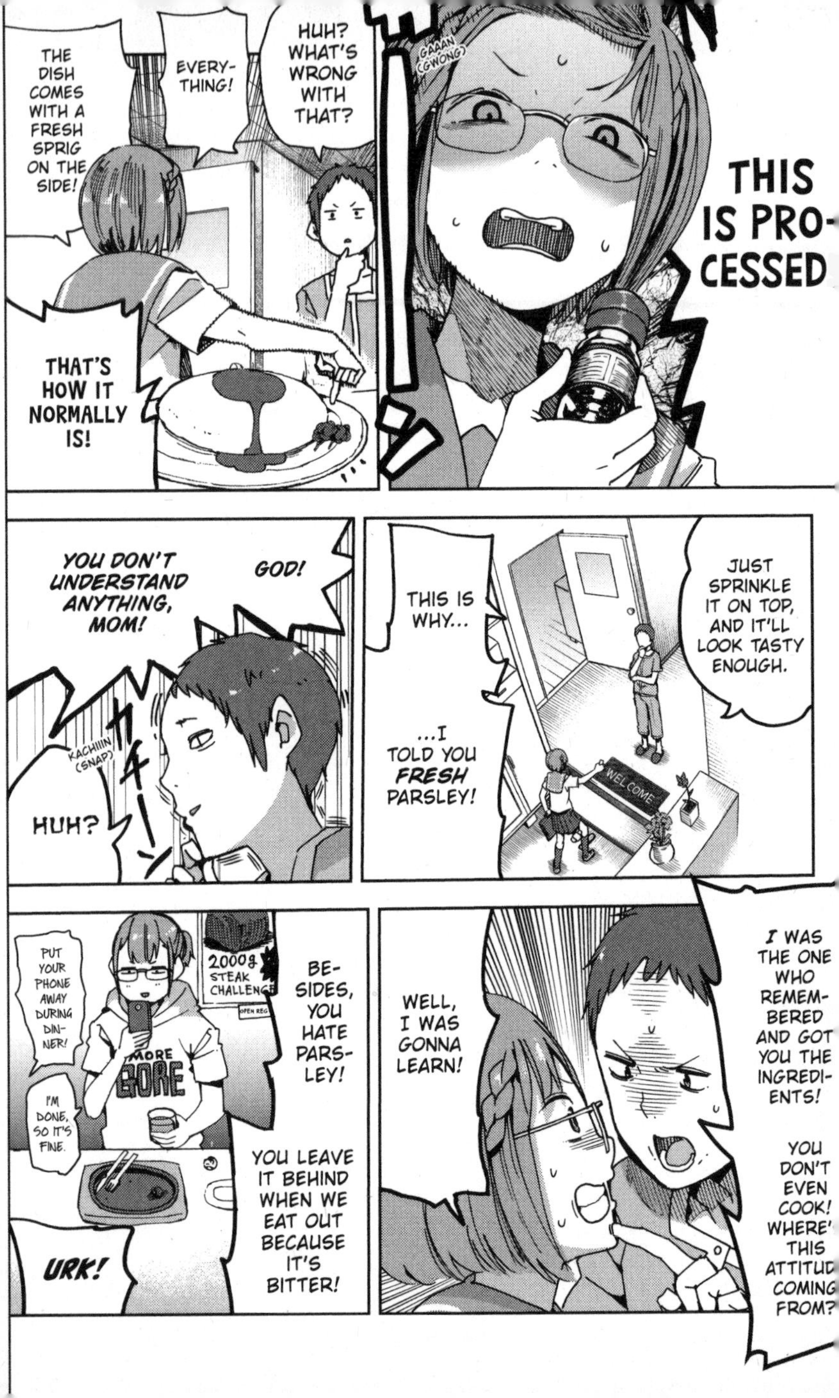
GAAAN (GWONG)
THIS IS PRO-CESSED
HUH? WHAT'S WRONG WITH THAT?
EVERY-THING!
THE DISH COMES WITH A FRESH SPRIG ON THE SIDE!
THAT'S HOW IT NORMALLY IS!
JUST SPRINKLE IT ON TOP, AND IT'LL LOOK TASTY ENOUGH.
THIS IS WHY...
...I TOLD YOU FRESH PARSLEY!
WELCOME
GOD!
YOU DON'T UNDERSTAND ANYTHING, MOM!
KACHIIIN (SNAP)
HUH?
I WAS THE ONE WHO REMEM-BERED AND GOT YOU THE INGREDI-ENTS!
YOU DON'T EVEN COOK! WHERE' THIS ATTITUD COMING FROM?
WELL, I WAS GONNA LEARN!
BE-SIDES, YOU HATE PARS-LEY!
YOU LEAVE IT BEHIND WHEN WE EAT OUT BECAUSE IT'S BITTER!
2000g STEAK CHALLENGE
PUT YOUR PHONE AWAY DURING DIN-NER!
MORE GORE
I'M DONE, SO IT'S FINE.
URK!

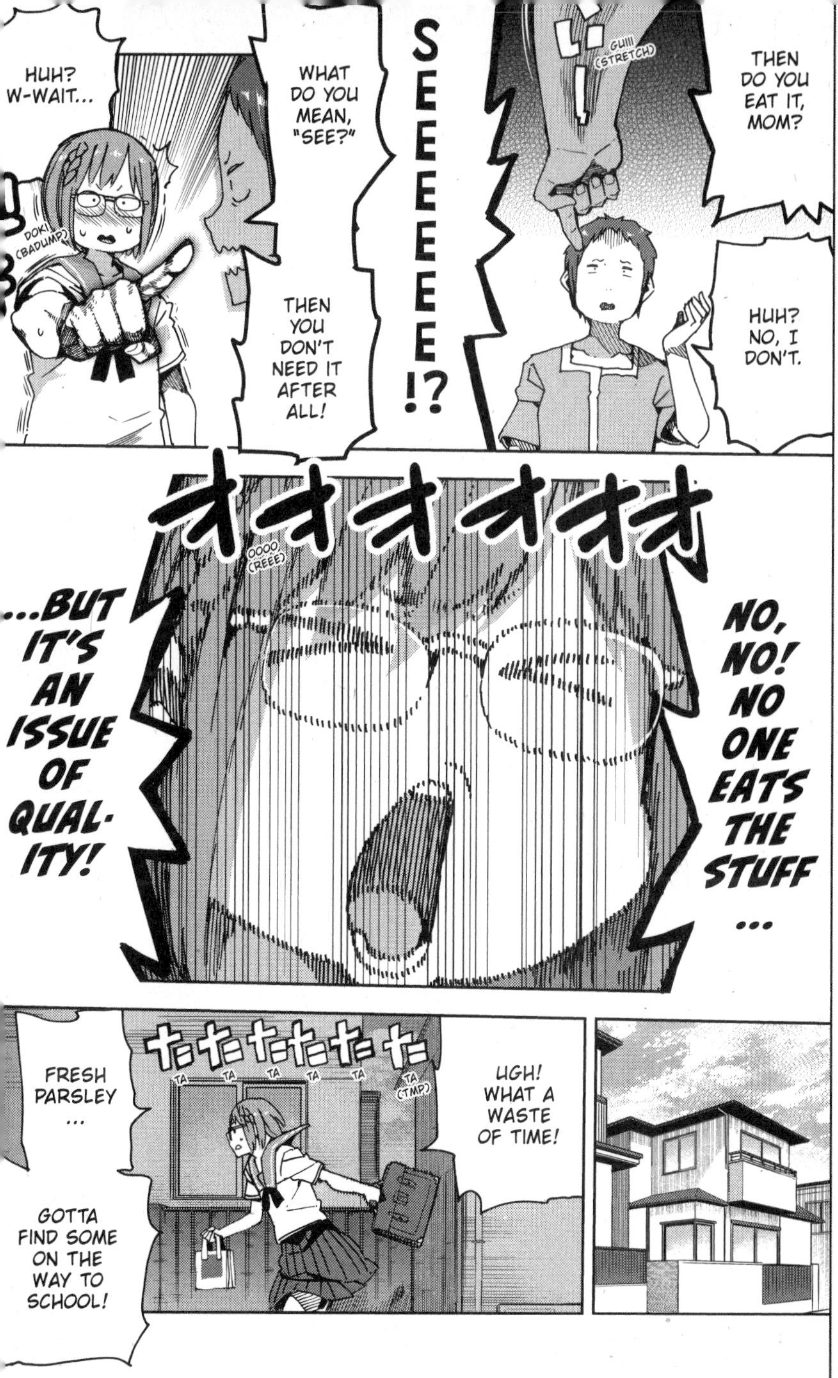
THEN DO YOU EAT IT, MOM?
GUIII (STRETCH)
HUH? NO, I DON'T.
SEEEEEEE!?
WHAT DO YOU MEAN, "SEE?"
THEN YOU DON'T NEED IT AFTER ALL!
HUH? W-WAIT...
DOKI (BADUMP)
オオオオオオ
OOOO (REEE)
NO, NO! NO ONE EATS THE STUFF...
...BUT IT'S AN ISSUE OF QUAL-ITY!
タタタタタタ
TA TA TA TA TA TA (TMP)
UGH! WHAT A WASTE OF TIME!
FRESH PARSLEY...
GOTTA FIND SOME ON THE WAY TO SCHOOL!

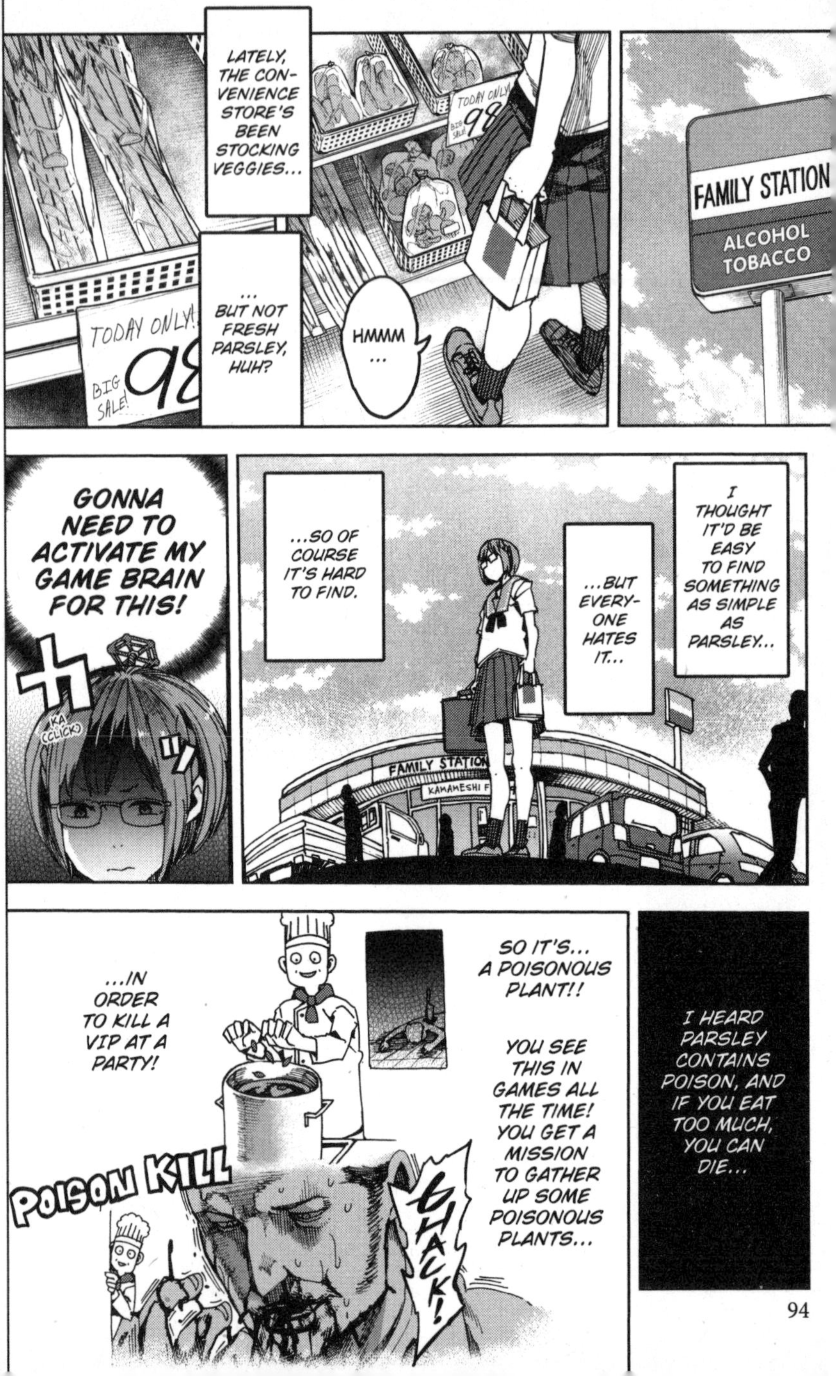
FAMILY STATION
ALCOHOL TOBACCO
LATELY, THE CON- VENIENCE STORE'S BEEN STOCKING VEGGIES...
TODAY ONLY 98 BIG SALE!
... BUT NOT FRESH PARSLEY, HUH?
HMMM ...
TODAY ONLY! 98 BIG SALE!
I THOUGHT IT'D BE EASY TO FIND SOMETHING AS SIMPLE AS PARSLEY...
...BUT EVERY- ONE HATES IT...
...SO OF COURSE IT'S HARD TO FIND.
FAMILY STATION
KAMAMESHI F
GONNA NEED TO ACTIVATE MY GAME BRAIN FOR THIS!
KA (CLICK)
I HEARD PARSLEY CONTAINS POISON, AND IF YOU EAT TOO MUCH, YOU CAN DIE...
SO IT'S... A POISONOUS PLANT!!
YOU SEE THIS IN GAMES ALL THE TIME! YOU GET A MISSION TO GATHER UP SOME POISONOUS PLANTS...
...IN ORDER TO KILL A VIP AT A PARTY!
POISON KILL
GHACK!

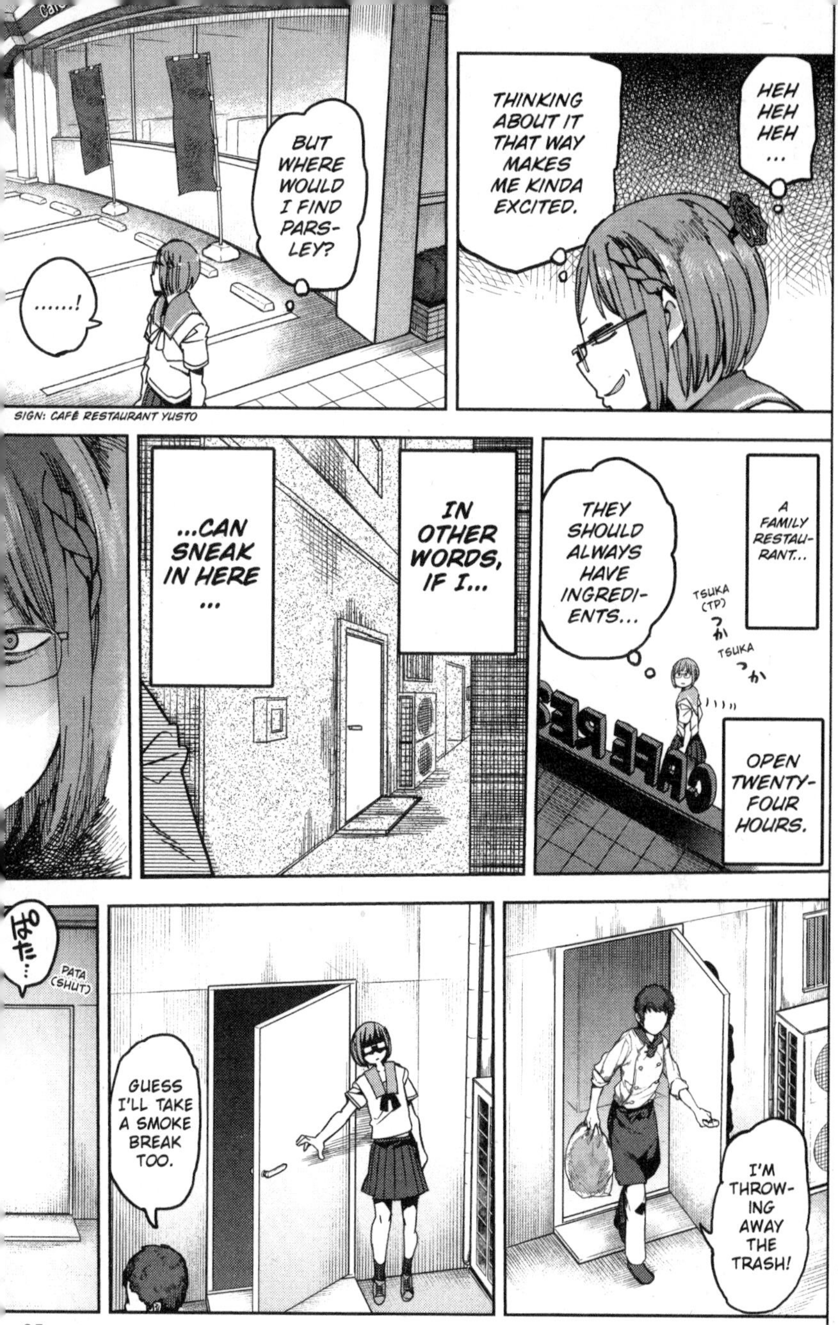
HEH HEH HEH ...
THINKING ABOUT IT THAT WAY MAKES ME KINDA EXCITED.
BUT WHERE WOULD I FIND PARS-LEY?
......!
SIGN: CAFÉ RESTAURANT YUSTO
A FAMILY RESTAU-RANT...
THEY SHOULD ALWAYS HAVE INGREDI-ENTS...
TSUKA (TP)
つか
TSUKA
つか
OPEN TWENTY-FOUR HOURS.
IN OTHER WORDS, IF I...
...CAN SNEAK IN HERE ...
I'M THROW-ING AWAY THE TRASH!
GUESS I'LL TAKE A SMOKE BREAK TOO.
ぱた…
PATA (SHUT)

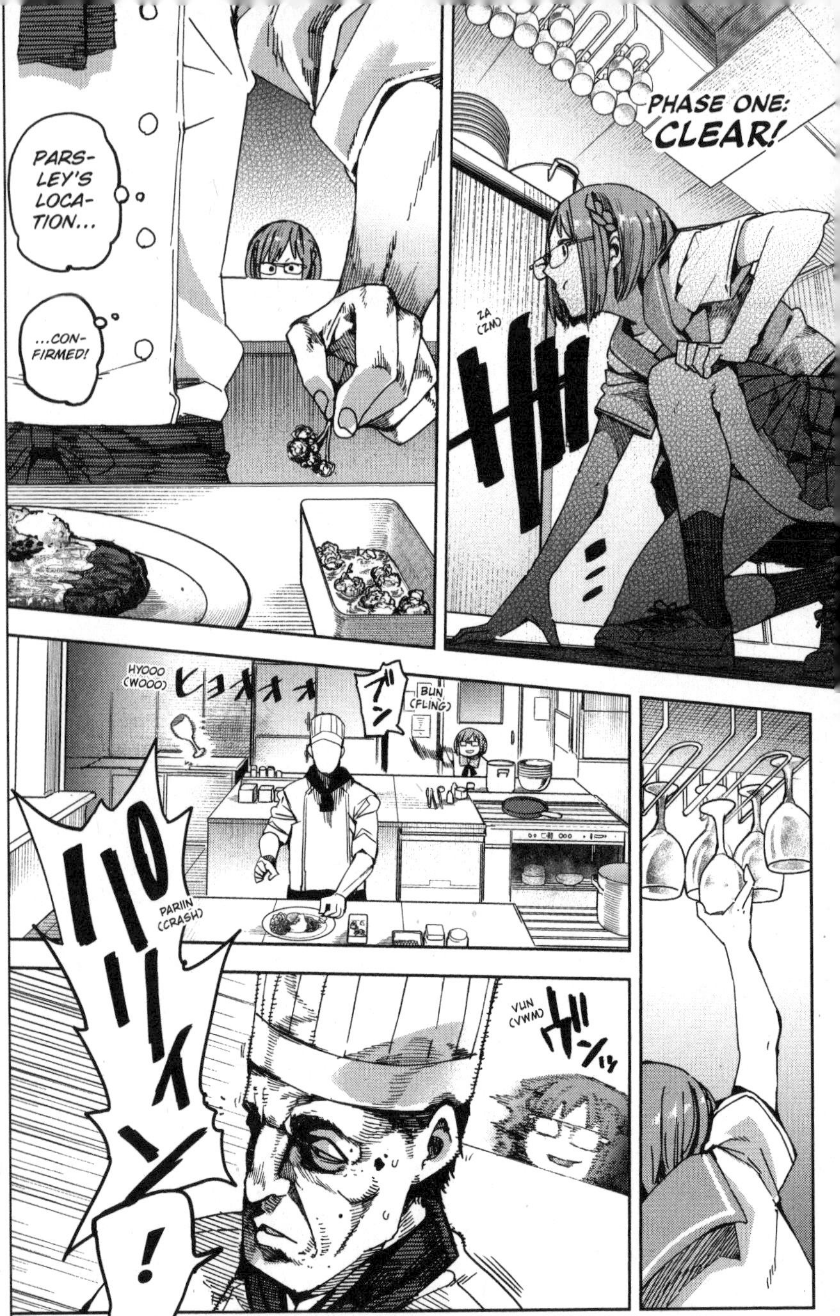

PHASE ONE: CLEAR!
ZA (ZM)
PARS-LEY'S LOCA-TION...
...CON-FIRMED!
BUN (FLING)
HYOOO (WOOO)
PARIIN (CRASH)
VUN (VWM)

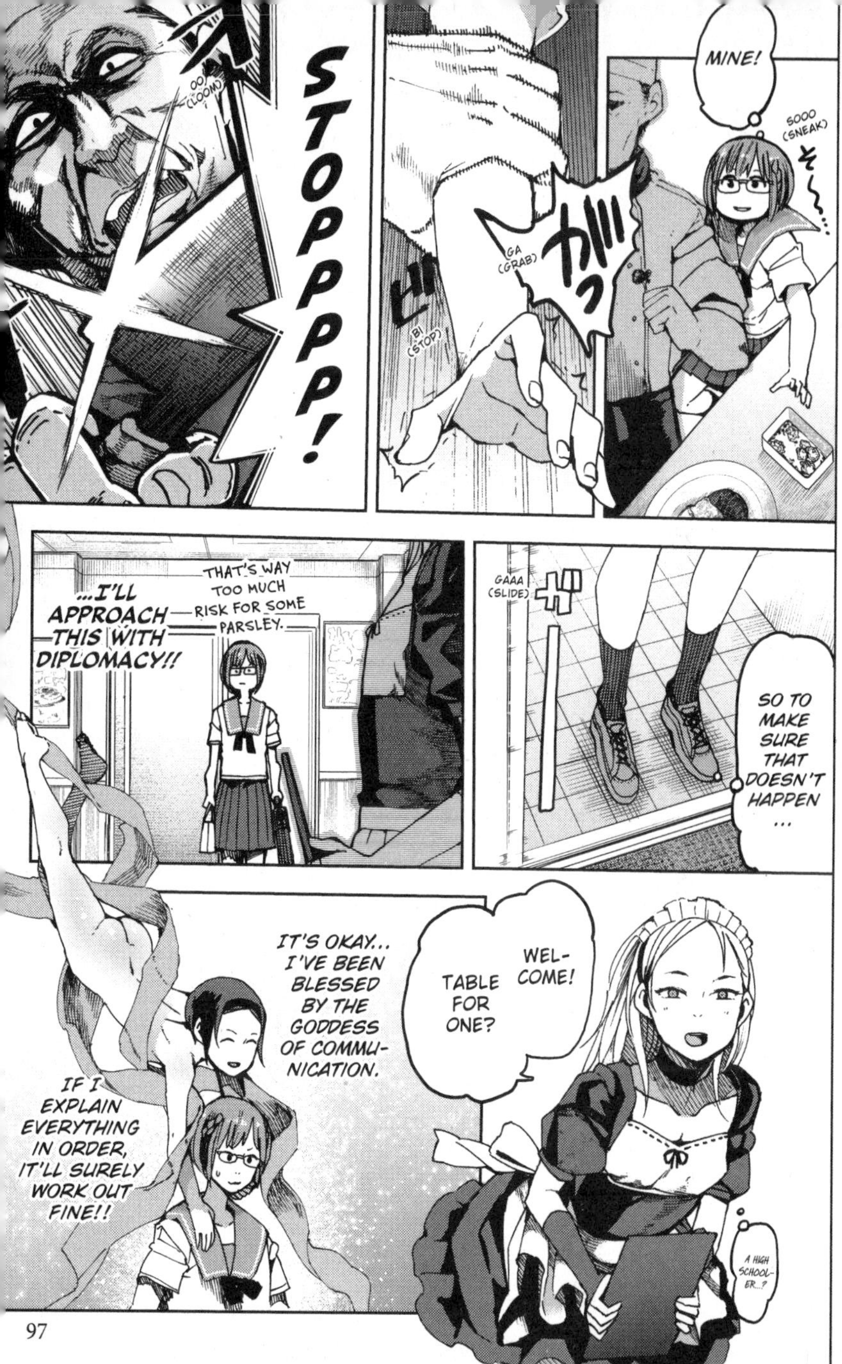
MINE!
SOOO (SNEAK)
GA (GRAB)
BI (STOP)
OO (LOOM)
STOPPPP!
GAAA (SLIDE)
SO TO MAKE SURE THAT DOESN'T HAPPEN...
THAT'S WAY TOO MUCH RISK FOR SOME PARSLEY.
...I'LL APPROACH THIS WITH DIPLOMACY!!
WEL-COME!
TABLE FOR ONE?
A HIGH SCHOOL-ER...?
IT'S OKAY... I'VE BEEN BLESSED BY THE GODDESS OF COMMU-NICATION.
IF I EXPLAIN EVERYTHING IN ORDER, IT'LL SURELY WORK OUT FINE!!

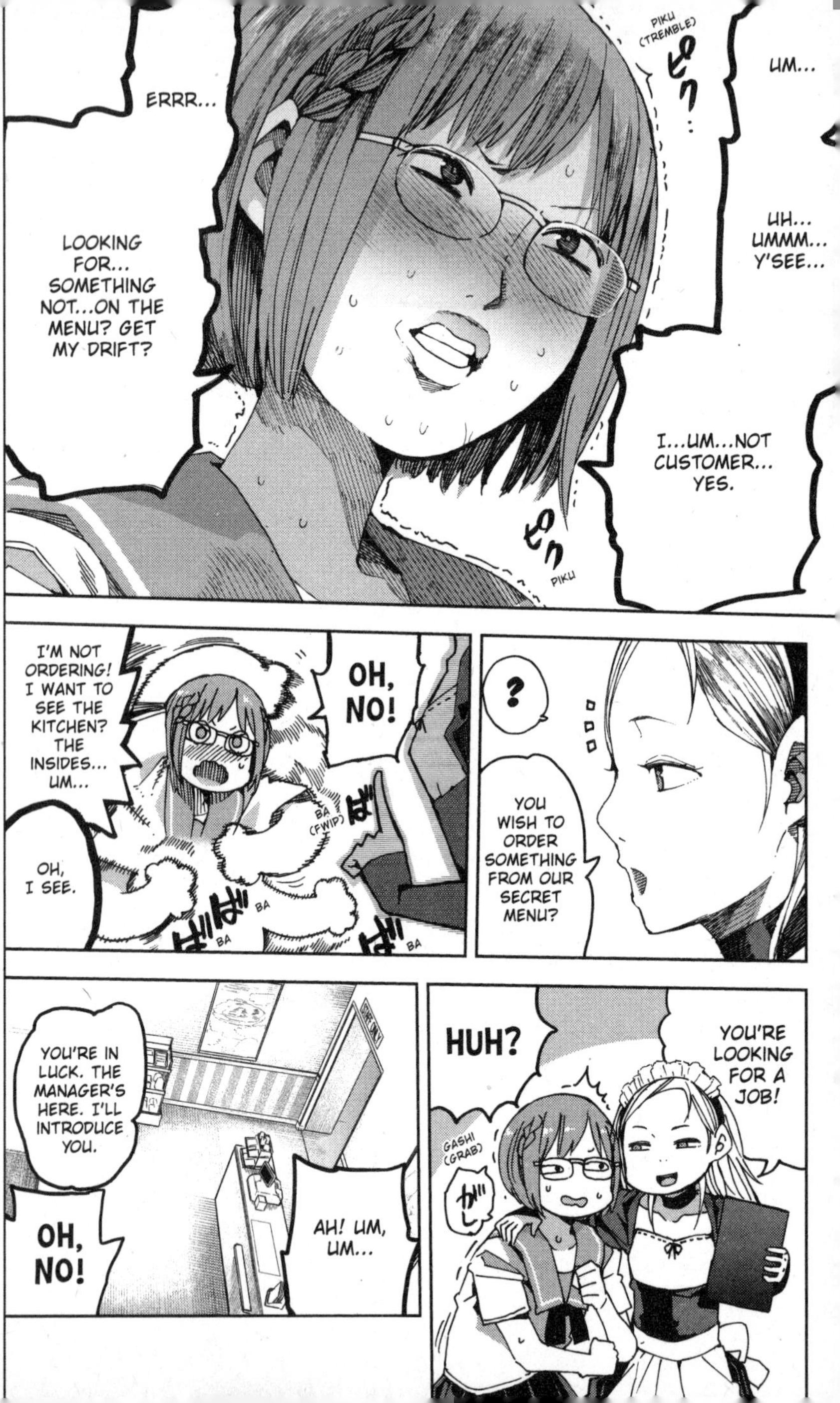
UM...
PIKU (TREMBLE)
ピク…
ERRR...
UH... UMMM... Y'SEE...
LOOKING FOR... SOMETHING NOT...ON THE MENU? GET MY DRIFT?
I...UM...NOT CUSTOMER... YES.
ピク
PIKU
?
YOU WISH TO ORDER SOMETHING FROM OUR SECRET MENU?
OH, NO!
I'M NOT ORDERING! I WANT TO SEE THE KITCHEN? THE INSIDES... UM...
BA (FWIP)
ば
OH, I SEE.
BA
BA
BA
YOU'RE LOOKING FOR A JOB!
HUH?
GASHI (GRAB)
がし
AH! UM, UM...
YOU'RE IN LUCK. THE MANAGER'S HERE. I'LL INTRODUCE YOU.
OH, NO!

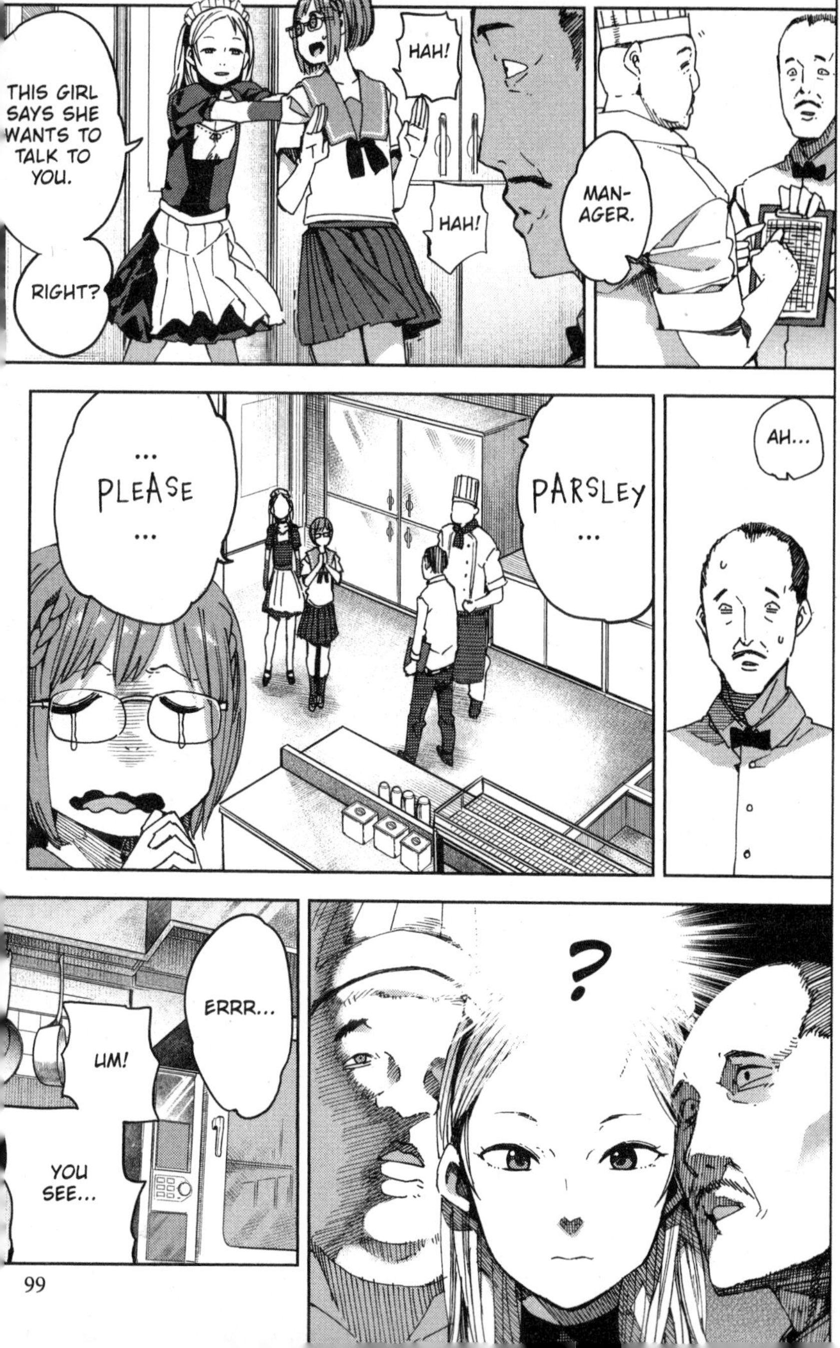
MAN-AGER.
HAH!
HAH!
THIS GIRL SAYS SHE WANTS TO TALK TO YOU.
RIGHT?
AH...
PARSLEY ...
... PLEASE ...
?
ERRR...
UM!
YOU SEE...

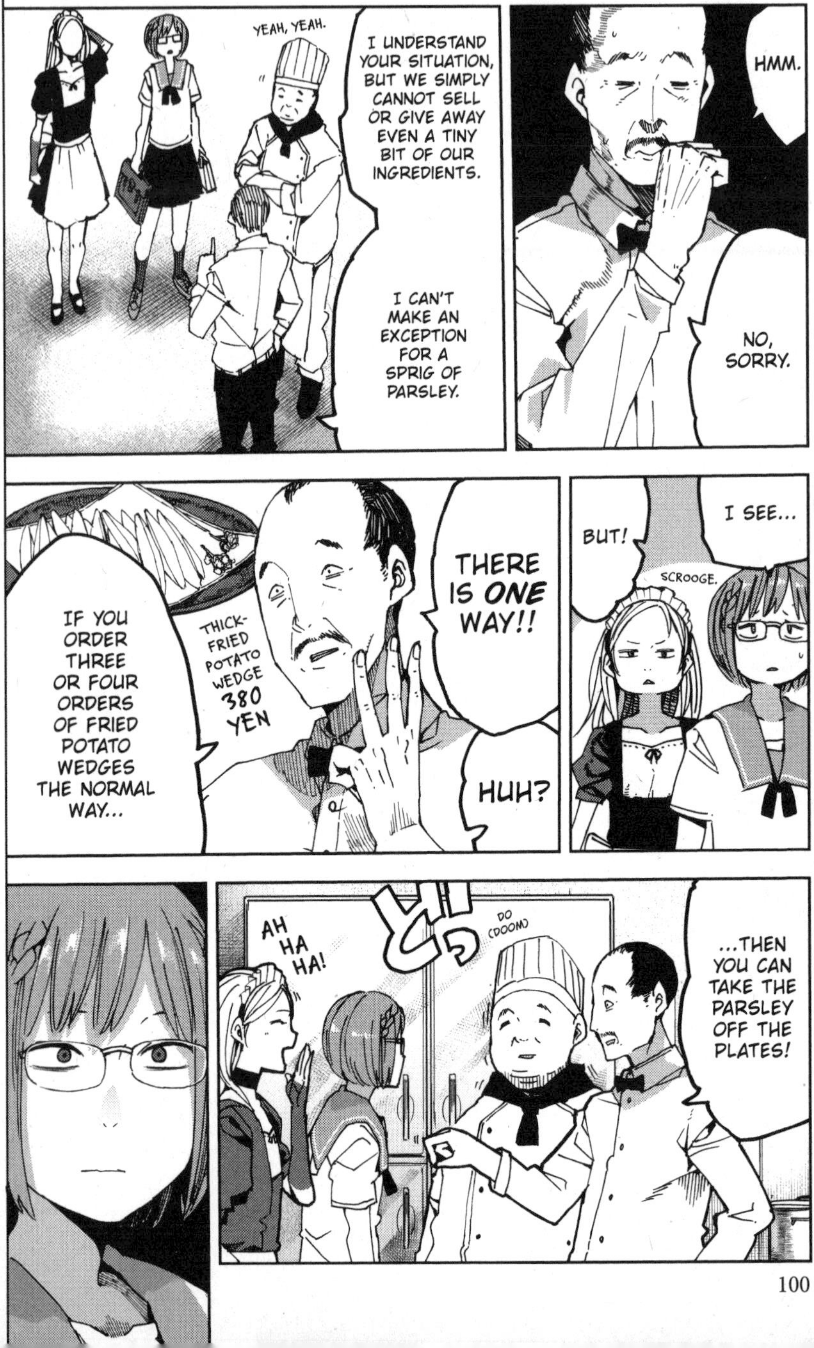
HMM.
NO, SORRY.
I UNDERSTAND YOUR SITUATION, BUT WE SIMPLY CANNOT SELL OR GIVE AWAY EVEN A TINY BIT OF OUR INGREDIENTS.
YEAH, YEAH.
I CAN'T MAKE AN EXCEPTION FOR A SPRIG OF PARSLEY.
I SEE...
BUT!
SCROOGE.
THERE IS ONE WAY!!
HUH?
THICK-FRIED POTATO WEDGE 380 YEN
IF YOU ORDER THREE OR FOUR ORDERS OF FRIED POTATO WEDGES THE NORMAL WAY...
...THEN YOU CAN TAKE THE PARSLEY OFF THE PLATES!
DO (DOOM)
AH HA HA!

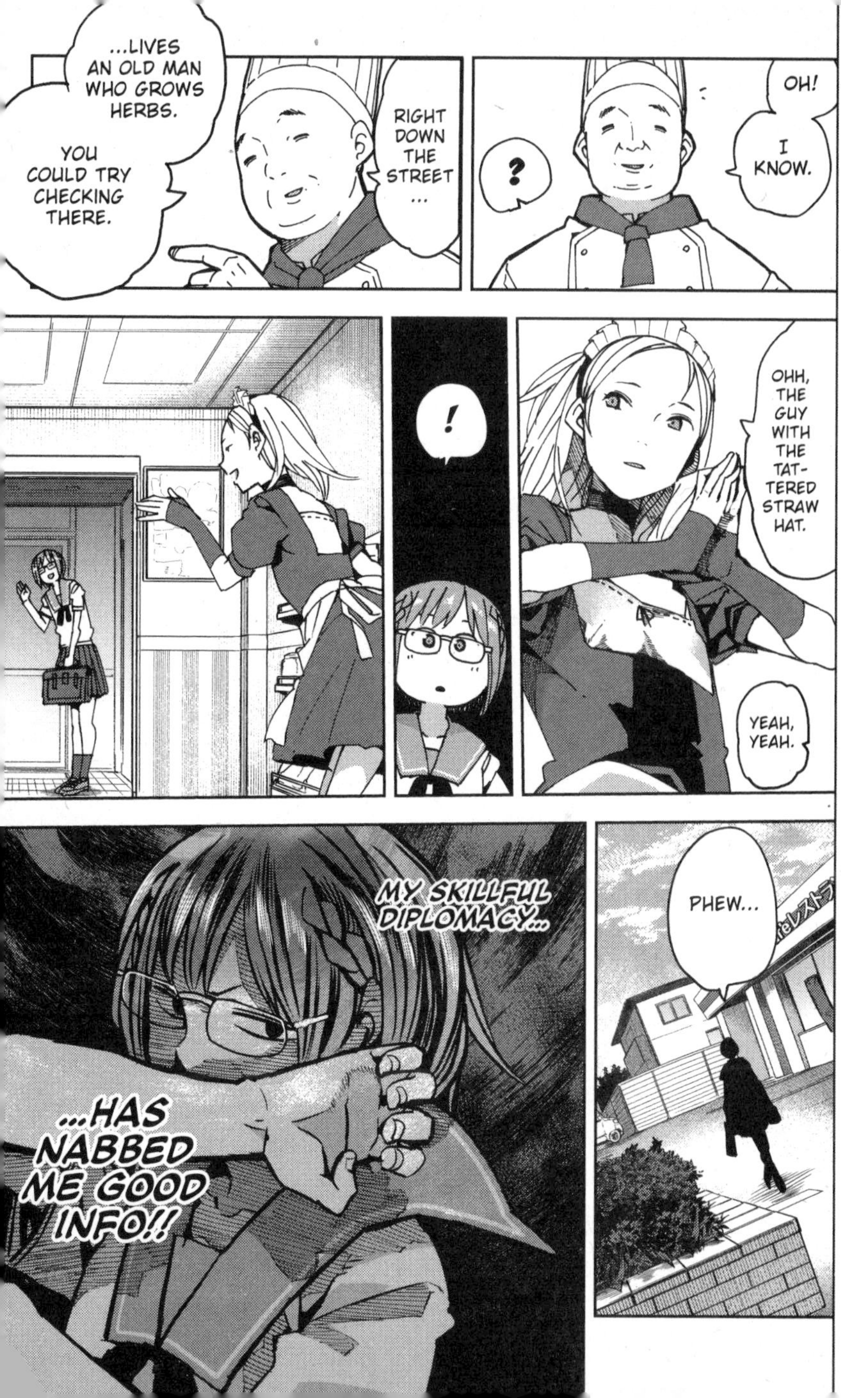
OH!
I KNOW.
?
RIGHT DOWN THE STREET...
...LIVES AN OLD MAN WHO GROWS HERBS.
YOU COULD TRY CHECKING THERE.
OHH, THE GUY WITH THE TAT-TERED STRAW HAT.
YEAH, YEAH.
!
PHEW...
MY SKILLFUL DIPLOMACY...
...HAS NABBED ME GOOD INFO!!

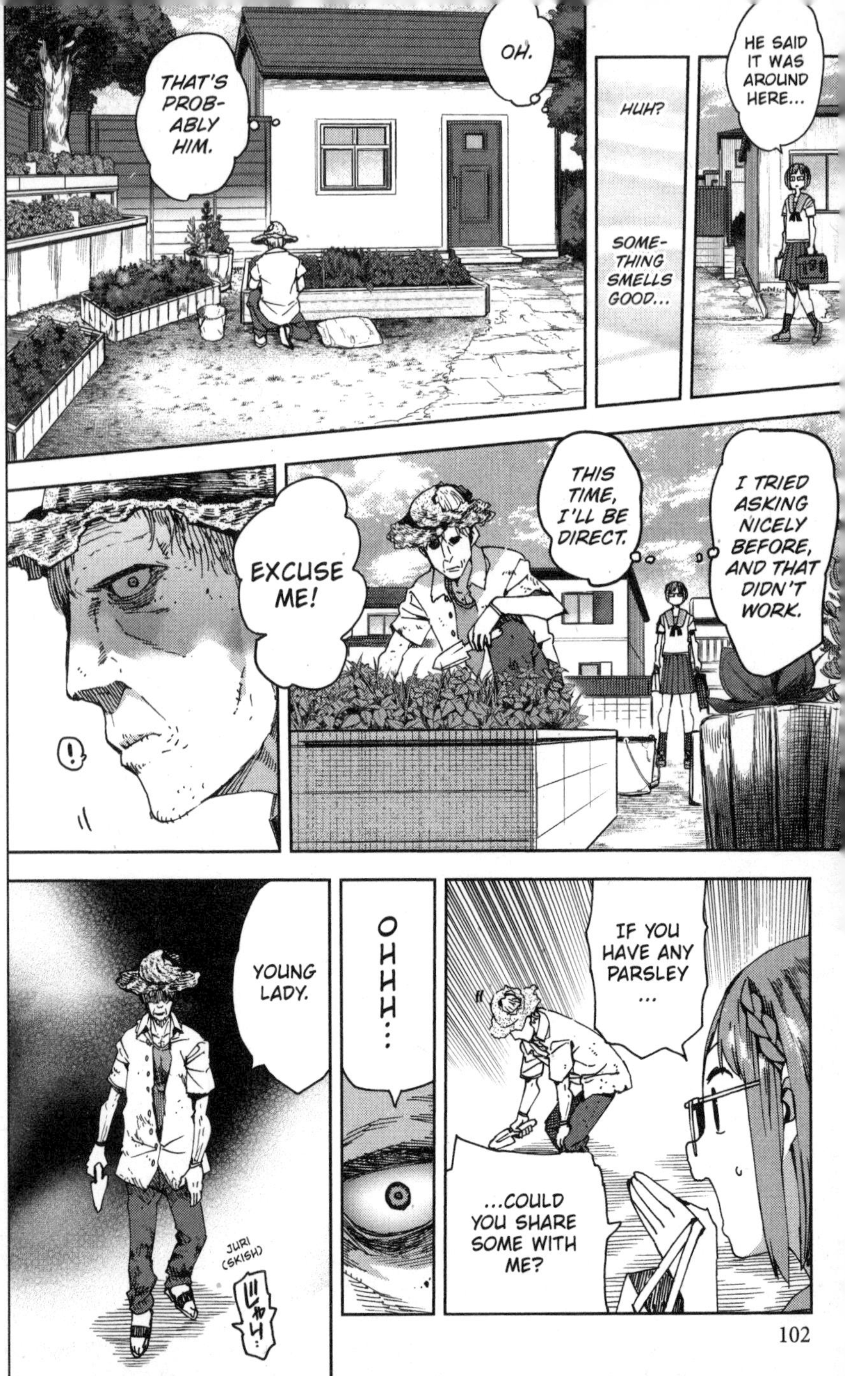
HE SAID IT WAS AROUND HERE...
HUH?
SOME-THING SMELLS GOOD...
OH.
THAT'S PROB-ABLY HIM.
I TRIED ASKING NICELY BEFORE, AND THAT DIDN'T WORK.
THIS TIME, I'LL BE DIRECT.
EXCUSE ME!
!
IF YOU HAVE ANY PARSLEY ...
...COULD YOU SHARE SOME WITH ME?
OHHH...
YOUNG LADY.
JURI (SKISH)
じゃり…

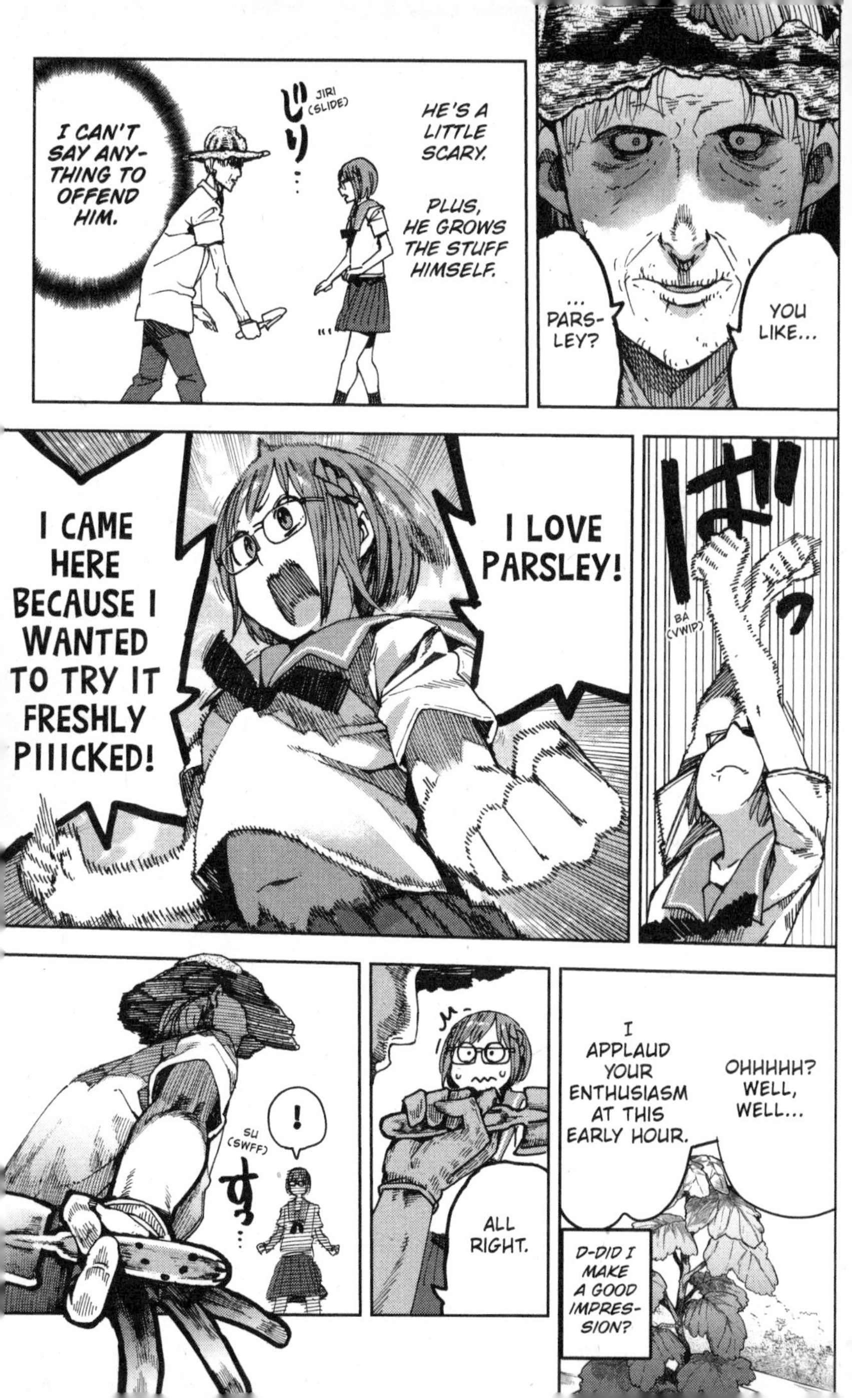
YOU LIKE...
...PARSLEY?
HE'S A LITTLE SCARY.
PLUS, HE GROWS THE STUFF HIMSELF.
じり…
JIRI (SLIDE)
I CAN'T SAY ANYTHING TO OFFEND HIM.
ぱっ
BA (VWIP)
I LOVE PARSLEY!
I CAME HERE BECAUSE I WANTED TO TRY IT FRESHLY PIIICKED!
OHHHHH? WELL, WELL...
I APPLAUD YOUR ENTHUSIASM AT THIS EARLY HOUR.
D-DID I MAKE A GOOD IMPRESSION?
ALL RIGHT.
!
すっ…
SU (SWFF)

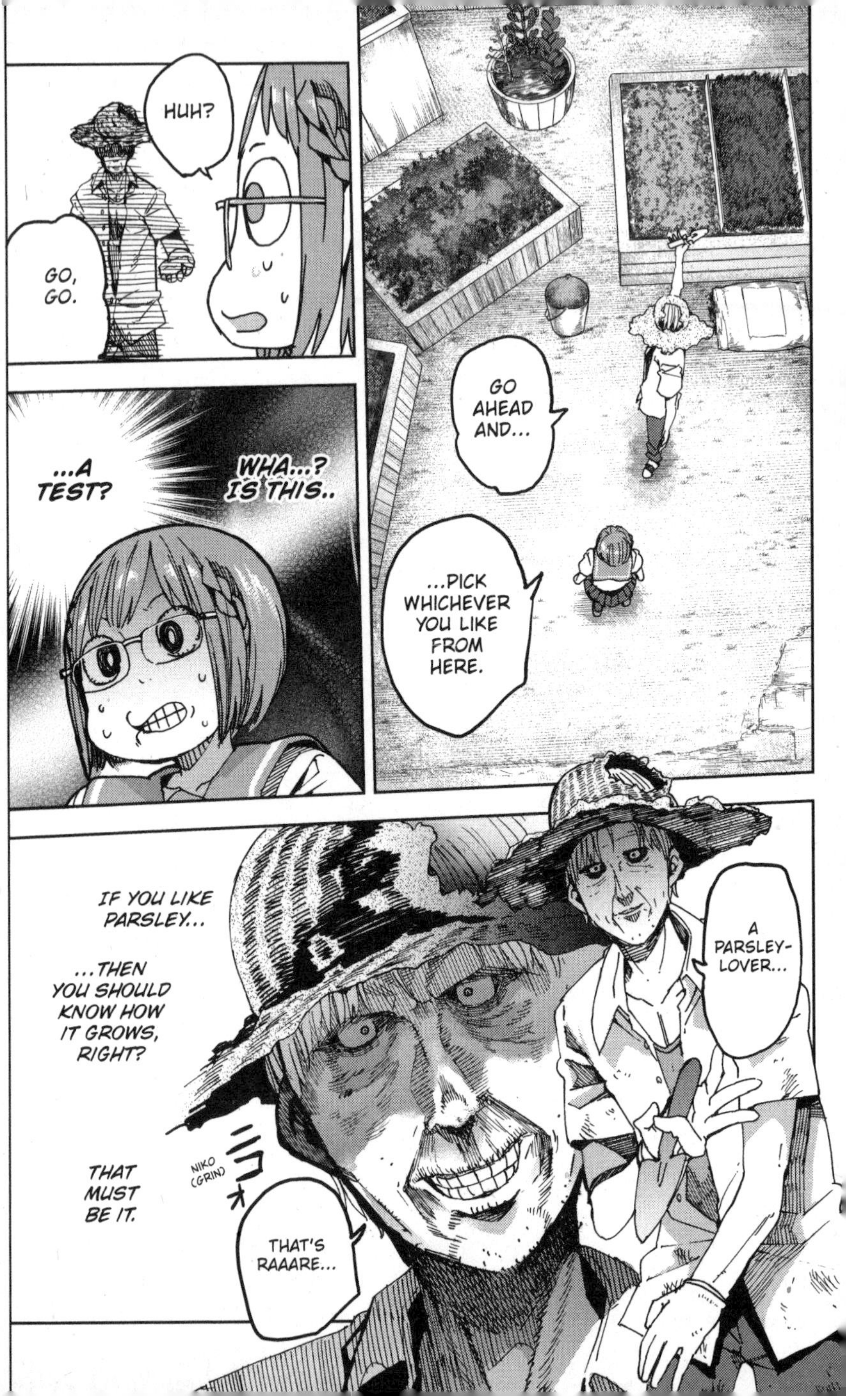
GO AHEAD AND...
...PICK WHICHEVER YOU LIKE FROM HERE.
HUH?
GO, GO.
WHA...? IS THIS..
...A TEST?
A PARSLEY-LOVER...
IF YOU LIKE PARSLEY...
...THEN YOU SHOULD KNOW HOW IT GROWS, RIGHT?
NIKO (GRIN)
THAT'S RAAARE...
THAT MUST BE IT.

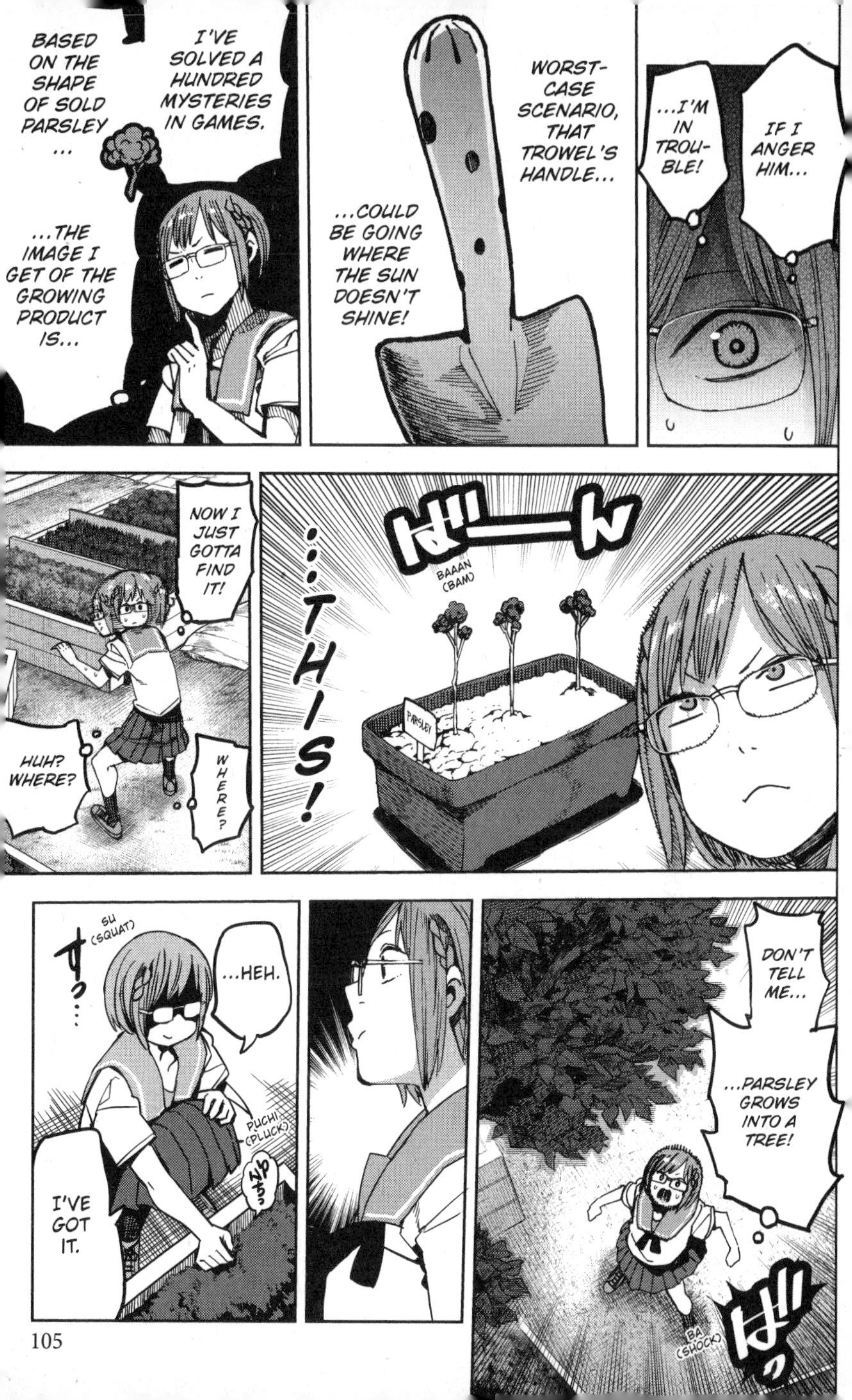
IF I ANGER HIM...
...I'M IN TROUBLE!
WORST-CASE SCENARIO, THAT TROWEL'S HANDLE...
...COULD BE GOING WHERE THE SUN DOESN'T SHINE!
I'VE SOLVED A HUNDRED MYSTERIES IN GAMES.
BASED ON THE SHAPE OF SOLD PARSLEY...
...THE IMAGE I GET OF THE GROWING PRODUCT IS...
ばーん
BAAAN (BAM)
...THIS!
PARSLEY
NOW I JUST GOTTA FIND IT!
WHERE?
HUH? WHERE?
DON'T TELL ME...
...PARSLEY GROWS INTO A TREE!
ばっ
BA (SHOCK)
すっ…
SU (SQUAT)
...HEH.
ぷちっ
PUCHI (PLUCK)
I'VE GOT IT.

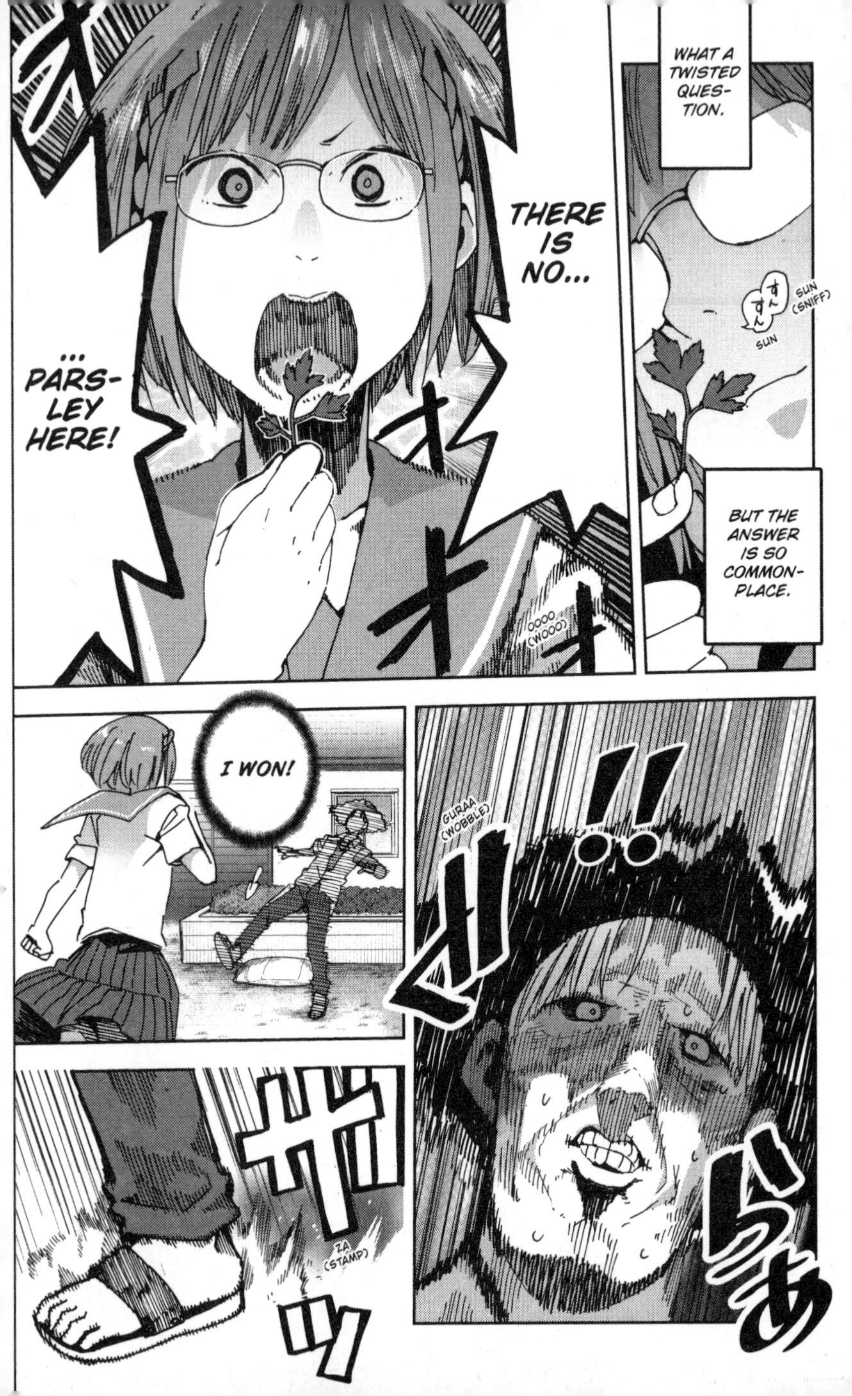
WHAT A TWISTED QUES-TION.
SUN (SNIFF)
SUN
BUT THE ANSWER IS SO COMMON-PLACE.
THERE IS NO...
...PARS-LEY HERE!
OOOO (WOOOO)
GURAA (WOBBLE)
I WON!
ZA (STAMP)

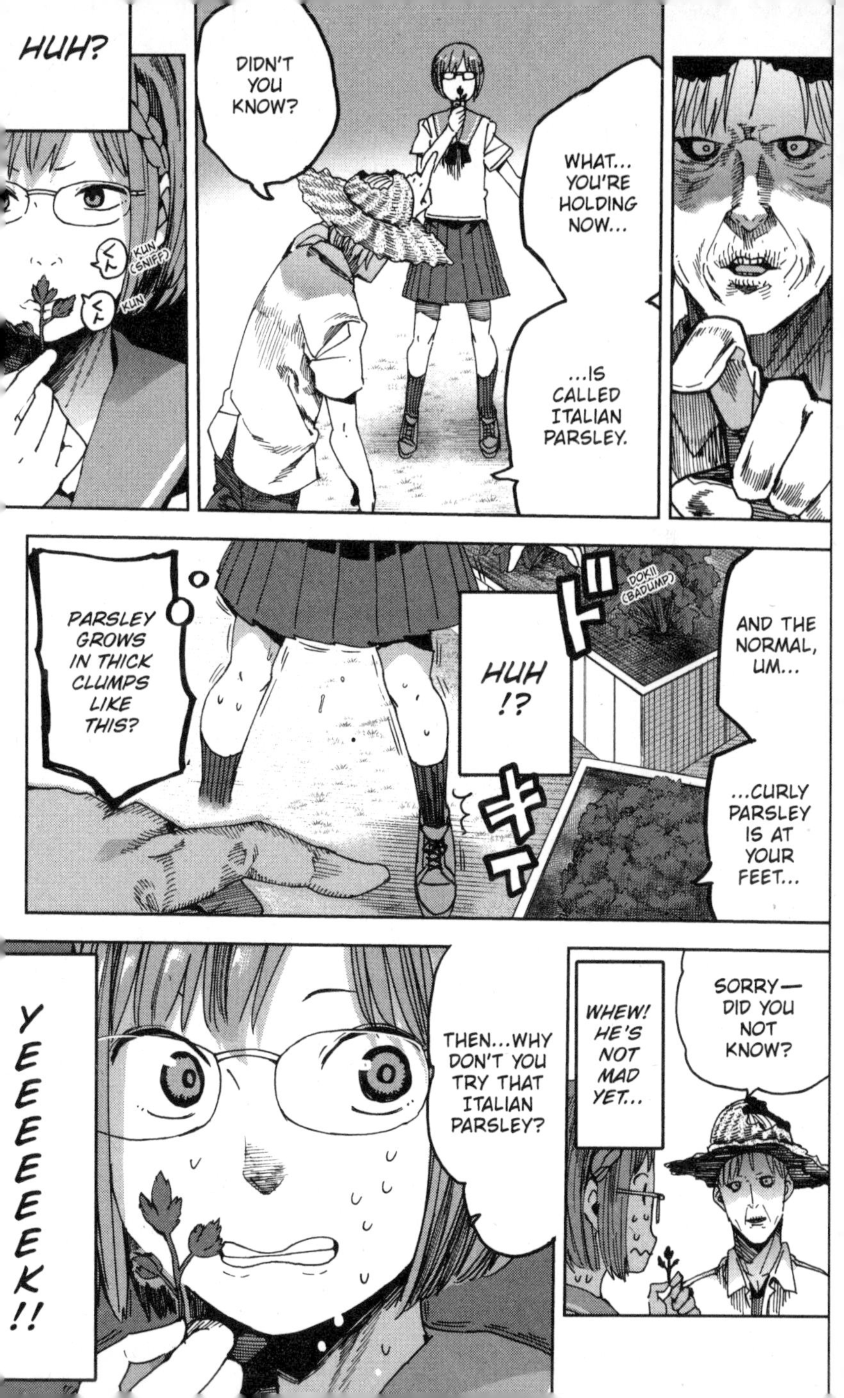
WHAT... YOU'RE HOLDING NOW...
...IS CALLED ITALIAN PARSLEY.
DIDN'T YOU KNOW?
くん KUN (SNIFF)
くん KUN
HUH?
AND THE NORMAL, UM...
...CURLY PARSLEY IS AT YOUR FEET...
ドキ DOKI (BADUMP)
HUH!?
PARSLEY GROWS IN THICK CLUMPS LIKE THIS?
SORRY— DID YOU NOT KNOW?
WHEW! HE'S NOT MAD YET...
THEN...WHY DON'T YOU TRY THAT ITALIAN PARSLEY?
YEEEEEEEEEK!!

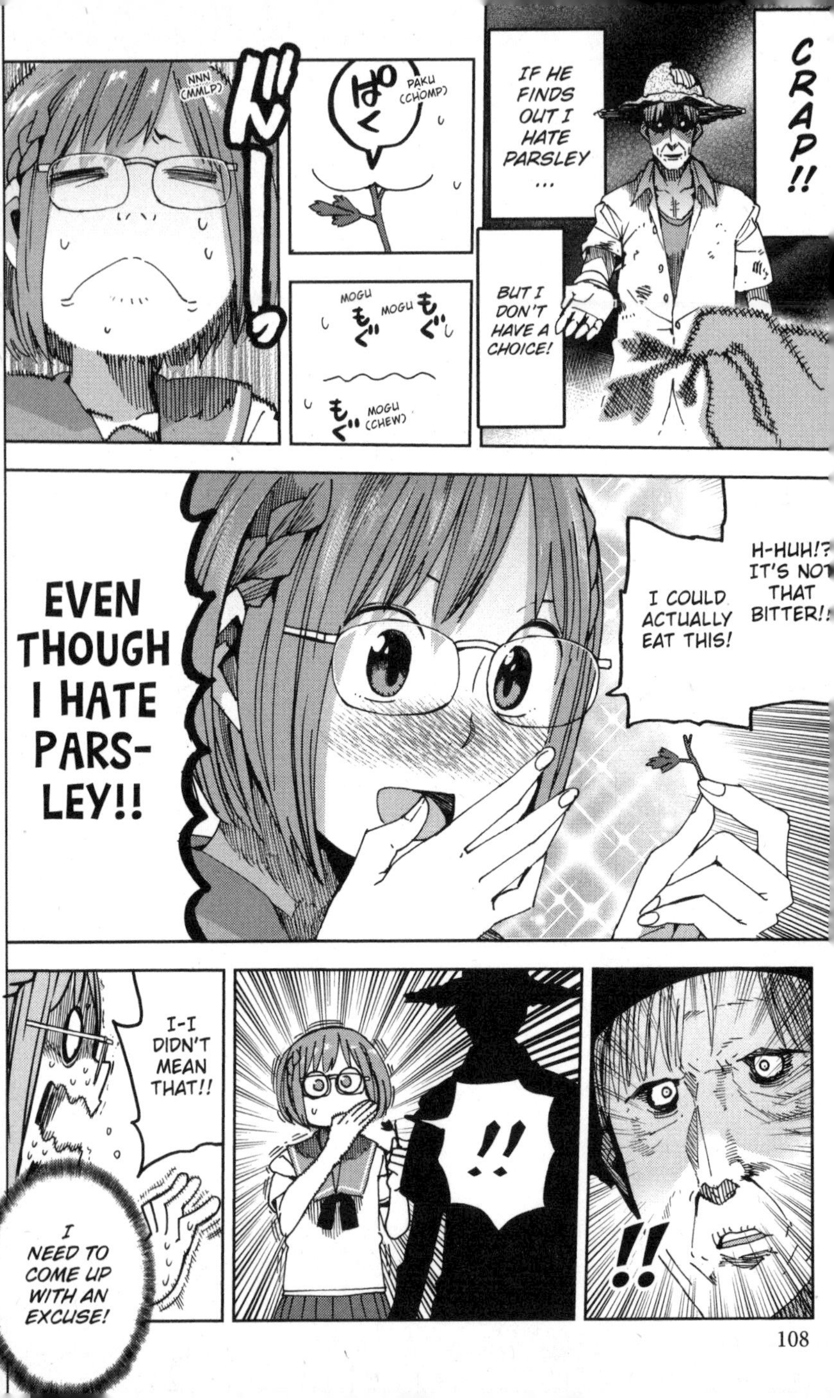
CRAP!!
IF HE FINDS OUT I HATE PARSLEY...
BUT I DON'T HAVE A CHOICE!
ぱく
PAKU (CHOMP)
もぐ もぐ もぐ
MOGU MOGU MOGU (CHEW)
んっ
NNN (MMLP)
H-HUH!? IT'S NOT THAT BITTER!!
I COULD ACTUALLY EAT THIS!
EVEN THOUGH I HATE PARS-LEY!!
!!
!!
I-I DIDN'T MEAN THAT!!
I NEED TO COME UP WITH AN EXCUSE!

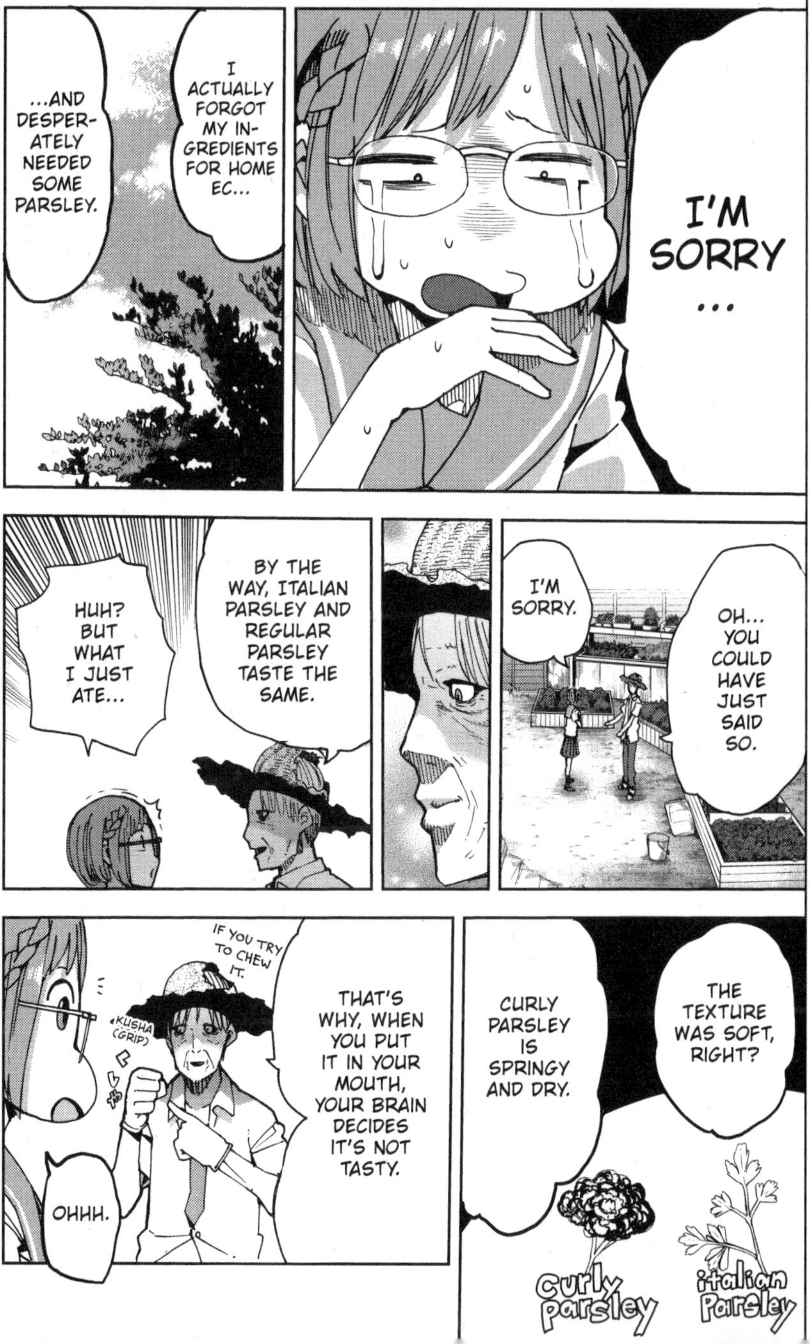
I'M SORRY ...
I ACTUALLY FORGOT MY IN-GREDIENTS FOR HOME EC...
...AND DESPERATELY NEEDED SOME PARSLEY.
OH... YOU COULD HAVE JUST SAID SO.
I'M SORRY.
BY THE WAY, ITALIAN PARSLEY AND REGULAR PARSLEY TASTE THE SAME.
HUH? BUT WHAT I JUST ATE...
THE TEXTURE WAS SOFT, RIGHT?
CURLY PARSLEY IS SPRINGY AND DRY.
italian Parsley
Curly parsley
THAT'S WHY, WHEN YOU PUT IT IN YOUR MOUTH, YOUR BRAIN DECIDES IT'S NOT TASTY.
IF YOU TRY TO CHEW IT.
KUSHA (GRIP)
OHHH.

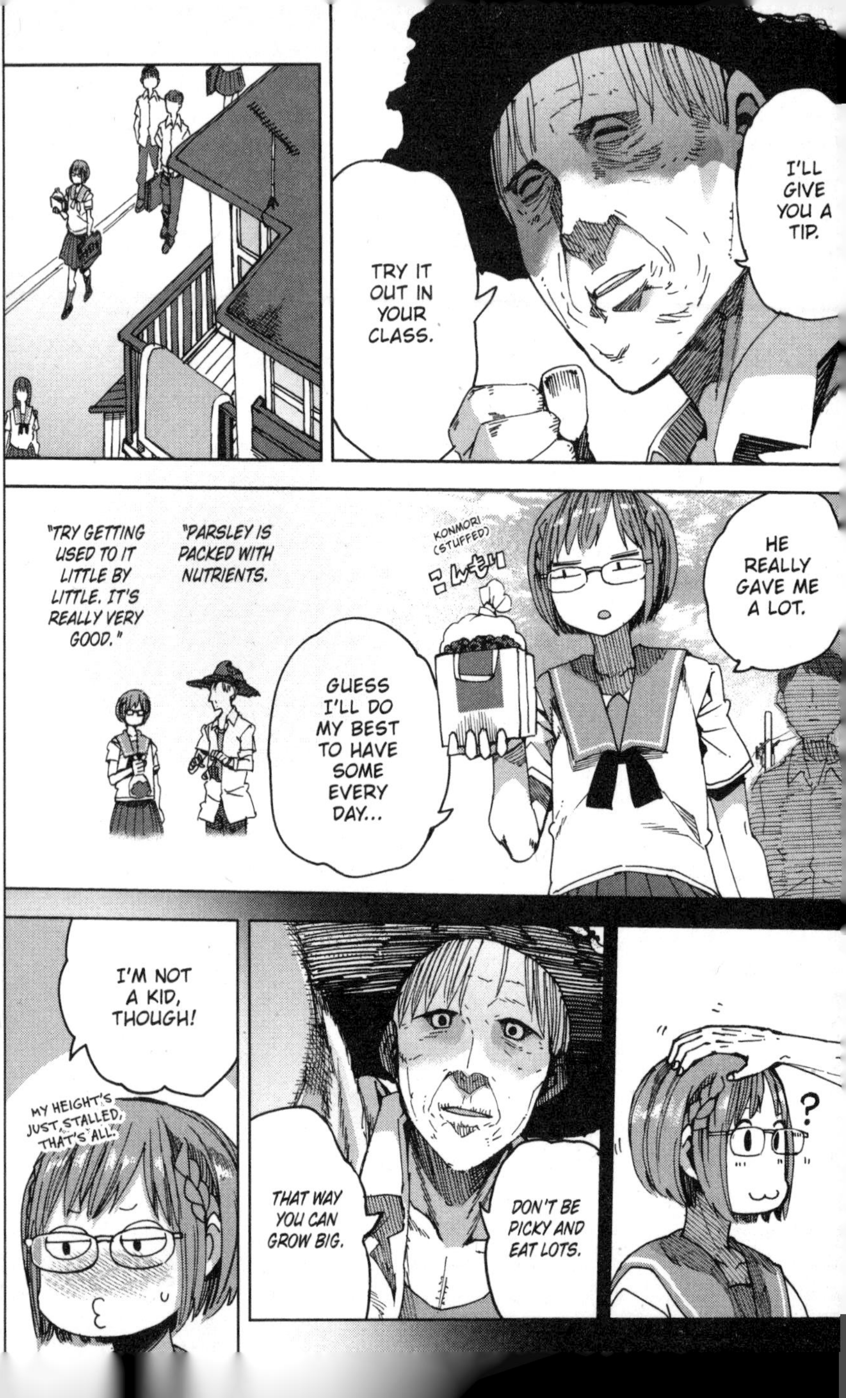
I'LL GIVE YOU A TIP.
TRY IT OUT IN YOUR CLASS.
HE REALLY GAVE ME A LOT.
KONMORI (STUFFED)
GUESS I'LL DO MY BEST TO HAVE SOME EVERY DAY...
"PARSLEY IS PACKED WITH NUTRIENTS.
"TRY GETTING USED TO IT LITTLE BY LITTLE. IT'S REALLY VERY GOOD."
?
DON'T BE PICKY AND EAT LOTS.
THAT WAY YOU CAN GROW BIG.
I'M NOT A KID, THOUGH!
MY HEIGHT'S JUST STALLED, THAT'S ALL.

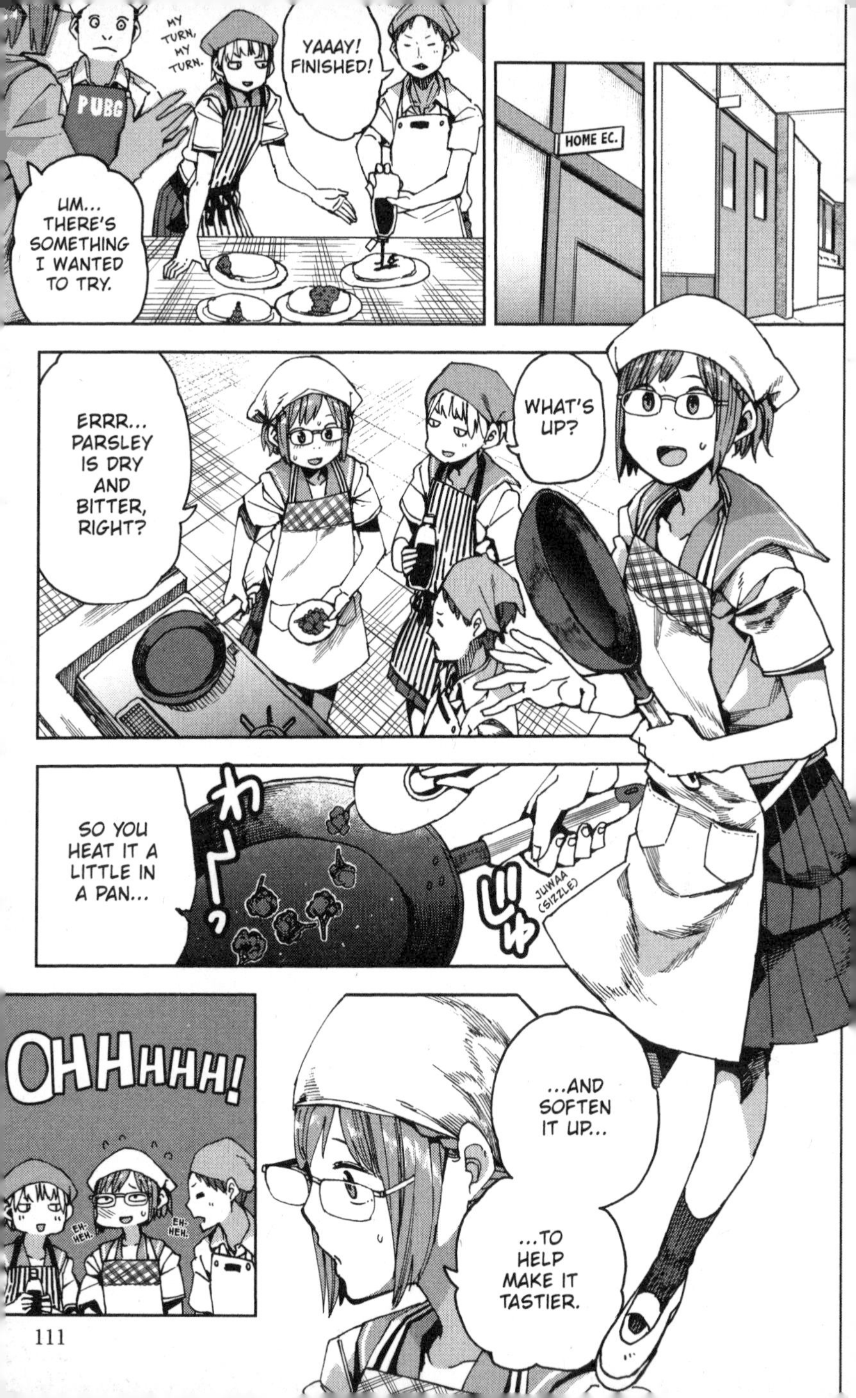
HOME EC.
YAAAY! FINISHED!
MY TURN, MY TURN.
UM... THERE'S SOMETHING I WANTED TO TRY.
WHAT'S UP?
ERRR... PARSLEY IS DRY AND BITTER, RIGHT?
JUWAA (SIZZLE)
SO YOU HEAT IT A LITTLE IN A PAN...
...AND SOFTEN IT UP...
...TO HELP MAKE IT TASTIER.
OHHHHH!
EH-HEH.
EH-HEH.

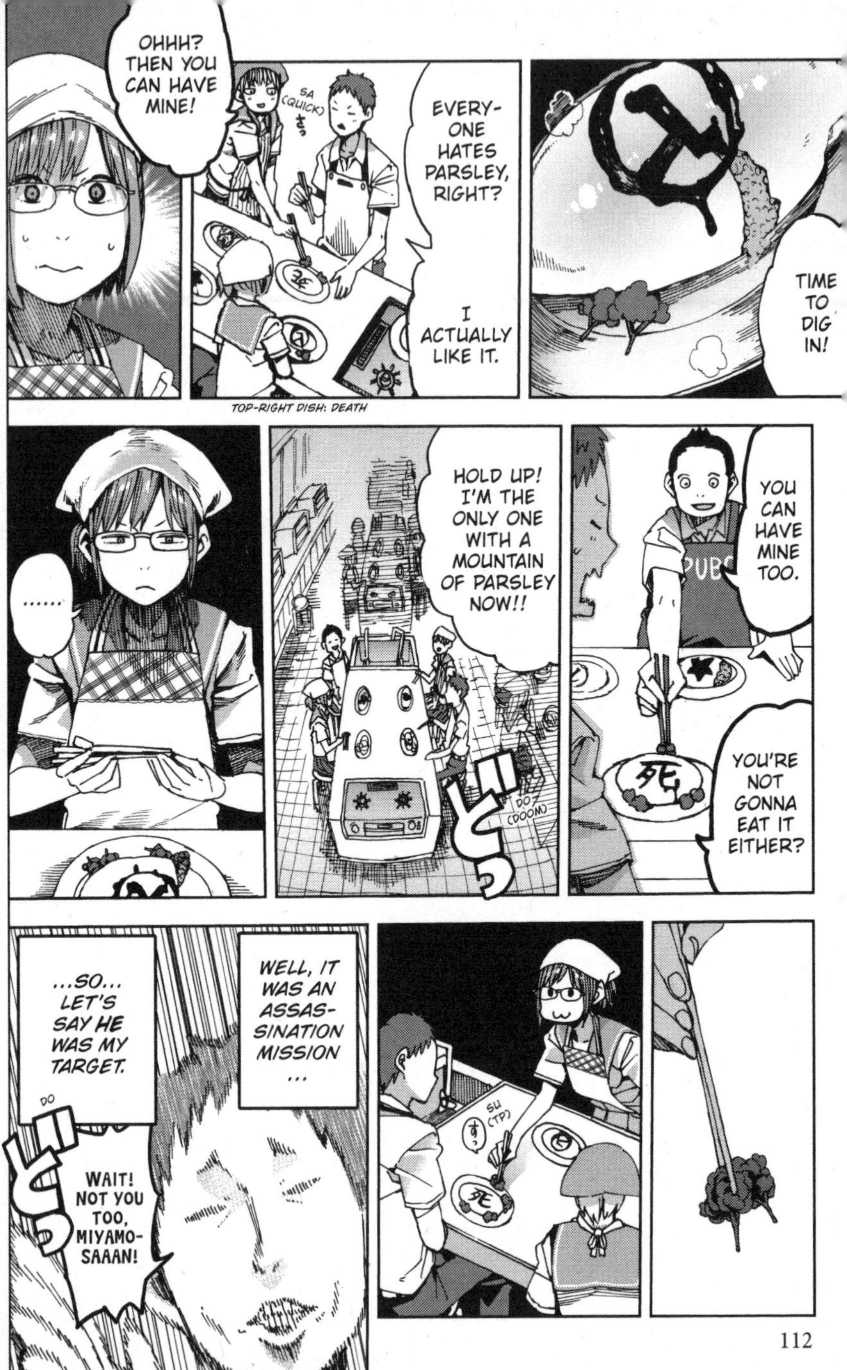
TIME TO DIG IN!
EVERY-ONE HATES PARSLEY, RIGHT?
I ACTUALLY LIKE IT.
SA (QUICK)
OHHH? THEN YOU CAN HAVE MINE!
TOP-RIGHT DISH: DEATH
YOU CAN HAVE MINE TOO.
YOU'RE NOT GONNA EAT IT EITHER?
HOLD UP! I'M THE ONLY ONE WITH A MOUNTAIN OF PARSLEY NOW!!
DO (DOOM)
......
SU (TP)
WELL, IT WAS AN ASSAS-SINATION MISSION...
...SO... LET'S SAY HE WAS MY TARGET.
DO
WAIT! NOT YOU TOO, MIYAMO-SAAAN!

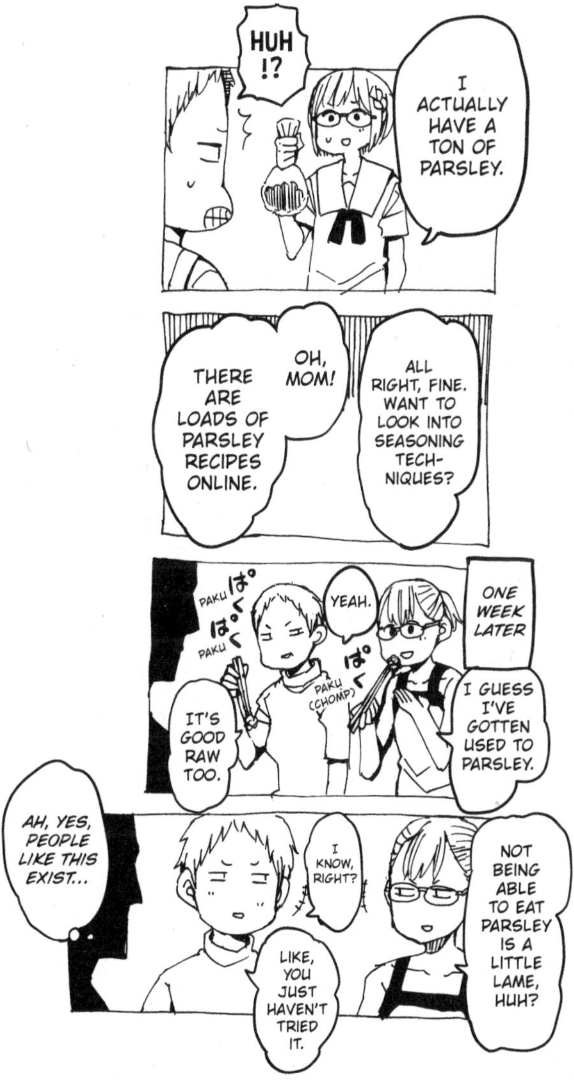
I ACTUALLY HAVE A TON OF PARSLEY.
HUH !?
ALL RIGHT, FINE. WANT TO LOOK INTO SEASONING TECH-NIQUES?
OH, MOM!
THERE ARE LOADS OF PARSLEY RECIPES ONLINE.
ONE WEEK LATER
I GUESS I'VE GOTTEN USED TO PARSLEY.
ぱく
PAKU (CHOMP)
YEAH.
ぱく
PAKU
ぱく
PAKU
IT'S GOOD RAW TOO.
NOT BEING ABLE TO EAT PARSLEY IS A LITTLE LAME, HUH?
I KNOW, RIGHT?
LIKE, YOU JUST HAVEN'T TRIED IT.
AH, YES, PEOPLE LIKE THIS EXIST...

Chio's SCHOOL ROAD

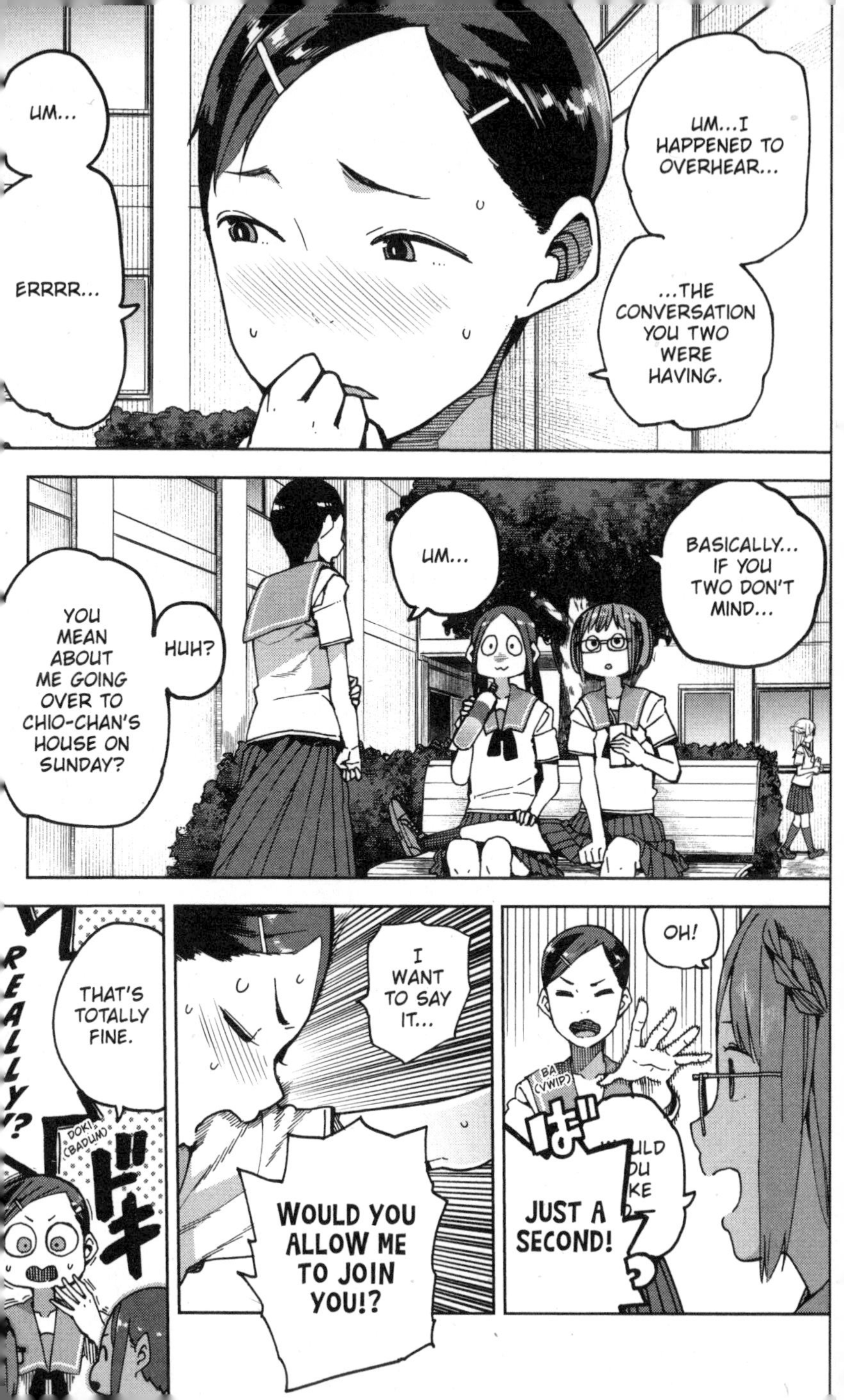
UM...I HAPPENED TO OVERHEAR...
...THE CONVERSATION YOU TWO WERE HAVING.
UM...
ERRRR...
BASICALLY... IF YOU TWO DON'T MIND...
UM...
HUH?
YOU MEAN ABOUT ME GOING OVER TO CHIO-CHAN'S HOUSE ON SUNDAY?
OH!
BA (VWIP)
JUST A SECOND!
I WANT TO SAY IT...
WOULD YOU ALLOW ME TO JOIN YOU!?
THAT'S TOTALLY FINE.
REALLY!?
DOKI (BADUMP)
ドキ

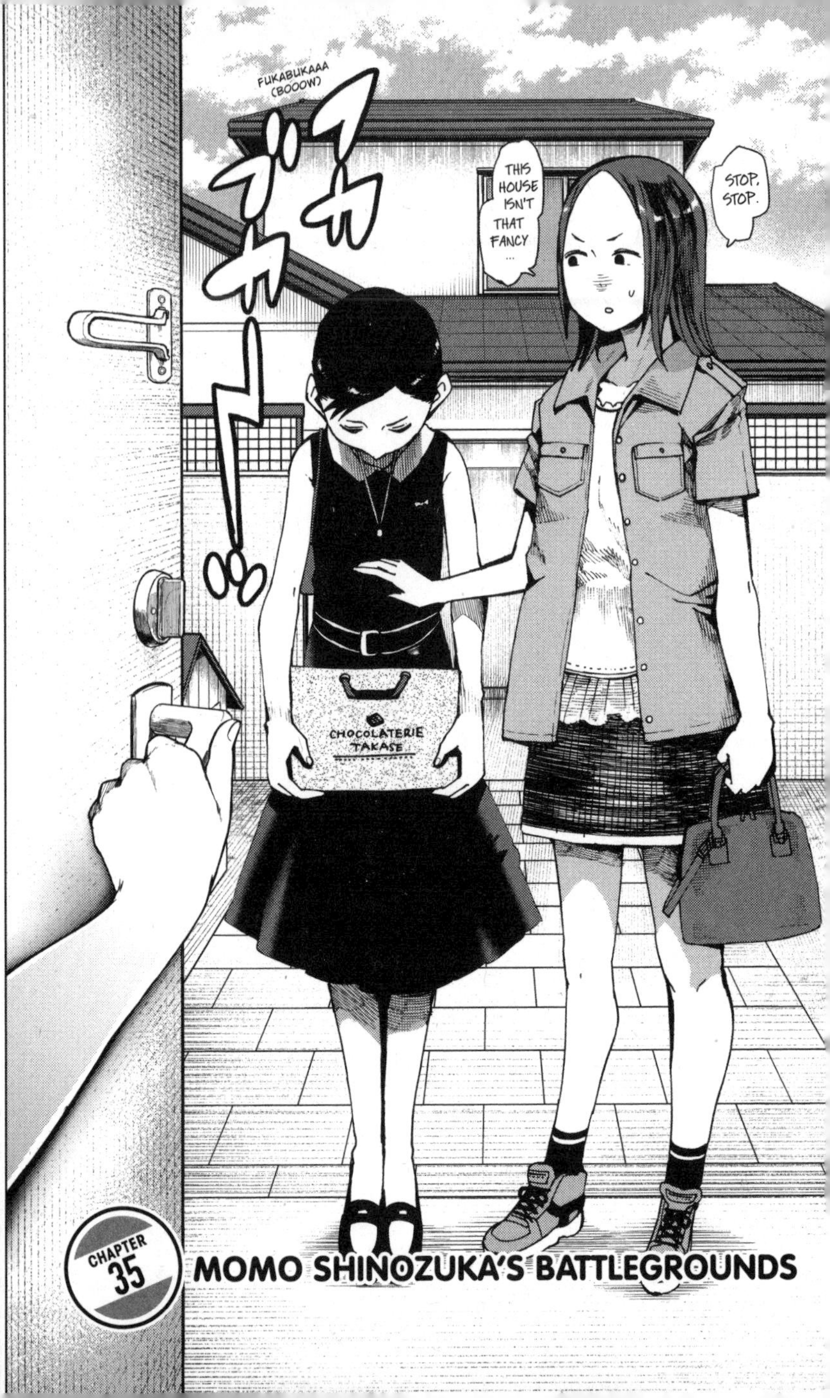
STOP, STOP.
THIS HOUSE ISN'T THAT FANCY...
FUKABUKAAA (BOOOW)
CHOCOLATERIE TAKASE

CHAPTER 35 MOMO SHINOZUKA'S BATTLEGROUNDS

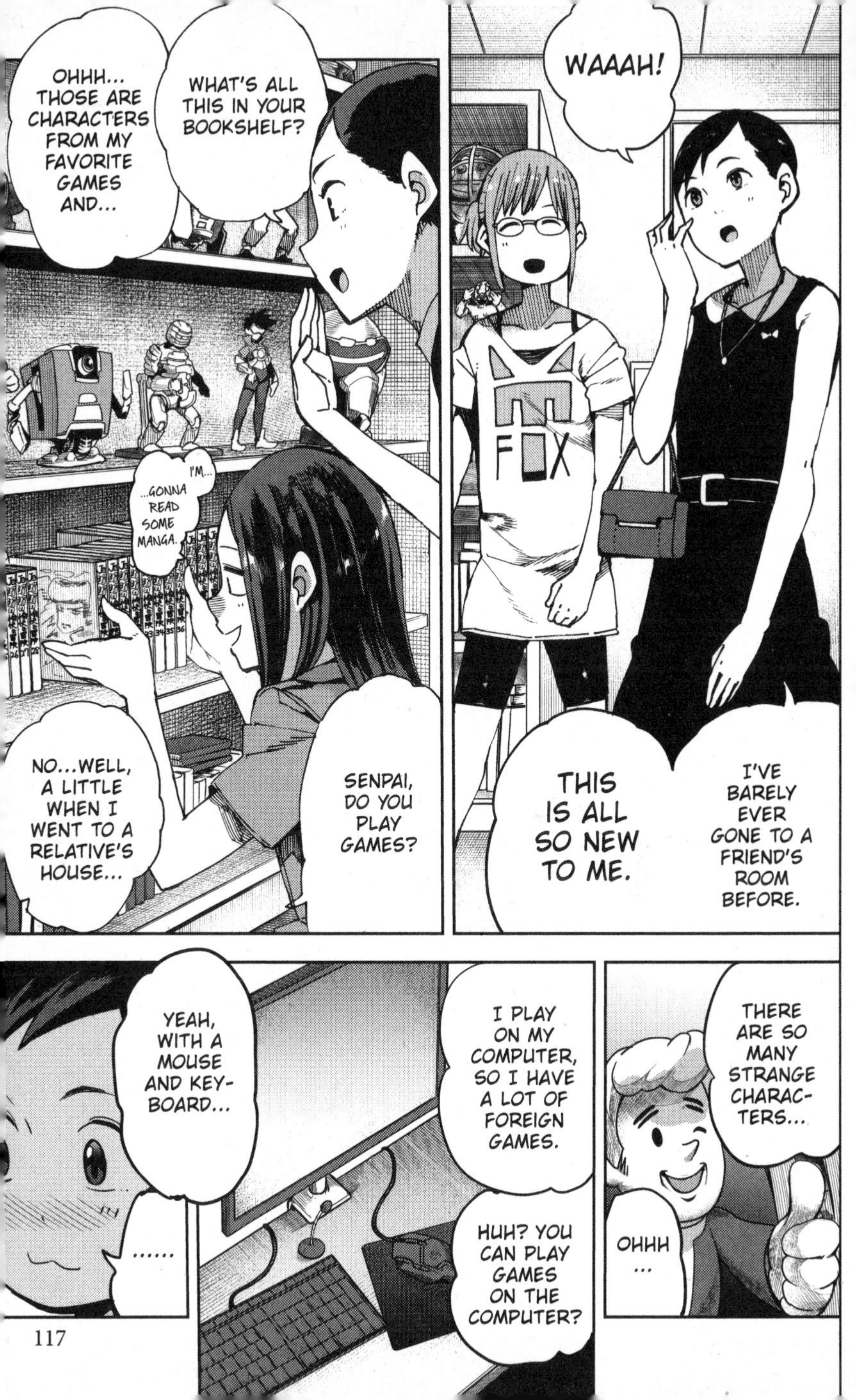
WAAAH!
I'VE BARELY EVER GONE TO A FRIEND'S ROOM BEFORE.
THIS IS ALL SO NEW TO ME.
WHAT'S ALL THIS IN YOUR BOOKSHELF?
OHHH... THOSE ARE CHARACTERS FROM MY FAVORITE GAMES AND...
I'M... ...GONNA READ SOME MANGA.
SENPAI, DO YOU PLAY GAMES?
NO...WELL, A LITTLE WHEN I WENT TO A RELATIVE'S HOUSE...
THERE ARE SO MANY STRANGE CHARAC-TERS...
OHHH ...
I PLAY ON MY COMPUTER, SO I HAVE A LOT OF FOREIGN GAMES.
HUH? YOU CAN PLAY GAMES ON THE COMPUTER?
YEAH, WITH A MOUSE AND KEY-BOARD...
......

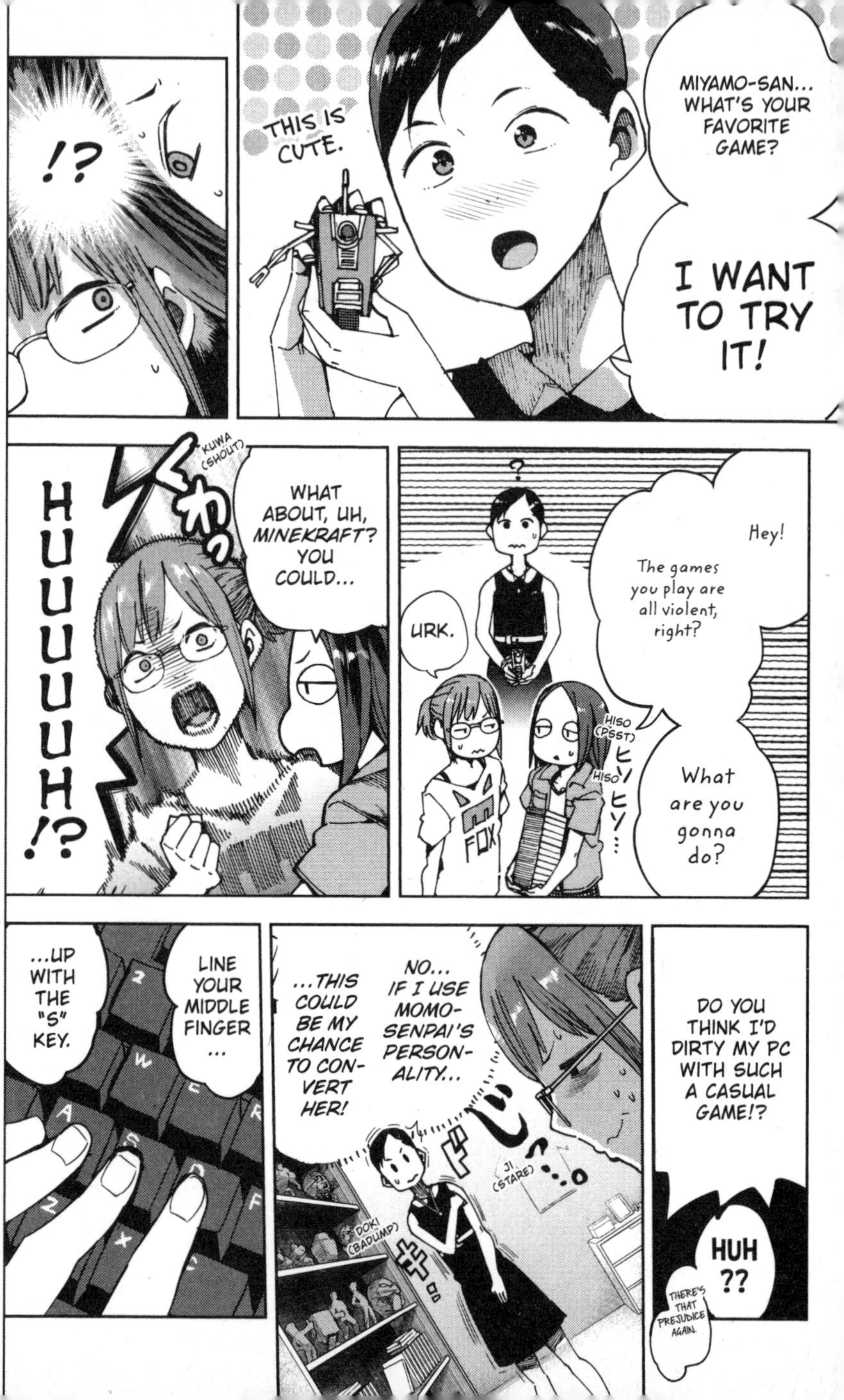

MIYAMO-SAN... WHAT'S YOUR FAVORITE GAME?
THIS IS CUTE.
I WANT TO TRY IT!
!?
Hey!
The games you play are all violent, right?
?
URK.
HISO (PSST)
ヒソヒソ…
HISO
What are you gonna do?
KUWA (SHOUT)
WHAT ABOUT, UH, *MINEKRAFT*? YOU COULD...
HUUUUUUUH!?
DO YOU THINK I'D DIRTY MY PC WITH SUCH A CASUAL GAME!?
HUH ??
THERE'S THAT PREJUDICE AGAIN.
NO... IF I USE MOMO-SENPAI'S PERSONALITY...
...THIS COULD BE MY CHANCE TO CONVERT HER!
JI (STARE)
DOKI (BADUMP)
LINE YOUR MIDDLE FINGER...
...UP WITH THE "S" KEY.

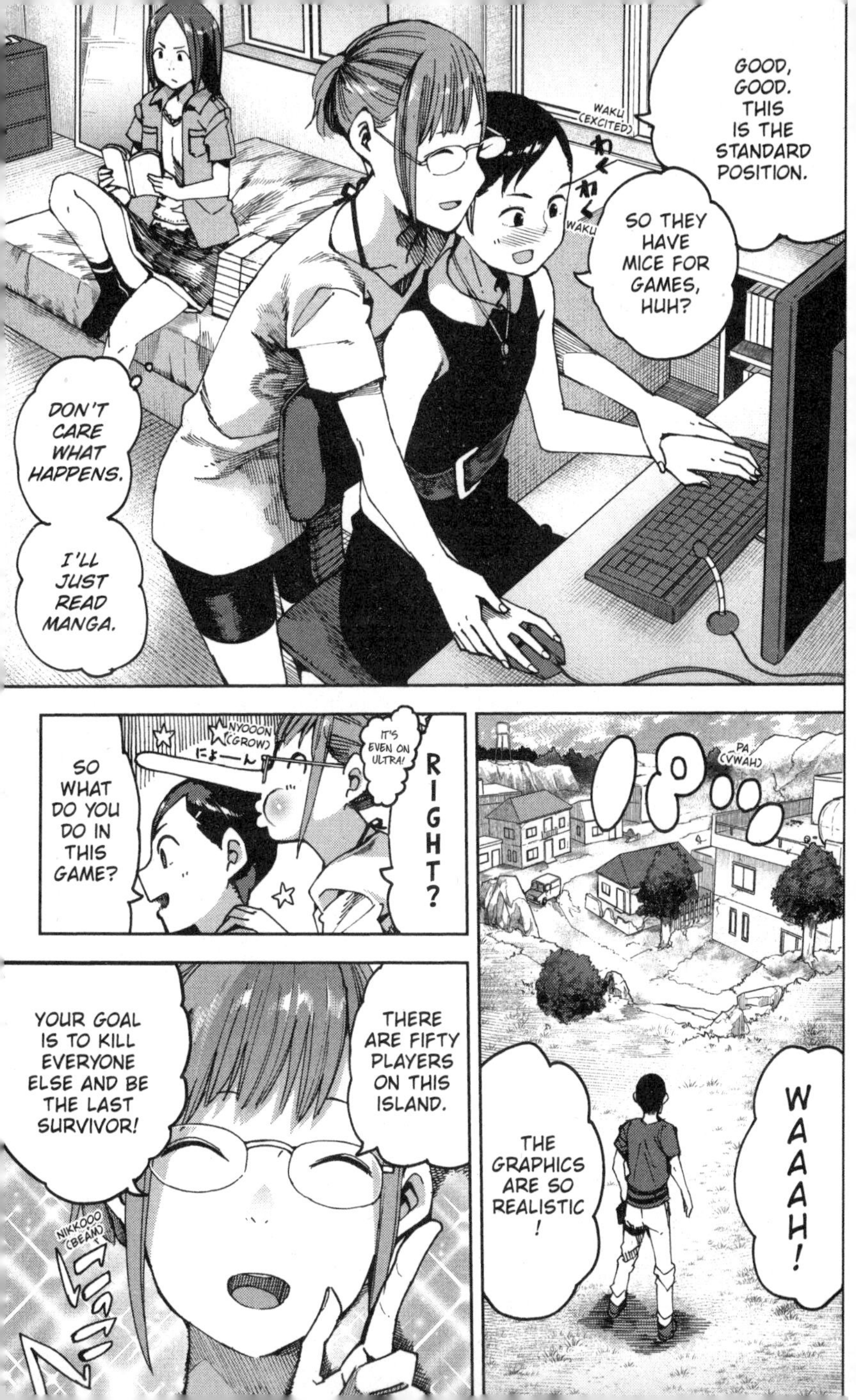
GOOD, GOOD. THIS IS THE STANDARD POSITION.
WAKU (EXCITED)
わくわく
WAKU
SO THEY HAVE MICE FOR GAMES, HUH?
DON'T CARE WHAT HAPPENS.
I'LL JUST READ MANGA.
PA (VWAH)
P...
WAAAH!
THE GRAPHICS ARE SO REALISTIC!
RIGHT?
IT'S EVEN ON ULTRA!
NYOOON (GROW)
によーん
SO WHAT DO YOU DO IN THIS GAME?
THERE ARE FIFTY PLAYERS ON THIS ISLAND.
YOUR GOAL IS TO KILL EVERYONE ELSE AND BE THE LAST SURVIVOR!
NIKKOOO (BEAM)

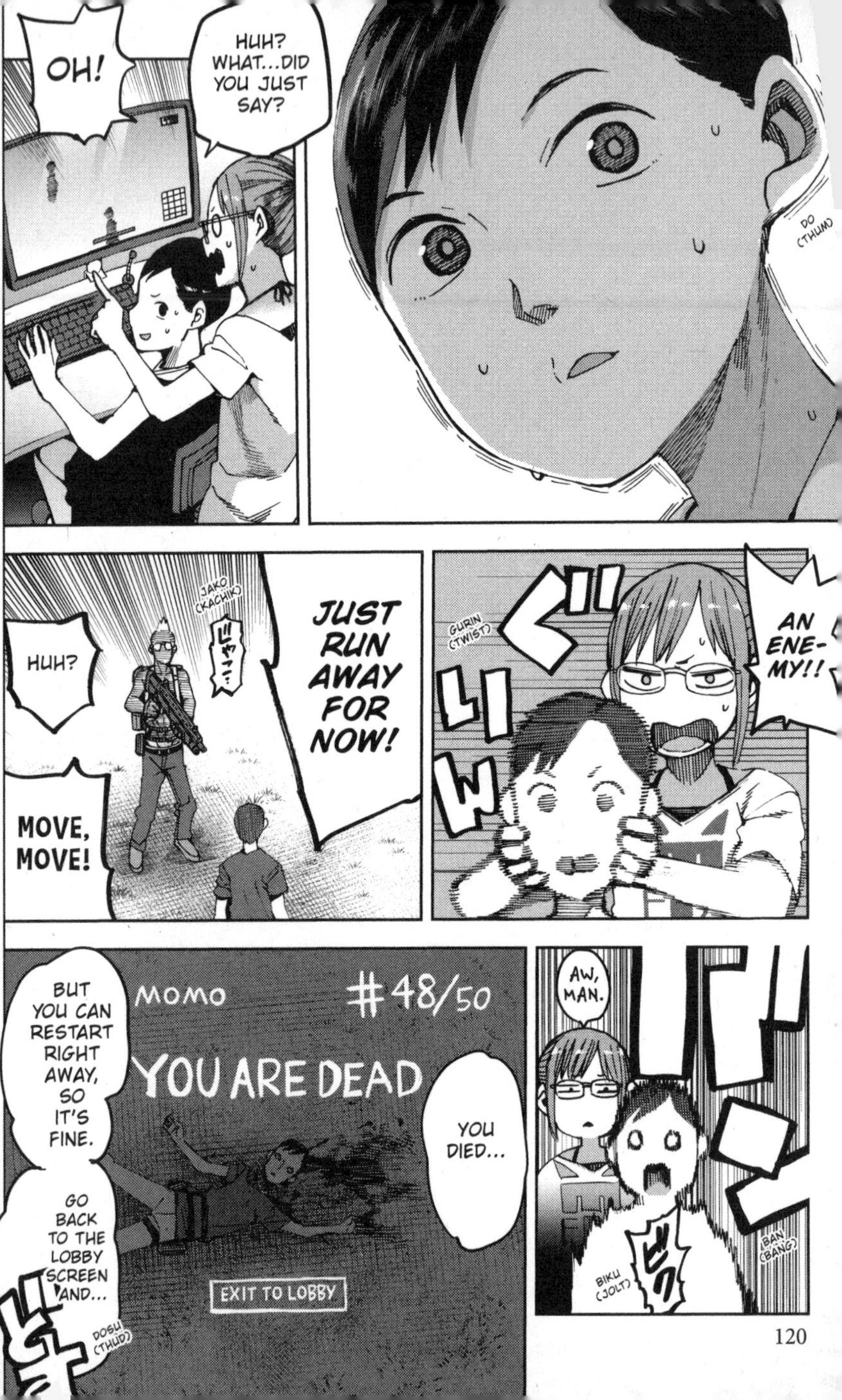
DO (THUM)
HUH? WHAT...DID YOU JUST SAY?
OH!
AN ENEMY!!
GURIN (TWIST)
JUST RUN AWAY FOR NOW!
JAKO (KACHIK)
HUH?
MOVE, MOVE!
AW, MAN.
BAN (BANG)
BIKU (JOLT)
#48/50
MOMO
YOU ARE DEAD
YOU DIED...
BUT YOU CAN RESTART RIGHT AWAY, SO IT'S FINE.
GO BACK TO THE LOBBY SCREEN AND...
EXIT TO LOBBY
DOSU (THUD)

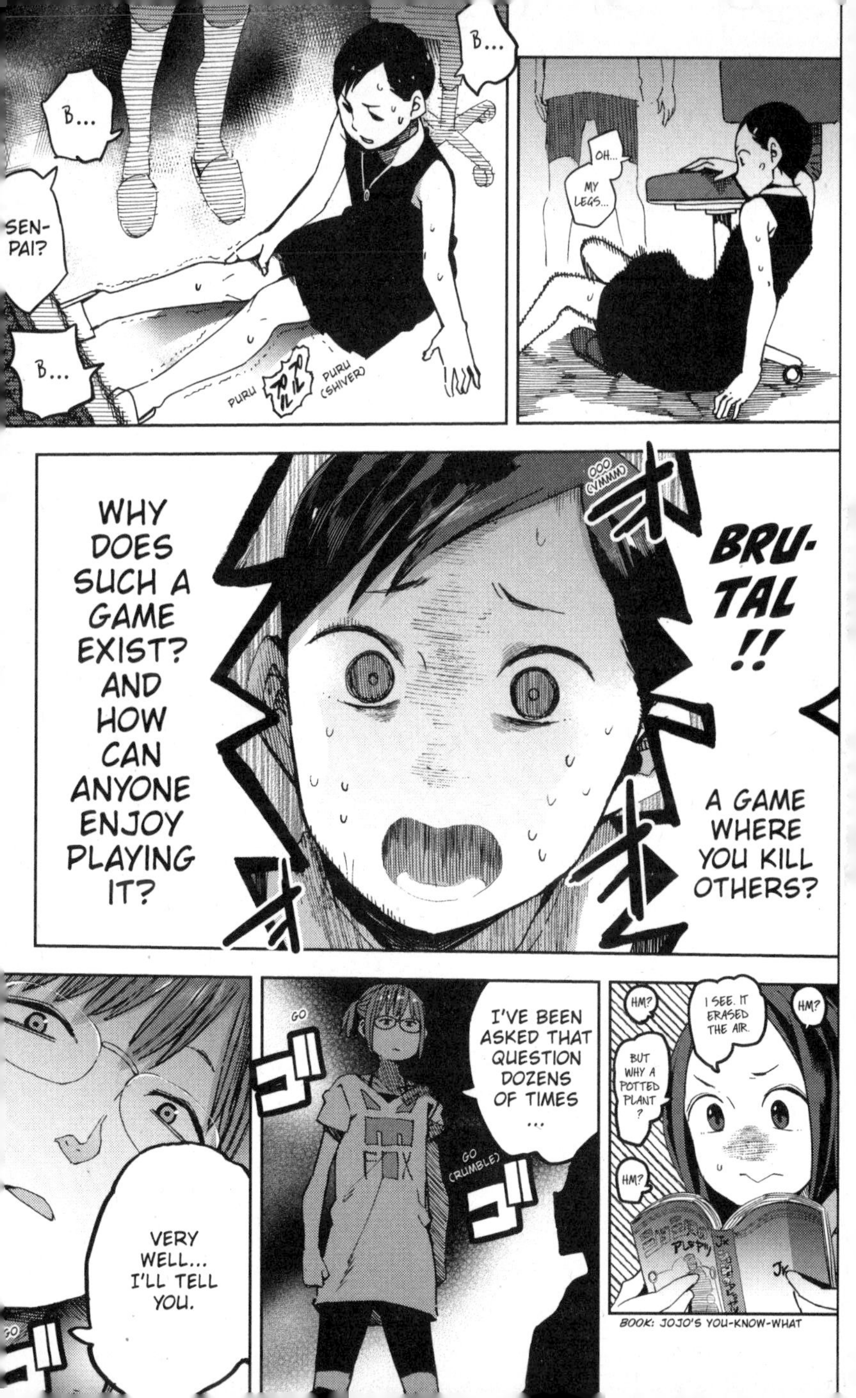
OH...
MY LEGS...
B...
B...
SEN-PAI?
B...
PURU
PURU (SHIVER)
BRU-TAL!!
A GAME WHERE YOU KILL OTHERS?
WHY DOES SUCH A GAME EXIST? AND HOW CAN ANYONE ENJOY PLAYING IT?
HM?
I SEE. IT ERASED THE AIR.
HM?
BUT WHY A POTTED PLANT?
HM?
BOOK: JOJO'S YOU-KNOW-WHAT
I'VE BEEN ASKED THAT QUESTION DOZENS OF TIMES...
GO
GO (RUMBLE)
VERY WELL... I'LL TELL YOU.
GO

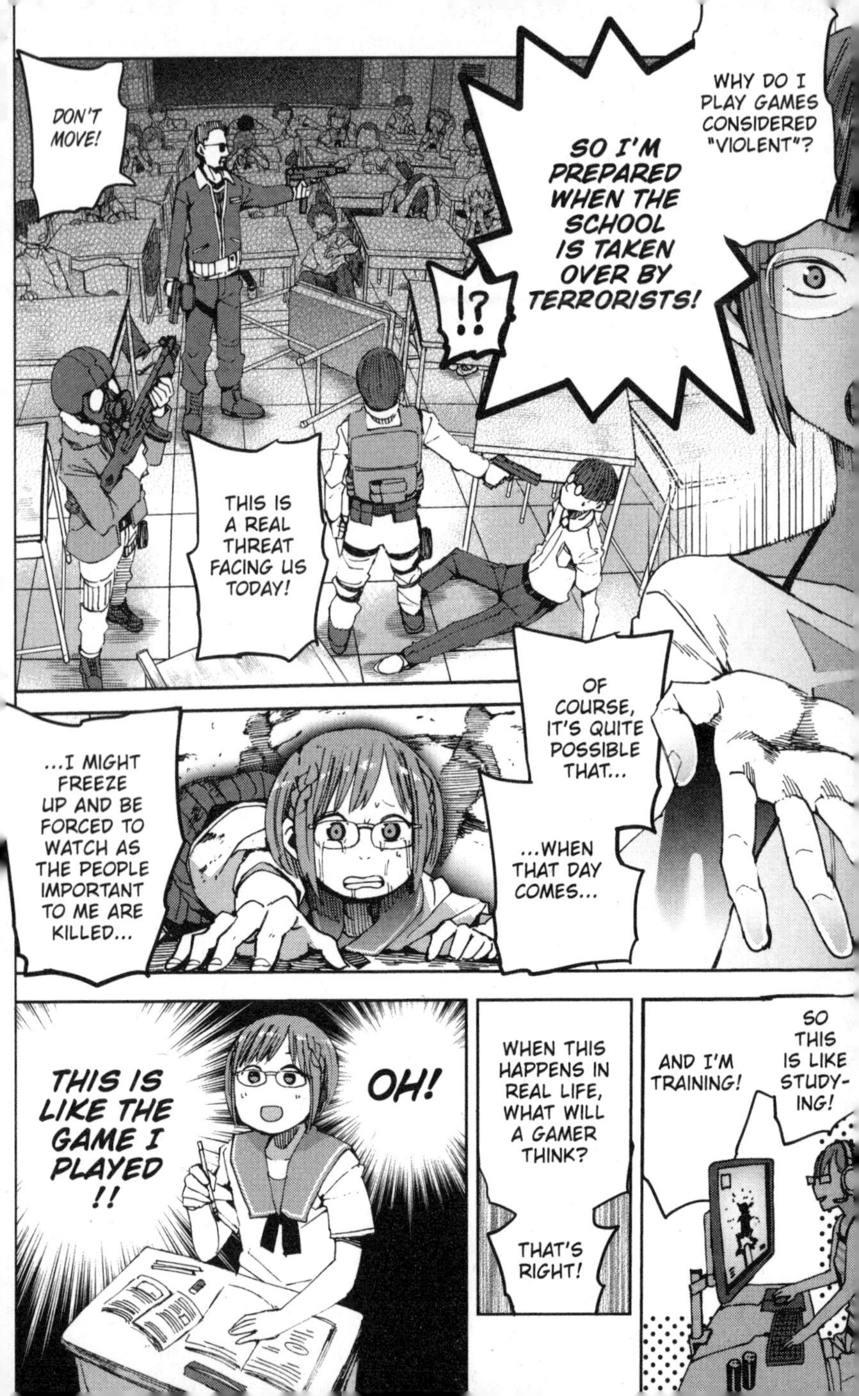
WHY DO I PLAY GAMES CONSIDERED "VIOLENT"?
SO I'M PREPARED WHEN THE SCHOOL IS TAKEN OVER BY TERRORISTS!
!?
DON'T MOVE!
THIS IS A REAL THREAT FACING US TODAY!
OF COURSE, IT'S QUITE POSSIBLE THAT...
...WHEN THAT DAY COMES...
...I MIGHT FREEZE UP AND BE FORCED TO WATCH AS THE PEOPLE IMPORTANT TO ME ARE KILLED...
SO THIS IS LIKE STUDYING!
AND I'M TRAINING!
WHEN THIS HAPPENS IN REAL LIFE, WHAT WILL A GAMER THINK?
THAT'S RIGHT!
OH!
THIS IS LIKE THE GAME I PLAYED!!

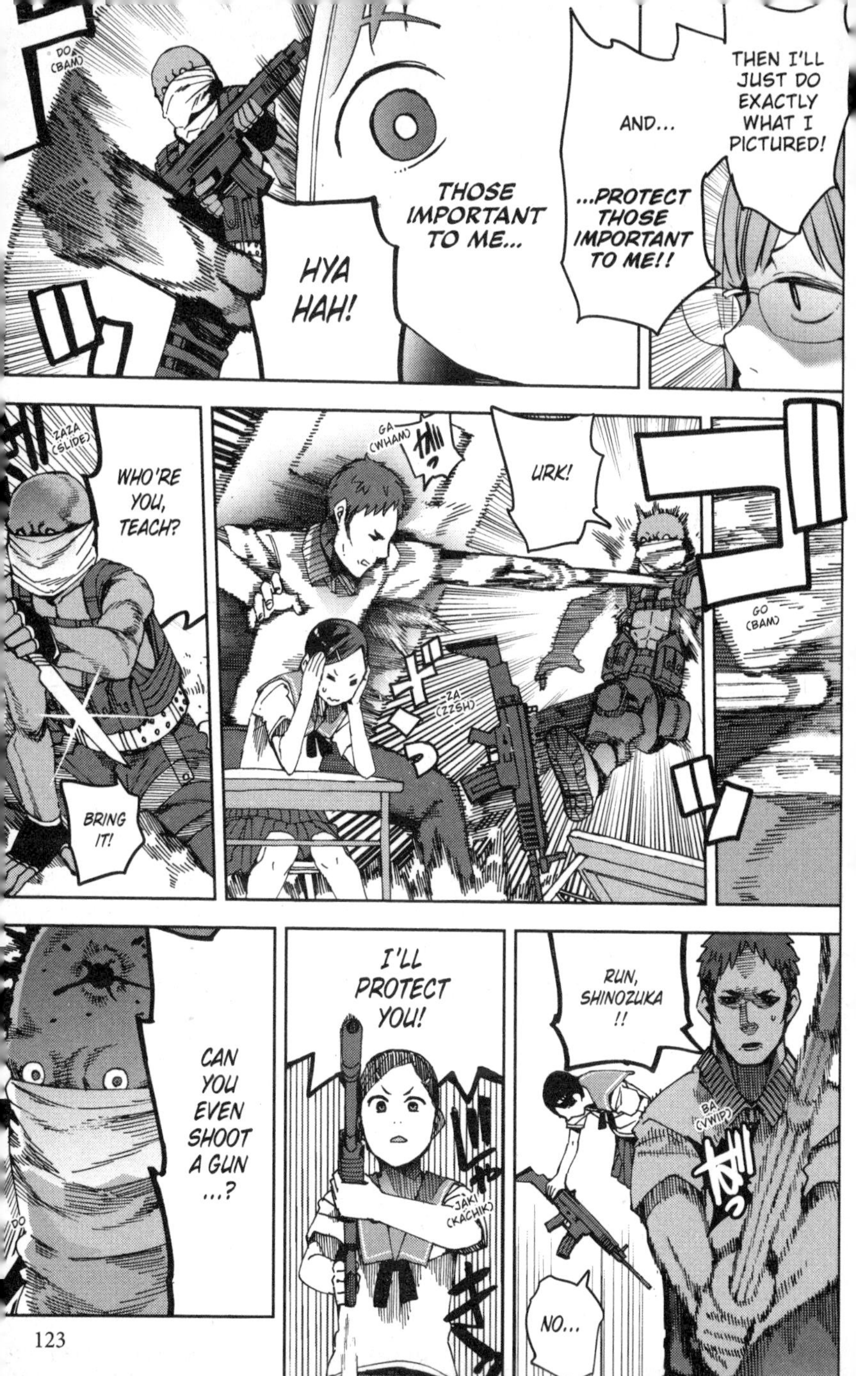
THEN I'LL JUST DO EXACTLY WHAT I PICTURED!
AND...
...PROTECT THOSE IMPORTANT TO ME!!
THOSE IMPORTANT TO ME...
DO (BAM)
HYA HAH!
GO (BAM)
URK!
GA (WHAM)
ZA (ZZSH)
ZAZA (SLIDE)
WHO'RE YOU, TEACH?
BRING IT!
RUN, SHINOZUKA!!
BA (VWIP)
NO...
I'LL PROTECT YOU!
JAKI (KACHIK)
CAN YOU EVEN SHOOT A GUN...?
DO

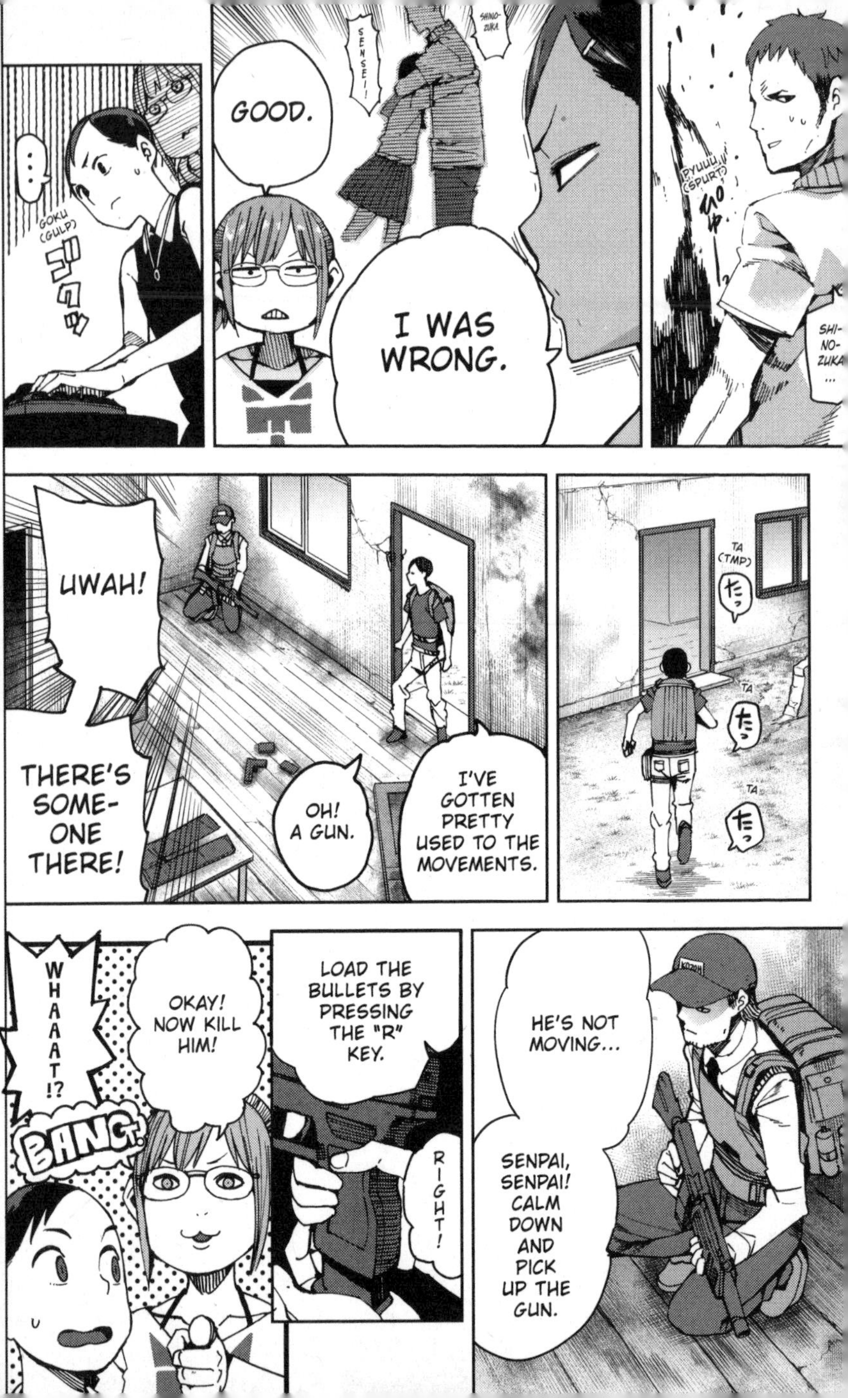
PYUUU (SPURT)
SHI-NO-ZUKA...
SHINO-ZUKA
SENSEI!
GOOD.
I WAS WRONG.
...
GOKU (GULP)
TA (TMP)
TA
TA
I'VE GOTTEN PRETTY USED TO THE MOVEMENTS.
OH! A GUN.
UWAH!
THERE'S SOME-ONE THERE!
HE'S NOT MOVING...
SENPAI, SENPAI! CALM DOWN AND PICK UP THE GUN.
LOAD THE BULLETS BY PRESSING THE "R" KEY.
RIGHT!
OKAY! NOW KILL HIM!
WHAAAAT!?
BANG!

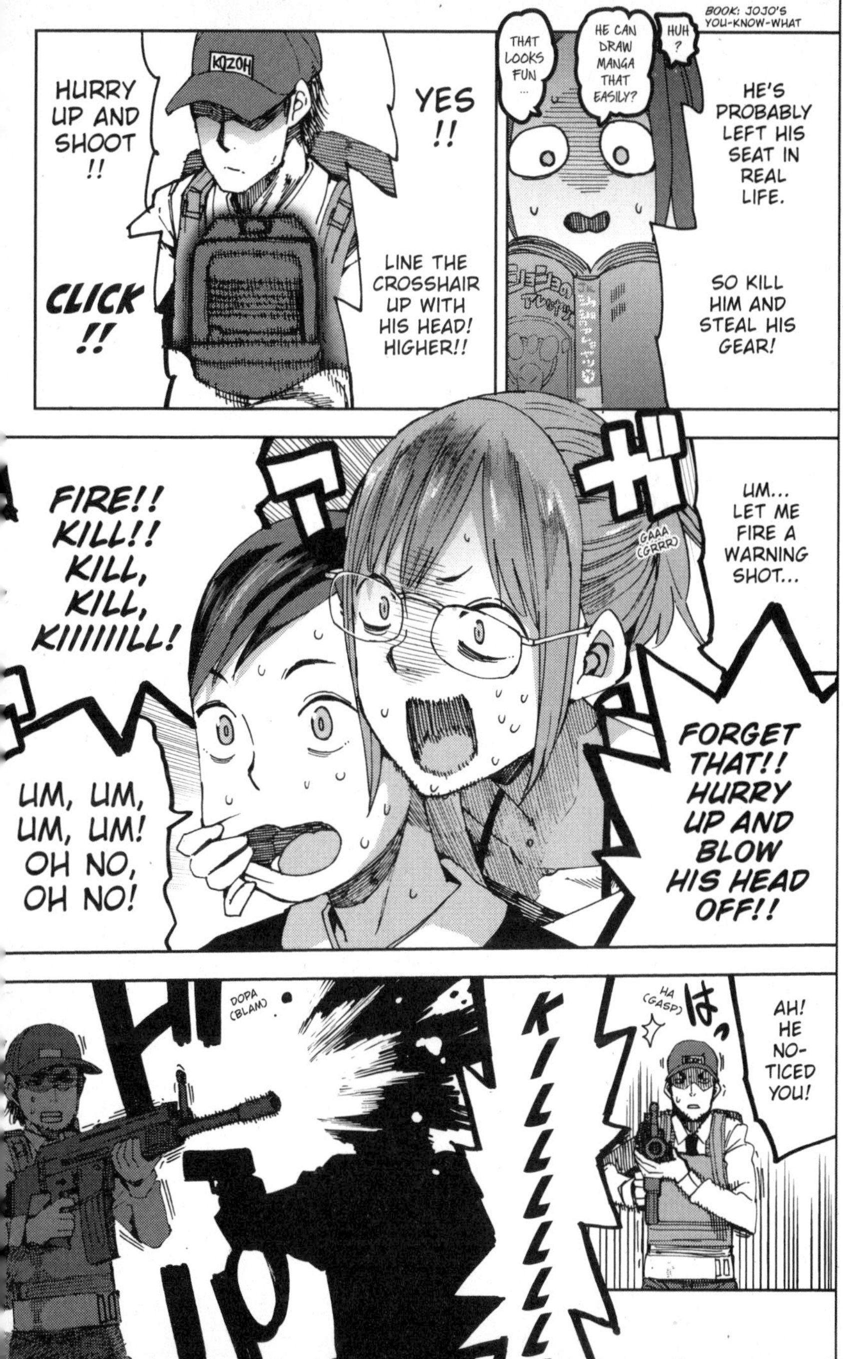
BOOK: JOJO'S YOU-KNOW-WHAT
HUH?
HE CAN DRAW MANGA THAT EASILY?
THAT LOOKS FUN...
HE'S PROBABLY LEFT HIS SEAT IN REAL LIFE.
SO KILL HIM AND STEAL HIS GEAR!
YES!!
HURRY UP AND SHOOT!!
LINE THE CROSSHAIR UP WITH HIS HEAD! HIGHER!!
CLICK!!
UM... LET ME FIRE A WARNING SHOT...
GAAA (GRRR)
FIRE!! KILL!! KILL, KILL, KIIIIIIILL!
FORGET THAT!! HURRY UP AND BLOW HIS HEAD OFF!!
UM, UM, UM, UM! OH NO, OH NO!
AH! HE NO-TICED YOU!
HA (GASP)
は
KILLLLLLLL
DOPA (BLAM)

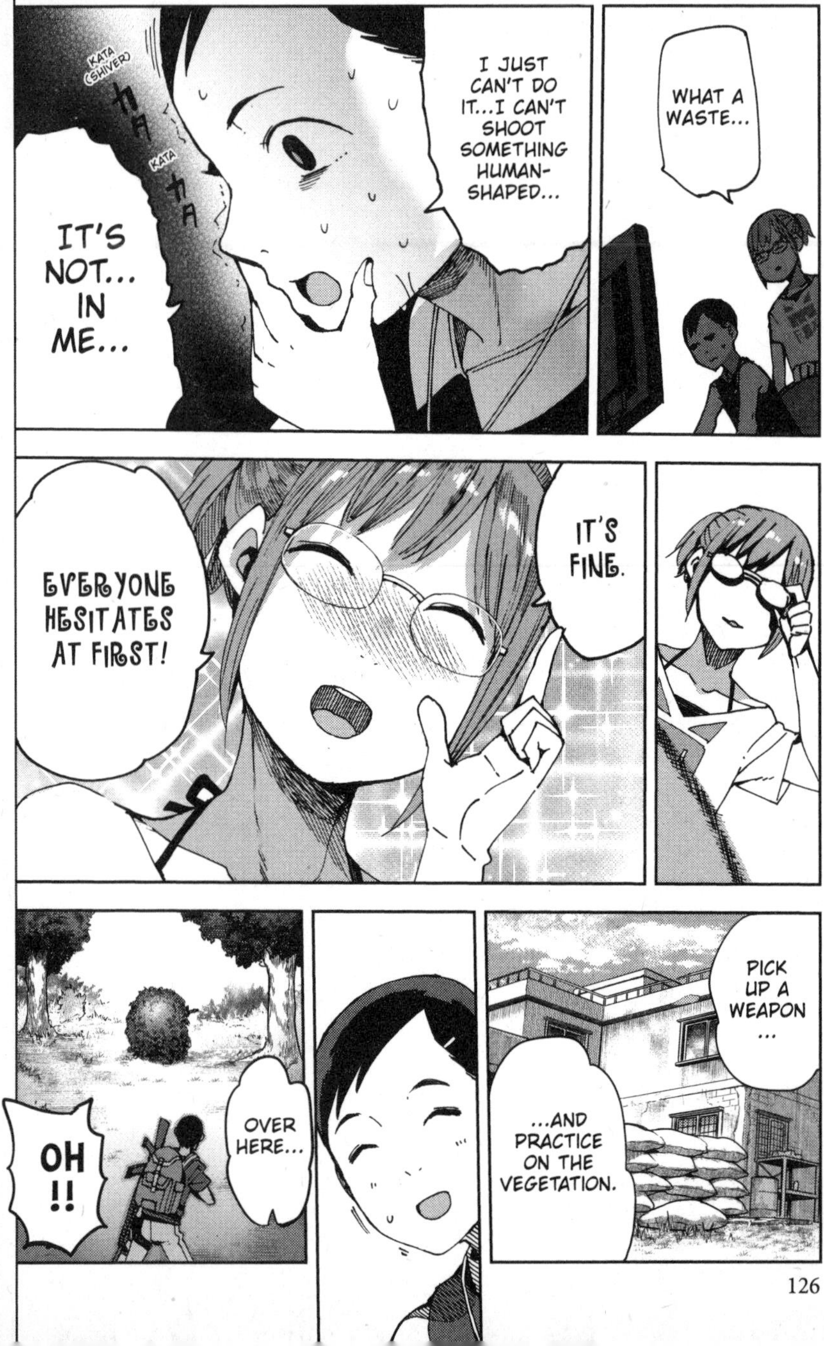
WHAT A WASTE...
I JUST CAN'T DO IT...I CAN'T SHOOT SOMETHING HUMAN-SHAPED...
KATA (SHIVER)
KATA
IT'S NOT... IN ME...
IT'S FINE.
EVERYONE HESITATES AT FIRST!
PICK UP A WEAPON ...
...AND PRACTICE ON THE VEGETATION.
OVER HERE...
OH !!

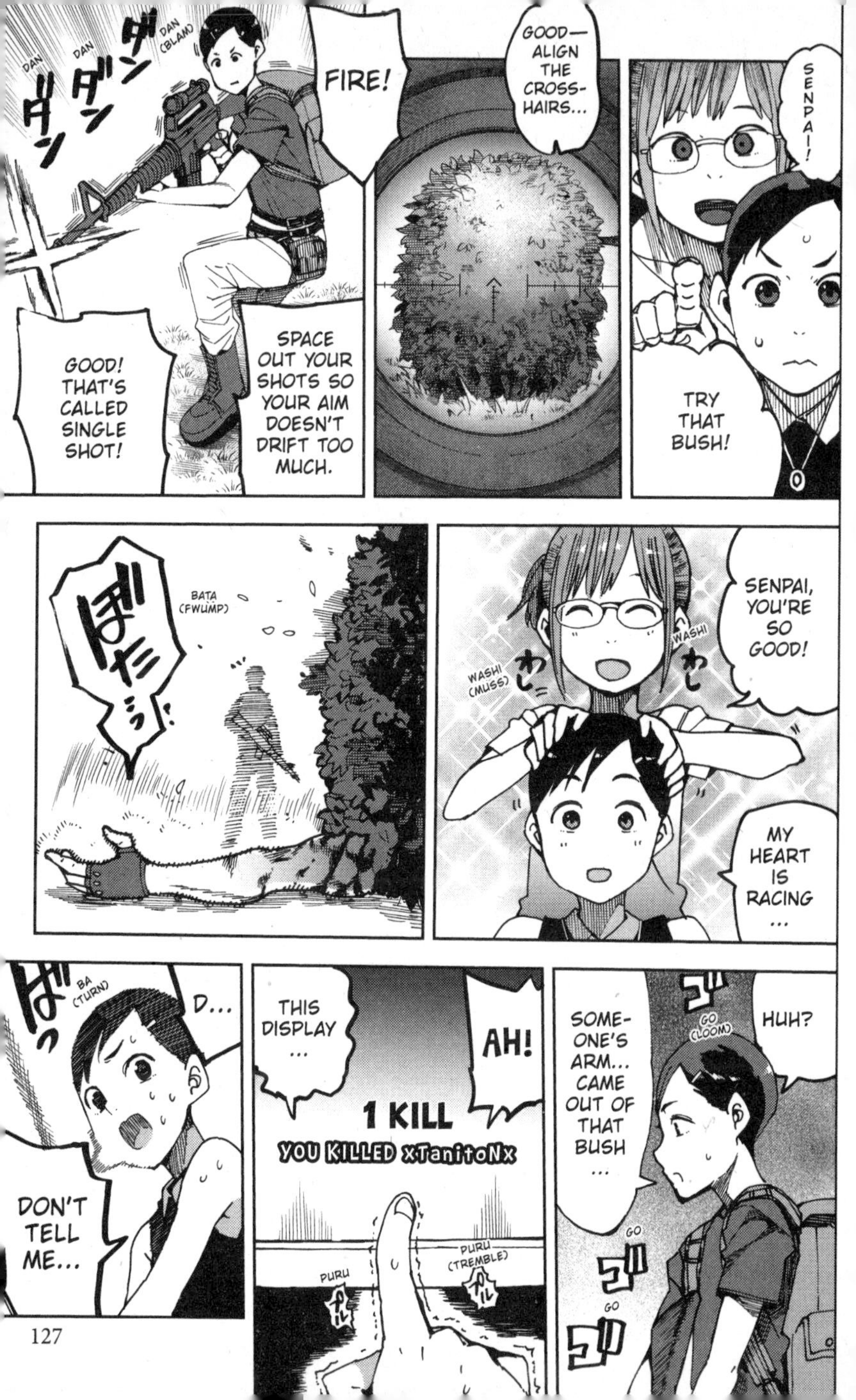
SENPAI!
TRY THAT BUSH!
GOOD—ALIGN THE CROSS-HAIRS...
FIRE!
DAN (BLAM)
DAN
DAN
SPACE OUT YOUR SHOTS SO YOUR AIM DOESN'T DRIFT TOO MUCH.
GOOD! THAT'S CALLED SINGLE SHOT!
SENPAI, YOU'RE SO GOOD!
WASHI
WASHI (MUSS)
MY HEART IS RACING...
BATA (FWUMP)
HUH?
GO (LOOM)
SOME-ONE'S ARM... CAME OUT OF THAT BUSH...
GO
GO
AH!
THIS DISPLAY...
1 KILL
YOU KILLED xTanitoNx
PURU (TREMBLE)
PURU
D...
BA (TURN)
DON'T TELL ME...

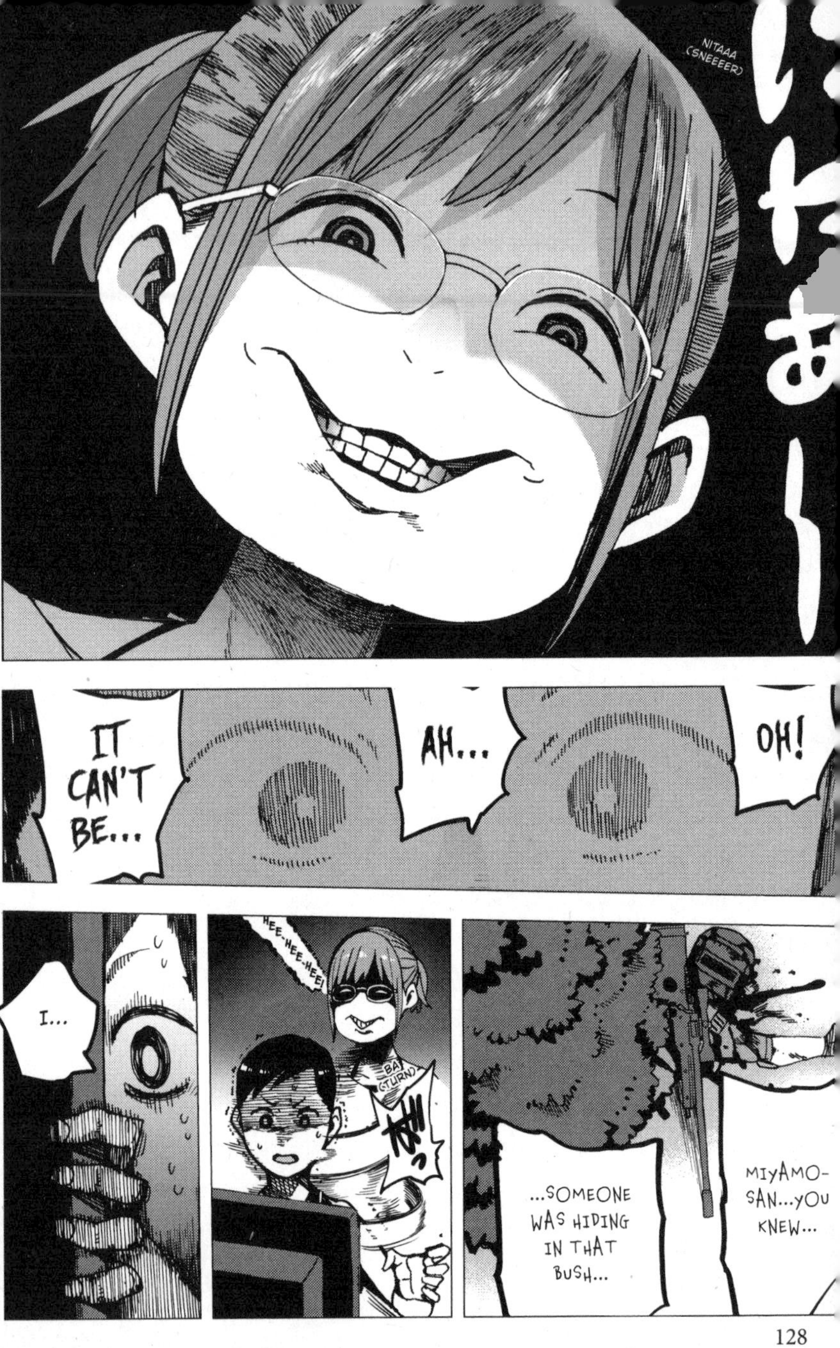
NITAAA (SNEEEER)
OH!
AH...
IT CAN'T BE...
MIYAMO-SAN...YOU KNEW...
...SOMEONE WAS HIDING IN THAT BUSH...
HEE-HEE-HEE!
BA (TURN)
I...

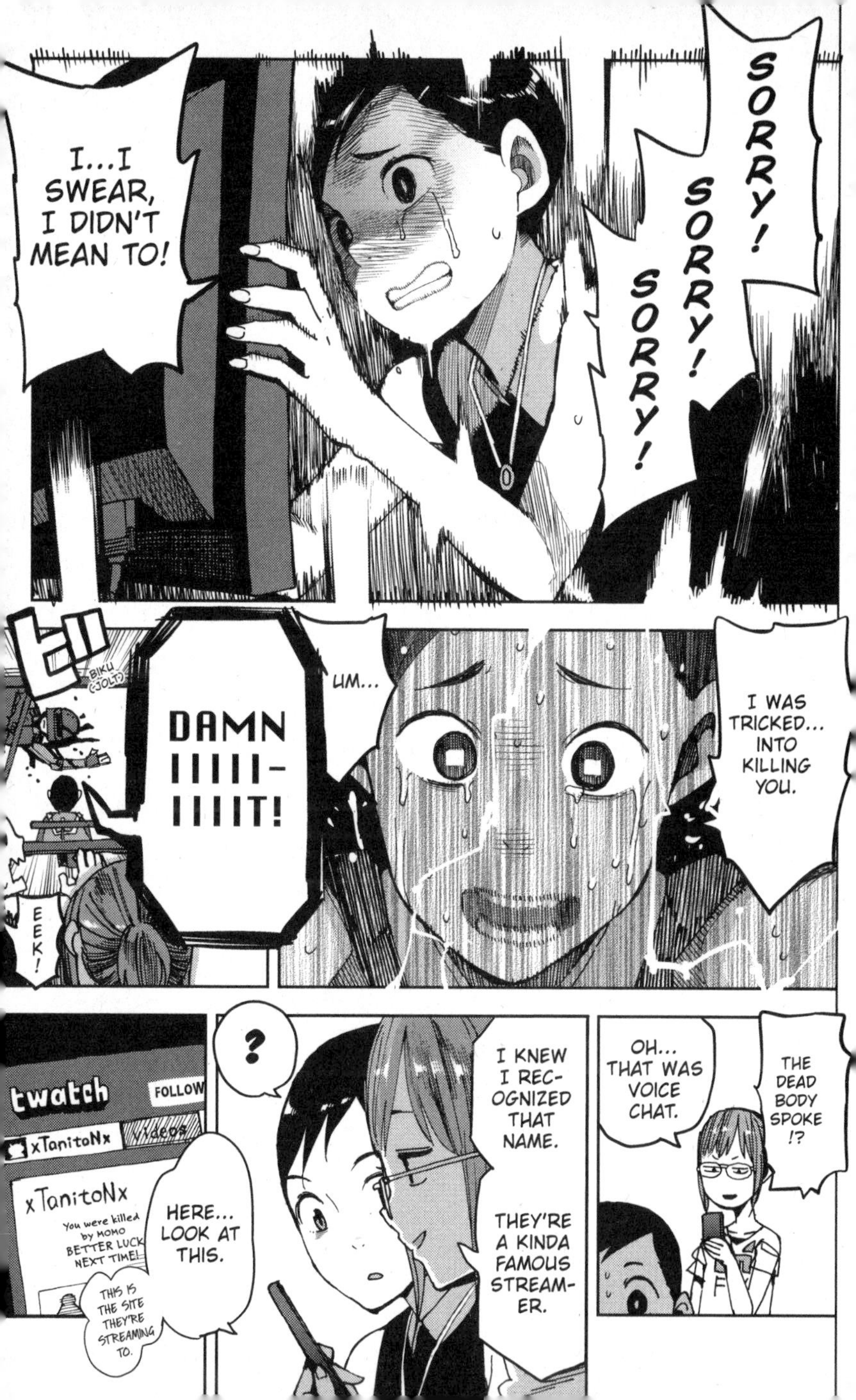
SORRY! SORRY! SORRY!
I...I SWEAR, I DIDN'T MEAN TO!
I WAS TRICKED... INTO KILLING YOU.
UM...
BIKU (JOLT)
DAMN IIIII-IIIIT!
EEK!
THE DEAD BODY SPOKE!?
OH... THAT WAS VOICE CHAT.
I KNEW I RECOGNIZED THAT NAME.
?
THEY'RE A KINDA FAMOUS STREAMER.
HERE... LOOK AT THIS.
THIS IS THE SITE THEY'RE STREAMING TO.
twatch
FOLLOW
xTanitoNx
videos
xTanitoNx
You were killed by MOMO
BETTER LUCK NEXT TIME!

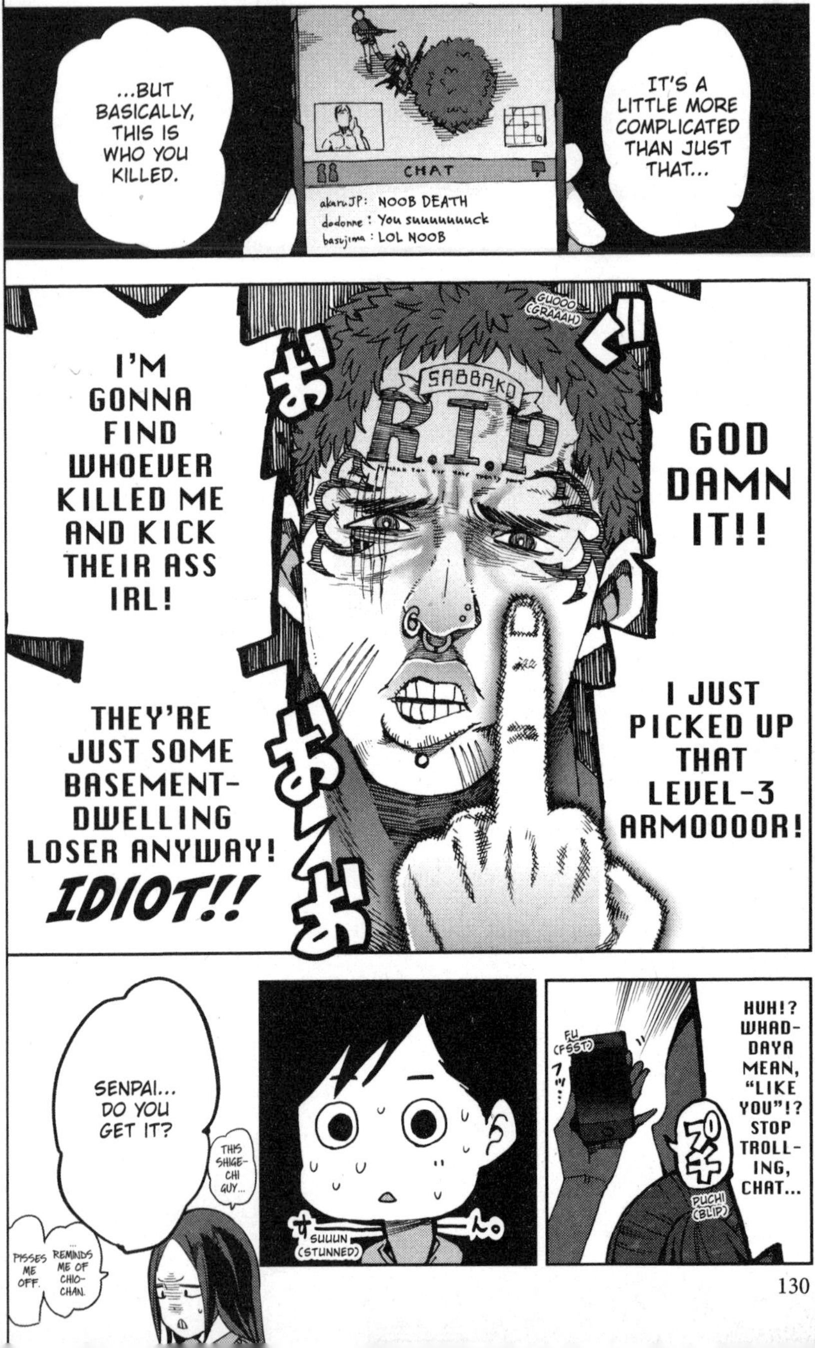
IT'S A LITTLE MORE COMPLICATED THAN JUST THAT...
CHAT
akaruJP: NOOB DEATH
dodonne: You suuuuuuuck
basujima: LOL NOOB
...BUT BASICALLY, THIS IS WHO YOU KILLED.
GUOOO (GRAAAH)
SABBAKO
R.I.P
GOD DAMN IT!!
I'M GONNA FIND WHOEVER KILLED ME AND KICK THEIR ASS IRL!
I JUST PICKED UP THAT LEVEL-3 ARMOOOOR!
THEY'RE JUST SOME BASEMENT-DWELLING LOSER ANYWAY! IDIOT!!
HUH!? WHADDAYA MEAN, "LIKE YOU"!? STOP TROLLING, CHAT...
FU (FSST)
PUCHI (BLIP)
SUUUN (STUNNED)
SENPAI... DO YOU GET IT?
THIS SHIGE-CHI GUY...
...REMINDS ME OF CHIO-CHAN.
PISSES ME OFF.

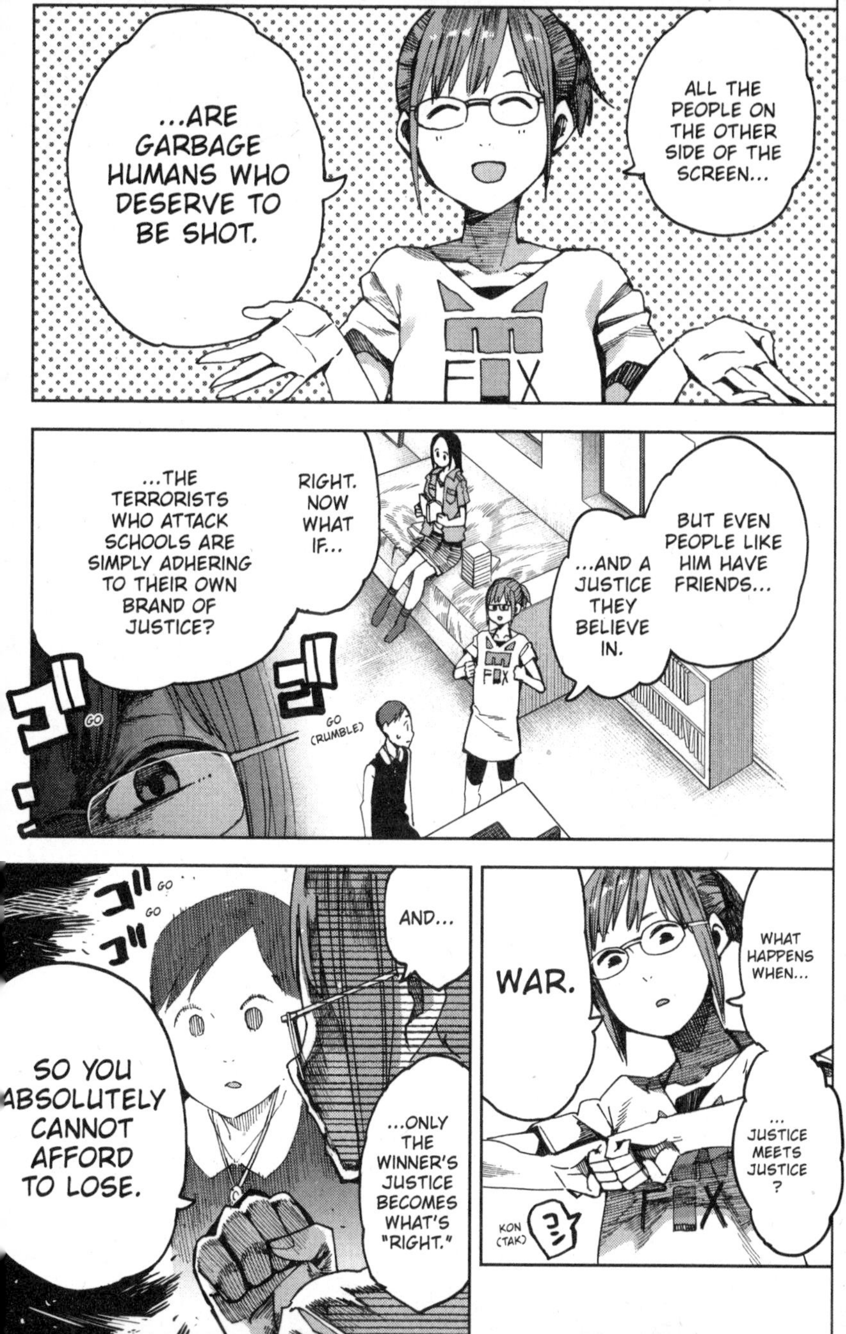
ALL THE PEOPLE ON THE OTHER SIDE OF THE SCREEN...
...ARE GARBAGE HUMANS WHO DESERVE TO BE SHOT.
BUT EVEN PEOPLE LIKE HIM HAVE FRIENDS...
...AND A JUSTICE THEY BELIEVE IN.
RIGHT. NOW WHAT IF...
...THE TERRORISTS WHO ATTACK SCHOOLS ARE SIMPLY ADHERING TO THEIR OWN BRAND OF JUSTICE?
GO
GO (RUMBLE)
WHAT HAPPENS WHEN...
...JUSTICE MEETS JUSTICE?
WAR.
KON (TAK)
AND...
...ONLY THE WINNER'S JUSTICE BECOMES WHAT'S "RIGHT."
GO
GO
SO YOU ABSOLUTELY CANNOT AFFORD TO LOSE.

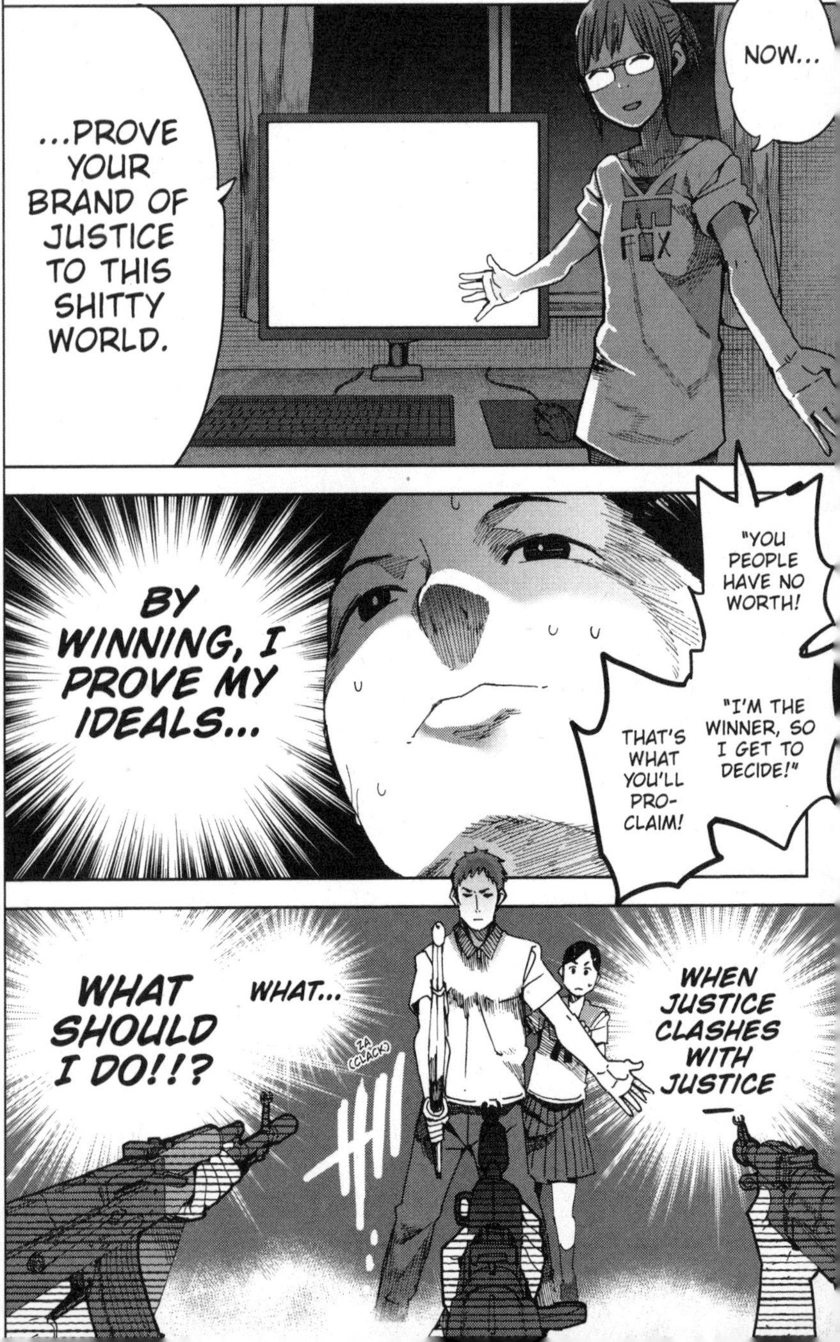
NOW...
...PROVE YOUR BRAND OF JUSTICE TO THIS SHITTY WORLD.
"YOU PEOPLE HAVE NO WORTH!
"I'M THE WINNER, SO I GET TO DECIDE!"
THAT'S WHAT YOU'LL PRO-CLAIM!
BY WINNING, I PROVE MY IDEALS...
WHEN JUSTICE CLASHES WITH JUSTICE —
ZA (CLACK)
WHAT...
WHAT SHOULD I DO!!?

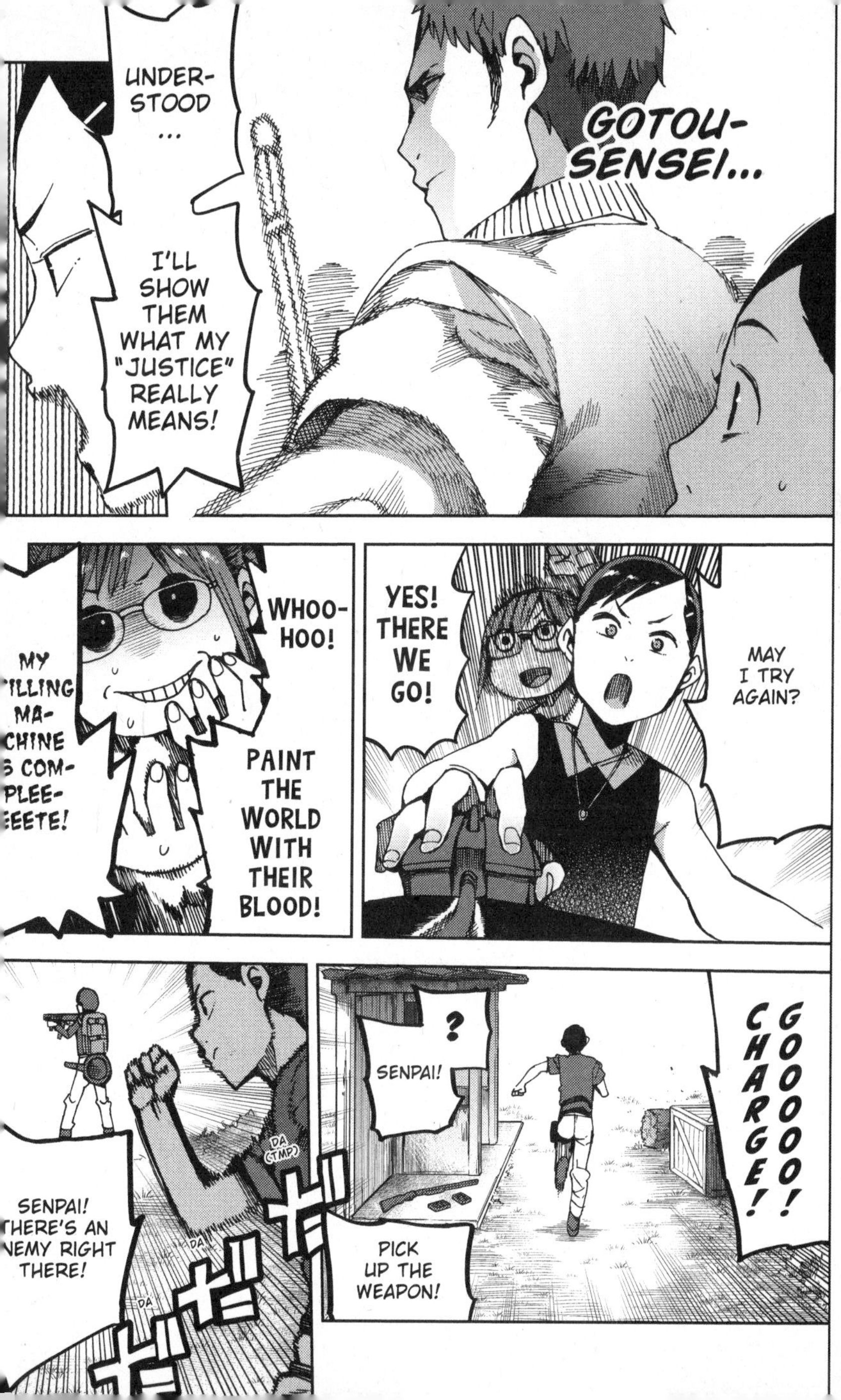
GOTOU-SENSEI...
UNDERSTOOD...
I'LL SHOW THEM WHAT MY "JUSTICE" REALLY MEANS!
MAY I TRY AGAIN?
YES! THERE WE GO!
WHOO-HOO!
PAINT THE WORLD WITH THEIR BLOOD!
MY ILLING MACHINE S COMPLEEEETE!
GOOOOOO!
CHARGE!
?
SENPAI!
PICK UP THE WEAPON!
DA (TMP)
DA
DA
SENPAI! HERE'S AN NEMY RIGHT THERE!

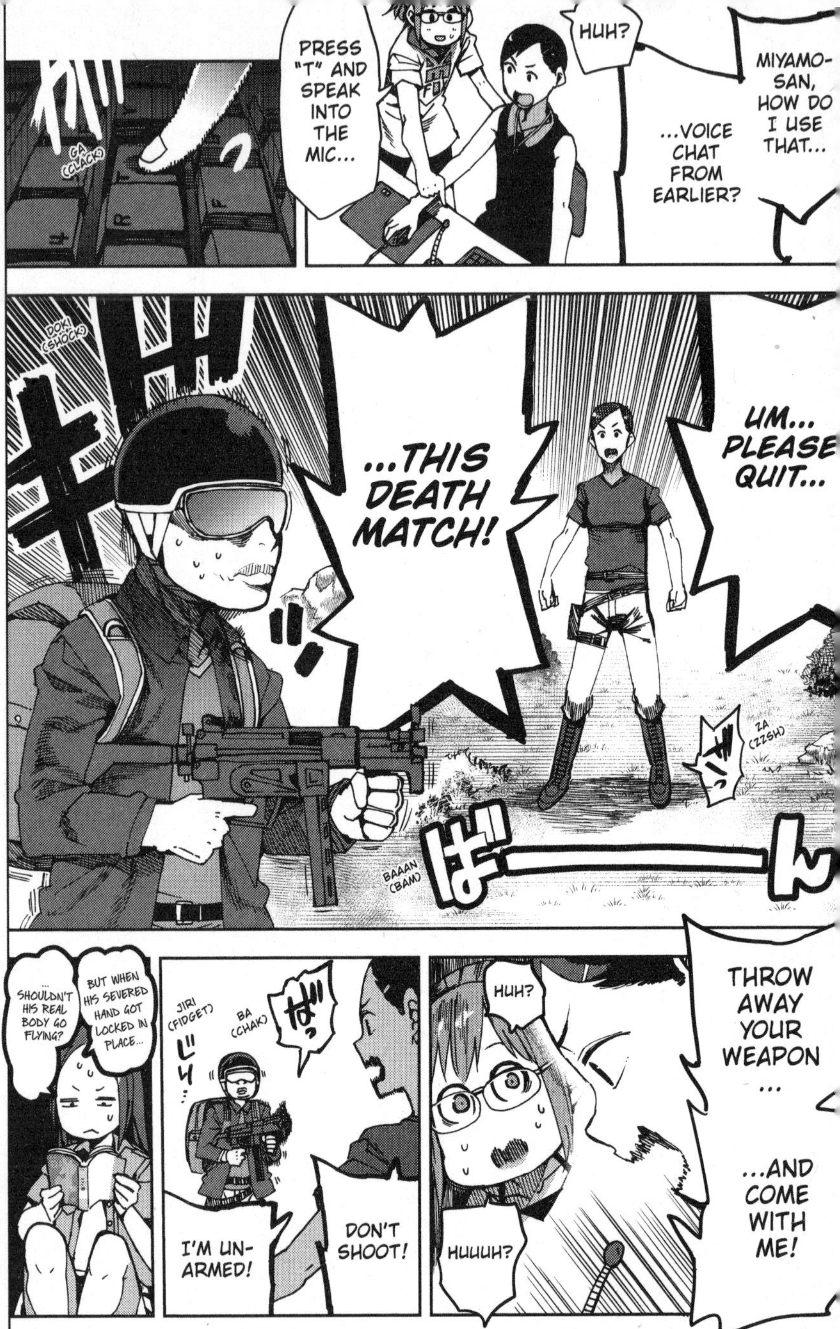
MIYAMO-SAN, HOW DO I USE THAT...
...VOICE CHAT FROM EARLIER?
HUH?
PRESS "T" AND SPEAK INTO THE MIC...
GA (CLACK)
UM... PLEASE QUIT...
...THIS DEATH MATCH!
DOKI (SHOCK)
ZA (ZZSH)
BAAAN (BAM)
THROW AWAY YOUR WEAPON...
...AND COME WITH ME!
HUH?
HUUUH?
BA (CHAK)
JIRI (FIDGET)
DON'T SHOOT!
I'M UN-ARMED!
BUT WHEN HIS SEVERED HAND GOT LOCKED IN PLACE...
...SHOULDN'T HIS REAL BODY GO FLYING?

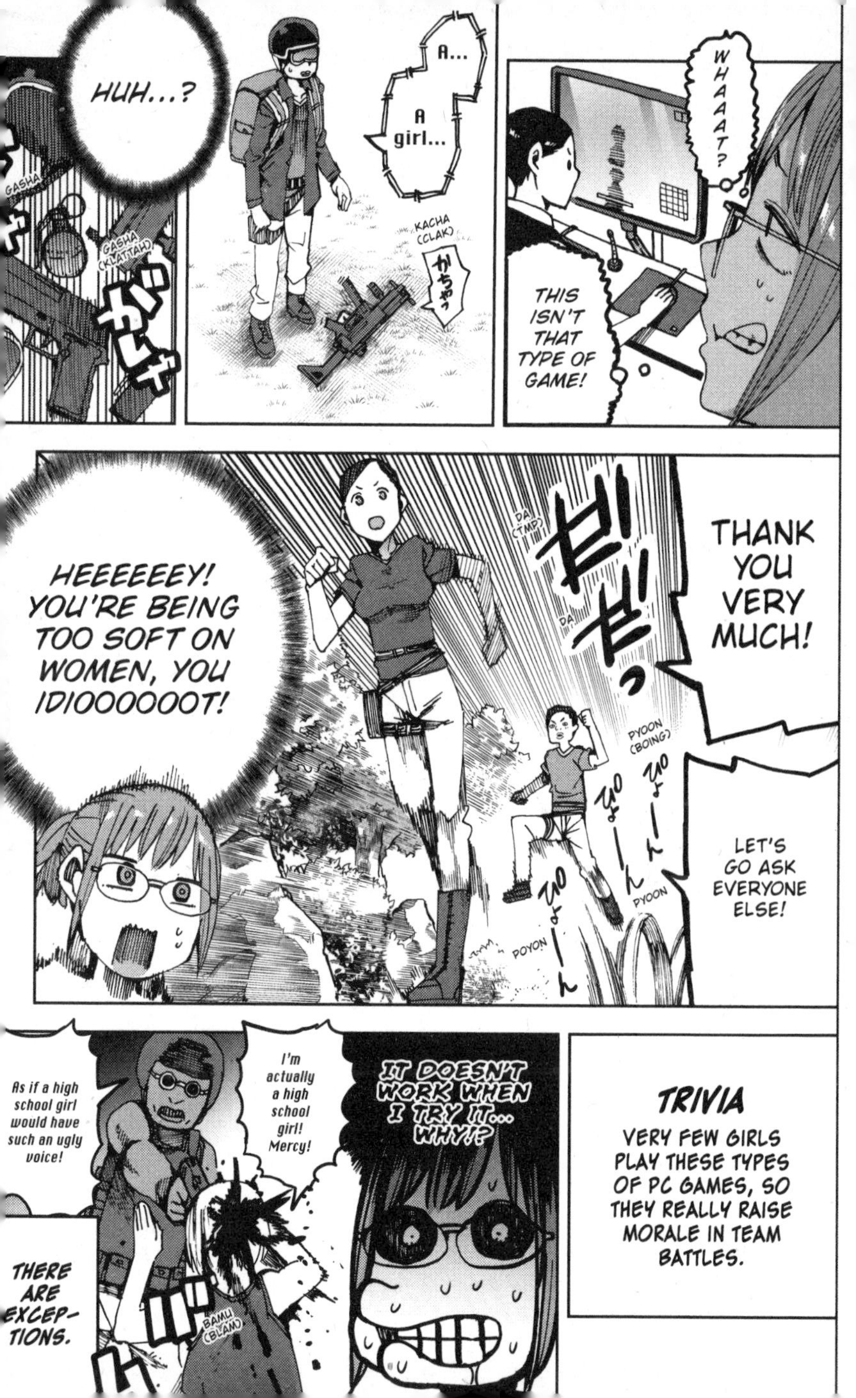
WHAAAAT?
THIS ISN'T THAT TYPE OF GAME!
A...
A girl...
KACHA (CLAK)
かちゃっ
HUH...?
GASHA
GASHA (KLATTAH)
THANK YOU VERY MUCH!
DA (TMP)
DA
だだっ
HEEEEEEY! YOU'RE BEING TOO SOFT ON WOMEN, YOU IDIOOOOOOT!
LET'S GO ASK EVERYONE ELSE!
PYOON (BOING)
PYOON
POYON
TRIVIA
VERY FEW GIRLS PLAY THESE TYPES OF PC GAMES, SO THEY REALLY RAISE MORALE IN TEAM BATTLES.
IT DOESN'T WORK WHEN I TRY IT... WHY!?
I'm actually a high school girl! Mercy!
As if a high school girl would have such an ugly voice!
BAMU (BLAM)
THERE ARE EXCEPTIONS.

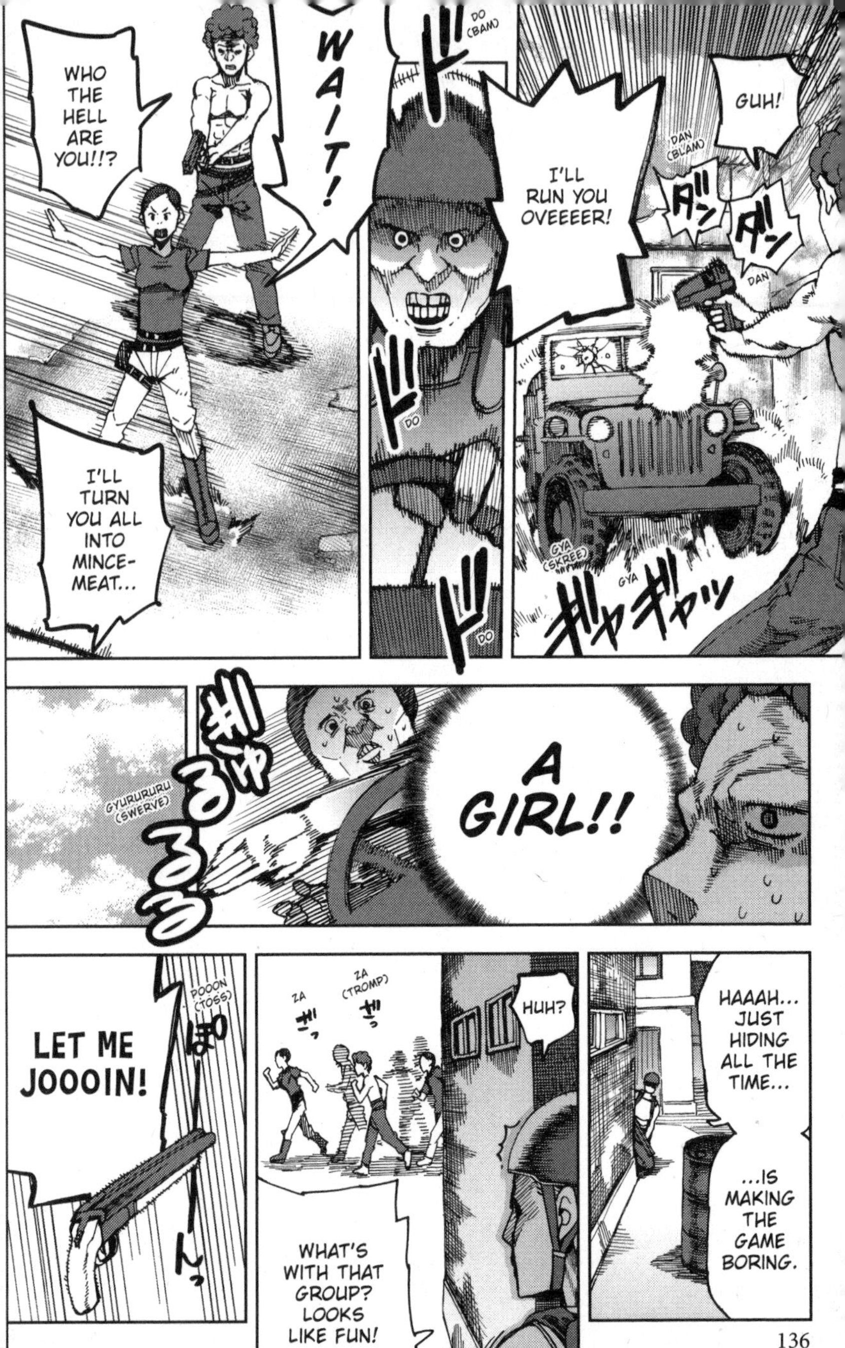
GUH!
DAN (BLAM)
DAN
GYA (SKREE)
GYA
WAIT!
DO (BAM)
I'LL RUN YOU OVEEEER!
DO
DO
WHO THE HELL ARE YOU!!?
I'LL TURN YOU ALL INTO MINCE-MEAT...
A GIRL!!
GYURURURU (SWERVE)
HAAAH... JUST HIDING ALL THE TIME...
...IS MAKING THE GAME BORING.
HUH?
ZA (TROMP)
ZA
WHAT'S WITH THAT GROUP? LOOKS LIKE FUN!
POOON (TOSS)
LET ME JOOOIN!

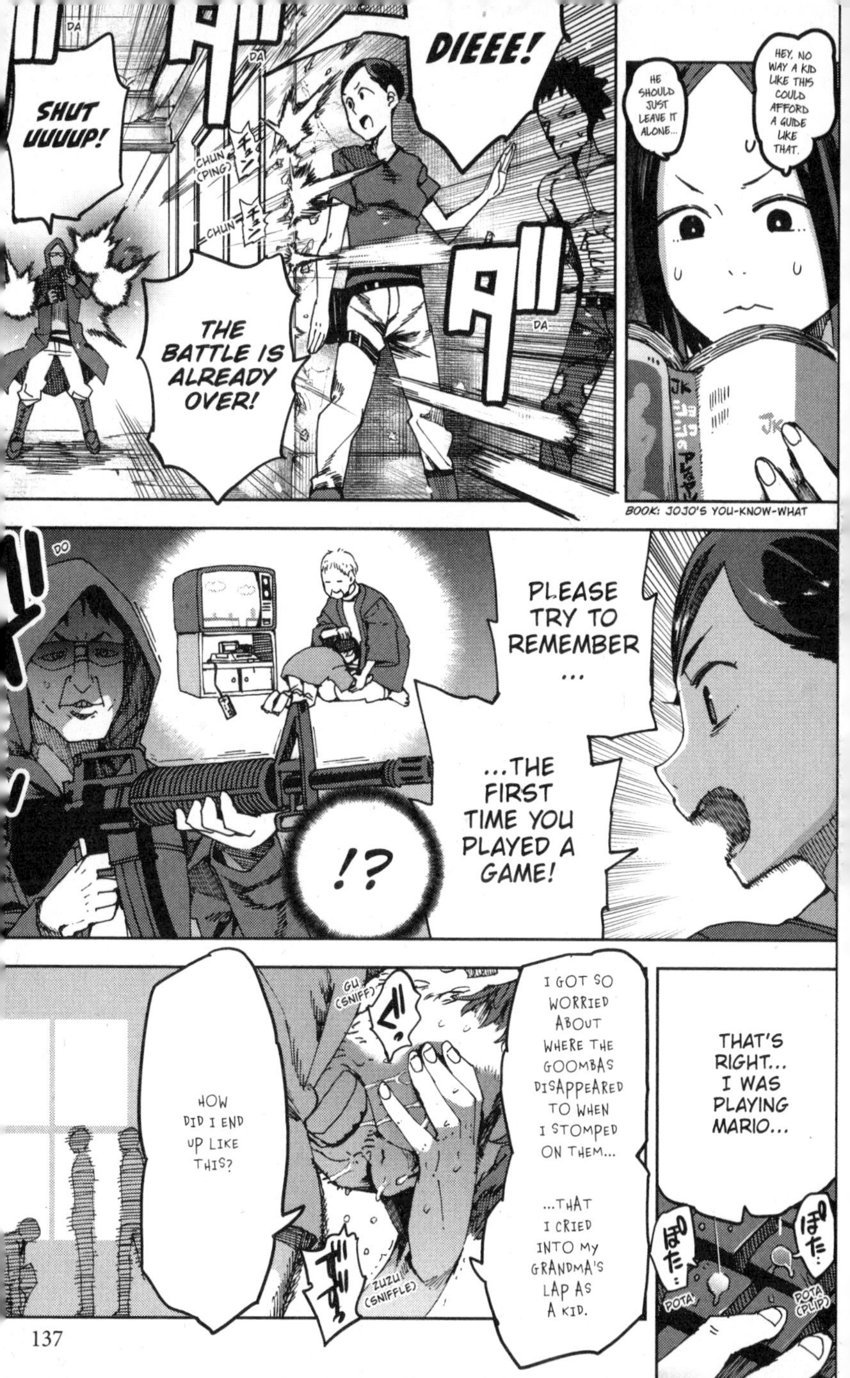
HEY, NO WAY A KID LIKE THIS COULD AFFORD A GUIDE LIKE THAT.
HE SHOULD JUST LEAVE IT ALONE...
BOOK: JOJO'S YOU-KNOW-WHAT
DIEEE!
DA
DA
SHUT UUUUP!
CHUN (PING)
CHUN
DA
THE BATTLE IS ALREADY OVER!
PLEASE TRY TO REMEMBER...
...THE FIRST TIME YOU PLAYED A GAME!
DO
!?
THAT'S RIGHT... I WAS PLAYING MARIO...
POTA (PLIP)
POTA
I GOT SO WORRIED ABOUT WHERE THE GOOMBAS DISAPPEARED TO WHEN I STOMPED ON THEM...
...THAT I CRIED INTO MY GRANDMA'S LAP AS A KID.
GU (SNIFF)
ZUZU (SNIFFLE)
HOW DID I END UP LIKE THIS?

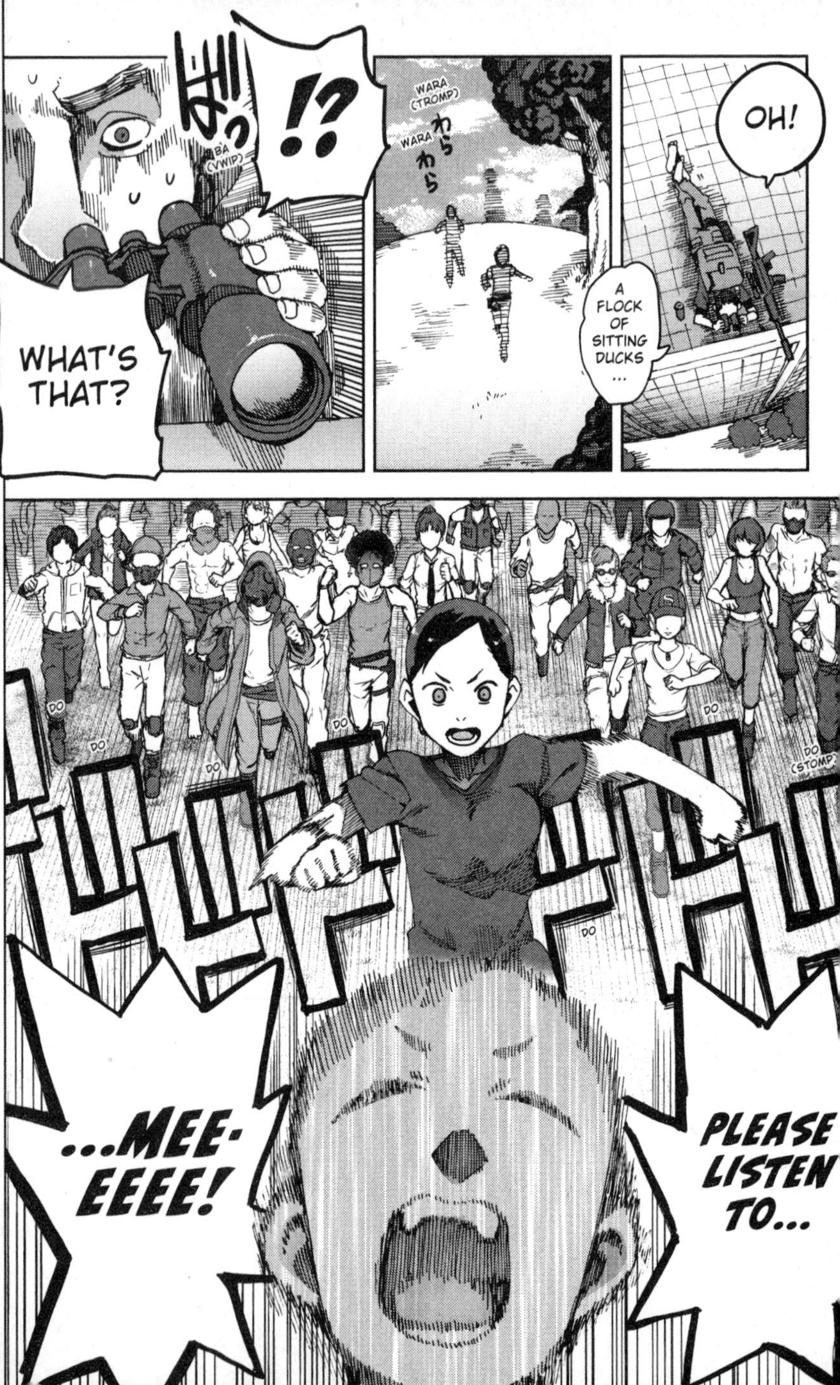
OH!
A FLOCK OF SITTING DUCKS...
WARA (TROMP)
わら
WARA
わら
ぱっ
BA (VWIP)
!?
WHAT'S THAT?
DO (STOMP)
DO
DO
DO
DO
DO
DO
PLEASE LISTEN TO...
...MEE-EEEE!

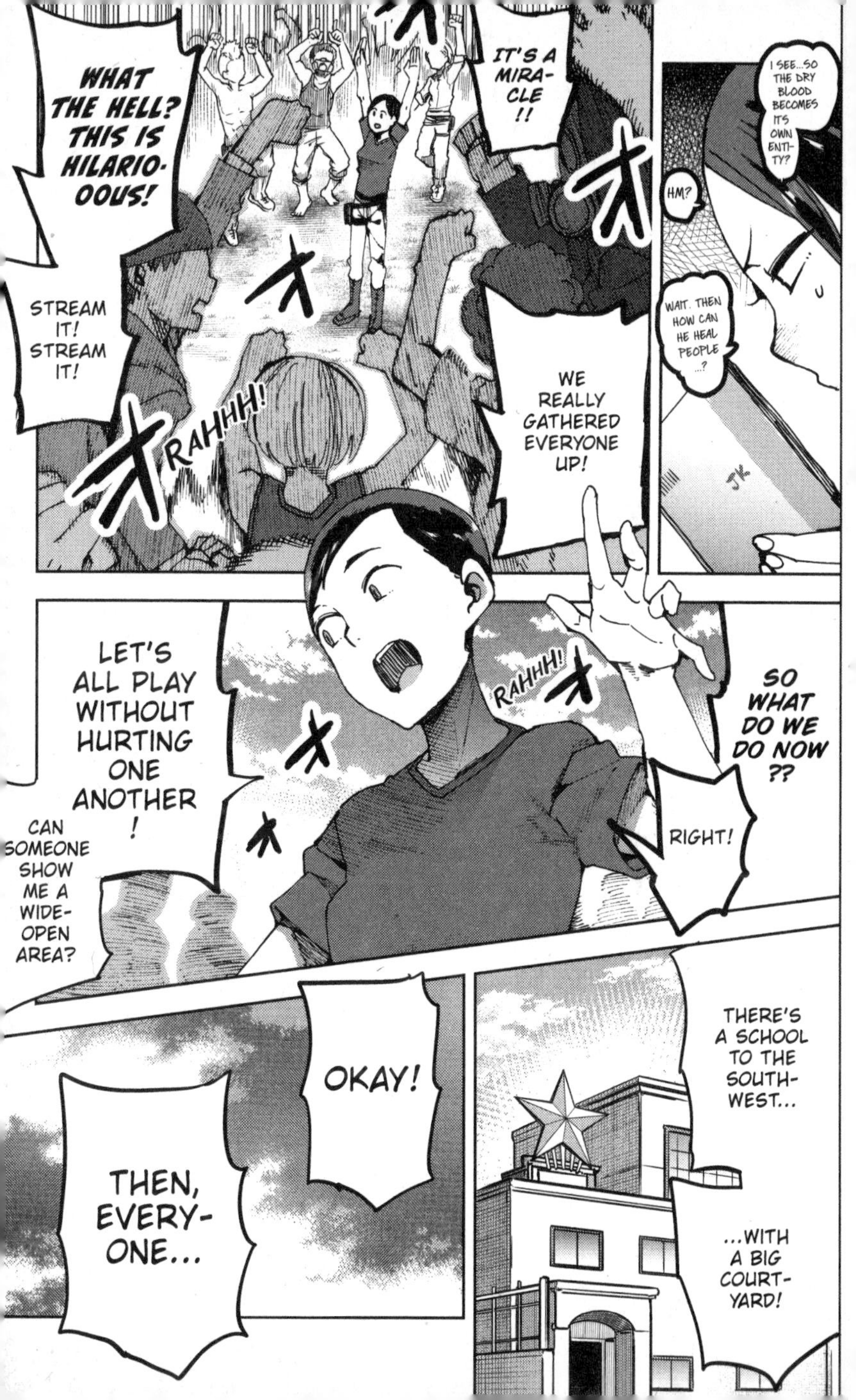
I SEE...SO THE DRY BLOOD BECOMES ITS OWN ENTITY?
HM?
WAIT. THEN HOW CAN HE HEAL PEOPLE...?
IT'S A MIRACLE!!
WHAT THE HELL? THIS IS HILARIOOOUS!
WE REALLY GATHERED EVERYONE UP!
STREAM IT! STREAM IT!
RAHHH!
SO WHAT DO WE DO NOW??
RIGHT!
RAHHH!
LET'S ALL PLAY WITHOUT HURTING ONE ANOTHER!
CAN SOMEONE SHOW ME A WIDE-OPEN AREA?
THERE'S A SCHOOL TO THE SOUTHWEST...
...WITH A BIG COURTYARD!
OKAY!
THEN, EVERYONE...

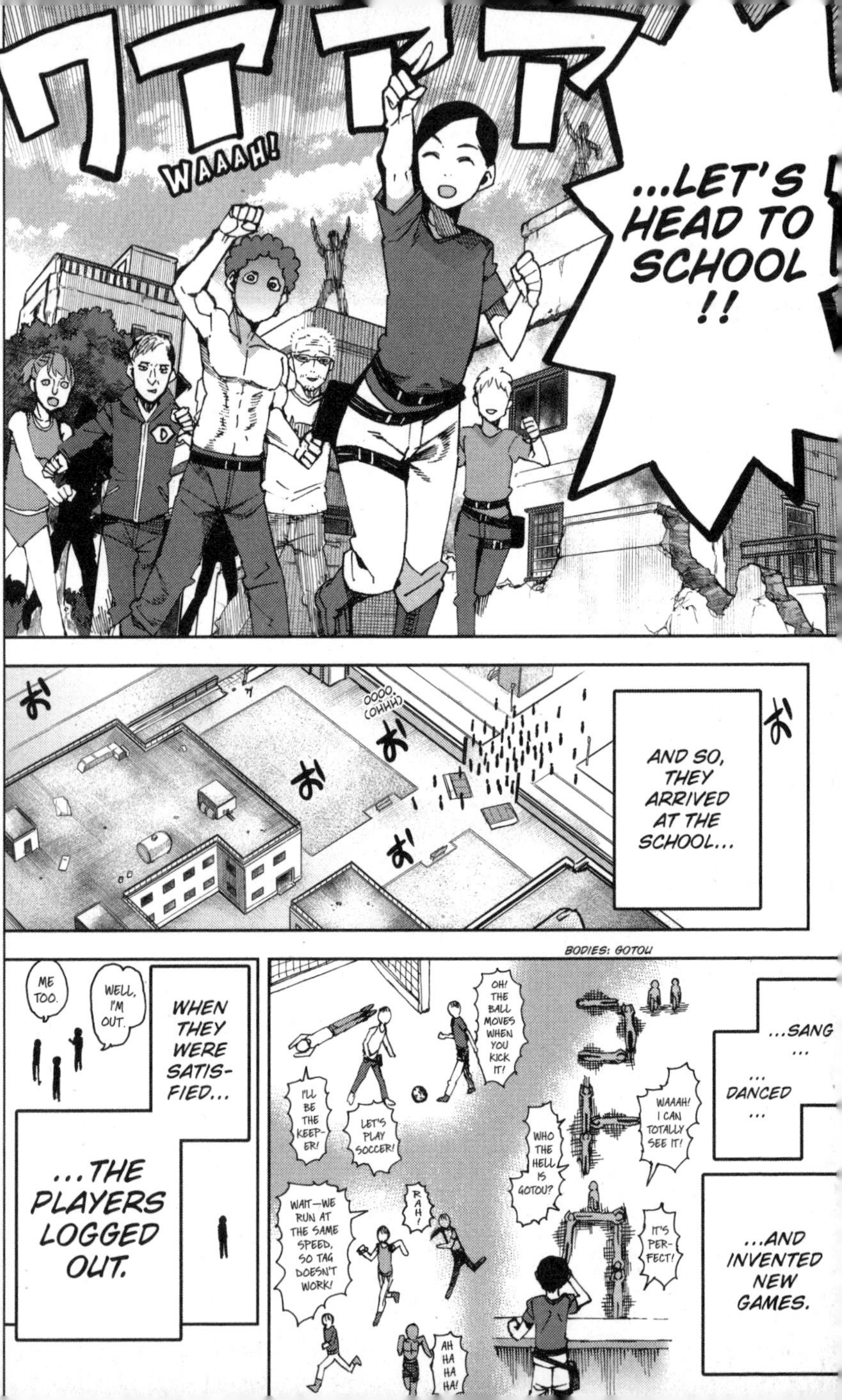
...LET'S HEAD TO SCHOOL!!
ワアアア
WAAAH!
AND SO, THEY ARRIVED AT THE SCHOOL...
お
お
お
お
お
OOOO (OHHH)
BODIES: GOTOU
...SANG...
...DANCED...
...AND INVENTED NEW GAMES.
WAAAH! I CAN TOTALLY SEE IT!
IT'S PERFECT!
WHO THE HELL IS GOTOU?
OH! THE BALL MOVES WHEN YOU KICK IT!
LET'S PLAY SOCCER!
I'LL BE THE KEEPER!
RAH!
WAIT—WE RUN AT THE SAME SPEED, SO TAG DOESN'T WORK!
AH HA HA HA!
WHEN THEY WERE SATIS-FIED...
WELL, I'M OUT.
ME TOO.
...THE PLAYERS LOGGED OUT.

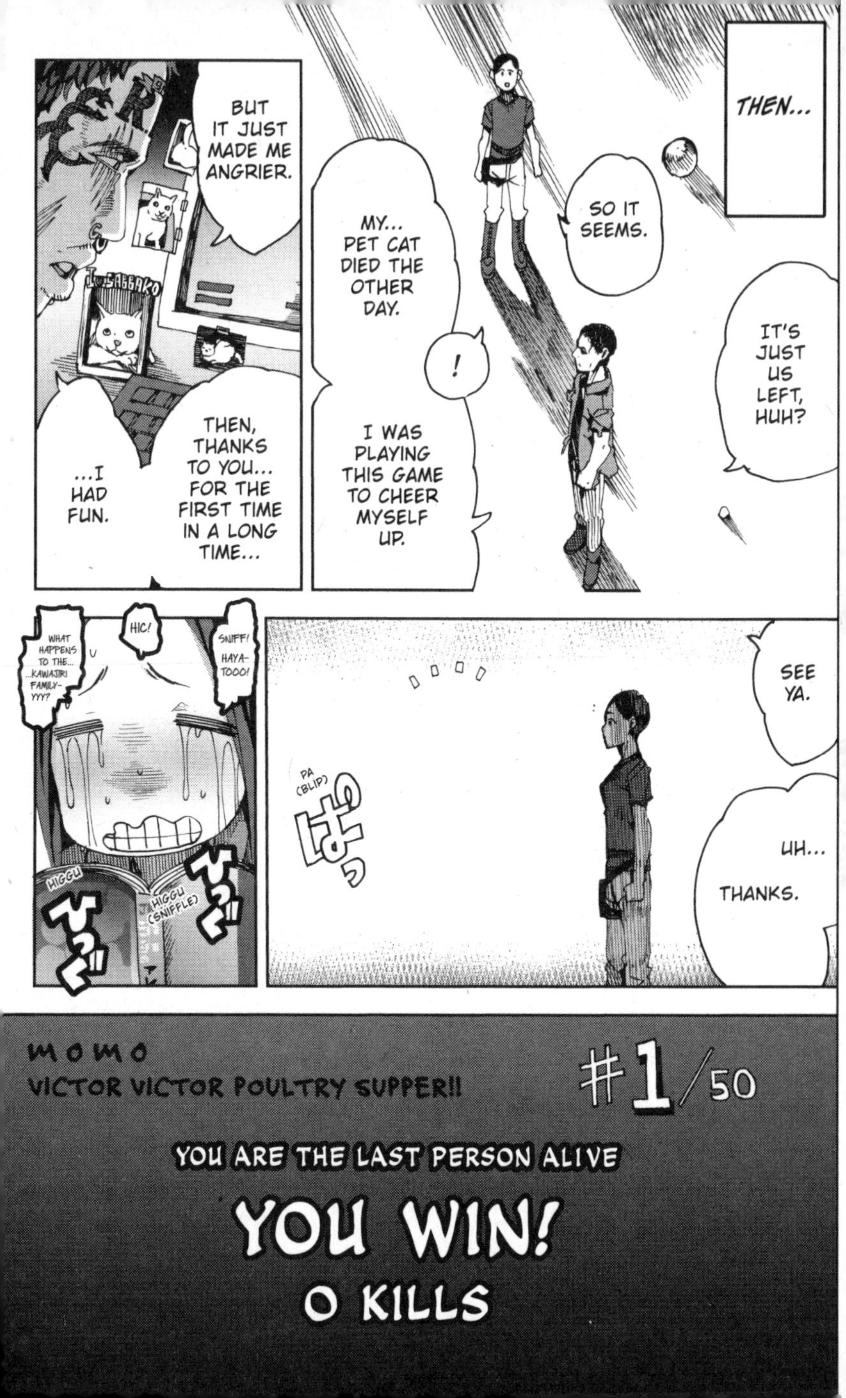
THEN...
IT'S JUST US LEFT, HUH?
SO IT SEEMS.
MY... PET CAT DIED THE OTHER DAY.
!
I WAS PLAYING THIS GAME TO CHEER MYSELF UP.
BUT IT JUST MADE ME ANGRIER.
THEN, THANKS TO YOU... FOR THE FIRST TIME IN A LONG TIME...
...I HAD FUN.
SEE YA.
UH... THANKS.
PA (BLIP)
SNIFF! HAYA-TOOO!
HIC!
WHAT HAPPENS TO THE... ...KAWAJIRI FAMILY-YYY?
HIGGU
HIGGU (SNIFFLE)
MOMO
VICTOR VICTOR POULTRY SUPPER!!
#1/50
YOU ARE THE LAST PERSON ALIVE
YOU WIN!
0 KILLS

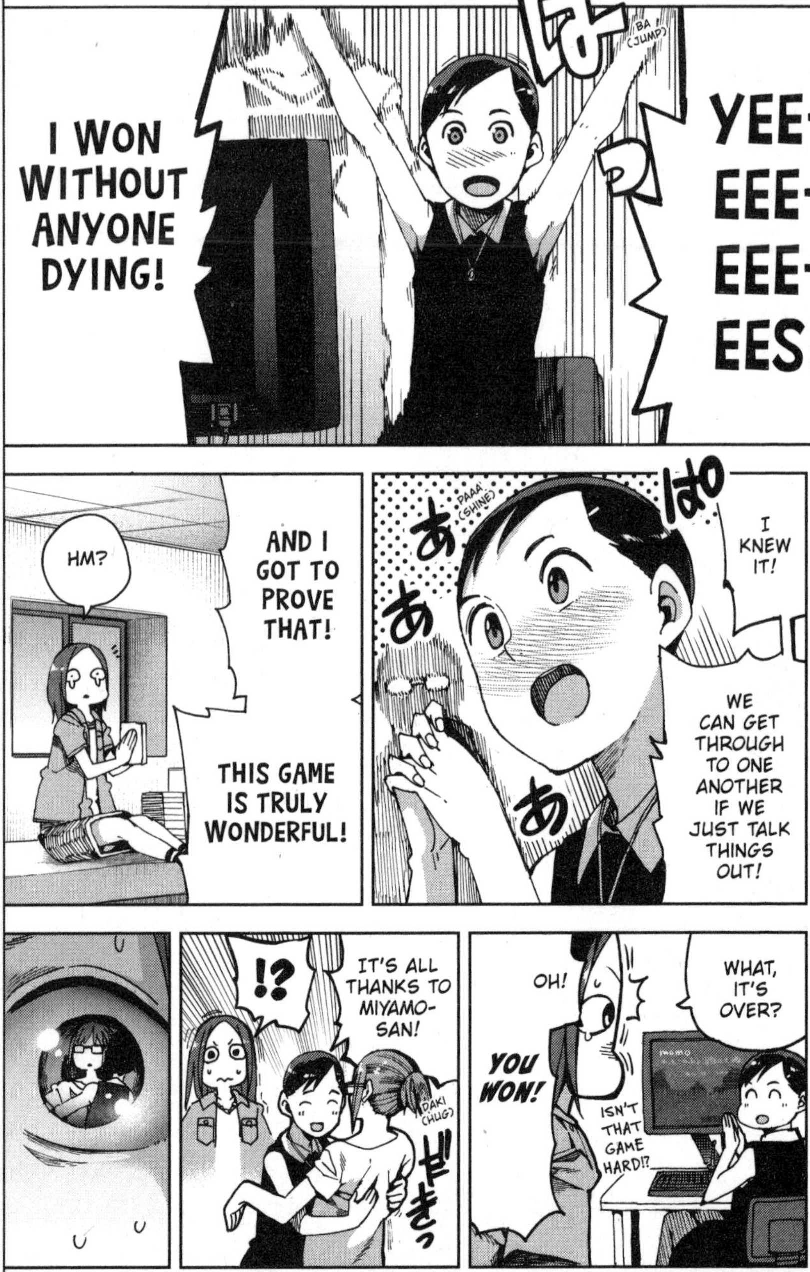
ばっ
BA (JUMP)
YEE-EEE-EEE-EES!
I WON WITHOUT ANYONE DYING!
ぱっ
PAAA (SHINE)
I KNEW IT!
WE CAN GET THROUGH TO ONE ANOTHER IF WE JUST TALK THINGS OUT!
あああ
AND I GOT TO PROVE THAT!
HM?
THIS GAME IS TRULY WONDERFUL!
WHAT, IT'S OVER?
OH!
YOU WON!
ISN'T THAT GAME HARD!?
IT'S ALL THANKS TO MIYAMO-SAN!
!?
DAKI (HUG)
だきっ

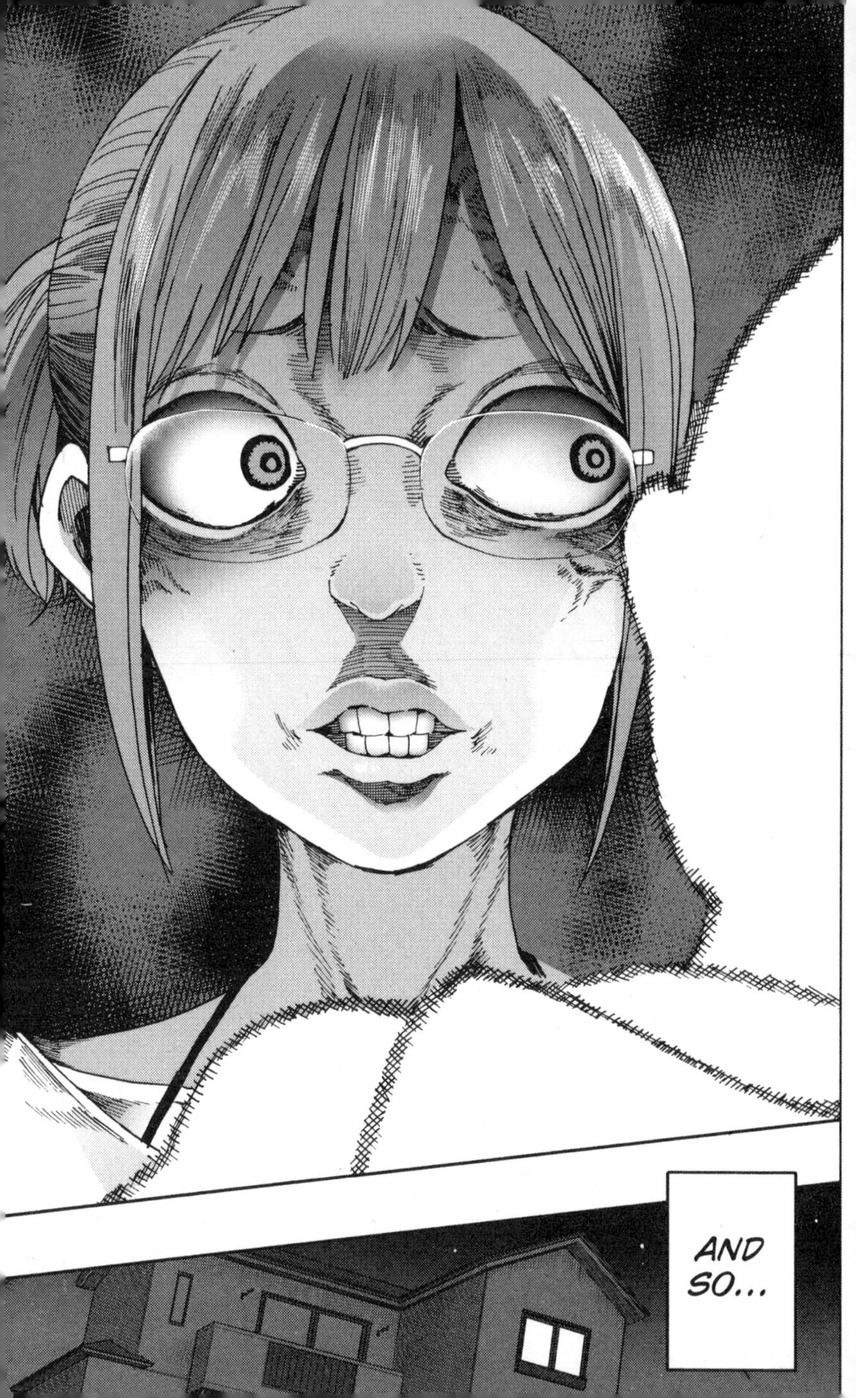
AND SO...

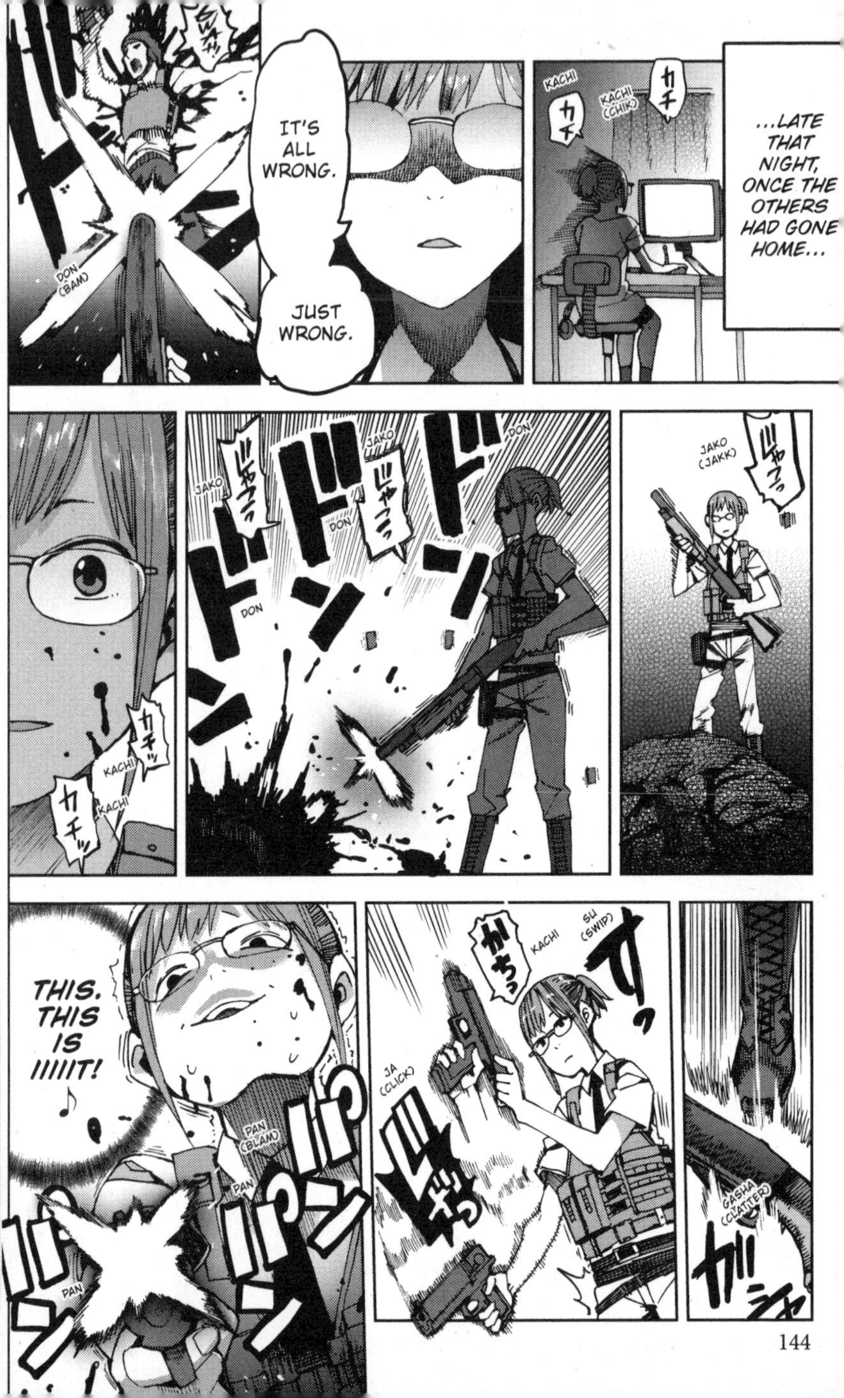

...LATE THAT NIGHT, ONCE THE OTHERS HAD GONE HOME...
KACHI (CHIK)
KACHI
IT'S ALL WRONG.
JUST WRONG.
GWAAH!!
DON (BAM)
JAKO (JAKK)
DON
JAKO
DON
JAKO
DON
KACHI
KACHI
GASHA (CLATTER)
SU (SWIP)
KACHI
JA (CLICK)
THIS. THIS IS IIIIIIT! ♪
PAN (BLAM)
PAN
PAN

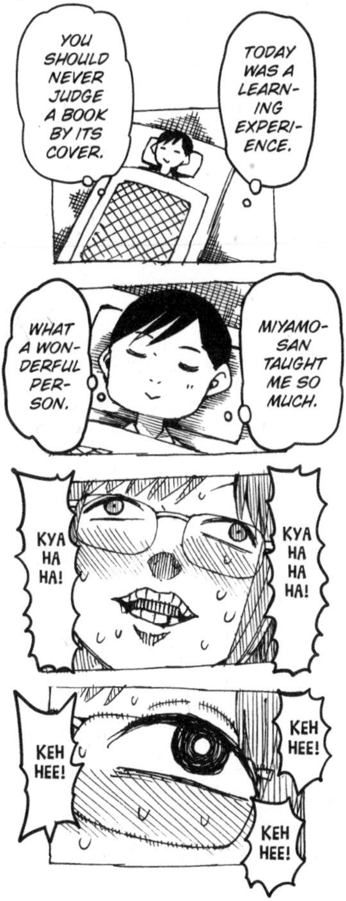
TODAY WAS A LEARNING EXPERIENCE.
YOU SHOULD NEVER JUDGE A BOOK BY ITS COVER.
MIYAMO-SAN TAUGHT ME SO MUCH.
WHAT A WONDERFUL PERSON.
KYA HA HA HA!
KYA HA HA!
KEH HEE!
KEH HEE!
KEH HEE!

BONUS MANGA **ONE SUNDAY AT CHIO-CHAN'S HOUSE**

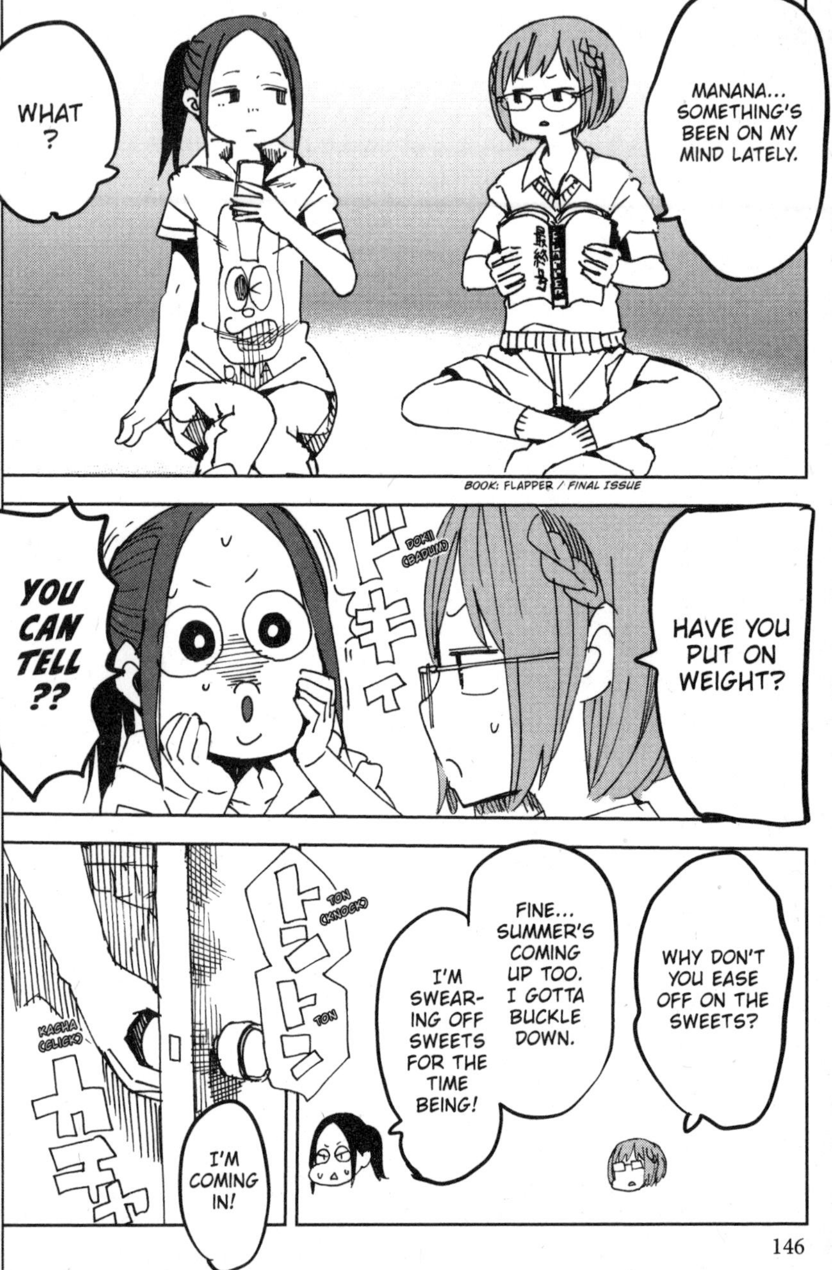
MANANA... SOMETHING'S BEEN ON MY MIND LATELY.
WHAT?
BOOK: FLAPPER / FINAL ISSUE
HAVE YOU PUT ON WEIGHT?
DOKI (BADUMP)
YOU CAN TELL??
WHY DON'T YOU EASE OFF ON THE SWEETS?
FINE... SUMMER'S COMING UP TOO. I GOTTA BUCKLE DOWN.
I'M SWEAR-ING OFF SWEETS FOR THE TIME BEING!
TON (KNOCK)
TON
I'M COMING IN!
KACHA (CLICK)

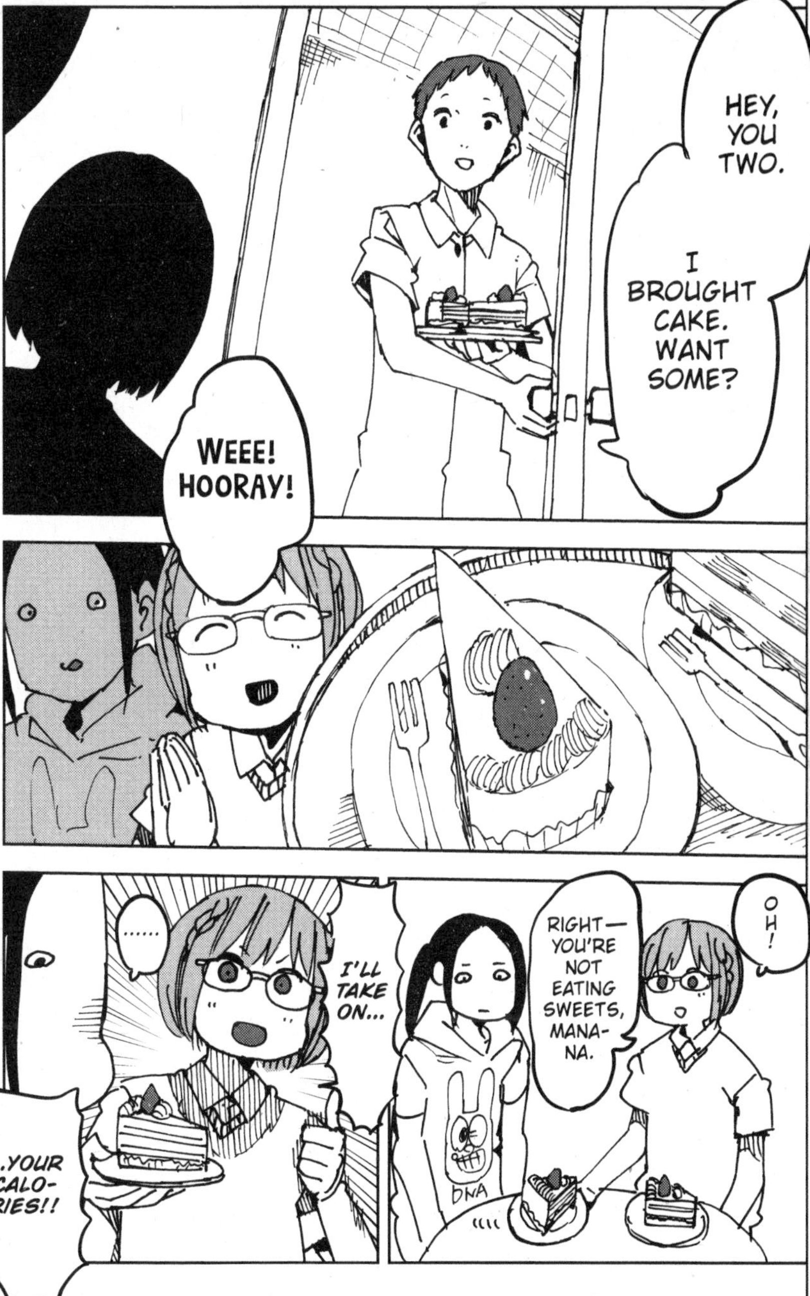
HEY, YOU TWO.
I BROUGHT CAKE. WANT SOME?
WEEE! HOORAY!
OH!
RIGHT— YOU'RE NOT EATING SWEETS, MANANA.
......
I'LL TAKE ON...
...YOUR CALORIES!!

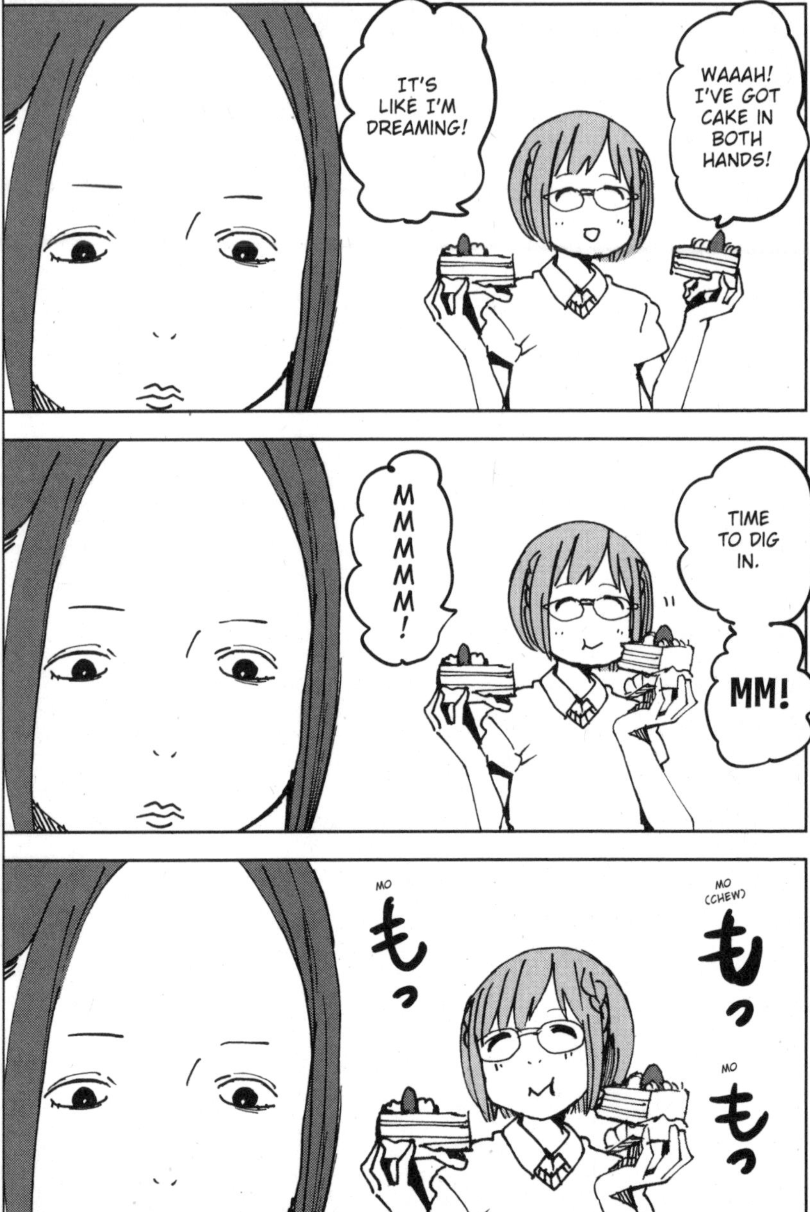
WAAAH! I'VE GOT CAKE IN BOTH HANDS!
IT'S LIKE I'M DREAMING!
TIME TO DIG IN.
MM!
MMMMMM!
MO (CHEW)
もっ
MO
もっ
MO
もっ

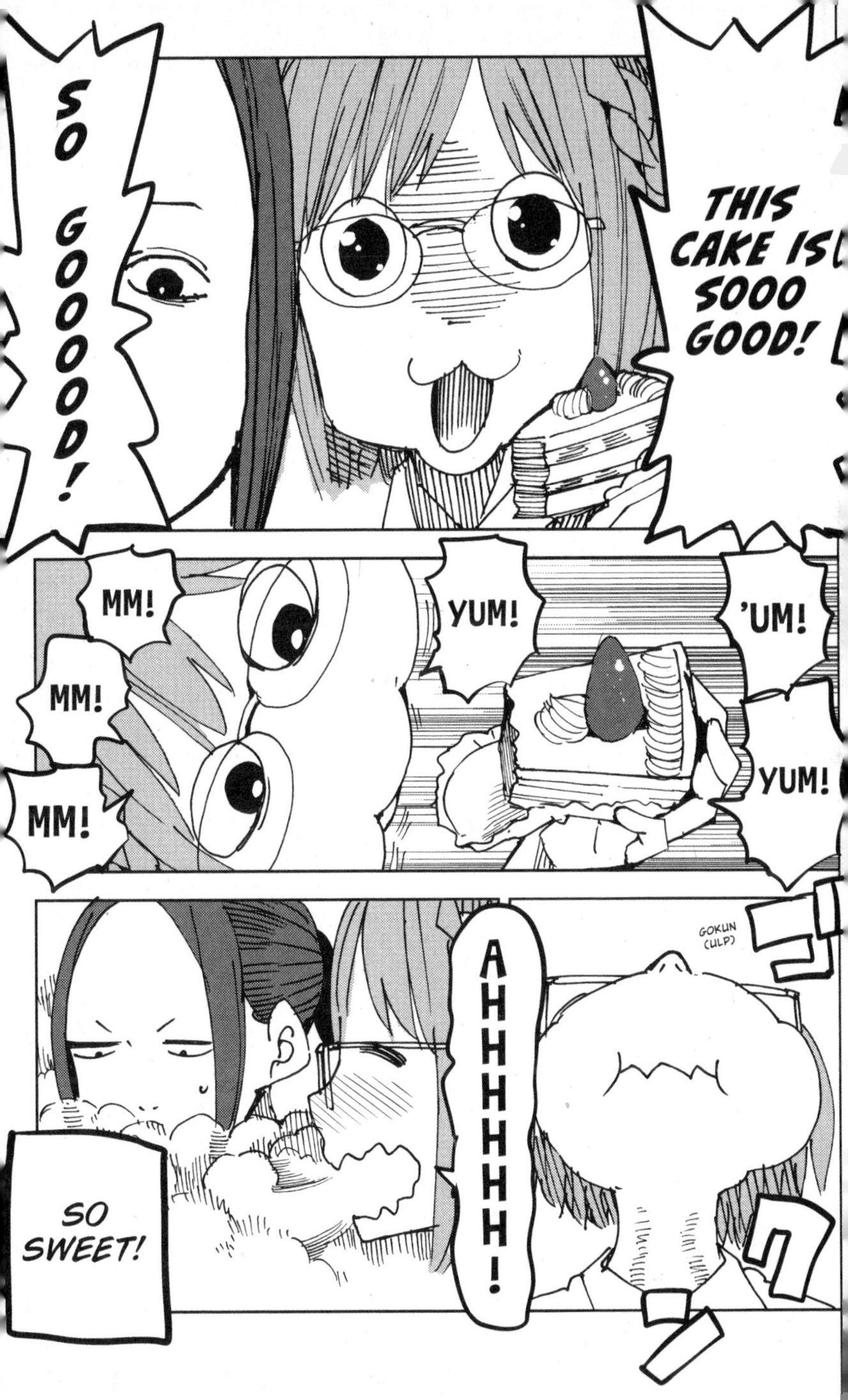
THIS CAKE IS SOOO GOOD!
SO GOOOOOD!
'UM!
YUM!
YUM!
MM!
MM!
MM!
GOKUN (ULP)
AHHHHHH!
SO SWEET!

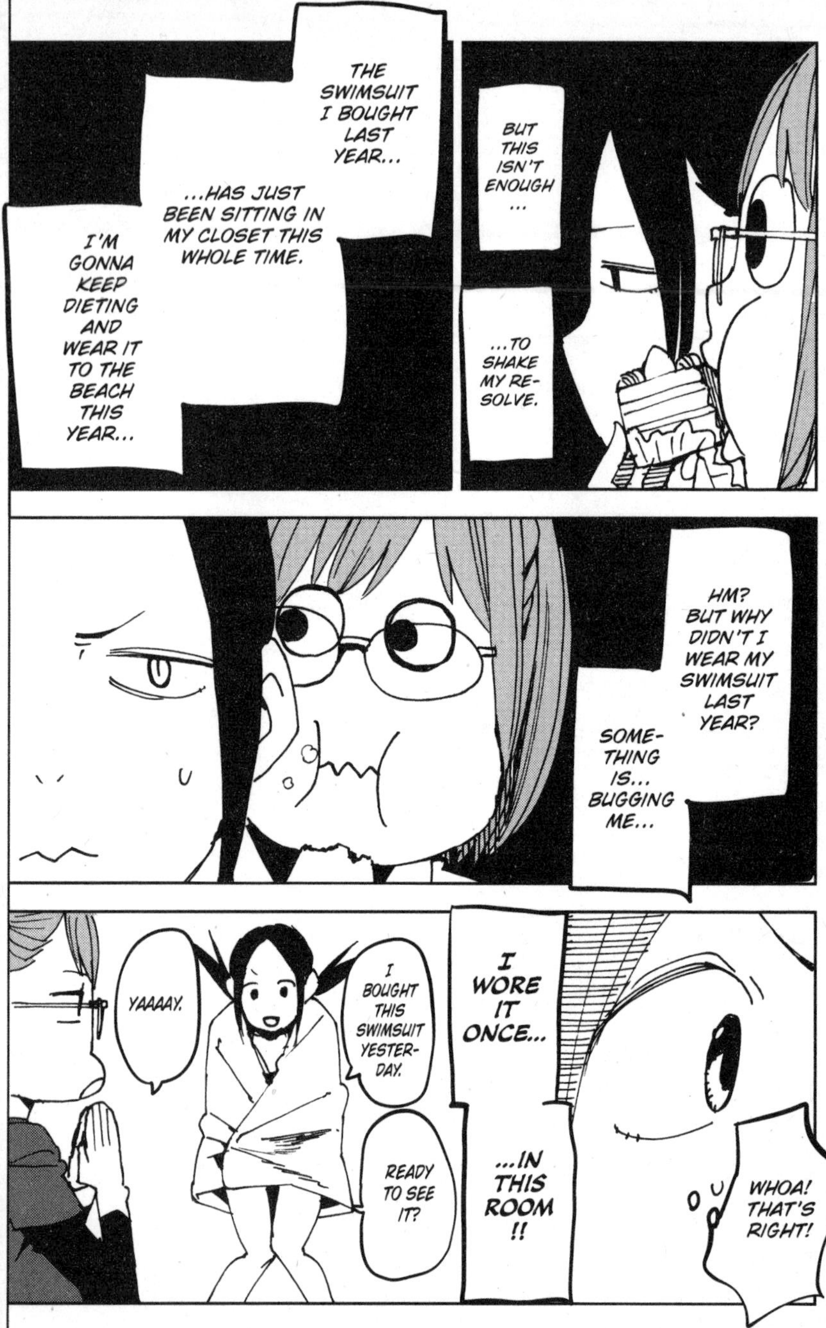

BUT THIS ISN'T ENOUGH...
...TO SHAKE MY RESOLVE.
THE SWIMSUIT I BOUGHT LAST YEAR...
...HAS JUST BEEN SITTING IN MY CLOSET THIS WHOLE TIME.
I'M GONNA KEEP DIETING AND WEAR IT TO THE BEACH THIS YEAR...
HM? BUT WHY DIDN'T I WEAR MY SWIMSUIT LAST YEAR?
SOMETHING IS... BUGGING ME...
WHOA! THAT'S RIGHT!
I WORE IT ONCE...
...IN THIS ROOM!!
I BOUGHT THIS SWIMSUIT YESTERDAY.
READY TO SEE IT?
YAAAAY.

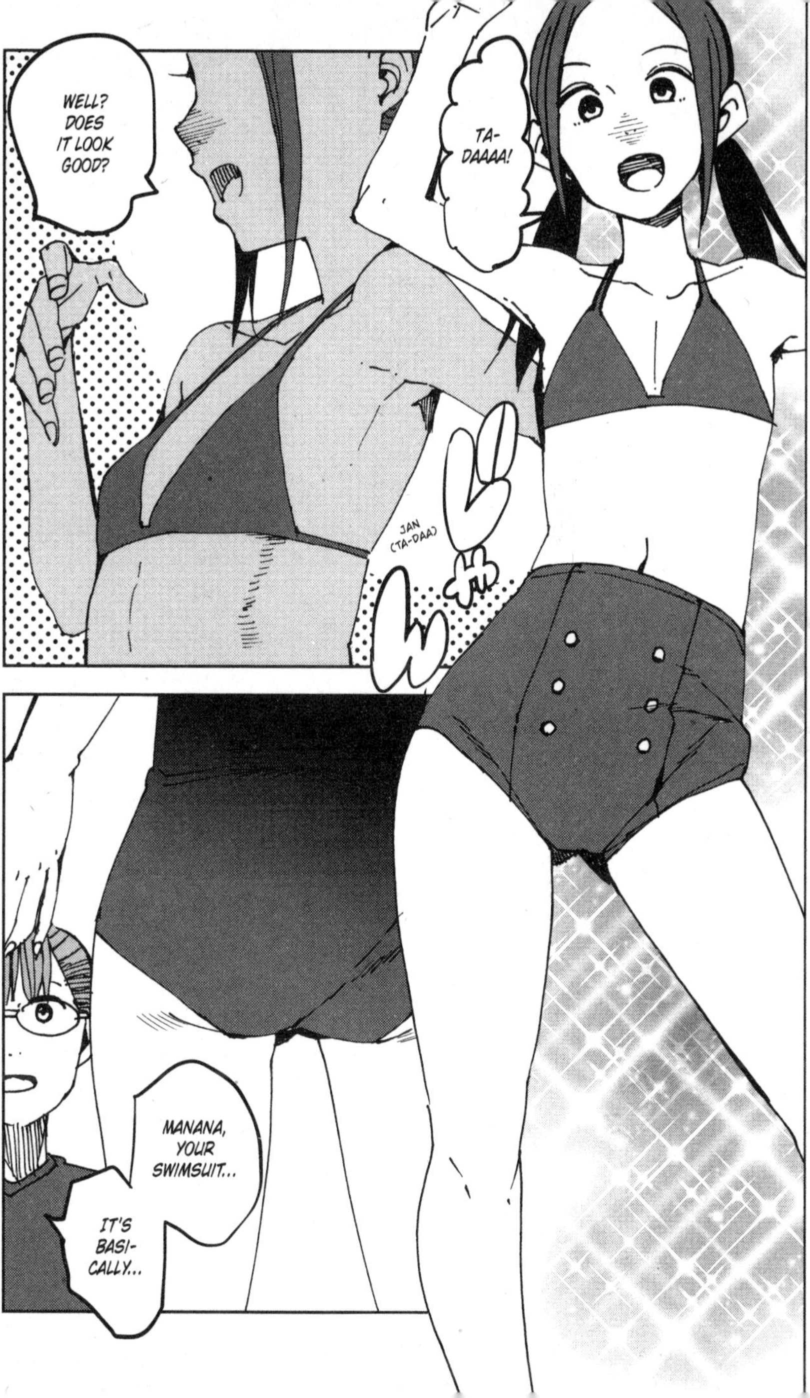
TA-DAAAA!
JAN (TA-DAA)
WELL? DOES IT LOOK GOOD?
MANANA, YOUR SWIMSUIT...
IT'S BASI-CALLY...

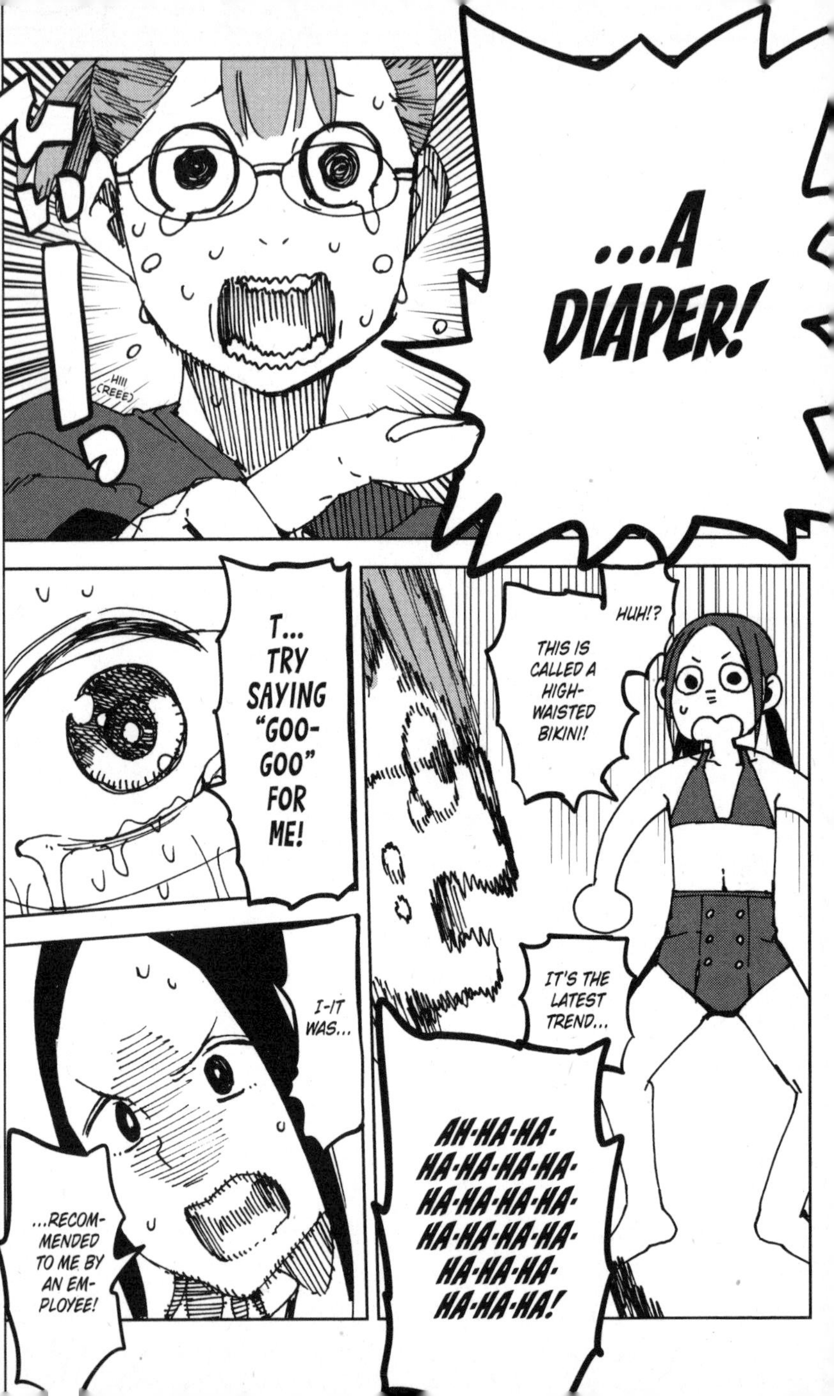
...A DIAPER!
HIII (CREEE)
HUH!?
THIS IS CALLED A HIGH-WAISTED BIKINI!
IT'S THE LATEST TREND...
AH-HA-HA-HA-HA-HA-HA-HA-HA-HA-HA-HA-HA-HA-HA-HA-HA-HA-HA-HA-HA-HA-HA!
T... TRY SAYING "GOO-GOO" FOR ME!
I-IT WAS...
...RECOMMENDED TO ME BY AN EMPLOYEE!

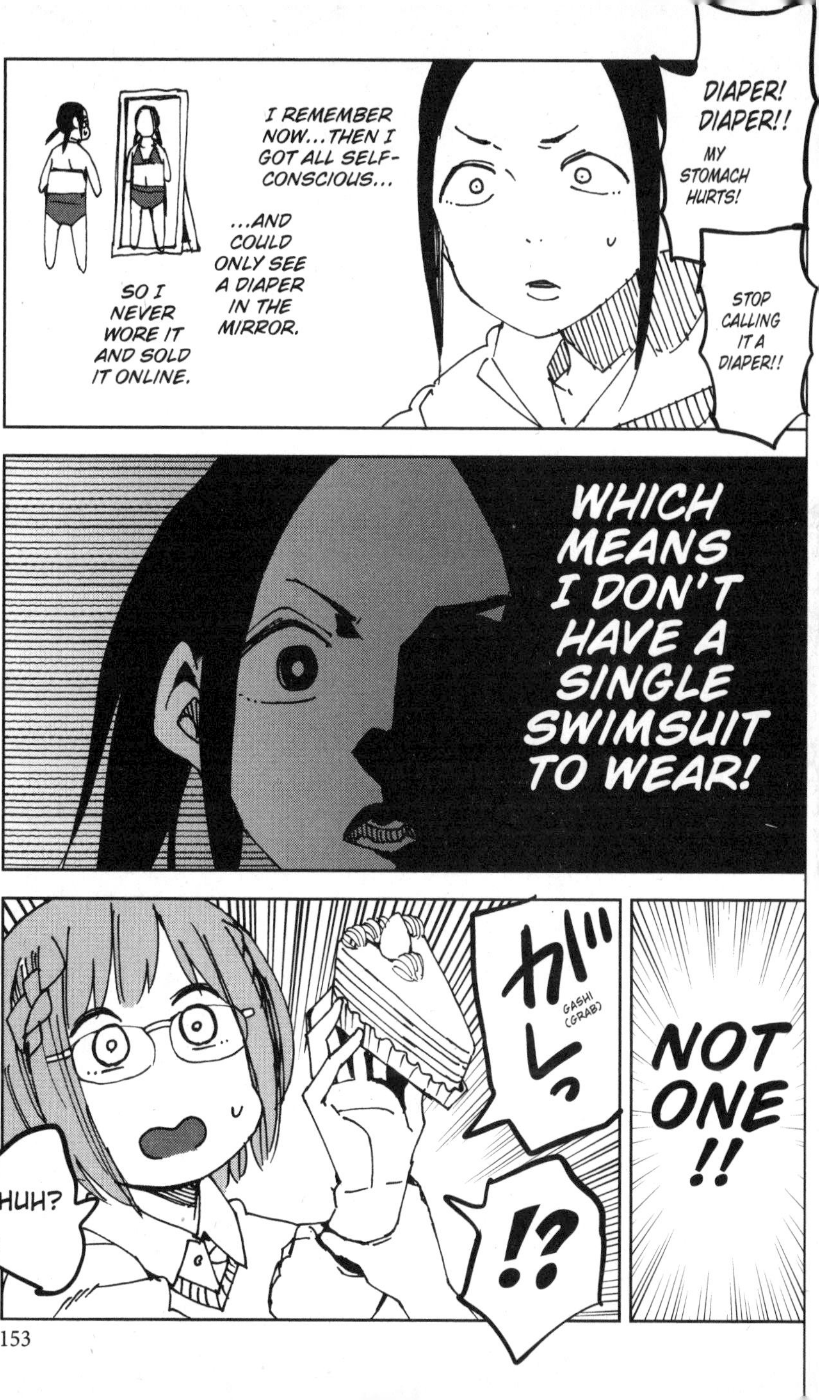
DIAPER! DIAPER!!
MY STOMACH HURTS!
STOP CALLING IT A DIAPER!!
I REMEMBER NOW...THEN I GOT ALL SELF-CONSCIOUS...
...AND COULD ONLY SEE A DIAPER IN THE MIRROR.
SO I NEVER WORE IT AND SOLD IT ONLINE.
WHICH MEANS I DON'T HAVE A SINGLE SWIMSUIT TO WEAR!
NOT ONE!!
がしっ
GASHI (GRAB)
!?
HUH?

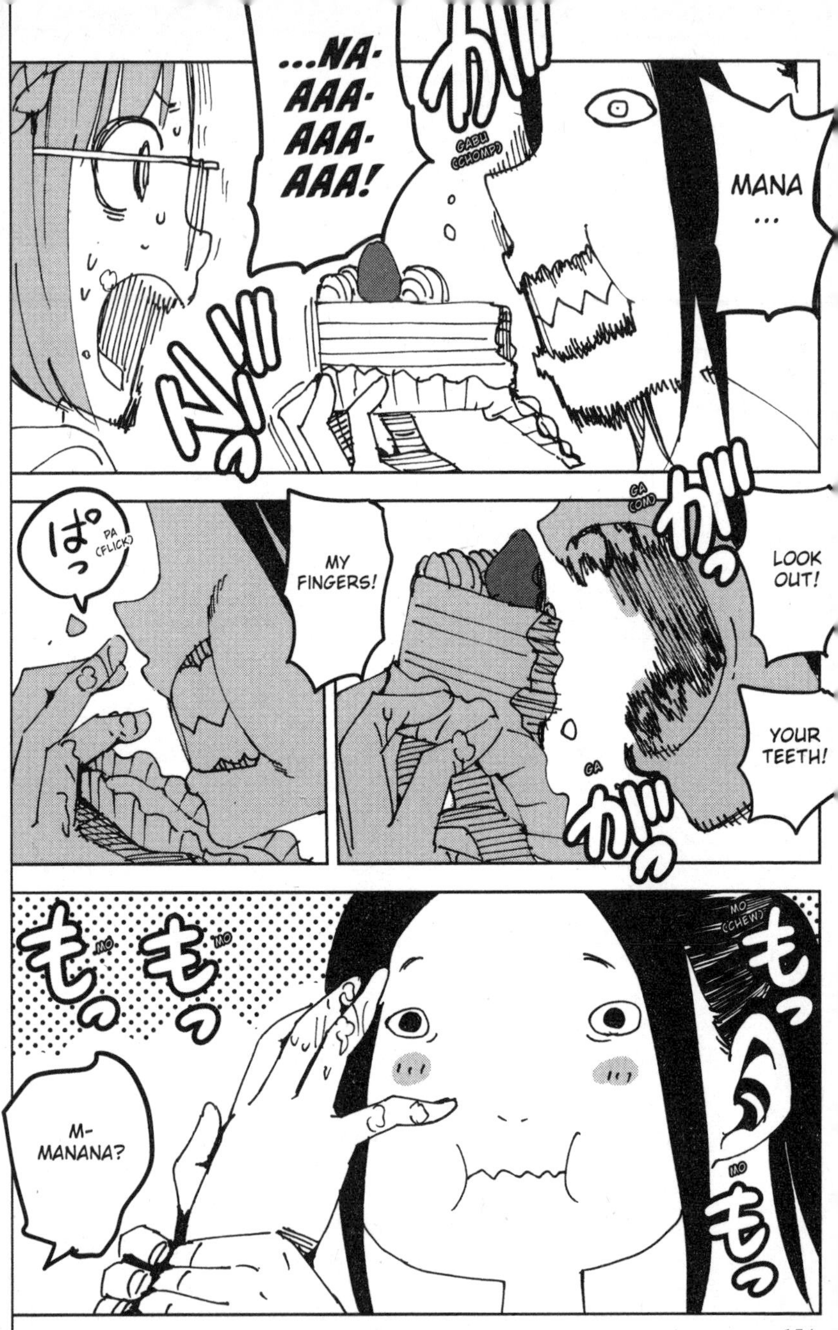
MANA ...
GABU (CHOMP)
...NA-AAA-AAA-AAA!
GA (COM)
LOOK OUT!
YOUR TEETH!
GA
MY FINGERS!
ぱっ
PA (FLICK)
MO (CHEW)
もっ
MO
もっ
MO
もっ
MO
もっ
M-MANANA?

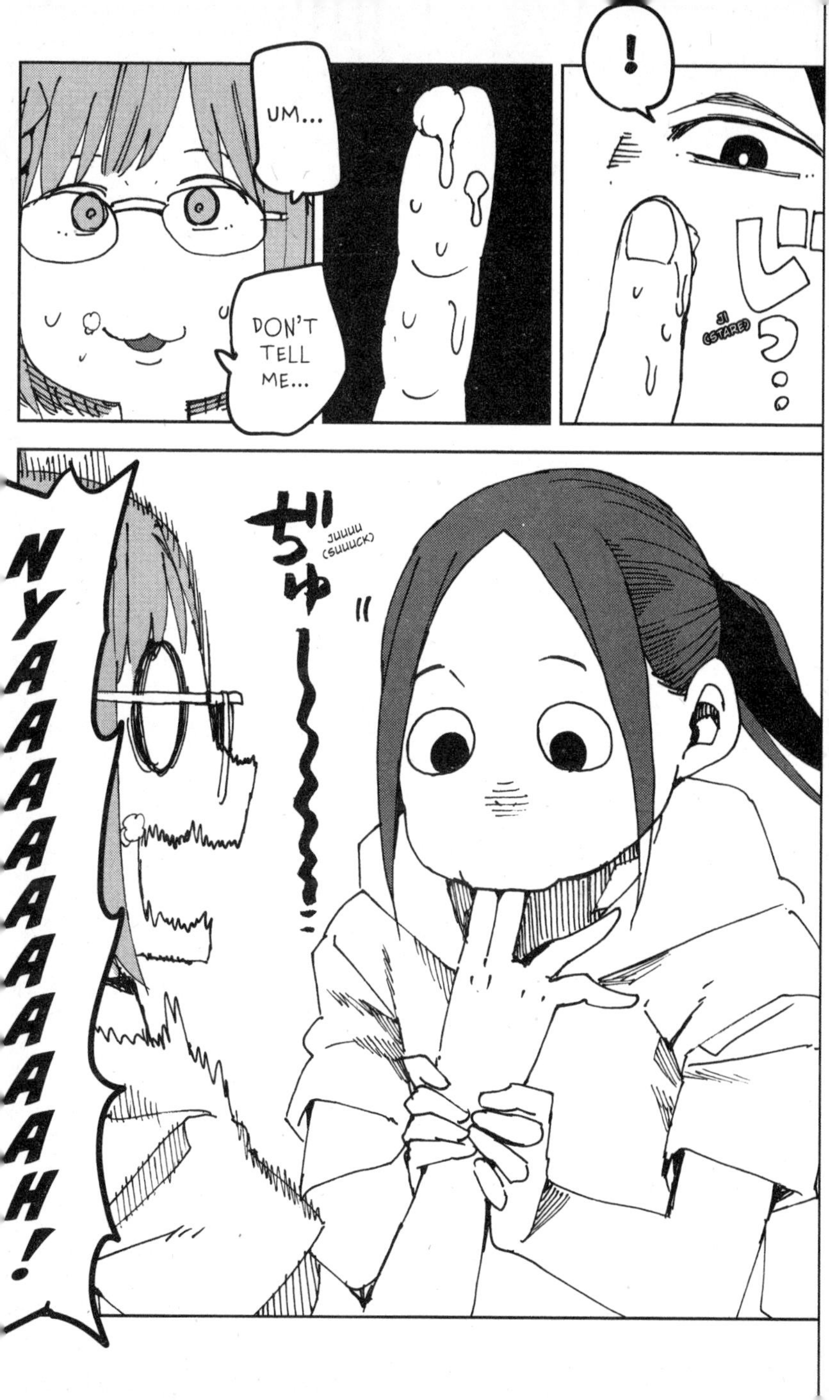
!
JI (STARE)
UM...
DON'T TELL ME...
JUUUU (SUUUCK)
NYAAAAAAAAAAAH!

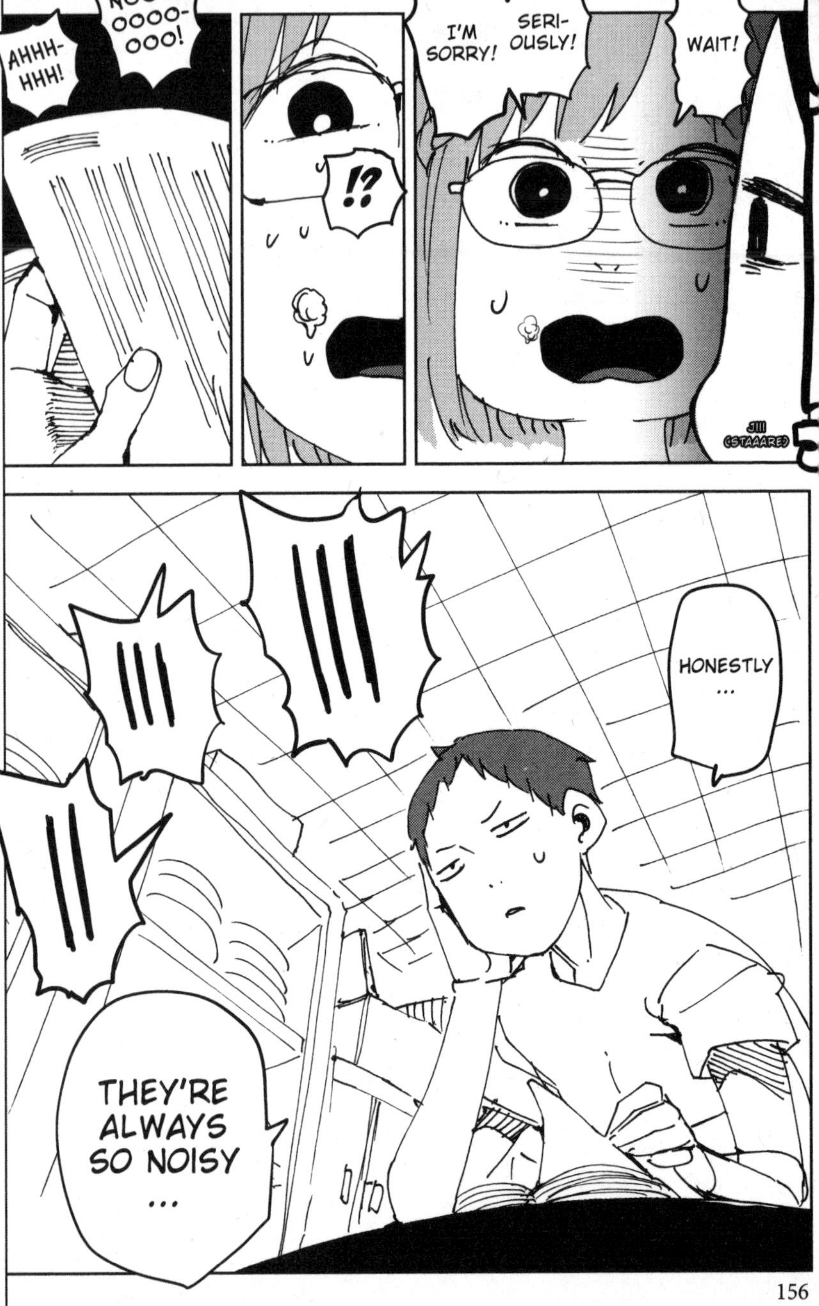
WAIT!
SERI-OUSLY!
I'M SORRY!
JIII (STAAARE)
!?
NOOO-OOOO-OOO!
AHHH-HHH!
HONESTLY ...
THEY'RE ALWAYS SO NOISY ...

THE FINAL BUTT BATTLE BEGINS.

GA (BARK)
I'LL BE WAITING HERE ONE WEEK FROM TODAY!
"MAD DOG" CHIHARU ANDOU
HMPH... KNOW YOUR PLACE.
KI (GLARE)
"THUMB PRINCESS" FUYUKI NOUJOU
"PSYCHO-PATH" ICHIGO TOONO
"MORIYAMA ASSASSIN" HIBIKI OGAWARA
"DUAL-WIELDER" YOUKO TAKAGI
"TYPHOON" MAKOTO AOZUKA
"TEACHER KILLER" CLAIRE HAMAE
"HERCULES" AYAME KAIRIKI
DO DO DO DO DO DO DO DO DO DO DO (DOOM)

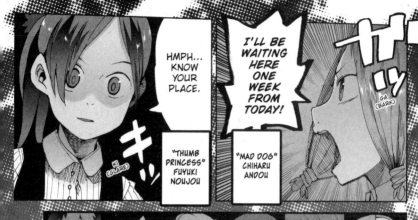

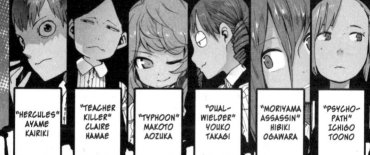

Chio's SCHOOL ROAD 8

ON SALE MARCH 2019

TRANSLATION NOTES

General
100 yen is approximately $1 USD in value.

Page 34
Bloodlust
In Japanese culture, *sakki* ("bloodlust" or "killing intent") is thought of as a mild pressure generated by hostility or threat. Everyone can sense it subconsciously, but experienced warriors can supposedly train their perception of it so it functions like a spider sense or amplify their own *sakki* to paralyze their opponents with fear.

Page 39
Deathscythe
This nickname refers to a certain mecha from a particularly famous mecha series.

Page 42
Popuko
Chio's face here makes her look just like Popuko, one of the protagonists in comedy manga *Pop Team Epic*.

Page 59
Babumicious
The package of gum Chio picked up is actually a reference to the Bubblicious brand of gum.

Page 60
Float of the Rings
The chapter title is a reference to the fantasy series *The Lord of the Rings*.

Page 67
"Push"
Chio mistakes Andou's *osu*, which means "push," for *ossu*, a way of saying "what's up?" often used by the kind of punk that Andou used to be.

Page 81
Life ring
In Japanese, Chio convinces herself that when Andou said *suki da* ("I love you"), he meant to say *ukiwa* ("life ring"), which is why she gets flustered when he later thanks her for giving him one.

Page 94
Kamameshi
Kamameshi is a traditional dish made from meat, vegetables, and rice that is cooked and served in a small pot.

Page 95
Cafe Restaurant
The restaurant Chio sneaks into is based on a certain chain of family restaurants that are well-known in Japan, as one can be found in every prefecture in the country.

Page 112
Ketchup art
Omelet rice is typically served with cutesy designs or messages written on top with ketchup; Chio has drawn the logo of a certain Western game series that has been awaiting a third installment for a long, long time on hers. Her classmate has written *shi* ("death") on his.

Page 116
MOMO SHINOZUKA'S BATTLEGROUNDS
The chapter title is a reference to a popular Western battle royale game.

Page 121
Manana's manga
Throughout Chapter 35, Manana sits in the background and nitpicks various events from the fourth installment of a long-running, famous series known for being "bizarre."

Page 146
Flapper
Chio is reading *Monthly Comic Flapper*, the Japanese magazine *Chio's School Road* is serialized in.

Chio's SCHOOL ROAD

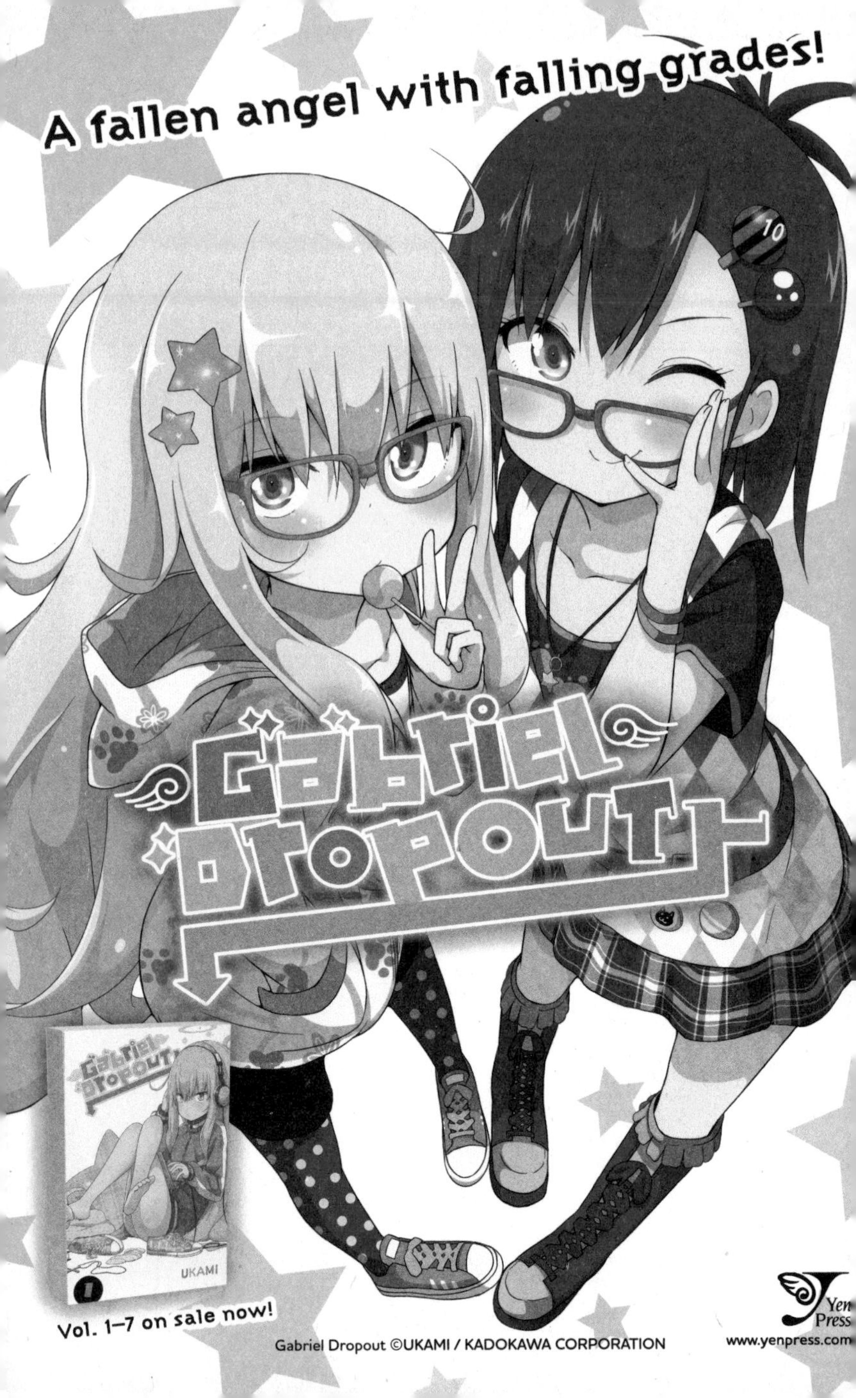
A fallen angel with falling grades!
Gabriel DropOut
Gabriel DropOut
UKAMI
1
Vol. 1–7 on sale now!
Gabriel Dropout ©UKAMI / KADOKAWA CORPORATION
Yen Press
www.yenpress.com

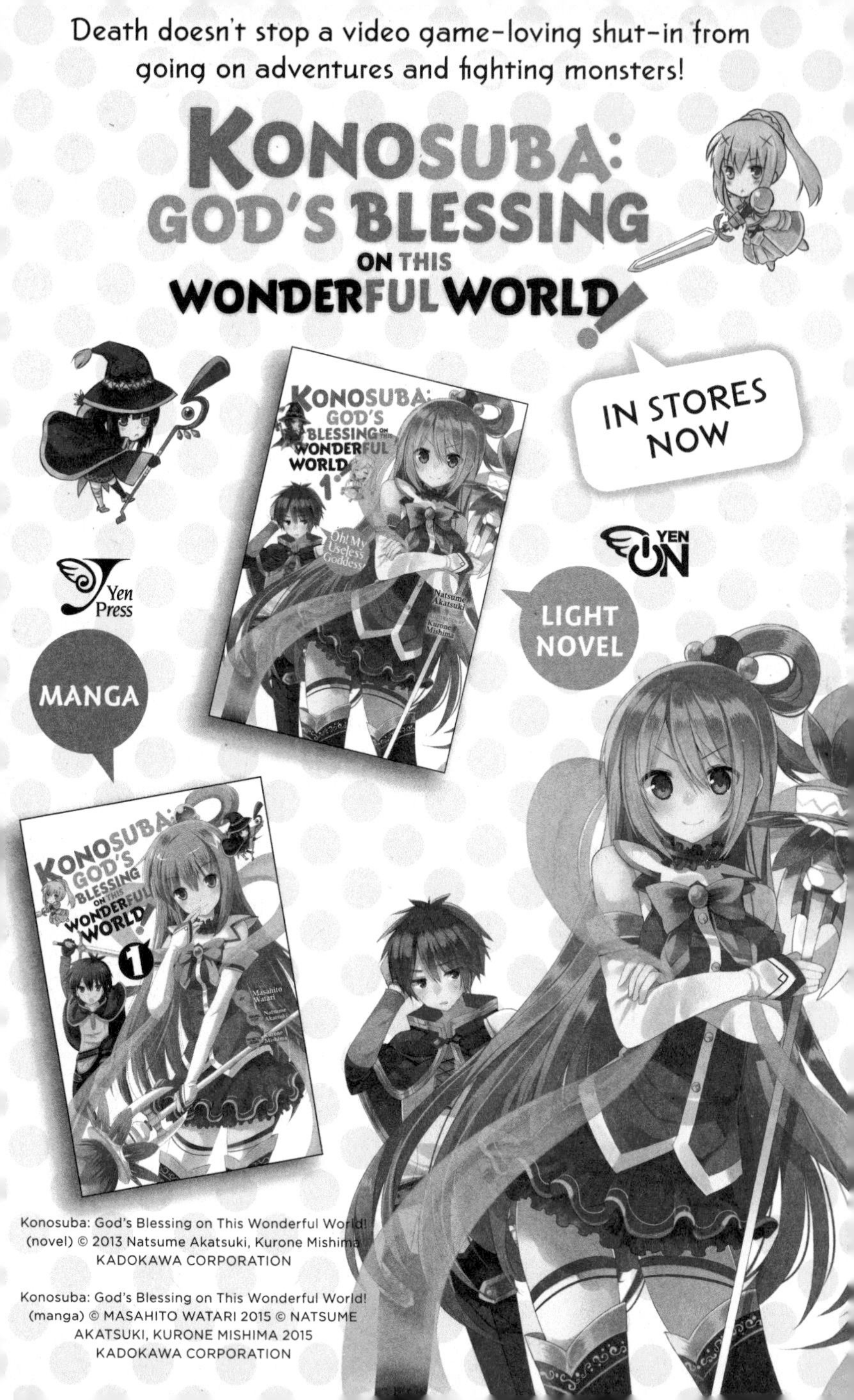
Death doesn't stop a video game-loving shut-in from going on adventures and fighting monsters!
KONOSUBA: GOD'S BLESSING ON THIS WONDERFUL WORLD!
IN STORES NOW
Yen Press
MANGA
YEN ON
LIGHT NOVEL
Konosuba: God's Blessing on This Wonderful World! (novel) © 2013 Natsume Akatsuki, Kurone Mishima KADOKAWA CORPORATION
Konosuba: God's Blessing on This Wonderful World! (manga) © MASAHITO WATARI 2015 © NATSUME AKATSUKI, KURONE MISHIMA 2015 KADOKAWA CORPORATION

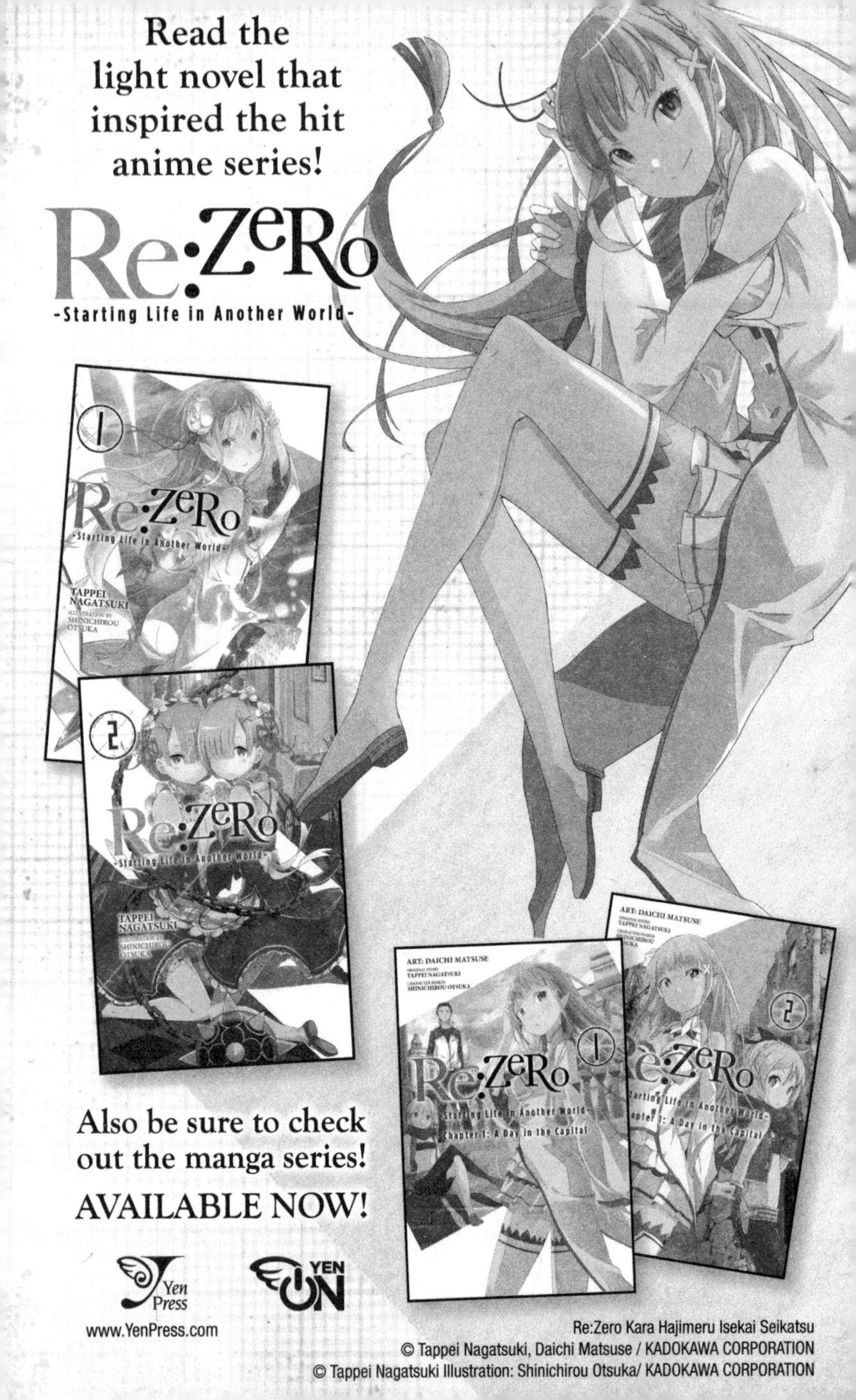
Read the light novel that inspired the hit anime series!
Re:ZeRo
-Starting Life in Another World-
Re:ZeRo -Starting Life in Another World-
TAPPEI NAGATSUKI
ILLUSTRATION BY SHINICHIROU OTSUKA
ART: DAICHI MATSUSE
ORIGINAL STORY: TAPPEI NAGATSUKI
CHARACTER DESIGN: SHINICHIROU OTSUKA
Chapter 1: A Day in the Capital
Also be sure to check out the manga series!
AVAILABLE NOW!
Yen Press
YEN ON
www.YenPress.com
Re:Zero Kara Hajimeru Isekai Seikatsu
© Tappei Nagatsuki, Daichi Matsuse / KADOKAWA CORPORATION
© Tappei Nagatsuki Illustration: Shinichirou Otsuka/ KADOKAWA CORPORATION

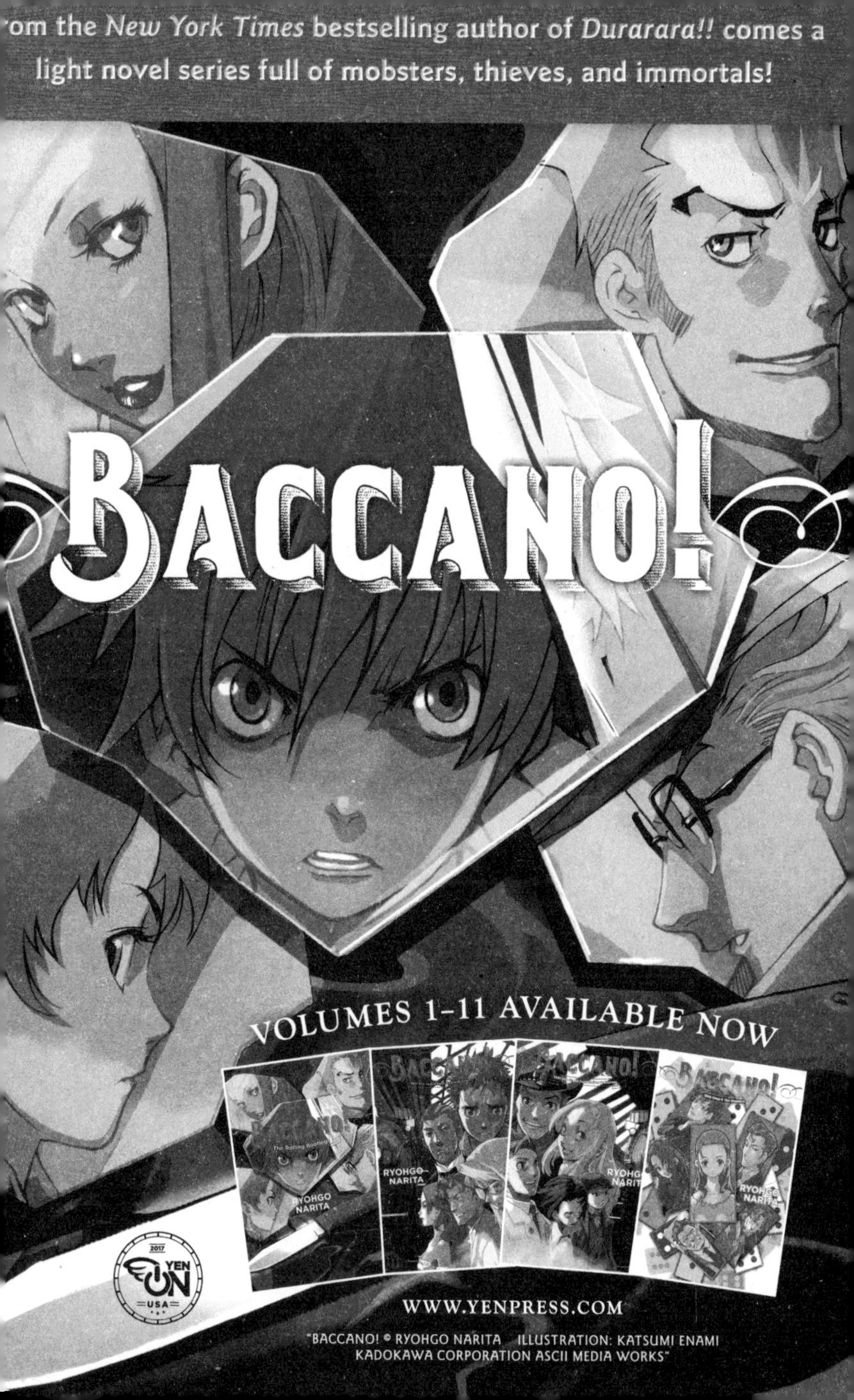
rom the New York Times bestselling author of Durarara!! comes a light novel series full of mobsters, thieves, and immortals!
BACCANO!
VOLUMES 1–11 AVAILABLE NOW
The Rolling Bootlegs
RYOHGO NARITA
RYOHGO NARITA
RYOHGO NARITA
RYOHGO NARITA
2017
YEN ON
USA
WWW.YENPRESS.COM
"BACCANO! © RYOHGO NARITA ILLUSTRATION: KATSUMI ENAMI
KADOKAWA CORPORATION ASCII MEDIA WORKS"

Hello! This is YOTSUBA!

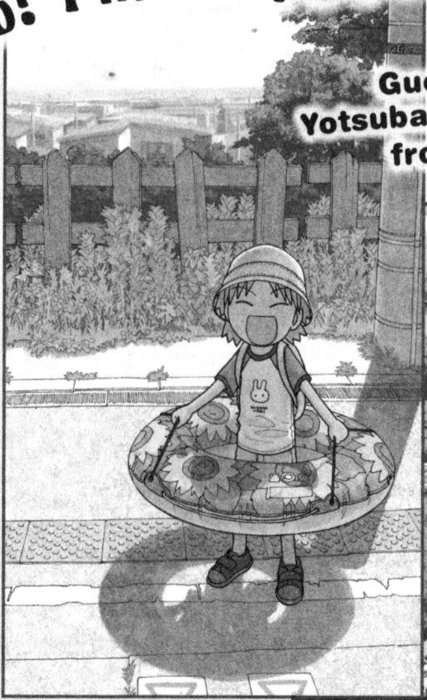

Guess what? Guess what?
Yotsuba and Daddy just moved here from waaaay over there!

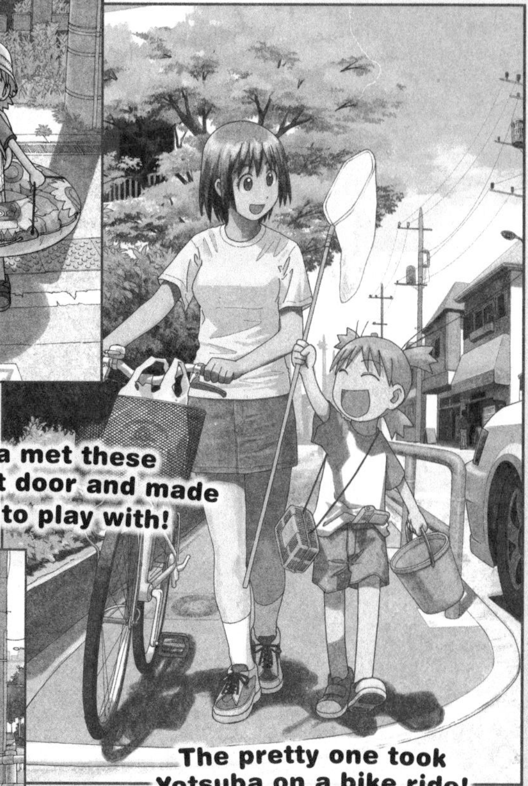

And Yotsuba met these nice people next door and made new friends to play with!

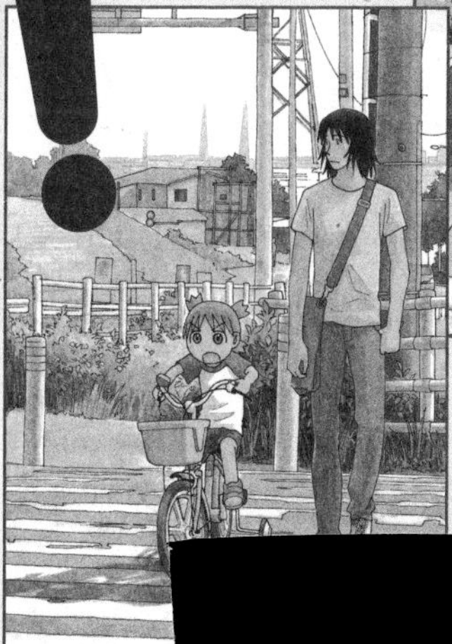

The pretty one took Yotsuba on a bike ride!
(Whoooa! There was a big hill!)

And Ena's a good drawer!
(Almost as good as Yotsuba!)

[redacted]

OHHHH!

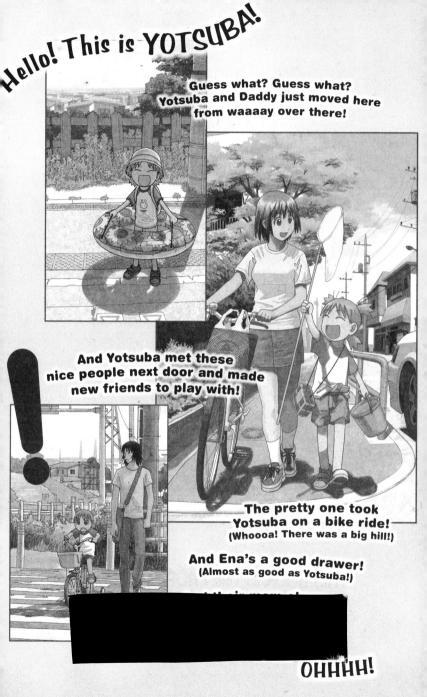

Chio's SCHOOL ROAD 7

TADATAKA KAWASAKI

- Translation: ALEXANDER KELLER-NELSON
- Lettering: ROCHELLE GANCIO

CHIOCHAN NO TSUGAKURO Vol. 7
© Kawasaki Tadataka 2017
First published in Japan in 2017 by KADOKAWA CORPORATION,Tokyo.
English translation rights arranged with KADOKAWA CORPORATION,Tokyo through TUTTLE-MORI AGENCY, INC., Tokyo.

English translation © 2019 by Yen Press, LLC.

Yen Press
150 West 30th Street, 19th Floor
New York, NY 10001

Visit us at yenpress.com ⬤ facebook.com/yenpress
twitter.com/yenpress ⬤ yenpress.tumblr.com ⬤ instagram.com/yenpress

First Yen Press Edition: December 2019

Yen Press is an imprint of Yen Press, LLC.
The Yen Press name and logo are trademarks of Yen Press, LLC.

Library of Congress Control Number: 2018948074

ISBNs: 978-1-9753-2776-7 (paperback)
978-1-9753-2777-4 (ebook)